Armed Forces Guide to Personal Financial Planning

Armed Forces Guide to Personal Financial Planning

Strategies for Managing Your Budget, Savings, Insurance, Taxes, and Investments

3rd Edition

Dr. J. Kevin Berner

and

LTC Thomas Daula

Contributing Associates, Department of Social Sciences,
U.S. Military Academy, West Point, New York:

CPT John Black, CPT Christopher Chambers, Holly Daula
CPT Kent Fasana, Dr. Mathew Fung, MAJ Vincent Grewatz
MAJ David Hoffman, CPT Daniel Mahoney, MAJ Michael Meese
MAJ Eric Nickerson, MAJ Michael Roane, Debra Roane, CPT Timothy Stanley

STACKPOLE BOOKS

Copyright © 1994 by Stackpole Books

Published by
STACKPOLE BOOKS
5067 Ritter Road
Mechanicsburg, PA 17055

All rights reserved, including the right to reproduce this book or portions thereof in any form or by any means, electronic or mechanical, including photocopying, recording, or by any information storage and retrieval system, without permission in writing from the publisher. All inquiries should be addressed to Stackpole Books, 5067 Ritter Road, Mechanicsburg, Pennsylvania 17055.

Cover design by Mark Olszewski

The ideas and opinions expressed in this volume are those of the authors and do not represent official policies of any governmental agency, the United States Military Academy, or the U.S. Army.

Printed in the United States of America

Third Edition

10 9 8 7 6 5 4 3 2 1

Library of Congress Cataloging-in-Publication Data

Berner, J. Kevin
    Armed Forces guide to personal financial planning : strategies for managing your budget, savings, insurance, taxes, and investments / J. Kevin Berner and Thomas Daula. ; contributing associates, John Black . . . [et al.]. — 3rd ed.
    p. cm.
    Rev. ed. of: Armed Forces guide to personal financial planning / Michael E. Edelson and Hobart B. Pillsbury, Jr. 2nd ed. ©1991.
    Includes bibliographical references and index.
    ISBN 0-8117-2501-4
    1. United States—Armed Forces—Finance, Personal. I. Daula, Thomas.
II. Edleson, Michael E. Armed Forces guide to personal financial planning. III. Title.
HG179. P55 1994
332.024'355—dc20   94-17278
                                                                              CIP

The Authors

THE AUTHORS are current or former members of the Department of Social Sciences at the U.S. Military Academy at West Point or military spouses. Together they bring to this work a total of 156 years of active-duty military service and 52 years of experience in teaching economics, personal finance, and related topics. Collectively, they have made more than 75 PCS moves; purchased more than 75 automobiles and bought or sold more than 20 homes; paid approximately 2,100 insurance premiums; spent, and occasionally saved, a total of about $4 million; and made most of the financial mistakes servicemembers can possibly make.

LTC Thomas V. Daula
Professor of Economics, USMA
B.S., USMA
M.S., Massachusetts Institute of Technology
Ph.D., Massachusetts Institute of Technology

J. Kevin Berner
Associate, McKinsey & Co., Inc.
(previously Associate Professor at USMA)
B.S., USMA
M.S., Massachusetts Institute of Technology
Ph.D., Massachusetts Institute of Technology

CPT John Black   Assistant Professor
BS, USMA
M.S., Carnegie Mellon University

CPT Christopher Chambers   Assistant Professor
B.S., USMA
M.B.A., Wharton School of Business

THE AUTHORS

Holly A. Daula
B.S., Roanoke College
M.B.A., University of Puget Sound

CPT Kent Fasana   Assistant Professor
B.S., USMA
MBA, Wharton School of Business

Dr. Mathew Fung
(previously Assistant Professor at USMA)
B.A., City College, CUNY
M.A., Columbia University
Ph.D., Rutgers University

MAJ Vincent Grewatz   Assistant Professor
B.S., USMA
M.P.A., Harvard University

MAJ David Hoffman   Assistant Professor
B.S., USMA
M.B.A., Wharton School of Business

CPT Daniel Mahoney   Assistant Professor
B.S., Lehigh University
M.B.A., Duke University

MAJ Michael Meese   Assistant Professor
B.S., USMA
M.P.A., Princeton University

MAJ Eric Nickerson, USAF   Assistant Professor
B.S., USAFA
M.A., University of Michigan

MAJ Michael Roane   Assistant Professor
B.A., University of Mississippi
M.B.A., Duke University

Debra Roane   Health Systems Specialist
B.A., Fresno State College

CPT Timothy Stanley   Assistant Professor
B.S., Virginia Military Institute
M.S., Massachusetts Institute of Technology

Contents

Tables	xiii
Preface	xv
Introduction	xix

PART I: PERSONAL FINANCIAL PLANNING

1 Assessing the Situation — 3
  The Balance Sheet

2 Financial Basic Training — 6
  Before-Tax and After-Tax Income
  Inflation
  Opportunity Cost
  Time Value of Money
  Risk and Reward
  Summary

3 Military Pay, Allowances, and Benefits — 15
  Military Pay and Allowances
  Travel Pay and Allowances
  Other Important Benefits
  Suggested References

4 Financial Planning and Budgeting — 25
  Establishing an Objective: Setting Financial Goals
  Developing a Plan: The Budget

PART II: FINANCIAL BASICS

5 Banking Smart   41
    Banking Services
    Selecting a Bank
    Bank Services
    Suggested References

6 Using Credit Wisely   55
    Consumer Credit
    Consumer Loans
    Credit and Debit Cards
    Borrowers' Rights
    Suggested References

7 Meeting Medical Expenses   71
    Uniformed Services Health Benefits Program
    Summary of Medical Benefits
    Dental Care for Dependents
    Supplemental Health Insurance
    The Evolving System for Military Medicine
    Suggested References
    Organizations Providing CHAMPUS Supplemental Health Insurance

8 Paying Your Taxes   89
    Personal Tax Responsibilities
    Federal Income Tax
    State and Local Taxes
    Recent Tax Developments
    Suggested References

PART III: BIG-TICKET ITEMS

9 Buying a Car   103
    Getting Started
    Financing
    Selecting an Automobile
    Buying a New Car
    Alternatives to Buying a New Car
    Disposing of Your Old Vehicle
    How Long Should You Keep Your Car?
    Suggested References

10 Automobile Insurance — 125
What Is Automobile Insurance?
The Insurance Policy: Explanations and Recommendations
Automobile Insurance Checklist
Suggested References

11 Housing — 136
The General Approach
Renting
Buying
Financing Your Purchase
Tax Considerations for Homeowners
Selling Your House
Rent versus Buy: A Quantitative Analysis
A Checklist for Home Buyers
Suggested References

12 Protecting Your Wealth with Insurance — 173
Homeowners' Insurance
Insurance for Other Circumstances
Liability Protection and Umbrella Policies
Homeowners' Checklist

PART IV: BUILDING YOUR NEST EGG

13 Investing in Financial Assets — 187
Debt Instruments
Equity Assets
Debt/Equity Assets
Commodity Speculation
Beware of Scams
Tax Avoidance for Small Investors
Summary of Financial Investing
Tips on Saving and Investing
Suggested References

14 Buying Mutual Funds — 207
Mutual Fund Basics
Mutual Fund Fees
Mutual Fund Prices
Types of Mutual Funds
Buying and Selling Mutual Funds
Mutual Fund Returns

Tax and Other Considerations
Summary
Suggested References

15 Investing in Real Assets — 231
Direct Real Estate Investment
Indirect Real Estate Investment
Some Final Comments on Real Estate Investment
Other Real Assets
Some Final Comments on Real Assets
Suggested References

PART V: PLANNING FOR RETIREMENT AND LATER

16 Military Retirement Benefits — 253
Retirement Pay for Length-of-Service Retirees
Disability Retired Pay
Dual Compensation
Other Retirement Benefits
Former Spouses
Conclusion
Suggested References

17 Estate Planning — 262
The Ownership of Property
Power of Attorney
Estate-planning Documents
Trusts
Income Shifting
Professional Assistance

18 Life Insurance — 281
The Principle of Insurance
Basic Life Insurance Terms
Types of Life Insurance Policies
Choosing the Right Policy
Estimating Your Life Insurance Needs
Suggested References

19 Social Security and Department of Veterans Affairs Benefits — 304
Social Security Benefits
Department of Veterans Affairs Benefits
Suggested References

20 Retirement Survivor Benefits 318
The Survivor Benefit Plan
Should You Take SBP?
Changes in Coverage
Supplemental Survivor Benefit Plan (SSBP)
The Bottom Line
Suggested References

PART VI APPENDIXES

A Sources of Assistance 333
Military Organizations and Associations

B Glossary of Financial Terms 338

C Military Pay, Benefit, and Entitlement Tables 354

D Time Value of Money and Present Value Tables 369
Application to Loans
Valuation of Assets
Application to Assets in General
Using the Financial Tables

E Sample Personal Affairs Record 377

Index 383

Tables

Table 1-1	A Comparison of Military and Financial Planning	3
Table 1-2	A Family Balance Sheet: Determining Your Net Worth	5
Table 4-1	Nominal and Real Future College Costs	26
Table 4-2	Real and Nominal Rates of Return	26
Table 4-3	Financial Goals Worksheet	28
Table 4-4	Historical Averages for Real Rates of Return	29
Table 4-5	Income Tax Brackets for 1993 and 1994	30
Table 4-6	Calculating the Required Lump-Sum Investment	31
Table 4-7	Converting the Lump Sum to an Equivalent Monthly Investment	32
Table 4-8	Budget Worksheet	36–37
Table 5-1	The Effect of Different Interest-Compounding Methods	52
Table 6-1	Comparison of Simple and Add-on Interest	59
Table 7-1	Annual Deductible Amounts for Outpatient Care	77
Table 7-2	CHAMPUS Costs	77
Table 7-3	Summary of Servicemembers' Health Benefits	79
Table 8-1	Income Tax Brackets for 1993 and 1994	99
Table 9-1	Monthly Payments (per $1,000) for a 24-Month Loan	105
Table 9-2	Monthly Payments (per $1,000) for a 36-Month Loan	105
Table 9-3	Monthly Payments (per $1,000) for a 48-Month Loan	105
Table 9-4	Monthly Payments (per $1,000) for a 60-Month Loan	105
Table 9-5	Depreciation Schedule/Resale Value	107
Table 9-6	Comparative Analysis	113
Table 9-7	Typical Automobile Operating Costs	119
Table 11-1	Worksheet—How Much House Can I Afford?	142
Table 11-2	Monthly Principal and Interest Payments on a 30-Year Mortgage	144
Table 11-3	Rent vs. Buy Cash-flow Summary	169
Table 12-1	Standard Types of Home Insurance Coverage	175

Table 14-1   Comparison of Net Returns in Load and No-Load Funds   209
Table 14-2   Mutual Fund Categories and Risk   214
Table 14-3   Mutual Fund Worksheet   218
Table 14-4   Dollar Cost Averaging   224
Table 14-5   Mutual Fund Quotations   225
Table 15-1   Projected Annual Income Statement: Four-plex Apartment   233
Table 15-2   Cash Flow Analysis: Tax Effects   236
Table 15-3   After-Tax Cash Flow (ATCF)   238
Table 15-4   Projected Equity Value at Resale (1997)   240
Table 16-1   Retirement Pay under the Three Retirement Systems   255
Table 16-2   Calculating Disability Retirement Pay   258
Table 17-1   Summary of Trusts   269
Table 17-2   Higher Education Cost Projections   275
Table 17-3   Income Shifting Summary   276
Table 18-1   Life Expectancies   296
Table 18-2   Life Insurance Worksheet   300
Table 19-1   Chart of Delayed Retirement Credit Rates   308
Table 19-2   Future Increases in Retirement Age   308
Table 19-3   Social Security Survivor Benefits   309
Table 19-4   Calculating the Average Indexed Monthly Earnings (AIME) and the Primary Insurance Amount (PIA)   312–13
Table 20-1   Present Value of SBP Premiums and Payoffs   325
Table 20-2   A Comparison of SBP and Term Life Insurance   327
Table C-1   Monthly Basic Pay, Officers   355
Table C-2   Monthly Basic Pay, Enlisted Members   356
Table C-3   Reserve Drill Pay, Officers   357
Talbe C-4   Reserve Drill Pay, Enlisted Members   358
Table C-5   Monthly Basic Allowance for Quarters   359
Table C-6   Other Special and Incentive Pay Categories   360
Table C-7   Aviation Career Incentive Pay   361
Table C-8   Aviation Crew Member Hazardous Duty Incentive Pay   362
Table C-9   Air Weapons Controller Pay   363
Table C-10   Career Sea Pay   364
Table C-11   Submarine Pay   365
Table C-12   Medical Officers' Special Pays   366
Table C-13   Dental Officers' Special Pays   367
Table C-14   Dependency and Indemnity Compensation (DIC) Monthly Payments to Surviving Spouses   368
Table D-1   Present Value of $1 Received in N Years   375
Table D-2   Present Value of $1 Received Annually for N Years   376

Preface

PERSONAL FINANCIAL PLANNING has become an intimidating enterprise for almost everyone in recent years. As the variety and complexity of spending, investment, and insurance options available have increased dramatically, so has the challenge of managing personal finances. New financial services and different kinds and combinations of investment and insurance programs seem to appear daily, while federal and state laws, tax rates, and existing programs are constantly changing. Under these circumstances, it is understandable if you feel intimidated or even overwhelmed by the prospect of managing your financial affairs. Clearly, wise financial decision-making today depends upon your understanding of the many available choices and upon your being familiar with changes in the laws that affect you and the programs available.

For most of us, a quick look through the financial pages of the daily newspaper is all we need to be convinced that a bewildering variety of financial options are available. There we find investments such as "junior subordinated discount debentures due 2006" and "triple tax free A-rated municipal bonds." In weekly newsmagazines we see advertisements for "universal," "variable," and "declining term" life insurance policies.

Meanwhile, as we struggle to stay abreast of what is going on in the financial marketplace, Congress and state legislatures routinely consider—and frequently approve—changes in Social Security, tax policy, and other laws that affect our financial affairs. Often these changes have far-reaching and unpredictable consequences. For example, revisions in the tax laws, which first substantially encouraged Individual Retirement Accounts and later restricted them as tax revenues declined, have had significant immediate and longer-range impacts both on how people save and on how much they save. Similarly, the reductions in military retirement benefits effective in 1980 and 1987 have left us now with three different ways of calculating retirement income, depending upon when members began their service. In addition to the uncertainty about future Social Security and retirement benefits, of course, military personnel must also be concerned with many other developments and their near-term consequences. The dramatic changes in the international political arena almost certainly will strengthen political pressure to hold down all of the costs of military manpower, including military pay.

In this complex and changing environment, financial planning by servicemembers must be thoughtful, careful, and well informed. The purpose of this book is to provide both the background knowledge and the "nuts-and-bolts" recommendations to help servicemembers manage their finances in precisely that manner.

We all have our own ideas about the best way to spend or save our money. Some of us spend every dollar as quickly as it comes in—occasionally even before. Others spend some and save some, depending on how they feel at any given time. When we do save, or "invest," as we often think of it, we again have some very different ideas about the best way to go about it. Many of us are not willing to risk our savings on investments that might drop in value, so we put our money in savings accounts that are insured by the government or we buy U.S. government savings bonds. At the other extreme, some of us buy the stocks of small companies, hoping to "get in on the ground floor" of the IBM or Apple Computers of the future.

In every stage of our personal financial management—spending, insuring, saving, and investing—we all have individual preferences and different ideas about risk that influence our decisions. Therefore, if you read through this book looking for "answers," you are likely to be disappointed. There are no right answers to personal financial management. There are intelligent choices, however, that you can make about every decision *if* you take the time to understand yourself, make an effort to learn the basics about each of the subjects presented, and perhaps do a little more work by reading or checking with someone you can trust before you commit yourself to any major financial obligation.

The contributors to this book have had a long-standing relationship with the armed services as commissioned officers, instructors at the U.S. Military Academy, or spouses of officers. Most are or have been assigned to the Department of Social Sciences at the U.S. Military Academy. With graduate degrees in economics, business administration, and public administration from many of the nation's leading universities, these faculty members provide instruction in economics and management courses offered at West Point. Along with their graduate education and teaching experience, they bring to this voluntary effort their extensive and varied experiences as military officers in managing their own financial affairs, counseling other servicemembers on financial matters, and teaching personal financial management both to cadets and to other units and organizations within the military and civilian communities.

Our purpose in writing this book, then, is to meet a recognized need of military personnel for a single reference and workbook to help them get their financial affairs in order and keep them that way. The intent is to provide a basic guide for servicemembers that shows them how to arrange their financial affairs—and how to counsel their subordinates—to meet immediate obligations effectively while working toward long-term financial goals.

No book such as this, of course, can provide a solution or specific blueprint for every individual's precise financial situation and problems. This one, however, provides the general information and techniques relevant to financial decision-making and suggests several approaches successfully used by servicemembers in managing their financial affairs. For several common financial decisions, the book contains detailed examples using realistic numbers to provide a starting point for you to use in evaluating your own situation. Also, sources of additional detailed information are provided at the end of most chapters. Before making any decision requiring up-to-date information, you would be wise to consult a current, original source for that information.

This book follows a line of publications on the subject of personal finance by associates in the Department of Social Sciences that dates back to 1967. Former contributors included Brig. Gen. Herman Beukema, Brig. Gen. George A. Lincoln, Lt. Gen. William S. Stone (USAF), Brig. Gen. Robert F. McDermott, Maj. Norbert W. Frische (USAF), Capt. Lloyd C. Briggs, Col. James R. Golden, Lt. Col. Robert Baldwin, Col. Hobart Pillsbury, and Maj. Michael Edleson.

The authors and editors are also grateful for the helpful advice and assistance from both private and government agencies, including the Army and Air Force Mutual Aid Association, Armed Forces Insurance, United Services Automobile Association, the Social Security Administration, the Department of Veterans Affairs, and the Finance and Accounting Office, USMA. Special thanks go to the following for their help in preparing this material: Brad Snyder, Walt Lincoln, Joyce Bond, and Ann Wagoner.

The current associates contributing to this work hope that it will be helpful to its intended audience of service comrades in planning their own financial affairs and in counseling their subordinates.

Introduction

FOR MOST SERVICEMEMBERS, the task of financial planning often appears so overwhelming that it is difficult to get started. Besides, it seems there are always more important things to take care of first. Unfortunately, just as no one else is going to be more interested in your military career than you are, no one else is going to manage your financial affairs for you. Having chosen a career in which you are unlikely ever to be rich, you really owe it to yourself and to your family to get the most from your income. This book is designed to help you do just that, and to help you counsel others so that they can do the same.

Part I, PERSONAL FINANCIAL PLANNING, provides the conceptual information you need to get started. In order to devise a plan to achieve your financial goals, you need to know your starting point. Chapter 1, "Assessing the Situation," explains how to prepare a balance sheet that summarizes your current financial situation. Chapter 2, "Financial Basic Training," explains terms and concepts that you must understand in order to manage your finances effectively. Chapter 3, "Military Pay and Allowances," provides essential background information about the wide range of pay, allowances, and benefits available to you and your dependents. This part closes with a chapter on "Financial Planning and Budgeting," which explains some basic "tools" and suggests some fundamental approaches for financial planning.

In Part II, FINANCIAL BASICS, we look at some important ways to manage routine finances. Although there isn't much that most of you can do to earn more—being in the service is already a twenty-four-hour-a-day job—everyone can better spend what he or she earns to get the most value out of every purchase. Simply put, every dollar saved in our regular purchases can give us just as much enjoyment as if it were an extra dollar earned through overtime or a second job. Best of all, for most Americans—and servicemembers are no exception—the effort required to save that dollar is usually a lot less than the work required to earn it in the first place. Being a smart consumer doesn't have to mean clipping thousands of coupons and tracking every price to the nearest penny, but it does mean paying attention to when and how things are sold and using some financial sense in decision-making about managing money. In this part of the book, we examine four major areas of spending where servicemembers are likely to make routine decisions that could cost them much more than is necessary—banking, credit, meeting medical expenses, and taxes.

Chapter 5, "Banking Smart," and chapter 6, "Using Credit Wisely," cover the fundamentals about day-to-day management of income and spending. Deregulation of the banking industry and the proliferation of new bank and credit arrangements have made these subjects appear thoroughly confusing, but there remain some very basic criteria for using such services that are easy to apply if you just know what to look for.

Chapter 7, "Meeting Medical Expenses," presents a detailed look at an important recurring expense that must be managed closely. Many servicemembers, including a surprisingly large number of officers and noncommissioned officers, have a strong misconception that all of their medical expenses and those of their dependents will be taken care of by the Department of Defense. That is simply not true, and every servicemember should understand the limits of care available under different circumstances and take positive measures to close the gap between what may be needed and what can reasonably be expected to be provided by the government.

Chapter 8, "Paying Your Taxes," looks at a second important recurring expense. Every servicemember has clear responsibilities for insuring that proper amounts are withheld for federal income taxes and for paying state taxes where required. The aggravation, embarrassment, and stiff financial penalties that may result from not knowing those responsibilities are significant.

Part III, BIG TICKET ITEMS, is geared to help you to plan for the most important major expenses you face from time to time. Chapter 9, "Buying a Car," and chapter 10, "Automobile Insurance," take a hard look at balancing the joys of owning and operating a car with the undeniable expenses involved. As is true for all consumers, servicemembers often overlook many important concerns in their initial enthusiasm over a particular car. It is a painful and expensive experience when the details become clear after the fact. The time to "get smart" is before you walk into the showroom or go to the seller's home. Fortunately, there are many excellent ideas and references available to help you do exactly that *before* you sign.

Chapter 11, "Housing," outlines the basics of the most important single financial decision most of us ever make. Although the recent performance of the Northeast housing market has shown that housing is not always a good investment, there *can* be real advantages to home ownership. Making a sound decision about whether to rent or buy when government quarters are unavailable, however, requires a basic understanding of just what is involved for each alternative in each new location where you may be stationed. All of the details this requires cannot possibly be covered in this book, but we do provide an outline of the questions to ask and some of the information needed to make a sound decision.

Chapter 12, "Protecting Your Wealth," presents a look at the most neglected area in most people's financial plan. After buying life insurance, automobile insurance, and usually some sort of medical coverage, servicemembers often neglect protecting their assets with property and liability insurance.

In Part IV, BUILDING YOUR NEST EGG, we explain principles for investing in financial and real assets. While previous sections of this book focus on building a stable financial base of operations, this section goes into the strategy and tactics needed to secure future objectives. Various means of *investment* are presented as possible "avenues of approach" as you move through life accumulating wealth to meet your objectives.

In Chapter 13, "Investing in Financial Assets," we look at the major categories of investments and consider their role in the typical servicemember's financial plan. While some of the language you will encounter may be unfamiliar, there is really nothing complex or mysterious about the subject. Just as personal financial goals will vary enormously, so will the mix of appropriate investments for each individual. Every type of investment will have some advantages and disadvantages. It is virtually impossible to recommend a single investment that will be appropriate for every person under all circumstances. But as you will see in chapter 14, "Buying Mutual Funds," mutual funds provide an ideal way for servicemembers to invest in financial assets.

Chapter 15, "Investing in Real Assets," examines buying such things as property and "collectibles" as investments. Real assets are often much more difficult to buy and sell than financial assets, but they also may offer above average growth in value, particularly during inflationary times, as well as the intangible joy of ownership.

In Part V we look ahead to retirement and the benefits available to the servicemember and to family members if the servicemember dies. Many servicemembers do not insure adequately against misfortunes that might affect them or their families. Although Americans today spend billions of dollars on insurance, too often what they buy is not what they need and may not even offer the protection they think they are getting.

Chapter 16, "Military Retirement Benefits," highlights existing entitlements for military retirees. Chapter 17, "Estate Planning," reviews the nuts and bolts for arranging your personal affairs to better guarantee that after your death your property is distributed according to your wishes. Chapter 18, "Life Insurance," looks at the many options available for replacing lost income in the event of your premature death for those who may be dependent upon you. Finally, chapter 19, "Social Security and Veterans Benefits," and chapter 20, "Retirement Survivor Benefits," look at the specific programs that servicemembers can integrate into a comprehensive plan for retirement and financial security for their heirs.

The final section, Part VI, presents several appendixes providing sources of assistance, a glossary, current pay tables, present value tables, and a sample personal affairs record. These are included to provide additional information and for your use in developing your personal financial plans.

Part I

PERSONAL FINANCIAL PLANNING

1

Assessing the Situation

AS MEMBERS OF the military, we plan continually as part of our job. Few of us, however, put the same effort into our personal financial planning. If we did, we'd more likely be able to avoid those "peanut butter and jelly" months that occur when an unexpected expense pops up.

TABLE 1-1
A Comparison of Military and Financial Planning

Military	Financial
Situation	Balance sheet / Net worth
Objective	Financial goals
Plan	Creating the budget
Execution	Implementing the budge
Consolidate / Redistribute	Review / Revise the budget

Table 1-1 shows a comparison between military and financial planning. Understanding the current situation is the first step in personal financial planning. In this chapter, we will help you assess your situation by assisting you in creating a balance sheet. The next few chapters will give you a quick introduction to some basic financial concepts and to setting financial goals. Once you know where you are and where you are going, all you need is a means to get there. The budget is a plan that enables you to achieve your goals. As with any plan, you must provide for contingencies and periodically review to check your progress. In all cases, you will need to revise your plan as your financial situation changes.

THE BALANCE SHEET

A balance sheet is nothing more than a snapshot of your financial situation at a specific point in time. As you can see in Table 1-2, the balance sheet has two sides. In order for it to "balance," the two sides must be equal; assets must equal the sum of liabilities and net worth.

Assets are simply the things that you own. They are listed at their "fair market value," which is the amount of money that a willing buyer would pay a willing seller for a particular item today. In some cases, the fair market value will be significantly lower than the price you paid for the item. A car is a good example. Once you drive across the exit ramp leaving the dealership, the amount that you could get for the car is considerably less than the check you just wrote. On the other hand, some of your assets should appreciate in value, and the amount that you list on the balance sheet will be more than what you paid.

Your debts, or liabilities, are listed on the right-hand side of the balance sheet. This is simply a list of all your creditors and the amount that you owe them.

The other section on the right-hand side of the balance sheet represents your net worth. This is an important number because it shows how much money you would have left over if you had to sell all your assets and pay all your creditors. Net worth is equal to assets minus liabilities. Many young couples, especially those with school loans and a car loan, will find that they have a negative net worth until they pay down some of the debt that they owe. A negative net worth is not a sustainable financial situation. If your net worth is negative, the financial plan that we are developing should help get you out of this situation. On the other hand, as your net worth becomes positive and grows larger, you may find that you are actually capable of living off the interest that your assets generate.

Once you total the liabilities and the net worth, the right-hand side will equal the left-hand side and the balance sheet will balance. Remember, the focus of the balance sheet is to give you a picture of your current financial situation. You may or may not like that picture. The purpose of this book is to help you to order your personal finances, and, over time, to improve your balance sheet. The chapters in this book will help you to understand some of the many aspects of personal finance. With some work on your part, some sacrifice in the near term, and some luck, you can improve your bottom line, set and achieve financial goals, and reduce the number of "peanut butter and jelly" months that you and your family have. As usual, we must begin with training in the basics.

TABLE 1-2
A Family Balance Sheet:
Determining Your Net Worth

ASSETS		LIABILITIES & NET WORTH	
LIQUID ASSETS		**SHORT-TERM DEBT**	
Cash	$_____	VISA	$_____
Savings Accts		MasterCard	_____
1.	_____	American Express	_____
2.	_____	Discover	_____
Checking Accts		Store Cards	
1.	_____	1.	_____
2.	_____	2.	_____
Money Market Fund	_____	3.	_____
		Signature Loan	_____
Total Liquid Assets	_____	Overdraft Protection Loan	_____
REAL PROPERTY		**Total Short-Term Debt**	_____
Primary Residence	$_____	**LONG-TERM DEBT**	
Autos/Recreational Vehicles		Auto/Recreational Vehicle Loan	
1.	_____	1.	_____
2.	_____	2.	_____
Recreation Equipment	_____	Appliance/Furniture Loan	_____
Other	_____	Bank Loan	_____
Total Real Property	_____	Finance Company Loan	_____
PERSONAL PROPERTY		College Loan	_____
		Loan from Family/Friends	_____
Furniture & Appliances	$_____	Primary Residence	_____
Stereos, TVs, Computer, etc	_____	Second Home	_____
Clothing	_____	Rental Property	_____
Jewelry	_____		
Other	_____	**Total Long-Term Debt**	_____
Total Personal Property	_____		
INVESTMENTS		**TOTAL LIABILITIES**	_____
CDs	$_____		
Bonds	_____	**NET WORTH**	_____
Mutual Funds	_____		
Stocks	_____		
Rental Property	_____	**TOTAL LIABILITIES &**	
Cash Value of Life Ins. Policy	_____	**NET WORTH**	_____
Other	_____		
Total Investments	_____		
TOTAL ASSETS	_____		

Notes:
1. Assets should be listed at "market value" (i.e. what you could get for them today if you had to sell them), not "cost."

2

Financial Basic Training

MOST READERS CAN digest most of this book without any special training or tools in economic or financial analysis. While this makes individual topics easily accessible, the old saying that "a little knowledge is dangerous" can prove to be true. Really understanding insurance, investments, mortgages, and car leases requires a basic understanding of a few simple principles of finance and economics, including before-tax versus after-tax income; inflation (real versus nominal values); opportunity cost; time value of money; and the relationship between risk and reward. You don't need an MBA to develop a rudimentary understanding of these concepts sufficient to aid in making solid financial decisions. This brief chapter provides the financial basic training you need to identify key issues, avoid confusion, and separate the gimmicks from the good ideas in the vast supermarket of financial products.

Many people ask, "Why worry about learning financial concepts? I can always consult a professional if I don't understand something." Unfortunately, professional advice costs money—money that can't go into your investment plan. Actually, the problem is that there are too many professionals out there willing to give you advice, often "for free." There are financial salesmen, advisors, planners, counselors, brokers, and consultants all hoping to share in a piece of your portfolio. They are as wide ranging as you can imagine in terms of qualifications, motivation, products offered, and sales tactics. There are many good professionals who are truly professional and worth their fees. But the less you know about financial basics, the more likely you are to fall prey to high-pressure salesmen more interested in a sizable commission than in your welfare. A skilled salesman can make any financial product look enticing, regardless of its true merits. You must defend your wealth by arming yourself with enough basic knowledge to sort out the ridiculous from the rewarding.

BEFORE-TAX AND AFTER-TAX INCOME

Taxes enter into every investment, saving, and spending decision so regularly and routinely that we often ignore them completely. But simply knowing the difference between before-tax income and after-tax income can be a major help in budget and investment decision-making. Chapter 8 is dedicated to personal tax issues.

A few everyday examples affecting servicemembers come immediately to mind. For illustration purposes, we'll consider a captain in the 28 percent tax bracket, with no state taxes. You probably know that the Basic Allowance for Quarters (BAQ) and Variable Housing Allowance (VHA) are not taxable. Receiving $644 in a combined BAQ and VHA allowance (*after-tax income*) is equivalent to receiving $1,000 in pay (*before-tax income*). Why? Because if you had received $1,000 in pay, $280 would come out for federal taxes, and about $76 more would be deducted for Social Security tax. These differences are often ignored (particularly state income tax and Social Security tax), causing servicemembers to underestimate their effective income. The true value of any out-of-pocket savings (such as lower commissary prices) is also underestimated.

The bottom line is that $1 in after-tax income is better than $1 in before-tax income. Seven dollars in coupon savings is better than $10 of additional pay (which provides only $6.44 after taxes to our captain above). This is particularly important information when you are budgeting. In actuality, a penny saved is *not* a penny earned: It is far more than a penny earned, because the taxing authority gets a big chunk of the penny earned.

As a result of this, work that you (or your family) do "for yourself" can pay off in a bigger way than you think. Paying a neighborhood kid $10 to mow the lawn really costs our captain $15.54 of his salary (he had to earn $15.54 to have $10 left over after taxes). By cutting it himself, he would effectively "earn" $15.54 of before-tax income.

Because every dollar we see is equally green, we forget that the after-tax dollars are so much better. Maybe it would be better if we received our gross pay, and then had to dole out, a dollar at a time, all of the tax deductions, so we'd treat the few remaining after-tax dollars with the respect they deserve.

Once you've earned income and had it taxed, and then saved and invested some, it gets taxed again. Well, not your investment itself; only the earnings (dividends, interest, capital gains) on your investment really get taxed. So by some measure, you have to worry about taxes *twice* with investments—once going into the investment, and once coming out of it. In general, the most powerful tax savings are on the front end, if you can get them. That is, unless you face much higher tax rates in the future, you are far better off investing all of your before-tax dollars (before the IRS gets hold of some of them) than to invest only those dollars left after taxes. But how can you invest before-tax dollars, since the IRS taxes your earnings before you get a chance to invest them? The most common way to do this (and almost all servicemembers can) is with an Individual Retirement Account (IRA). As long as your adjusted gross income is under $50,000 (married), you have the opportunity to put at least some before-tax dollars to work in an IRA investment without losing any of them to the tax man. Also, if you have a spouse working in the civilian sector and any retirement plan (401k is the most common) is offered, money can be deducted from salary *before* taxes are paid to fund a retirement investment. Similar deals exist for anyone with a sideline business or self-employment income. These are phenomenal opportunities that are passed up by most servicemembers.

Tax savings are also available on the back end of your investment, depending on the investment vehicle that you choose. Just remember that there may be a difference between what you earn on an investment *before* taxes and what you earn *after* taxes. While Social Security taxes do not apply to investment income, other taxes do. A major who thinks her earnings on a bond are 10 percent will get only 7.2 percent after taxes. While the range of tax strategies is far too varied to cover here and in the tax chapter, a few brief points are so obvious but generally overlooked that they must be mentioned.

Retirement plans not only allow front-end tax savings, but also allow investment income to compound tax-free within the fund. (Actually, all these tax savings are really only tax deferrals, because the money is taxed when it is withdrawn. Even so, such tax deferrals are valuable to the individual.) Money grows much faster this way, particularly over longer periods of time. The advantages are so overwhelming that if you had some money you could do without for at least a few years, you would need a pretty convincing reason *not* to fill up your IRA or other retirement fund. See chapters 8 and 13 for more information.

Other general strategies have to do with the fact that capital gains are not taxed until they are realized (sold). A capital gain is the difference between the price at which you sell an asset and the price at which you bought it. If held until your death, capital gains are totally untaxed. Thus, it makes sense to put investments that generate interest income (bonds and CDs) into your tax-deferred retirement funds and to have equity investments (stocks, which are usually held for their capital gain potential) outside your IRA. Many people have it backward, for whatever reason. Also, don't carelessly sell a long-term stock investment, as you'll have to pay taxes on the full capital gain now, instead of deferring the tax until later or avoiding it completely.

If you are in a high income tax bracket, it might be to your advantage to purchase the stocks of companies that pay low dividends in order to retain earnings for financing future growth. This makes sense because dividend income is taxed immediately, whereas capital gains are not taxed until you have realized them by selling your stocks. If you concentrate on stocks that will appreciate in market value in the future, you can defer payment of taxes on your investment income. As you will see in the "Time Value of Money" section later in this chapter, it is always advantageous to speed up receipts and defer payments of money as much as possible.

Also, remember that college expenses for children generally get paid out of after-tax income. That is, your college fund investments are generally taxed "on both ends." But this need not be the case. In chapter 17, some income-shifting strategies are discussed, and there are some financial instruments such as Series EE savings bonds described in chapter 13 that will keep investment income from being taxed, or at least tax it at a lower rate.

If you itemize your deductions when you file your income tax return, you can minimize your tax liability by claiming all deductions to which you are entitled. One deduction that is commonly underreported is the state and local income taxes you paid during a tax year. In the "Taxes You Paid" section of Form 1040, Schedule A, you can deduct the sales taxes you have paid during the year. If you keep receipts of significant purchases you have made, you can add up all the sales taxes you have paid and claim them as a deduction against your taxable income. Of course, how many receipts you should keep depends on how beneficial the deduction is and how willing you are to spend time performing addition. It may not be worthwhile to save a receipt for a $5 meal you bought for lunch, but it is prudent to save a receipt for a $1,000 furniture purchase. Finally, the purchase of a home provides perhaps the best available tax shield. Because mortgage interest is tax deductible, you should consider buying a home if you currently do not own one.

Although some of these strategies may appear obvious, many military families fail to take advantage of them. Such failures probably result from a lack of understanding of the substantial difference between before-tax and after-tax income.

INFLATION

We're all aware of inflation; we just do a poor job of working it into our financial planning. Since purchasing power tends to decline over time, we need an increasingly higher number of dollars to purchase the same level of goods. This raises the important distinction between *real* and *nominal* values. If we speak in terms of *nominal* dollars, we mean whatever a dollar can buy at a given time, even if that's a head of lettuce today and a single pinto bean in the year 2010. Thus, if we set our financial goals in nominal dollars, it's extremely important to make sure we account for inflation properly. It wouldn't make much sense basing our 1995 budget on the same figures we used in 1990, because we would need more nominal dollars due to inflation, and our income, in nominal dollars, is likely to increase with inflation as well. If we speak in terms of a *real* dollar, we refer to its purchasing power in a base year. Thus, if you expect to purchase something at some point in the future that costs $100 in 1994, you'll need a (larger) sum of money that will buy the same as $100 bought in 1994. In 1995, $100 in *real* 1994 dollars would be the equivalent of $104 in *nominal* 1995 dollars if the inflation rate is 4 percent in 1994.

Although it is a bit confusing, this doesn't seem too terribly difficult—so where is the problem? Well, often problems arise when there is an inconsistency in your planning; either you ignore inflation altogether, or you somehow get real and nominal figures mixed up. Many whole life insurance policies and investment contracts have been using projections of a million nominal dollars sometime in the future. The salesman is talking in nominal dollars (where a Yugo might cost a quarter million!), while you are dreamily thinking in real dollars (gosh, if I could have a million dollars just think what I could buy!). Another problem is failing to forecast projected numbers consistently. In evaluating a rental property investment, you could figure that your rents would go up by 5 percent a year but make no adjustment to expenses for inflation, causing you to overvalue the deal. Or you could make no adjustment for any inflation at all and undervalue the deal. We must be careful to treat inflation correctly when analyzing any investment situation.

Just as there are real and nominal dollars, there are also real and nominal rates of return on investments. If you purchase a $1,000 one-year bond that pays 8 percent interest, you will have $1,080 dollars next year. But if inflation was 4 percent over the year, it takes $1,040 nominal dollars to buy what could be bought with $1,000 real dollars. Although your nominal rate of return on this investment was 8 percent, your real rate of return was only 4 percent. Your purchasing power increases at the real rate of return, not at the nominal rate. It is easy to convert the nominal rate of return to a real rate of return—simply subtract the inflation rate. (Note: This is actually an approximation that works well only over short periods of time, say one to two years.) It is possible to have a negative real rate of return if the inflation rate is larger than the nominal rate of return. When this happens, your purchasing power declines.

Because inflation erodes purchasing power, it is important to protect your savings against inflation. Some investments, like savings accounts and life insurance policies, provide relatively low nominal rates of return—at times even negative real rates of return—and therefore provide inadequate protection against inflation. Stocks and tangible assets such as real estate, precious metals, and art objects have historically performed better in protecting purchasing power. If you expect inflation to be high in the future, you should consider investing in some of those assets.

OPPORTUNITY COST

The opportunity cost of any action or decision is simply the value of the best alternative that was forgone. Cost in this sense may not be purely monetary but may also include your time or even something intangible. The opportunity cost of getting an M.B.A. degree is not just the $40,000 or so you will pay in tuition and fees, but would also include the two years of lost wages, two years of forgone seniority, perhaps the cost of two moves, and some additional stress.

Opportunity cost is a concept best understood in conjunction with the saying "There is no free lunch." You will be confronted with many situations that claim to offer something for free, at least monetarily. "Free" financial advice often comes in conjunction with hidden or even explicit commissions or fees. Be on guard, and use your common sense when offered a deal that seems too good to be true.

Whole life insurance provides an excellent example of the opportunity cost idea. Some insurance agents will proudly show how you can buy their insurance product and ten years later get all of your premium money back, making it sound like free insurance! But if you stop to analyze the opportunity cost, you see that the money you spent on whole life premiums could have bought cheaper term insurance with no cash value. You could have invested the difference and possibly had even more cash to show for it than with the whole life policy. In fact, the saving in premium payments that term insurance affords is one of the places you should look when trying to find funds to set aside for your financial goals.

TIME VALUE OF MONEY

Would you rather pay your $200 grocery bill right at the store, or pay the $200 a month later? Would you rather receive a $1,000 gift right now, or wait a year? Of course, we like to get money as soon as possible and delay giving it up as long as possible. This actually has more to do with interest rates than it does with any human quality like greed or impatience. With a bank account paying you 3 percent interest (that's .25 percent per month), all you would need is $199.50 in the bank right now to cover the delayed $200 grocery bill next month. That's better than paying $200 right now. The $1,000 gift received right now will grow to $1,030 by next year; that beats getting $1,000 next year. In fact, the interest rate is the *opportunity cost* of money, reflecting its time value.

At this time, it would be a good idea for you to read through appendix D, which gives a more detailed treatment of the time value of money and the related concept of *present value*. An example of this has already been given: The present value of $200 received a month later is $199.50 if the interest rate is 3 percent. The $200 future value is said to be "discounted" to the present at a *discount rate* of 3 percent per annum, or .25 percent for the one-month period in question. Present value techniques are quite useful in analyzing such problems as which mortgage or car loan to take, whether to buy property or not, and how much a particular financial contract is worth.

Specific applications of interest rates and present values are given throughout this book. It's a good idea to understand the techniques and even to be able to replicate them. You should have an inexpensive ($10 to $20 range) financial calculator that will easily and quickly solve numerically complicated formulas. Most computer spreadsheet software (like Quattro Pro, Excel, and Lotus 1-2-3) will also perform these calculations. But unless you know what a present value is, and how to use it once it's calculated, this technology will be useless.

A conceptual application of the importance of the time value of money involves contract funds, which are explained in the mutual fund chapter. Basically, you sign a contract to purchase an investment on a periodic basis, but you pay most of your fees to the salesman in the first twelve months (and very little in the way of fees in later months). While *on average* you pay 8.5 percent of your gross investment to the salesman in fees over the entire contract period, the reality is far worse. Because most of the fees you pay are up front, their present value is extremely high. The fee "savings" in later years have a present value that is extremely low. By using present value techniques, you can calculate that the percentage commission you are effectively paying the salesman is more than 12 percent in present value, even though it looks like only 8.5 percent "on paper." With an understanding of the concept of the time value of money, you could have figured out without calculating any numbers at all that this type of a fee structure is a bad deal for you.

RISK AND REWARD

We all take risks when we invest our money. You may need the money in a certificate of deposit before it matures; your money market fund could dip in value; house, stock, and bond prices fluctuate constantly. Even a "risk-free" investment like a Treasury bill is subject to some price risk while you own it. That is, the price at which you could resell the T-bill varies from day to day. *Risk* is the amount of uncertainty or variance in your possible future returns on an investment over some holding period. Investments vary greatly in the amount of risk involved. You get to choose your own risk level for your investment program.

Most investors would prefer less risk, everything else held equal. Thus, if an investment is risky, investors would not be very likely to purchase it at the same rates of return as a safe investment. In the late 1980s, when Treasury bonds were yielding about 9 percent, there was no way that investors would purchase corporate bonds also yielding 9 percent, because there is a significantly greater chance that a corporation will default on its debt than that the U.S. government will default. At 10 percent, however, investors were willing to purchase the bonds of very solid corporations. And at 15 to 20 percent, they were even tempted to invest in very risky corporate bonds that came to be known as "junk bonds." Because the typical investor doesn't like risk, market returns on risky investments are higher to compensate investors for incurring the "cost" of that risk.

As a rough guideline, historical returns over the past several decades show this relationship at work. The very long-run average return on nearly riskless T-bills is just barely over inflation. Long-term T-bonds are riskier (more volatile in their price movements, not at risk of default) and have averaged a 1 percent real rate of return. Assuming the additional risk of corporate bonds earns an average real return of almost 2 percent. But common stocks, which have the most price uncertainty, have returned almost 7 percent over inflation on average over the past six decades. Based on a rough estimate of expected inflation of 3 to 4 percent annually, you might expect an *average* return in the stock market of about 12 percent per year in the long run. That's quite a reward, but then the risk has been fairly substantial as well—stock prices move fairly wildly, even if you hold a diversified portfolio.

Don't confuse the long-run averages with what actually happens on a year-to-year basis. Stock market returns have an annual standard deviation of about 20 percent. As a general rule, you can expect results within a standard deviation of the average about two-thirds of the time. This means that *most of the time,* your returns in the market will range between losing 8 percent of your value and gaining a sizable 32 percent. About one year in six you could expect to do *better* than a 32 percent gain, but the bad news is that you will just as frequently have a year where you lose even more than 8 percent, perhaps a lot more. And although the 1980s were far better than average for market performance, there were still some particularly bad years. The high risk inherent in stock investments means that you are less likely to be able to predict future performance with any confidence or accuracy. So, to earn high returns in the stock market, either you must be willing to subject your annual outcome to substantial uncertainty and even be willing occasionally to lose money, or you must have a rather long time horizon (retirement planning or college funding) to let these year-to-year gyrations average out. Over a four-year time frame, the risk in your average annual return on stocks is approximately cut in half, so that two-thirds of the time your annualized return over the entire four-year period will fall in a range between roughly a 4 percent gain and a 24 percent gain. Remember, though, that there is still some likelihood that you might lose money over even a four-year period.

From the discussion so far, it might seem that there is a definite relationship between risk and reward—as you take more risk, your expected (long-run average) reward goes up as well. That's a good general sense to have, but it is not quite accurate. Unreasonable and unnecessary risk is generally not rewarded. Risk in a well-crafted, *diversified* portfolio (i.e., a collection of investments in different financial assets) usually is rewarded (although not every year, of course). This is a finer point, but one that is crucial particularly for the small investor to grasp.

Someone who invests in a single risky stock, XYZ, and nothing else, may experience returns with a standard deviation of 40 to 50 percent per year. That's a lot of risk. It is also a lot of unnecessary risk. The typical investor in XYZ stock holds a little bit of it (perhaps through a mutual fund) in conjunction with several other stocks and bonds. That investor has a diversified portfolio of investments. The risk of wild movements in XYZ stock is absorbed and averaged out with the differing movements of the many other investments in the portfolio; some go up, others go down, but on average the overall return is positive.

Diversification reduces risk, but it does not eliminate risk. Even a diversified portfolio of investments experiences price risk, and it is this nondiversifiable risk that the market rewards. If you do not diversify your portfolio, then the market assumes that either you have a high tolerance for risk, or you are ignorant of the benefits of diversification. *The market will reward you only for the risk that you must bear.* Being somewhat stingy, it will not reward you for your excessive risk tolerance or your ignorance.

A purer example of this is gold-mining stocks. By themselves, they are incredibly risky; almost no investors would choose to hold a gold stock without diversifying their holdings. Yet for all this incredible risk, gold stocks actually return (on average) several percentage points lower than the average stock. The reason for this is a little complex, but quite instructive. Gold stocks' price movements seem to be completely unrelated to other stocks: When most stocks are moving down, there's no telling what a gold stock will be doing; it could easily be going up. By taking a little of this individualistic gold stock and putting it in a portfolio with a lot of "typical" stocks, you might actually *reduce* the overall risk of the portfolio's return. That is, because of the rebel movements the gold stock adds to your portfolio, a bad day for the market now won't be quite as bad for your portfolio, but a good day for the market won't be quite as good, either. This risk reduction is a nice quality for which diversified investors are willing to "pay" by accepting a slightly lower average return on the gold stock. This is ironic, given the outrageous level of risk in the gold stock *by itself,* but market returns are not driven by the needs of a few irrational and overly risky holdings of a few investors.

So in this seemingly contradictory world of "risk gets rewards" but "unreasonable individual risk gets no rewards," what is a small investor to do? First, determine the level of risk with which you are comfortable. You're never going to make enough on a moderate portfolio to make it worth losing sleep over. Then, pick a diversified portfolio of investments that will achieve your risk target. If you hold only one or two stocks or bonds, either you will give up a sizable return to achieve your risk goal, or else you will accept much more risk than you were comfortable with to achieve a return goal. With a diversified portfolio, you get to have your cake and eat it too.

But do not include too many securities in your portfolio; you incur a brokerage fee every time you buy or sell, and the benefits from diversification decrease rather quickly. Academic research has shown that as a portfolio is expanded from one to five securities, the gain in diversification is substantial. Further additions to the portfolio, until it contains ten securities, will still yield significant gains, but beyond ten securities the improvement is slight. Also, remember that the more securities you include in your portfolio, the more time you will have to spend tracking their performance as you manage your portfolio. For investors who are willing to spend time managing their portfolios, picking three to ten securities in which to invest may be the best choice.

For those who do not want to manage their portfolios, a *mutual fund* may be the appropriate instrument for achieving their goals. More information on investing in financial assets, mutual funds, and real assets is available in chapters 13 through 15.

SUMMARY

Saving and investing are certainly not easy for most of us. In a complex world of investment bankers, convertible subordinated debentures, and put options on commodities futures, you cannot be blamed for feeling a bit overwhelmed sometimes. But you don't need to learn everything at once; just master a few basic concepts, and internalize them into your thinking about your personal financial options. This, we hope, will keep you from buying financial products that you don't want or need and will help you avoid misunderstanding what various products offer to you. Many financial products that servicemembers buy are overpriced, oversold, and should be avoided. We're not stupid, and we're certainly not more stupid than the next guy. Bad or mediocre products are usually distorted by a skilled seller to look better than they are. How is this done? In almost all cases, the "magic" is a simple twisting around or violation of one of the five basic concepts presented above. It is easy to make a deal seem too good to be true when you confuse present and future values; ignore taxes, inflation, and the time value of money; ignore the opportunity cost; or avoid risk analysis and comparison. Once you understand these concepts, it is easier to sort out the truth from the exaggeration or even misrepresentation. You may not be able to convince an eager salesman of your more accurate point of view, but at least you'll know when to shut the door or hang up the phone. Just remember, it's your money, and no one (except the IRS) can tell you what you ought to do with it.

3

Military Pay, Allowances, and Benefits

DETERMINING YOUR INCOME is one of the initial steps toward establishing a personal financial plan. Total income can include service pay and allowances, returns from savings and investments, part-time work, and the earnings of other members of your family. This chapter will focus on the portion of income earned from military service. This includes military pay and allowances and the other benefits available to you while you are on active duty.

MILITARY PAY AND ALLOWANCES

All branches of the armed forces provide a monthly Leave and Earnings Statement (LES) that lists your pay and allowances, allotments, and any collections made for that month. You should also receive a midmonth Military Net Pay Advice.

If you examine your LES, you should be able to identify the following sections:

- Entitlements: pay and allowances you received.
- Deductions: federal and state taxes, FICA–Social Security and Medicare, collections from your pay for past overpayments, fines, forfeitures, and so on.
- Allotments: portions of your entitlements paid at your direction to family members, financial institutions, or charities.
- Summary: take-home pay paid to you or sent to your bank (end-of-month pay).
- Leave Information: your leave days accrued during the current fiscal year and your current balance.
- Tax Information: a summary of federal, FICA, and state income taxes withheld.

Before discussing benefits, we will focus on the entitlements section of your LES. *The Department of Defense Military Pay and Allowances Entitlements Manual,*

16 • PERSONAL FINANCIAL PLANNING

which can be found at your local finance office, provides a more detailed description of all available pay and allowances.

There is a key distinction between military entitlements identified as "pay" and those identified as "allowances." By law, federal and state taxes are deducted from "pay," whereas "allowances" are tax exempt. When comparing military and civilian pay, you will frequently see "tax advantage" adjustments for allowances to show how much one actually shields from taxes.

Basic Pay

Basic pay can be received twice a month or once at the end of the month. The twice-a-month option provides you with half of your pay on the fifteenth of each month and the remaining pay at the end of the month. Take advantage of this option, because it allows you more flexibility in paying bills. Even if you don't need it to pay bills, you can earn two weeks' interest on half your pay every month.

Appendix C shows monthly basic pay rates for officers and enlisted personnel by pay grade and length of service as of 1 January 1994. Pay rates are reviewed annually by Congress; changes are usually made effective January 1.

For pay purposes, length of service includes all periods of active and inactive service as a commissioned officer, warrant officer, flight officer, or enlisted person in any regular or reserve component of any of the uniformed services. It does not include time served as a cadet, midshipman, or ROTC student.

Housing Allowances

Servicemembers are authorized a Basic Allowance for Quarters (BAQ) according to pay grade and family composition when government quarters are not available. The BAQ rates as of 1 January 1994 are shown in Appendix C. Single members normally receive BAQ at the "without dependents" rate; married members receive BAQ at the "with dependents" rate. If you reside in government quarters considered substandard because of size or condition, BAQ may be paid at the "partial rate."

You may receive a Variable Housing Allowance (VHA) in addition to BAQ if you live in a high-cost area. The amount of VHA depends on your pay grade, the type of BAQ you received, and the average cost of civilian housing in the area to which you are assigned. As an example, an E-5 with dependents would receive a VHA of $44.20 at Fort Hood, Texas; $155.24 at Norfolk, Virginia; and $164.57 at Edwards AFB, California. An O-3 stationed at the same locations would receive $46.51, $228.14, and $156.69, respectively. Under the Rent Plus program in overseas areas, monthly housing allowances are based on actual rent, up to a ceiling for each pay grade and area. Check with your local finance office to determine the amount of VHA or Rent Plus (if any) authorized for your area.

Subsistence and Clothing Allowances

These allowances are designed to help defray the cost of food and clothing. As of 1 January 1994, all officers receive the Basic Allowance for Subsistence (BAS) at a fixed rate of $142.46 per month. Enlisted members are paid BAS only when meals are not provided by the government. Rates for BAS for enlisted members as of 1 January 1994 are as follows:

- $6.80 per day if on leave or authorized separate rations.
- $7.67 per day if government meals are unavailable.
- $10.16 per day under emergency conditions if no government dining facilities exist.

Clothing allowances are paid monthly to enlisted personnel to help defray the cost of clothing repair and replacement. Payment amounts vary with branch of service, length of service, and gender. Check with your finance office for specifics.

Other Pay and Allowances

Many servicemembers receive additional pay and allowances based on categories such as special skills, type of duty, and location of duty. The following listings summarize the most important categories. Your local finance office will have the complete details.

Hazardous Duty Incentive Pay

This type of pay applies to the following hazardous duties:

1. Duty involving parachuting.
2. Duty involving frequent participation in flight operations on the decks of ships from which aircraft may be launched.
3. Duty inside a high- or low-pressure chamber.
4. Duty as a human acceleration or deceleration experimental subject.
5. Duty involving the servicing of aircraft or missiles using toxic fuels or propellants.
6. Duty involving the demolition of explosives, including training for such duty.
7. Duty as a human test subject in thermal stress experiments.
8. Duty involving handling of chemical munitions.

With the exception of a High-Altitude Low-Opening (HALO) parachutist receiving $165 per month, servicemembers who qualify for Hazardous Duty Incentive Pay as non-crew members will receive $110 per month. Instead of hazardous duty pay, crew members receive incentive pay based on their rank and years of accrued service.

Hostile Fire/Imminent Danger Pay

Except in time of war declared by Congress, servicemembers are paid $150 per month for any month in which they are present in a designated "hostile fire/imminent danger area." If wounded in a hostile fire area, members are entitled to up to three months' hostile fire pay while hospitalized.

Foreign Duty Pay

Enlisted members assigned to duty at certain places outside the forty-eight contiguous states may be entitled to foreign duty pay. The amounts range from $8.00 per month for an E-1/E-2 to $22.50 per month for those in pay grades E-7 through E-9. Contact your local finance officer for pay rates for specific locations.

Family Separation Allowance

Married members whose assignments separate them from their families for thirty or more consecutive days receive a monthly allowance of $75. If members are not assigned to government quarters while separated from their families, they also may be entitled to draw an extra monthly BAQ at the "without dependents" rate to defray the costs of maintaining two homes.

Sea Pay

Some officers and enlisted members receive sea pay as an incentive for service on ships at sea. The rates will vary with pay grade and cumulative years of sea duty and are shown as of 1 January 1994 in appendix C.

Submarine Duty Pay

Naval personnel who meet certain submarine duty qualifications are entitled to monthly submarine duty pay. Rates as of 1 January 1994 are in appendix C.

Nuclear Duty Pay

Officers having nuclear qualifications and who are performing duties involving nuclear operations and equipment are authorized special pay. There are three general categories of nuclear pay:

1. New accessions to nuclear specialties receive a bonus of up to $8,000.
2. Members extending their obligations in nuclear specialties for three, four, or five years may receive bonuses of up to $12,000 per year of extension.
3. Members serving in nuclear specialties beyond an obligated extension may receive an incentive bonus of up to $10,000 per year.

Diving Duty Pay

Members assigned to diving duty are entitled to special pay for periods of actual diving performance. A master diver can receive up to $300 a month.

MILITARY PAY, ALLOWANCES, AND BENEFITS • 19

Flying Pay
Servicemembers who participate in regular and frequent aerial flights as crew or non-crew members are entitled to flying pay. The monthly amount of pay depends on a number of factors; see appendix C for details.

Foreign Language Proficiency Pay
Members who have qualified as proficient in certain foreign languages will receive a monthly allowance of between $25 and $100.

Special Pay for Health Care Professionals
Veterinarians and optometrists are entitled to special pay of $100 per month. Several types of special pays are authorized for dentists, medical doctors, nurse anesthetists, and chiropractors, depending on rank, years of service, and qualifications. The details are shown in appendix C.

TRAVEL PAY AND ALLOWANCES

Permanent-change-of-station (PCS) and temporary duty (TDY) travel can be a genuine drain on your financial resources. Fortunately, you are entitled to financial assistance to help defray the cost of travel. For a complete reference, see the *Joint Travel Regulations for the Uniformed Services,* commonly called the JTR, available at your finance office.

Permanent Change of Station

Moving yourself, your family, and your household goods will be easier if you know what type of assistance the government will provide. We have moved enough times to realize that not all costs are covered, so make the best use of what the government offers.

Travel Pay
The pay you receive will depend on whether the government provides the transportation (either using its own vehicle or a common carrier) or you provide your own privately owned vehicle (POV). If you provide your own transportation, you are entitled to a Monetary Allowance in Lieu of Transportation (MALT) of 15 cents per mile for yourself, 17 cents per mile if one family member is traveling with you, 19 cents with two family members, or 20 cents with more than two family members. The official distance between permanent duty stations, including travel to TDY locations en route to the new duty station, will be used to calculate your mileage allowance. In addition, the servicemember receives a flat rate of $50 per diem (less BAS for enlisted members), family members twelve years and older receive $37.50 per diem, and those

under twelve receive $25 per day. When a spouse travels separately from the servicemember, the spouse receives $50 a day.

Most overseas moves are accomplished by government or common carrier. You can also request such "transportation-in-kind" when moving within the United States. You will not receive the mileage allowance when you use transportation-in-kind, but per diem will still be paid. In addition, certain expenses such as cab fares, tips to porters, visa fees, and even the fee for traveler's checks are reimbursable. Keep a good record of such costs and report them when you arrive at your next duty station.

Transportation of Household Goods

The government will pay to move your belongings to your next duty station, within certain weight limitations that depend on your grade and length of service. The government will use the lowest-cost mode of transportation that provides the required service. Your local transportation office will make all the necessary arrangements.

You also may elect to move yourself under the voluntary "Do-It-Yourself" (DITY) program. This program provides a way for some servicemembers to earn extra money by moving themselves using their own truck or van or a rented vehicle (but not a passenger car). If you want to do a DITY move, be certain to apply for it at your transportation office. You must fill out a counseling form and have the empty vehicle weighed before making this type of move. The government will pay you 80 percent of what it would have cost to move you commercially, with 60 percent paid up front. The government may withhold some portion of the final settlement for federal, state, and local taxes.

If you make a DITY move, some problems may arise if government housing is not immediately available when you arrive at your destination. Storage costs can accumulate rapidly. When you finally receive government housing, you must rent a vehicle to move your stored household goods. Clearly, when deciding whether to make a DITY move, your comparisons must be based on a door-to-door analysis. If you have a large household, you may find it much easier to let the government move you. Also, remember that the cost of the DITY move should include your own time and labor.

If you own a mobile home, the government will pay for all or part of the cost of moving it to your next duty station within the continental United States and Alaska. The following three conditions must be met:

1. You bought the home on or before the effective date of the orders.
2. The home will be your residence at your new duty station.
3. The body and chassis, including tires, are in fit condition to the satisfaction of the government.

Moving your mobile home will, in most cases, substitute for shipping your household goods. Note that if the move costs more than it would cost to move your household goods, you must agree in writing to pay the difference. This is fairly common and can be an added expense of several hundred, or thousands, of dollars. To ensure that you will have a place to set up your home, reconnoiter your new duty sta-

MILITARY PAY, ALLOWANCES, AND BENEFITS • 21

tion. Many areas no longer allow mobile homes. One final note: Mobile homes do not always arrive undamaged from the journey, so there may be some additional expenses if the repair costs exceed the amount of government insurance.

If your PCS orders limit the amount of household goods to less than your normal weight allowance, the government will pay for nontemporary storage of what you must leave behind. (The weight shipped plus the amount stored cannot exceed your weight allowance). The government will also pay for ninety days of temporary storage to allow you to locate quarters at your new duty station. Under certain circumstances, this period can be extended an additional ninety days.

For overseas moves, each servicemember may ship one privately owned vehicle (POV) at government expense. Certain restrictions apply for various destinations, so check with your transportation office for specific details.

Other Help

Finally, servicemembers are authorized other types of allowances to help defray the cost of moving.

Except for moving to your first duty station, you are authorized a *Dislocation Allowance* (DLA) equal to two months' BAQ when you relocate your household. You may not receive more than one DLA per fiscal year. Also, if you are a member without dependents and are assigned government quarters at your new duty station, DLA will not be authorized. Single servicemembers are eligible for DLA only if they are not assigned to government quarters.

Servicemembers are authorized to receive a *Temporary Lodging Expense* (TLE) for CONUS moves of up to $110 per day for a maximum of ten days ($1,100).

Overseas Station Allowances are paid to help cover the extra cost of living overseas. If you must stay in a hotel while waiting for quarters overseas, you may be entitled to a TLA for up to sixty days upon arrival. You may be authorized up to ten days of TLA prior to your departure from overseas. You may also receive an *Overseas Housing Allowance* (OHA) and a *Cost of Living Allowance* (COLA) based on the location of the duty station. Rates and conditions vary by overseas location. Check with your local finance office for details.

Your travel pay and the allowances described above are payable in advance. In addition, you may receive one month's base pay in advance and two months' base pay once you've arrived at your new duty station. Be forewarned, however, that you will be required to repay any excess travel and relocation allowances in addition to a monthly deduction for the advance on your base pay.

Temporary Duty

The *Joint Travel Regulation for Uniformed Services* (JTR) governs the travel pay for TDY. Generally, local transportation facilities provide tickets for TDY travel, and the local finance office authorizes per diem allowances to cover food, lodging, and personal care. For enlisted personnel drawing separate rations, per diem will be reduced by the daily BAS rate. The total per diem paid cannot exceed the local maximum rate as authorized by the JTR. For specific details on per diem rates by locality, contact your servicing finance office.

OTHER IMPORTANT BENEFITS

Medical and Dental Care

As a servicemember you are entitled to any medical and dental care you require while on active duty. Medical and dental care for your family, however, will be provided on a space-available basis. See chapter 7 for further information regarding family health care.

Department of Veterans Affairs Benefits

The VA offers a number of programs for your benefit while you are on active duty and after you have resigned or retired. Chapter 19 contains a detailed discussion of the most significant benefits. For complete information, visit, call, or write your nearest VA facility, which you can find listed in your local phone book under U.S. Government, Veterans Affairs.

Servicemen's Group Life Insurance

All members of the armed forces are automatically insured under Servicemen's Group Life Insurance (SGLI) for $100,000 unless they elect in writing not to participate or to be covered for a lesser amount. Servicemembers also have the option to increase their coverage up to $200,000 as of 1 December 1992. Premiums are automatically deducted from your pay. SGLI represents a low-cost method of providing some excellent insurance coverage. Additional insurance will depend on your family situation. SGLI can be converted without a medical exam to Veterans Group Life Insurance (VGLI) when you leave the service. VGLI is a nonrenewable five-year term policy that, upon expiration, can be converted to a permanent individual policy. VGLI premiums are based upon the insured's nearest age on the effective date of the policy.

Survivor Benefits

If you die while on active duty, your family or other designated beneficiaries may be entitled to several lump-sum payments, monthly benefits, and funeral and burial rights. Chapters 17 and 18 discuss the planning for support of your loved ones in the event of your death. This section identifies the types of payments your family may be authorized if you die while on active duty.

MILITARY PAY, ALLOWANCES, AND BENEFITS • 23

Lump-sum Benefits
The following benefits are paid on a one-time basis, at the death of the servicemember.

1. Death Gratuity: A payment equal to six months' pay of the deceased, but not less than $800 or more than $3,000, is paid as soon as possible.
2. Social Security Lump-sum Death Benefit: A one-time payment of $255 is made by the Social Security Administration. This is payable only to the surviving spouse or to an eligible child.
3. Pay for Accrued Leave: Survivors will receive the deceased's basic pay for up to sixty days of earned but unused leave.
4. Arrears of Pay: All pay due but unpaid up to the date of death will be paid to the designated beneficiary of the deceased.

Monthly Payments
1. Dependency and Indemnity Compensation (DIC): A payment based on your pay grade is provided by the VA to surviving family members of deceased active-duty servicemembers. Information on the amount of this entitlement is provided in chapter 19.
2. VA Dependents' Education Allowance: Your surviving spouse and children between the ages of eighteen and twenty-six (extended up to age thirty-one in certain cases) may be eligible for up to forty-five months of education benefits. Spouses must use the benefits within ten years of your death. Training may be in any approved vocational or business school, college, professional school, or establishment providing apprentice or on-the-job training. Current (1994) monthly rates are $404 for full-time attendance, $304 for three-quarter-time, and $202 per month for half-time. Some states may also offer additional assistance (free tuition, loans, grants, and so on) for the survivors of deceased servicemembers who were legal residents of that state.
3. Social Security Survivor Benefits: Benefits are paid to eligible beneficiaries depending on the amount of your average monthly earnings. Computations of the payment are complex. See chapter 19 for a discussion of Social Security benefits.
4. Survivor Benefit Plan: Upon reaching twenty years of service and, thus, eligibility for retirement, active-duty personnel are automatically covered by the Survivor Benefit Plan (SBP). SBP is essentially a life insurance plan that extends your retirement pay to your family in the event of your death. See chapter 20 for a full discussion of the SBP program.

Funeral and Burial Benefits
If you die while on active duty, the government will bury you in any national cemetery (if space is available) designated by your next of kin. Burial of your spouse, minor children, and, in some restricted cases, adult children in the same grave as the servicemember may also be authorized. The nearest national cemetery can provide details.

Arlington National Cemetery is under the jurisdiction of the Department of the Army. For information, write to the Superintendent, Arlington National Cemetery, Arlington, VA 22211, or call (703) 695-3250.

24 • PERSONAL FINANCIAL PLANNING

The government will provide headstones and markers for all persons buried in national cemeteries. For servicemembers, the government will arrange for shipment and preparation of remains and provide a burial flag. If death occurs near a military installation, and the next of kin makes the funeral arrangements, reimbursement may not exceed what the government would have had to pay for preparation of the remains. A maximum reimbursement of $750 will be paid for a death occurring away from a military installation's contracting area.

A servicemember buried in a private cemetery will receive a maximum of $2,140, in addition to preparation costs, to help defray other expenses. If you are buried in a national or post cemetery and the next of kin contracts for a funeral director to conduct the burial, a maximum of $1,390 will be paid in addition to reimbursement for preparation of the remains. For burial in a national or post cemetery with government preparation of the remains, a maximum of $110 is paid to cover other expenses incidental to burial.

SUGGESTED REFERENCES

Army Times, Navy Times, and *Air Force Times* all contain current information on military pay and allowances, and any anticipated changes.

The Handbook for Military Families is published each year as a newspaper supplement to *Army, Navy,* and *Air Force Times* during the first week in April.

DOD Military Pay and Allowances Entitlements Manual.

Joint Travel Regulations for the Uniformed Services (JTR).

4

Financial Planning and Budgeting

ARMED WITH OUR balance sheet, our basic training in financial topics, and our understanding of military pay and allowances, we are ready to undertake the basic tasks of financial planning: setting financial goals and establishing a budget to achieve them. Both of these topics are discussed in this chapter.

ESTABLISHING AN OBJECTIVE: SETTING FINANCIAL GOALS

While most of us have thought about financial goals, few have probably taken the time or effort to calculate just how much achieving these financial goals will "cost." A key part of the goal-setting process is determining how much money you need to set aside, either now or each month, to achieve these goals. Clarifying your objectives and deciding exactly how much to save are important first steps in your personal financial planning. Establishing specific goals can provide the motivation necessary to achieve them.

When calculating what it will cost to achieve your goals, you can use either nominal or real values. The first three rows of Table 4-1 show the projected nominal cost of sending a child to college in 1994, 1999, and 2004. The nominal cost increases from year to year for two reasons. First, inflation erodes the purchasing power of the dollar, so a dollar in 1999 will purchase less than a dollar in 1994. Second, providing a college education in the future may require an increasing amount of real resources, as would be the case if, over time, colleges built new science laboratories and had to charge more for the better educational experience that resulted. Predicting such real price changes is very difficult, and for personal financial planning purposes it is sufficient to ascribe all of these price increases from year to year to inflation. That is, we assume that if we could pay for a year of education at a four-year public college in 2004 with "real" 1994 dollars, the real price would be $7,630. Due to the effect of inflation, however, the nominal price will be $16,613.

TABLE 4-1
Nominal and Real Future College Costs

Average Annual College Expenses (in year)*	Public College		Private College	
	2-Year	4-Year	2-Year	4-Year
1994	$4,991	$7,630	$13,388	$20,455
1999 (nominal, 1999 dollars)	6,945	11,248	20,394	32,415
2004 (nominal, 2004 dollars)	9,686	16,613	31,153	51,442
2004 (real, 1994 dollars)	4,991	7,630	13,388	20,455

*Annual college expenses represent the sum of annual tuition, room, and board charges.

Source: The projected annual college expenses have been estimated by the authors using historical costs for the period 1976–1990 published in National Center for Education Statistics, *Digest of Education Statistics,* 1991 (Washington, DC: U.S. Department of Education, Office of Education Statistics, 1991).

Just as there are nominal and real prices, so too there are nominal and real interest rates. Because we earn interest on our investments, interest rates are often referred to as a "rate of return." We earn interest at the nominal rate of return. That nominal interest rate is composed of two parts: the real rate of return, which is compensation for not consuming our income but saving it instead, and an inflation premium that protects the purchasing power of the investment. Stated differently, the nominal rate of return is equal to the real rate of return plus the inflation rate. Table 4-2 shows average nominal and real rates of return over five-year periods, dating back to 1955, earned by short-term Treasury securities.

TABLE 4-2
Real and Nominal Rates of Return

5-Year Period Ending Dec.	Nominal Rate of Return	Inflation Rate	Real Rate of Return
1955	1.48%	1.43%	0.05%
1960	2.55	2.12	0.42
1965	3.09	1.33	1.73
1970	5.45	4.54	0.88
1975	5.78	6.90	−1.05
1980	7.77	9.21	−1.32
1985	10.30	4.85	5.20
1990	6.83	4.13	2.59

Rates are 5-year averages; rates of return are short-term Treasury bill rates.

Source: Roger G. Ibbotson and Rex A. Sinquefield, *Stocks, Bonds, Bills, and Inflation (SBBI) 1993 Yearbook* (updated annually by Ibbotson Associates).

In personal financial planning, it is easiest to work with real prices and real interest rates. Working with nominal prices and nominal interest rates requires making predictions about inflation, a task that is difficult even for professional economists. If we have a goal of sending a child to a four-year private college in 2004, and if it costs, on average, $20,455 per year in 1994, we will want to set a goal of having $20,455 real dollars (that is, $20,455 dollars with 1994 purchasing power) in each year from 2004 to 2007. We will then choose a savings plan and investments that earn the real rate of return necessary to achieve our goal.

Now we are ready to determine the cost of our financial goals. Use the financial goals worksheet (Table 4-3) as a guide. The following seven-step process will help.

Step 1: Brainstorming

List your financial objectives. If you are married, talk them over with your spouse. Achieving these objectives will require that you save some amount each month, and it will be much easier to do this if you and your spouse agree that the objective is worth the sacrifice.

Decide which objectives must be achieved in the short term, which in the medium term, and which in the long term. An example of a short-term goal would be an emergency fund (if you don't already have one). Most financial planners recommend three to six months' after-tax income as a reasonable amount for such a fund. Depending on your circumstances, that sum may be too large. Think about the types of emergencies for which you want to save, and then set aside an appropriate amount. Deductibles on your insurance policies or the cost of buying last-minute airline tickets to get your family home in case of an emergency might be typical uses. As you get closer to leaving the service, you should consider increasing the amount of money you keep in your emergency fund.

Medium-term goals might include paying cash for a new car, refurnishing a room in your home, or replacing that old television set. Medium-term goals often find themselves in conflict with more important long-term goals. In the long term, most of us are concerned with putting our children through college and planning for retirement. Since our military pension won't be enough for us to live on, we should plan on saving an additional amount to supplement our pension.

The reason you should separate the goals by time period is that the suitable types of investments and their expected rate of return vary with the planning horizon. It is often possible to achieve longer-term goals by making riskier investments that earn a higher rate of return. We will use an example of sending a child to a year at a four-year private college in 2004. This is a long-term objective that requires saving enough each month to have $20,455 in real 1994 dollars in 2004.

Step 2: Determine Today's Cost of Your Goals

As explained above, one of the advantages of using real values is that you don't have to try to predict the future cost of your goal. All you need to know is what it would cost you today. From Table 4-1, you know that, on average, a year's tuition, room, and board at a four-year private college costs $20,455 dollars in 1994. Enter that value in the column for today's cost.

TABLE 4-3
Financial Goals Worksheet

Expected Annual Before-tax Rates of Return (Table 4-4)	Marginal Income Tax Rates	Expected Real After-tax Rates of Return	
		Annual	Monthly
Short-term: _____	Federal: _____	Short-term: _____	
Medium-term: _____	State: _____	Medium-term: _____	
Long-term: _____	Combined: _____	Long-term: _____	

	Today's Cost	Date Required	# of Months	Lump Sum	Monthly Amount to Meet Goal
Short-term goals (within 1 year)					
Emergency fund	_____	_____	_____	_____	_____
Major purchase	_____	_____	_____	_____	_____
Christmas gifts	_____	_____	_____	_____	_____
Other	_____	_____	_____	_____	_____
Medium-term goals (1 to 5 years)					
Major purchase	_____	_____	_____	_____	_____
Down payment on home	_____	_____	_____	_____	_____
Education	_____	_____	_____	_____	_____
Other	_____	_____	_____	_____	_____
Long-term goals (over 5 years)					
Education	_____	_____	_____	_____	_____
Business start-up	_____	_____	_____	_____	_____
Retirement income	_____	_____	_____	_____	_____
Care for dependent parents	_____	_____	_____	_____	_____
Other	_____	_____	_____	_____	_____

Step 3: Set a Target Date
Make your objective more concrete by setting a deadline. Determine the amount of time until the target date. Because most military families are paid monthly and will save some amount each month, you want the number of months until the money is needed. For the purposes of the example, it is ten years, or 120 months, until you need the annual tuition, room, and board to send your child to college. Enter the date required and the number of months in the appropriate column in Table 4-3.

Step 4: Calculate the "Lump Sum"
The lump sum represents the amount of money that you would have to invest today at your expected real rate of return in order to achieve your financial goal by the target date. To calculate this value, you must be able to fill in the values at the top of Table 4-3 (that is, the expected real rates of return on short-, medium-, and long-term investments consistent with your tolerance for risk, as well as your income tax bracket).

TABLE 4-4
Historical Averages for Real Rates of Return
(1926–1992)

Investment Alternatives	Rate of Return[a]	Corresponding Mutual Funds
Small stocks[b]	8.8%	Aggressive growth funds
		Sector or international funds
Common stocks[c]	7.0%	Growth funds
		Growth and income funds
		Equity-income funds
		Balanced or income funds
Long-term corporate bonds	2.3%	Bond funds
Long-term government bonds[d]	1.7%	Government funds
U.S. Treasury bills[e]	0.5%	Money market funds

[a] Approximate historical rates of return are "real," that is, after deducting inflation. The returns shown are "pre-tax," that is, with no adjustment for taxes. The average is calculated as the geometric mean. Inflation is measured by the Consumer Price Index.

[b] Small-company stocks are represented by the fifth capitalization quintile of stocks on the New York Stock Exchange for 1926–81 and the performance of the Dimensional Fund Advisors (DFA) Small Company Fund thereafter.

[c] Common stocks are represented by the Standard & Poor's 500 Stock Composite Index (S&P 500).

[d] Long-term government bonds are represented by 20-year U.S. government bonds.

[e] Treasury bills refer to 30-day U.S. Treasury bills. The real return on Treasury bills measured the real riskless rate of return.

Source: Roger G. Ibbotson and Rex A. Sinquefield, *Stocks, Bonds, Bills, and Inflation (SBBI) 1993 Yearbook* (updated annually by Ibbotson Associates).

Rates of return depend on the level of risk that you are willing to accept (see chapter 2 for a discussion of financial risk). Although this risk tolerance varies for each individual or family, Table 4-4 should provide some assistance in determining an expected real rate of return (that is, after deducting inflation) for your goals. This table shows the historical average real rate of return for several investment alternatives. Since many people do not invest in individual securities, we have included the corresponding categories of mutual funds. (These investment instruments are explained in more detail in part IV of this book.) The expected rate of return increases with the amount of risk that you are willing to accept. For short-term goals, you may be unwilling to take on as much risk as for longer-term goals. As your long-term goals become your medium-term goals and your medium-term goals become your short-term goals, you may want to change the investment vehicle you have chosen so that you can protect yourself from the greater risks associated with longer-term investments.

The other bit of information you will need is your combined marginal income tax rate, which is the tax rate that applies to the last or next dollar of taxable income you earn. Look at your most recent federal income tax returns to determine your taxable income, which is the total income you earn that is subject to taxation minus itemized or standard deductions and the value of your exemptions (see chapter 8). Find the column in Table 4-5 that corresponds to your filing status, then find the row that contains your taxable income. Your federal income tax bracket is in the left-most column of that row. You can find your state income tax bracket from last year's state income tax return. Enter your federal and state tax brackets in Table 4-3 as decimals (e.g., a 15 percent tax bracket is 0.15). Add your state and federal income tax brackets to get your combined marginal tax rate.

Now you are ready to do the necessary calculations. First, you need to calculate the expected, real after-tax rate for the investment period. Begin by adding the expected real return and the expected rate of inflation to get the expected nominal return for each investment period. Next, subtract your combined marginal tax rate from 1, then

TABLE 4-5
Income Tax Brackets for 1993 and 1994[1]

	Taxable Income Range, Based on Filing Status		
Tax Rate	Joint (Married)	Head of Household	Single
15%	≤ $36,899	≤ $29,599	≤ $22,099
28%	$36,900–89,149	$29,600–76,399	$22,100–53,499
31%	$89,150–$139,999	$76,400–$127,499	$53,500–$114,999
36%	$140,000–$249,999	$127,500–$249,999	$115,000–$249,999
39.3%	≥ $250,000	≥ $250,000	≥ $250,000

[1] These brackets will be adjusted for inflation beginning in 1995.

Source: Omnibus Budget Reconciliation Act of 1993.

multiply the result by each of the before-tax nominal rates of return to get the after-tax, nominal returns. Finally, subtract the expected rates of inflation for each period to obtain the after-tax, real returns. An example of these calculations is shown in part 1 of Table 4-6. We'll use a 6.5 percent expected real rate of return and a 4 percent expected rate of inflation for our example, but you should use the rate of inflation you expect to occur over the investment period and the expected real rate of return that corresponds to the amount of risk you are willing to take.

This gives you an annual after-tax real rate of return, but you need a monthly rate to correspond to the monthly time periods you will use in your calculations. Always ensure that the interest rate and the time period are for the same length of time (e.g., annual rate and years, monthly rate and months). To convert the annual rate to a monthly rate, simply divide by twelve as shown in part 2 of Table 4-6, and enter these real, after-tax monthly rates of return in Table 4-3. Now you can calculate the lump sum required to achieve each goal as shown in part 3 of Table 4-6.

Today's cost is the cost of your goal in today's dollars, or $20,455 in this example. The expected real after-tax rate of return, "r," is 0.004 percent per month, and the number of months, "n," is 120 months. The lump sum of $12,669 is the present value of the $20,455 that you need in ten years. Stated differently, investing $12,669 at a real interest rate of 6.5 percent per year will yield $20,455, after taxes, in ten years. It is important to remember that this is $20,455 in 1994 purchasing power. Actually, the money will accrue interest at the nominal rate, which is higher than the real rate, and in 2004, you will have considerably more than $20,455. But due to inflation, you will need to have more than that to buy what you could have bought in 1994 with $20,455.

Table D-1 (in appendix D) contains discount factors for several rates of return and time periods. These discount factors replicate the calculations described above for spe-

TABLE 4-6
Calculating the Required Lump-sum Investment

[1] Calculate the annual after-tax real rate of return.

$$r_{after\ tax} = [(r_{before\ tax} + inflation\ rate) \times (1 - tax\ rate)] - inflation\ rate =$$
$$[(.065 + .04) \times (1 - .15)] - .04 = .049$$

[2] Convert the annual rate of return to a monthly rate of return.

$$r_{monthly} = r_{after\ tax} \div 12 = .049 \div 12 = .004$$

[3] Calculate the lump-sum amount you would have to invest today in order to achieve your financial goal as planned.

$$Lump\ Sum = \frac{Today's\ Cost}{(1 + r)^n} = \frac{\$20,455}{(1 + .004)^{120}} = \$12,669$$

cific interest rates and may be used instead of the formulas in Table 4-6 to obtain lump-sum amounts that are approximately correct. To calculate the lump sum using the discount factors, merely multiply the future real amount by the discount factor that applies to the real, after-tax annual rate of return you are assuming. In the above example, we calculated the real, after-tax annual return to be .049. Because Table D-1 only reports discount factors for certain real rates, you would either interpolate or use the nearest rate to obtain your discount factor. If you decided that .05 is sufficiently accurate, the discount factor would be .614 and the lump sum would be $12,559 (i.e., $12,559 = .614 × $20,455). Because the discount factor is based on an approximate interest rate, the lump sum we calculate using the factor is only approximately correct. Also, the factors in Table D-1 are based on annual and not monthly compounding. Therefore, we recommend that you use the formulas in Table 4-6 if you have a calculator available.

Step 5: Calculate the Monthly Allotment

Since most of us won't have the lump sum available to invest to meet our goals, we will need to chip away at the cost of our goal by setting aside a certain amount of money each month. Table 4-7 shows the calculation for our example. The complicated expression in the denominator is called the annuity factor. An annuity is a series of payments at fixed intervals, invested at the same rate of return. An allotment from your monthly paycheck to a mutual fund is an example of an annuity. (Actually, it is not quite an annuity, because the rate of return available through mutual funds changes over time. But for our purposes, it is close enough.) Dividing the lump sum by the annuity factor converts it into an equivalent monthly amount. Investing $133 each month for 120 months at a real rate of return of 7 percent per year is equivalent to investing $12,669 at a real before-tax 7 percent annual rate of return for ten years.

An investment of $133 a month is a lot of money, but it is considerably easier than finding $12,669 to invest all at once. And this is only for one year's tuition, room, and board! If we invested for eighteen years instead of only ten years, it would cost us only $88 per month, which is 33 percent less. That is why it is important to begin saving early for long-term financial goals like putting children through college.

Table D-2 contains annuity factors that approximate the calculations shown in Table 4-7, as the discount factors in Table D-1 approximated a portion of the calculations in Table 4-6. Using .05 to approximate .0495, we see that the annual annuity fac-

TABLE 4-7
Converting the Lump Sum to an Equivalent Monthly Investment

Using the figures from Table 4-6, convert the lump sum into an annuity of equivalent value.

$$\text{Allotment} \frac{\text{Lump Sum}}{\left(\frac{1}{r} - \frac{1}{r \times (1+r)^n}\right)} = \frac{\$12,669}{\left(\frac{1}{.004} - \frac{1}{.004 \times (1+.004)^{120}}\right)} = \$133$$

tor is 7.722. If we divide our lump sum by this factor, we obtain the annual amount to be saved ($12,669 ÷ 7.722 = $1,641). If we divide this annual amount by 12, we obtain the amount we would have to set aside each month. In our example, this would be $137 ($1,641 ÷ 12 = $137). Once again, we see that using a published factor provides an answer that is only approximately correct. Therefore, we recommend that you perform the calculations shown in Table 4-7.

Step 6: Set Priorities

If you sum the monthly allotments required to meet all your future spending goals, you will probably find that you cannot possibly afford to set aside that much money each month and still meet your monthly living expenses. So you must choose among your savings goals and living expenses according to your priorities. If you do not have an adequate emergency fund, establishing one may be your top priority. Once you have an emergency fund, you can begin to set aside money toward your other goals. Remember, though, that if you do not make contributions to your long-term goals until they become short-term goals, it will be impossible to set aside the monthly allotment to meet them.

Step 7: Determine the Appropriate Investment

Determine the investment vehicle you will use for each goal. It is important that the mutual fund you select has the performance characteristics that you assumed in your calculations. Again, see part IV for more information on investing.

DEVELOPING A PLAN: THE BUDGET

Now that you have established where you are and where you want to go, you need to develop a plan that will enable you to achieve your financial goals. That plan is the budget. Budgets allocate all of your income against all of your expenses in a way that is consistent with your priorities. In the typical family, the result of a budget will be to reduce your spending to satisfy your current consumption desires in order to save some of your income each month for longer-term financial goals. Because it involves current sacrifice, even the mention of the "B" word can conjure up resentment in some families. It doesn't have to be that way if you follow a few simple principles in developing a budget. We'll discuss these important principles before we delve into the mechanics of the budget using Table 4-8.

Budget Principles

Gain Consensus

If you are married, then the budget *must* be a family project. Without the cooperation of everyone involved, your plan is doomed to failure. Once you've completed the budget, consider it a family contract to which all members are dedicated.

Pay Yourself First
Any financial planner will tell you this. If you wait to see how much you have left after monthly expenses, you won't have any money to set toward your financial goals. Set a minimum percentage of your income that you want to dedicate to achieving financial goals. Then, see how many of your goals you can work toward given that amount. Also, when you get a raise, try to set aside at least half of it to put toward your financial goals. If you were meeting your expenses before the raise, you should be able to save a significant portion of it. Don't forget about those expensive long-term goals for which you need to start saving.

Make the Big Payments Little Ones
Most of us cannot afford to write a check for several hundred dollars out of our monthly paycheck to meet the large expenses that must be dealt with periodically. Christmas comes on December 25 every year. The Christmas spirit is often reflected in our generosity toward our family and friends. Instead of saving a little each month for Christmas, we end up using our credit cards, making a large expense larger because of the interest we will be charged.

Why not take those big payments that come up every year and divide them by twelve, setting aside that much each month? Then, when an expense comes up, you'll have the money in your savings or money market account to write out the check, and save the interest charge in the bargain.

Minimize Unanticipated Expenses
The budget format in Table 4-8 may seem extremely long and cumbersome, but it is helpful in that it focuses on the principle of minimizing unanticipated expenses. If you can avoid unexpected expenses, you can avoid those "peanut butter and jelly" months.

Budget Mechanics

If you know how to use a spreadsheet on a personal computer, this is the time to turn your computer on and start up your spreadsheet program. Family budgets are easiest to make on a spreadsheet, because it permits you to make the entries while the machine calculates totals and recalculates them every time you adjust an entry. There is a fair amount of iterative work in developing a budget. Let the machine make it easy for you.

If you do not know how to use a spreadsheet, don't worry. The budget involves only addition and subtraction, operations that are still easy to do with a calculator or by hand.

Step 1: List Income Sources
List the amounts for each source of income. We will discuss more about investments and the income they generate in part IV and about sources of retirement income in part V.

Step 2: List Expenses

Although the list in Table 4-8 is extensive, you may have expenses not listed there. Be sure to include them. Estimate an amount for each expenditure, and write it in the column for preliminary estimates. You can use any record of previous expenditures to develop these estimates.

Notice that we have divided the expenses into three categories: fixed, variable, and cumulative. Fixed expenses are those that occur every month and that you cannot readily influence (e.g., rent). Variable expenses are those that depend directly on the amount of use (e.g., your long-distance phone bill). Cumulative items are those big expenses or financial goals that you chip away at each month by setting some money aside for when the bill comes due.

Step 3: Determine the Amount Remaining to Be Reallocated

When all of your income is allocated to an expense and your income exactly equals your expenses, you have a workable budget. You almost certainly will have to do some reallocation to make this happen. If your expenses are greater than your income, you will have to reduce some of your expenses or you will have to find some way to earn extra income. If your expenses are less than your income, then you have the happy task of increasing the amount you can spend on one or more of your expenditure categories.

Step 4: Allocate or Reallocate Income and Expenses

It is typically the case that your income is less than your desired expenditures. Having classified your expenditures as fixed, variable, or cumulative, you can more easily determine where to cut. Surprisingly, we recommend that you should examine some of your "fixed" expenditures first. They are not always "fixed" at the level that best suits your needs. For example, many military families are overinsured or improperly insured, and it is possible to obtain equal or better insurance protection for a smaller premium. (See chapters 12 and 18 for a discussion of insurance.)

Examine your variable expenses next. Variable expenses are variable in that if you use less of them, then your expenditures fall. This clearly requires that your entire family agree to change its behavior to achieve the desired result. For example, you might want to reduce your long-distance telephone bill by $20 per month or reduce your utilities bill by $30 per month.

Finally, avoid trimming money set aside for cumulative goals. The whole point of this exercise is to make room for them in the monthly budget.

When you have allocated your entire income to monthly expenditures and there is nothing left over, you're finished. Write the final estimates of income and expenditure in the column for your revised numbers.

Step 5: Establish Budget Item Accounts and Method of Payment and Receipt

This step and the next are primarily bookkeeping functions intended to help you with implementing your budget. You pay for most of your regular monthly expenses with cash or a check, so you will want the money for those items readily accessible in your

TABLE 4–8
Budget Worksheet

	Preliminary	Revised
Monthly income		
Salaries, wages, commissions, tips, etc.	_____	_____
Interest earned on savings accounts	_____	_____
Interest earned on bonds	_____	_____
Dividend income	_____	_____
Other investment income	_____	_____
Social Security and VA cash benefits	_____	_____
Pensions and annuities received	_____	_____
Other income	_____	_____
	_____	_____
	_____	_____
	_____	_____
	_____	_____
Total monthly income	_____	_____
Fixed monthly expenses		
Taxes due or withheld	_____	_____
Mortgage payment or rent	_____	_____
Automobile loans	_____	_____
Bank or finance company loans	_____	_____
Automobile insurance premiums	_____	_____
Health insurance premiums	_____	_____
Life insurance premiums	_____	_____
Other insurance premiums	_____	_____
Minimum payments for credit cards	_____	_____
Local service phone bill	_____	_____
Other fixed monthly expenses	_____	_____
	_____	_____
	_____	_____
	_____	_____
	_____	_____
Total fixed monthly expenses	_____	_____

continued

**TABLE 4-8
Budget Worksheet
(continued)**

	Preliminary	Revised
Variable monthly expenses		
Food		
Transportation		
Clothing		
Utilities		
Long-distance phone bill		
Recreation		
Babysitting		
Church donations		
Charitable contributions		
Gifts for birthdays, Christmas, etc.		
Personal allowances:		
Husband		
Wife		
Child		
Child		
Child		
Child		
Other variable monthly expenses		
Total variable monthly expenses		
Cumulative monthly expenses		
Long-term goal		
Long-term goal		
Long-term goal		
Medium-term goal		
Medium-term goal		
Medium-term goal		
Short-term goal		
Total cumulative monthly expenses		
Total monthly expenses		
Total monthly income (compare)		
Amount to be allocated/reallocated		

checking account. On the other hand, many of your cumulative expenses occur only occasionally, so you don't need the accessibility that a checking account provides. In fact, you will want to put that money to work earning interest in either a money market fund or a savings account. When such occasional bills come due, you can charge them and then write a check out of your money market account to pay for them before interest starts coming due. Once you have decided where the expense money should be held, you can divide your paycheck appropriately to match your expenses.

Step 6: Implement

There are as many ways to implement and monitor a budget as there are people. The key is to find a way that works for you and stick with it. At a minimum, you need to track your expenses. Fixed and cumulative expenses usually occur only monthly, so a journal of accounts with a page for each expense is perfectly adequate. The more frequent expenses, like food and entertainment, require closer scrutiny. An inexpensive and easy way to track these expenses is to keep a record of them in a pocket notebook. Just title a page to correspond to each of the variable expenses, and record transactions as they occur. Then, at the end of the month, total the amount and post it to the journal of accounts. Then post the monthly total to a ledger that shows all of your accounts on one page. The ledger gives you a mechanism to see quickly how well you're doing at sticking to your budget.

Step 7: Review Periodically

Just as you must routinely check up on the implementation of any plan, so too you must check up on your budget. Look at the ledger to see whether you're consistently over or under budget in any of the accounts. If so, make adjustments. You will also have to make adjustments each time you get a raise or one of your fixed expenses changes. The budget is not locked in concrete.

There you have it—the basics of a financial plan. With a little discipline and determination, you should be well on your way to achieving your financial goals. But don't stop reading here. The rest of this book will show you how to be an educated consumer of financial products and services, to get the most from your investments, and to plan for your retirement.

Part II

FINANCIAL BASICS

5

Banking Smart

IF YOU ENTERED active duty after 1 October 1985, you are required by law to have a Sure Pay account. Even if the law doesn't require it, common sense does. Only Sure Pay will ensure that you have access to your funds if you are on leave, temporary duty (TDY), in the middle of a permanent-change-of-station move (PCS), or deployed overseas. Check to unit simply doesn't work for anyone who isn't in the unit on payday. All servicemembers run that risk. Check to unit has been a major source of financial hardship to servicemembers worldwide.

Because you must deposit your monthly earnings at some financial institution, we dedicate this chapter to helping you select the bank that suits you best. You need a framework to compare services offered at these institutions and to choose where to place your trust and your money.

Distinctions between the various kinds of financial institutions (e.g., bank, savings and loan, credit union, and thrift) have become less and less clear with continuing deregulation within the banking industry. Since the traditional roles have become so blurred, we will refer to all financial institutions as banks in this chapter and focus less on the diverse services offered and more on your financial needs. The financial plan you developed in part I of this book will determine some of the services you need. But first, let's look at the general services offered by financial institutions.

BANKING SERVICES

Commercial banks, savings and loans, mutual savings banks, and credit unions all can now offer most of the primary services that households will use. In the recent past, government regulations prevented credit unions and thrifts from providing some services banks could offer. For example, until 1980 it wasn't legal for thrifts and credit unions to offer checking accounts. Federal Reserve Regulation Q also placed ceilings on the interest rates that banking institutions could pay on deposits of different types.

42 • PERSONAL FINANCIAL PLANNING

Changes in bank regulations made in the 1980s and early 1990s seem to be removing completely the distinctions among the various types of banking institutions. Consumers can usually find all the banking services they require at a single institution. However, regulatory changes have also given banking institutions much greater freedom to determine interest rates paid and charged, fees for services, policies on withdrawal of funds, and minimum required balances in accounts. Though it's possible to find all the services you will want under one roof, to find the best deal on all your needs you may have to shop carefully and use several institutions.

As government regulations on banking activities have been relaxed, banks, thrifts, and credit unions have attempted to become "financial supermarkets" that can offer a variety of products. Aside from the traditional deposit and loan services, many banks now provide services that in the past were available only through insurance agencies, stock brokerages, and other specialized financial firms. At the same time, firms that formerly offered only stock brokerage or insurance services have begun to provide accounts that behave much like bank accounts and now even offer loans to consumers.

Banking institutions provide the following services:

1. Traditional bank services
   - Checking accounts.
   - Savings accounts.
   - Time deposits and certificates of deposit.
   - Credit cards.
   - Trust services.
   - Safe deposit boxes.
   - Consumer and business loans.
2. New banking services.
   - Stock and bond brokerage services.
   - Mutual fund sales.
   - Financial planning services.
   - Tax preparation and advice.
   - Travel services.

Families have many financial needs. First, people need a transactions account for paying their recurring bills. Second, they need emergency funds that are quickly and easily available to meet short-term emergencies. Third, they need to save for their medium- and long-term goals, such as buying a house, sending their children to college, or saving for retirement. Additionally, they need a source for borrowed funds to purchase certain big-ticket items too large to be purchased directly from savings.

Transactions Account

Most people are paid once or twice a month but must be able to make payments for purchases throughout the month. One alternative is to carry currency at all times. This is both bulky and dangerous. A far more convenient method of meeting this need is to deposit funds in a transactions account for use whenever you need them.

Whether your transactions account is a checking account or a share draft account (a checking account at a credit union), it is an excellent way of ensuring the immediate availability of cash. You can write checks to anyone who will accept them. You have a written document to help you record where you spend your money. Debit cards and charge cards are additional services offered by banks that can be used to pay for transactions. Whether you solve your transactions need with checks, share drafts, debit cards, or charge cards, you'll find that banks and their close relatives offer the only convenient services for meeting this need.

Emergency Fund Account

The second crucial piece needed in a financial plan is an emergency fund. The emergency fund provides immediate cash if a disaster occurs. You must determine the size of this fund. Most financial advisors suggest between two and six months' pay. We feel two months' base pay may be sufficient if you have quick and easy access to credit, unless you anticipate voluntarily leaving the service or a PCS into a high-cost area. Ask yourself what emergencies might arise that require immediate payments. Certainly you would want a fund large enough to purchase a plane ticket home for the entire family. You would want to be able to cover the deductible and depreciation of parts to repair your car should you suffer an accident. You may need much more if you anticipate a loss of income due to illness or lost employment.

With emergency funds, you are much more concerned with the ability to use your money quickly than in the return such funds receive. You are willing to trade away higher rates of interest for liquidity (the ability to spend it quickly if necessary) and safety. The most liquid portion of this fund could be kept in a checking account, but the opportunity cost of lost interest on this money makes this a poor choice. Savings accounts paying money market rates (money market deposit accounts) and money market funds with check-writing privileges are ideal for emergency funds. Even if you can't manage to accumulate an emergency fund, you should get overdraft protection or a credit card with a sufficient line of credit to provide you with the peace of mind that you can pay for your family's immediate emergency needs.

Long-term Savings Account

A third crucial piece to your financial plan is long-term savings. Each of us has a need to accumulate funds to support our future goals. When you made your budget in chapter 4, you forecasted the amounts of money needed at certain times in the future for retirement, home ownership, or additional education. You didn't intend and don't want to spend this money soon. Exercise patience and invest this savings in longer-term securities offering a higher rate of return.

Banks are one of several sources competing for your long-term savings dollar. A certificate of deposit (CD) is a good long-term investment for the risk-averse investor. We will discuss CDs later in this chapter. The more aggressive investor could place all of these funds in other investments (e.g., stocks, bonds, or mutual funds) and not use bank CDs. Refer to chapters 13 through 15 for higher-risk, higher-return alternatives for long-term savings. Where you choose to place your long-term investments will affect the banking services you demand. This decision should be made before you begin to choose a specific bank to use.

Loans

Most people, from time to time, find it necessary to borrow money. You may not have the cash available to pay for big-ticket items like major appliances, cars, and houses. Sometimes, you would rather spread the cost over the period of time you anticipate using the goods and are willing to borrow and pay interest for that convenience. Chapter 6 helps you to evaluate the credit services offered by banks.

SELECTING A BANK

An effective and convenient relationship with a bank is especially important to the military family. Military duties often take us away from home and make family separations necessary. Servicemembers need ready assets they can draw upon away from home and also must provide for the needs of the family members left behind. Similarly, permanent-change-of-station moves frequently require military families to rely on their cash reserves in checking or savings accounts for a month or more until a new financial routine can be established. Many banking institutions located near military installations take special interest in the needs of servicemembers and their families. The services these banks can provide are crucial to the operation of a family financial plan.

There are three primary factors to consider when selecting a bank. The first and most important is whether the institution is in sound financial condition. A second factor is convenient access to your deposits. Finally, the cost of the services is also important. The cost of banking services is affected by much more than the interest rates paid on deposits and charged on loans. Methods used to calculate the amount of interest due, service fees, and policies on minimum sizes of accounts and penalties for early withdrawals make major differences in the real cost. We'll discuss each of these factors in detail in the paragraphs that follow.

Bank Safety

Banking is a risky business. Banks loan their depositors' money to other people, businesses, or countries. When choosing a bank, consider foremost the safety of your deposits. Ensuring that your bank is safe is relatively easy. The federal government insures deposits up to $100,000 in participating institutions through the Federal Deposit Insurance Corporation (FDIC), the Federal Savings and Loan Insurance Corporation (FSLIC), and the National Credit Union Share Insurance Fund. Actually, more than $100,000 of deposit insurance is available, because the limit applies to the amount in a single account. If you are fortunate enough to have more than $100,000 on deposit in a single institution, you can have it all insured by registering separate accounts, each under the limit. Congress is considering changing these rules and limits, but most servicemembers will not be affected.

All you really need to do is make sure that your bank, thrift institution, or credit union is a member of one of the federal insurance programs. Most institutions participate in these programs, but not all. There is no reason to use a bank, thrift, or credit union that isn't covered by federal deposit insurance. Eliminate them from consideration; accept no substitutes for federal insurance. Depositors in state-insured institutions have experienced significant delays in gaining access to their deposits after their banks failed. Once you have narrowed your search for banking services to federally insured institutions, turn your attention to the convenience and cost of the services offered and to the interest rates paid on deposits and charged on loans.

Convenience

We use banks because we want to make convenient purchases and because we want to ensure that our money is quickly available if an emergency arises. Since convenience is a major reason for using a bank, it's a major factor to consider when choosing a bank.

When most of us need money, we write a check. A check is simply a note to our bank telling it to transfer some money in our account to someone else. In this function, most checking/share draft accounts differ little, if at all. There is a major difference, however, when we need to convert that check to cash. It may be difficult for you to get currency close to work or home and after bank operating hours.

For servicemembers, post and base exchanges almost always cash checks; so do officers' and NCO clubs. For check cashing, these facilities are often closer and easier to use than the bank, but they offer only a limited solution to the problem of getting cash after working hours. The use of twenty-four-hour banking machines, known as automatic teller machines (ATMs), is increasing rapidly as banks attempt to meet their customers' needs for convenient currency. The better ATM networks share sites and allow you to obtain cash from machines far removed from your individual bank; some even allow international access. Look for a bank having ATM locations convenient to your home or work.

One of the most important features banks offer servicemembers is direct deposit of military and federal government paychecks into checking or savings accounts. A direct deposit arrangement sets up a direct link between the military or governmental pay system and your bank. On payday, your pay is automatically sent to the bank and deposited in your account while you continue to receive your Leave and Earnings

Statements. Your paycheck gets deposited and your money is made available even if you are away from your duty station on leave, TDY, or deployment. The convenience and security of this feature are hard to overestimate. We highly recommend it for all. Your local finance activity has the necessary forms to set up this most useful service. Virtually every bank will participate; you should not bank at one that does not.

An intangible factor related to the convenience of services involves the bank's attitude toward consumer-oriented banking in general and banking for military personnel in particular. Some banks pursue primarily firms and very large individual customers. Such banks may discourage small accounts, which are often more expensive to manage. You'll be able to tell whether a bank is interested in your business by observing employees' attitudes as they describe their services and by checking over the fees charged for small accounts.

Don't bank where your banking business isn't enthusiastically welcomed. Thrift institutions and credit unions have historically been oriented to small customers. There are many fine individual-oriented banks as well, especially around military installations. Some have grown up specifically to provide service to the military population. These banks often specialize in understanding and helping with the financial problems arising in the course of a military career.

Many military families maintain bank accounts in the locality where they are assigned. If this is the only account they keep, they close out accounts in the area they are leaving and open new ones at their new duty station. Some also maintain a "permanent" bank so they can continue to write checks and maintain savings balances while in transit from one assignment to the next. To say the least, closing and opening bank accounts and shopping for the best banking services are time-consuming and unpleasant chores. It's worth asking, then, if a local bank really is necessary. If you have a good permanent bank with which you can easily deal by phone and mail, you may not need a local bank.

Do you need a new local bank at each duty station? Ask yourself the following questions:

- Do you use credit cards instead of checks for local retail purchases?
- Can you easily and conveniently get cash with an out-of-state account?
- Is your bank a member of a national ATM network?
- Is an officers' club, NCO club, or exchange conveniently located where you can easily cash checks?
- Does your permanent bank offer convenient loan service by mail or phone?
- Does your permanent bank offer convenient ATM deposit or deposit-by-mail services including free postage-paid deposit envelopes?
- Can you easily move savings balances into your checking account by phone in your permanent bank?

If you can answer most of these questions with a yes, you may not need a local bank at all. You can establish a relationship with a bank offering the services you want, and do all your banking by phone or mail. Minimizing the number of accounts you have can simplify your life and hold down the cost of your financial services.

Cost of Services

Many of us grew up in the days when banks were regulated. Banks with lower operating costs weren't allowed to compete by offering higher interest rates. The maximum interest rates allowed were prescribed by law. The costs and benefits of checking and savings accounts were nearly identical from bank to bank. This era of equivalent rates was thrown out with the deregulation of the banking industry. Today, vast differences exist in the cost of, and interest earned on, bank accounts. Now, banks are allowed to compete head to head in both price and service. It's more common to package a set of services at a fair price to increase customer loyalty. In setting a price strategy, most banks try to attract the most profitable customers. In doing so, their pricing schemes encourage or discourage specific types of customers. You should understand these pricing schemes and seek a bank desiring accounts like yours.

Even when two banks claim to offer or charge the same interest rate, the amount of interest received depends on the method used to calculate interest. There are a variety of methods in use. You need to understand how banks compute interest and charges if you are to choose the best bank and get the most value from its services.

BANK SERVICES

Now let's explore the three major services that banks offer to meet your three basic needs: checking and share-draft accounts for transactions; savings accounts or money market deposit accounts for emergency funds; and certificates of deposit for long-term savings.

Checking Accounts

No service provides for your need for transactions as well as a checking/share draft account. Checking accounts come in two basic varieties: non-interest-bearing and interest-bearing. As their name implies, non-interest-bearing accounts offer no interest on the deposited funds. Since there is no interest cost to the bank, these accounts are cheaper to run. Banks generally encourage depositors who plan to keep very small balances (less than $500 or $1,000) to use non-interest-bearing checking accounts.

Several varieties of interest-bearing checking accounts are offered.The most common of this type are called negotiable order of withdrawal (NOW) accounts. NOW accounts pay a modest rate of interest (generally about 3 percent). They are best for medium-size consumer deposits having typical balances of $1,000 to $2,500. When the account balance falls below a specified amount, banks often pay no interest or charge a service fee.

Banks also offer super-NOW accounts. Typically, these accounts pay a money market rate of interest, the rate of interest available to the largest and most sophisticated investors in short-term government and corporate debt securities. Since the bank's interest cost on super-NOW accounts is relatively high in comparison to other checking accounts, large average balances (generally $2,500 to $5,000 or more) are normally required. In the past, money market rates have varied from roughly 6 percent to 8 percent. More recently, these rates have ranged from 2 percent to 4 percent.

Banks typically charge both "per-check" and service fees for checking accounts. Per-check fees are levied on each check written on the account; they are intended to cover the expenses involved in processing and clearing checks. Typical fees are in the range of 15 to 25 cents per check, but you may find them as low as 10 cents and as high as 50 cents. Service fees, designed to compensate the bank for the costs of maintaining small accounts, are levied every month on some checking accounts. Many banks will waive these fees for direct-deposit customers. Most military credit unions will not have them at all. These fees can really add up, so it is worth shopping around.

You will often see advertisements for "free" checking accounts, with no per-check or service fees. The catch on many free checking accounts is that the fees are waived only if the average balance in the account is greater than a minimum amount, usually $1,000 or more. In other cases, free checking is offered if the depositor has savings accounts or time deposits greater than a required minimum, perhaps $2,500 or more.

The key ingredient in measuring value in an interest-bearing checking account is the cost and interpretation of the minimum balance requirement. We will examine common methods used to compute the minimum balance, and then look at an example of the costs and benefits of an interest-bearing account.

Computing Minimum Balance

Your minimum balance determines whether service and check fees are charged and, sometimes, the rate of interest paid. You must understand the specific method your bank uses to compute this balance. The two most common methods are the "average daily balance" and the "largest continuous balance."

The average-daily-balance method takes the balance in the account each day of the month, adds up all these figures, and divides by the number of days in the month. With the largest-continuous-balance method, the bank simply determines the largest amount in the account for the entire month. Of course, this will be the smallest balance on any day during the month. The largest-continuous-balance method thus yields a much smaller number (meaning less interest, higher fees, or both) than the average-daily-balance method. For example, if you had $1,000 in your account for twenty-nine days during the month and withdrew $500 on the thirtieth day, the average-daily-balance calculation would put your average balance at about $983 [{(29 days × $1,000) + (1 day × $500)} ÷ 30 days]. The largest-continuous-balance calculation would give you credit for only $500 because only that amount was continuously on deposit for the entire month. Many credit unions and a few small banks use this approach.

Clearly, the method used in determining the balance in the account and the required minimums are important. They affect whether or not you are charged for checking services. If you fail to maintain the required minimum balance and are charged per-check and service fees, you could easily wind up paying $5 per month or more for your checking account. Read the fine print about checking account operations before opening an account, and ask if you don't see a clear explanation of fees, minimum balances, and interest rates.

It isn't unusual to see checking accounts paying interest and also charging fees if the minimum balances aren't maintained. On small account balances, the fees will probably be greater than the interest payment. In such cases, it may pay to investigate a non-interest-bearing account, because the maintenance fees may be lower. In other cases, banks will pay interest on the checking deposit only if the minimum balance is maintained. Some banks tailor special low-cost checking accounts especially for small depositors. Thrift institutions and credit unions tend to be more oriented toward consumers and small depositors than are commercial banks. In your search for the right checking account, don't overlook thrift institutions.

Interest-bearing Accounts
Your objective with a checking account is to enjoy convenient checking at the lowest possible cost. Earning interest is nice but is not your primary concern. It may be financially wise to obtain an interest-bearing account, but it is not necessarily so. If the balance in your account is larger than you need for transaction purposes, you incur an opportunity cost, because the excess funds could be invested elsewhere at a higher rate of return. If the balance is too small, you may incur a service charge for the privilege of quick access to your money. Both costs should be considered when selecting an interest-bearing checking account. To illustrate how to make this calculation, consider the following example.

Suppose a bank offers free checking if you maintain at least $1,000 average daily balance in your checking account, and will pay 3 percent interest on the average balance. If you fail to maintain that minimum, you continue to earn interest but will pay 30 cents per check and a $5 monthly service charge. You normally keep only $500 in a checking account and write twenty checks per month. You have $500 in a savings account paying 4 percent. Should you move $500 from the savings account to the checking account?

Strategy number 1 keeps $500 in savings at 4 percent and $500 in checking at 3 percent. You will earn $1.67 each month in interest on your savings account (4 percent per year equals 0.3333 percent [4 ÷ 12] per month, so $500 × 0.003333 = $1.67) and $1.25 in interest on your checking account. Additionally, you will be charged a $5 service fee and a $6 fee (20 × 30 cents) for checks each month. Strategy 1 earns $2.92 in interest but pays $11 in fees, for a net cost of $8.08 per month.

Strategy 2 moves $500 from savings into checking so that the minimum balance is maintained. Since the savings account goes down by $500, interest earned declines by $1.67, but the interest earned on the checking account rises to $2.50 a month. More important, the checking service is now free, so the $2.50 per month is net earnings on the account.

In this example, moving funds from your savings account to your checking account is like getting a raise of $10.58 per month *after taxes*. The answer could be different if your savings account paid higher interest or if the service and per-check fees were lower. Look at your old bank statements and see what you were charged and how many checks you wrote each month. Experiment with the example to see how the various factors affect the decision. Take the time to figure out the best place to have your checking account and whether it is worthwhile to maintain the minimum balance if one is required. In the example, the difference between the two strategies is almost $127 per year.

As mentioned earlier, some banks offer free and interest-paying checking if a customer keeps a minimum balance in other accounts, including savings. For example, the bank might agree to pay 3 percent interest on the average checking balance and to levy no fees on the account if the average balance in checking and savings accounts together is more than $2,500. These arrangements are usually best for most of us, because they keep savings and checking deposits separate while allowing for checking services at the lowest possible cost. While it may be cheaper to consolidate savings into checking accounts in some cases, only the disciplined consumer should do so for the purpose of getting free checking. It's too easy to spend money in a checking account. You could wind up spending your savings in an effort to keep a large enough balance to qualify for free checking. We recommend keeping enough in savings accounts in a bank to qualify for free checking. In so doing, you get money market interest rates for your savings accounts and federal deposit insurance as well.

Savings Deposits

The liquidity offered by checking accounts makes them ideal for handling your frequent financial transactions. Giving you immediate access to your funds makes the bank's job harder, so the bank charges you for that liquidity. One of the purposes of your financial plan is to be able to save some of your monthly income and invest it to achieve your financial goals. You do not need as much liquidity with these funds, and the banks are happy to oblige by providing two basic types of savings deposits: savings accounts and certificates of deposit (CDs). These non-checkable deposits are relatively low-risk instruments for achieving your short- and medium-term financial goals.

There are institutional arrangements that make savings deposits less liquid than checkable deposits. A customer purchasing a CD agrees not to withdraw the funds before the specified maturity date, and the bank makes its business plans based on that agreement. Therefore, CDs have an *early withdrawal penalty*, typically requiring a depositor to forfeit three to six months' interest if the funds are withdrawn early. Savings accounts are open-ended deposits, and there is no early withdrawal penalty; however, banks may technically require advance notice of a withdrawal of funds deposited in a savings account, although in practice savings accounts offer few restrictions on the immediate availability of the funds in the account. Because the funds in CDs are less liquid than the funds in savings accounts, CDs typically pay a higher rate of return.

Savings Accounts
The deregulation of the financial industry has had an even larger impact on non-checkable savings deposits than on checkable deposits. A decade ago, most banks offered very similar savings accounts; regulation permitted few differences across institutions. Today, banks are free to set interest rates as they choose. New financial

products appear routinely. There is much more flexibility in the financial services market, and that is good news for the educated consumer.

Savings accounts are perhaps the financial products most affected by financial reform. Some banks still offer the old "passbook" accounts, where deposits and withdrawals are usually recorded in a passbook kept in the depositor's possession. Increasingly, however, banks are offering products with easier access to funds in savings accounts (competing directly against checkable accounts), and with higher rates of return (competing directly against money market mutual funds).

Originally, passbook accounts paid 5.25 percent interest. Federal regulations used to preclude higher interest, but they no longer do. Banks hope that uninformed depositors will continue giving them deposits at low interest cost, and they have no incentive to get these customers to change their behavior. As of this writing, hundreds of billions of dollars remain in passbook accounts at below-market rates of interest. If you are the owner of some of these deposits, switch to accounts that pay money market rates while still offering immediate access to funds.

As the line between checking accounts and savings accounts continues to blur, some banks are offering savings accounts with check-writing capability that compete directly with money market mutual funds (chapter 14) for your emergency fund account. They compete favorably only if they pay money market rates. A passbook savings account paying only 2 percent is a poor location for your emergency fund.

Competitive savings accounts, often called money market deposit accounts (MMDA), offer rates of interest just below the money market rate. Frequently the rates are tied to those currently prevailing in the money markets. The rates earned in savings accounts aren't guaranteed for any length of time but are adjusted up and down with market rates.

Much of what we said about checking account minimum balances also applies to savings accounts. It's common for banks to require a minimum balance—at least $1,000 to $2,500 and sometimes more—before the money market rate of interest is paid. As with checking account balances, the method used to compute the average balance is most important. In savings as in checking, the average daily balance method (ADB) is much better than the largest continuous balance method (LCB), and for the same reason. The amount of interest credited is calculated by multiplying the average balance by the interest rate, so the larger your average balance, the more interest you will earn. Be sure you understand the method used in calculating the balance on which interest will be paid. Bank advertising generally emphasizes the interest rate paid on savings deposits, while the method used to compute the average balance is relegated to the fine print. An account paying a lower interest rate can pay more interest than an account with a higher rate that gives the depositor credit for a smaller average balance.

Accounts using the LCB method aren't necessarily to be avoided. Many credit unions use the LCB method on their share-draft accounts. A typical credit union may offer 3 percent annual interest compounded quarterly on the LCB. Since 3 percent may be an attractive rate in comparison with bank savings accounts, the credit union may have a better deal for you than the bank. Be careful, however, when making

52 • PERSONAL FINANCIAL PLANNING

deposits and withdrawals from an LCB account. For example, if your share account credits interest quarterly on the LCB and you withdraw $1,000 on the next to last day of the quarter, you could lose interest on $1,000 for the entire quarter. At 3 percent annual interest, that loss amounts to $7.50. Similarly, if you deposited $1,000 two weeks before the end of a quarter, you wouldn't be paid any interest on it for that quarter even though it was on deposit for two weeks. Many credit unions, however, give a full month's credit for deposits made by the tenth of the month. If you deposit and withdraw funds frequently, you are probably better off with an account using the ADB method. Whatever your situation, know the rules and play by them.

Another important factor to consider is the compounding method used. Compounding refers to the payment of interest on interest earned previously. Bank advertisements almost always note how the interest rate is compounded. To illustrate the difference compounding makes, consider Table 5-1, showing six different methods of compounding 8 percent annual interest on $1,000. If the 8 percent interest rate is "simple," that is, no compounding of interest, the interest earned is $80. If the bank uses quarterly compounding, the account balance rises at the end of each quarter by 2 percent (8 percent divided by 4 quarters) of the previous quarter's balance. Since the first quarter's interest earns interest in the second quarter and so on, the amount in the account at the end of the year is $1,082.43 and the annual effective rate of interest is 8.24 percent. A common interest method pays interest daily and credits it monthly to your account. This is really monthly compounding, and the annual effective yield here would be 8.30 percent. Actual daily compounding yields 8.33 percent. The final two methods illustrated in the table are seldom used. You will often see "continuous compounding" advertised. This involves the assumption that compounding of interest occurs every instant and results in the theoretically largest possible interest earned for a stated annual rate. Eight percent compounded continuously gives an annual effective rate of 8.33 percent, only a penny better than daily compounding. Sometimes banks calculate daily interest on the assumption of a 360-day year, which results in a larger daily interest rate (because the annual rate is divided by 360 rather than 365) and an effective annual rate higher than the continuous compounding rate. For example, assuming a 360-day year, the daily interest rate is .0222 percent (8 percent divided by 360), which compounded for 365 days (the actual number of days in a year) is an

TABLE 5-1
The Effect of Different Interest-Compounding Methods: $1,000 at 8%

Method	End-of-year Balance	Effective Yield
Simple interest	$1080.00	8.00 %
Quarterly compounding	$1082.43	8.24 %
Daily w/ monthly credit	$1083.00	8.30 %
Daily compounding	$1083.28	8.33 %
Continuous compounding	$1083.29	8.33 %
Daily compounding, 360-day	$1084.48	8.45 %

effective annual rate of 8.45 percent (1.000222 to the 365th power is 1.0845, or 8.45 percent growth).

It's obvious from Table 5-1 that the actual effective rate of interest earned on a savings account depends on the compounding method used. We saw that an 8 percent annual rate can result in an effective interest rate ranging from 8 percent to 8.45 percent. Always ask about the method used to compute the average balance and to compound the interest in the account. Your job is made easy, though, in that most institutions will quote the "annual effective yield," which you can compare to other like numbers from other institutions.

Use the following general principles when evaluating savings accounts:

1. Accounts using the ADB rather than the LCB will pay more in interest given the same stated interest rate. The difference is important only if deposits and withdrawals are made during a compounding period. If none are made, both methods result in the same number. You can usually identify ADB accounts as those promising to pay "daily interest" or to use the "day of deposit to day of withdrawal" method.

2. Accounts compounding interest more frequently pay more interest than those compounding less frequently, given the same interest rate. Look for the highest annual effective rate, or effective yield.

3. Avoid savings accounts having service fees or maintenance charges. These fees are sometimes levied if the required minimum balance isn't maintained. In accounts of this type, it's possible that the fees could be larger than the amount of interest credited, so that the balance in the account is actually declining. Be sure to read the fine print carefully to look for any applicable fees.

4. You should be able to find a savings account paying money market rates on a reasonable balance ($1,000 to $2,500). Since we recommend maintaining an emergency savings balance equal to two months' pay, you should have an account large enough to qualify. If banks in your area don't offer money market interest rates on deposits of the size you want to maintain, look at credit unions and thrift institutions. Don't accept the old "passbook" rate on a balance large enough to qualify for money market rates.

Certificates of Deposit

Finally, banks offer certificates of deposit to compete for our long-term investments. (see chapters 13 through 15 for other types of long-term investments.) Certificates of deposit (CDs) pay higher interest rates than regular savings accounts but levy an early withdrawal penalty if the funds are taken out before the maturity date. Generally, you should use CDs when you have funds in excess of your requirements for emergencies and short-term needs. For example, if you have already established an emergency fund with a balance two times your monthly pay and you have no other short-term need for the excess funds, a CD paying higher interest than the savings account is one way to save for your longer-term goals.

In part IV of the book, we'll discuss investing in debt instruments as a means of accumulating funds for long-term financial objectives. Bank CDs are one type of debt instrument (the bank owes you money if you have one of its CDs) that may be very useful in meeting your financial goals. Many Americans use bank CDs as their primary long-term savings vehicle. The bank CD is the most popular investment in individual IRA accounts.

It is impossible to generalize about which CD offerings are best among the many available. In analyzing CDs, you'll find that the interest rates are usually higher for longer maturity periods. A great advantage of CDs is that the interest is guaranteed for the entire life of the certificate, so a CD enables you to "lock in" an attractive rate of interest for a known amount of time. Savings accounts don't offer this advantage, because they typically pay very low interest rates or money market rates that fluctuate up and down weekly or monthly.

The "advantage" of being able to lock in a rate of interest for several years is a double-edged sword, however. You can't tell what will happen to money market rates in the future. For example, a CD rate of 4 percent guaranteed for five years (and locking your deposit in for five years) may seem attractive today if savings deposits are paying 3 percent. If next year money market rates go to 6 percent, however, your guaranteed 4 percent rate doesn't look so good.

You shouldn't be too concerned about "locking up" your money in a CD. If you really need the money, or if interest rates in the money market and on new CDs shoot way up, you can always get your deposit out of the CD by paying the withdrawal penalty. Forfeiting three to six months' interest may not be as severe as it seems. The penalty may take away some interest earned, but the principal remains intact. As with all bank deposits, it's important to understand fully the terms of a CD before you commit your funds to it. Remember, however, if interest rates on new CDs rise significantly, the early withdrawal penalty can be more than recovered by earning interest at the higher rate. See chapter 13 for additional details on this attractive feature of CDs.

The problem in selecting an appropriate CD, then, is to identify the period of time over which you can afford to leave your money tied up and to find the most attractive interest rate available for CDs of that maturity. Shopping for CDs can really be worthwhile. The offers made by different banks vary significantly. The *Wall Street Journal* publishes interest rates in the money markets daily and frequently shows the rates offered on consumer CDs. *Money, Barron's,* and other financial publications often report CD rates as well. Look for this published information to determine whether the CD rates you are being quoted are competitive with those being offered around the country.

SUGGESTED REFERENCES

The following periodicals, available at virtually all military and public libraries, frequently include articles on the latest trends and services in the banking industry:

Money. Published monthly by Time, Inc.
Changing Times. Published monthly by the Kiplinger Washington Editors, Inc.
The Wall Street Journal. Published on business days by Dow Jones, Inc.
Barron's. Published weekly by Dow Jones, Inc.

6

Using Credit Wisely

BORROWING TO FINANCE the purchase of durable goods like cars, furniture, and appliances has long been a prominent feature of American life. In this chapter, we discuss the wise use of consumer credit, the operation of traditional bank-loan services, and some of the different types of collateralized loans being offered to consumers. Additionally, we will discuss the uses, abuses, and costs of consumer credit and debit cards.

CONSUMER CREDIT

Today, consumer credit is relatively easy to get—so easy that many families find themselves in financial distress. The danger in taking on too much debt is that there is not enough income both to amortize (pay off) the debts and to provide for the basic needs of food and shelter, much less save for future needs. As we have emphasized in chapter 4, success in personal financial management requires planning and perseverance in implementing the plan. An absolute requirement for any family is a regular savings plan. If having to make large monthly installment debt payments makes regular saving impossible, you should take immediate steps to reduce the amount you owe. Although this situation is easier to prevent than it is to cure, it is never beyond hope.

This is not to say that military families should never borrow. Virtually everyone, at one time or another, needs to borrow money to finance major purchases such as automobiles and furniture or to pay educational expenses. Additionally, there are very few people who can afford to buy a house with cash alone. Without credit, some of these costly items could not be bought at all unless a family has successfully saved enough money to pay outright for certain major purchases. In this case, it is almost always more advantageous for people to use their own funds, to "borrow from themselves," than to borrow from a lending institution. The interest rate they lose on savings is generally lower than the interest rate they would be charged on a consumer loan. In fact, it is even possible, using the concepts in appendix D, to calculate the "loan payment" to be repaid each month to oneself. Most military families never achieve this level of financial independence, however, and find it convenient to use credit to finance major purchases.

Notice that in discussing credit, we have used as examples durable goods (e.g., furniture, cars) and long-lasting assets (e.g., education). Our point is that *it is inappropriate to use consumer credit to finance day-to-day needs.* It is good practice to ensure that the item financed has a useful life at least as long as the time it will take to repay the debt. We do not think that military families should routinely carry unpaid credit card balances for purchases of clothes, entertainment, groceries, and other such nondurable items. Such routine spending should be covered by current income. Using credit to finance routine purchases or to splurge on "extras" is a sure sign of personal financial *mis*management.

Since it is improbable that everyone reading this book will adhere to our rather strict view of the proper use of consumer credit, it is worth discussing how much consumer debt is "too much." When we talk about consumer debt, we mean all debts incurred to finance a purchase, including car loans and credit card debt, but excluding real estate mortgages. Several rules of thumb have been developed as guidelines for the maximum amount of debt a family should have. One very useful rule is that *monthly payments on consumer debt* should be no more than 20 percent of "monthly disposable income" (income after mortgage or rent, food, utilities, and taxes have been paid). Another guideline is that the *total outstanding consumer debt* should be less than one-third of your annual disposable income. To see how these guidelines might be applied, consider the following examples.

Debt-payment Guideline: A captain with more than ten years of service who occupies government quarters will have after-tax take-home pay of approximately $2,500 per month. If the officer has no utilities or other housing expenses, we need only estimate spending for food to find his "disposable income." Let's assume that the officer is responsible for a family of four and that his family's food costs are $500 per month. This means that the officer has $2,000 a month in disposable income. According to the first guideline, the officer's installment debt payments should not exceed $400 per month (20 percent of $2,000). How much debt could be carried for $400 per month? If we assume that the average maturity of the debt is two years and that the average interest rate is 12 percent, the outstanding debt that could be serviced with $400 per month is about $8,500. If the debt had an average maturity of three years, $400 would be adequate to service about $12,000. (These total debt amounts are found by multiplying the monthly payment by the annuity factor. See Table 4-7 for the formula and appendix D for a table of annuity factors.)

Now suppose that the officer's family did not occupy government quarters and that the housing allowance plus variable housing allowance (VHA) were $200 per month less than the additional expenses for rent, utilities, and other housing costs. This would make the officer's monthly disposable income about $1,800. In this case, the 20 percent guideline suggests a limit of $360 per month maximum for consumer debt service and proportionately less total installment debt, about $7,650 for debt maturing in two years.

Total-debt Guideline: This rule is a bit stricter than the debt-payment guideline. Continuing with our example, the officer living in government quarters with an annual disposable income of $24,000 should not owe more than one-third of that, or $8,000, in consumer debt. The officer living off post who has an annual disposable income of $21,600 should owe less than $7,200 in consumer debt.

Military servicemembers and their spouses should continue to monitor their levels of consumer debt especially during these days of "drawing down" the armed forces and the federal civilian workforce. Involuntary or voluntary separations or loss of employment by a spouse can disrupt family income and cause financial problems if you cannot service your consumer debt. Thus, it is wise for military families to stay comfortably below the upper limits of consumer indebtedness suggested above. Consumer debt should be carefully planned as one component of a monthly budget that continues to include adequate provisions for regular savings and an emergency reserve.

CONSUMER LOANS

The most common type of loan arrangement used by consumers is the *installment loan,* in which the amount borrowed, plus interest, is amortized (repaid) over a predetermined period in equal monthly payments. The familiar automobile loan and the home mortgage are common examples. *Single-payment loans* are also used, but much less commonly. In a single-payment loan, the full amount borrowed plus interest is repaid at the maturity date of the loan. A loan having a combination of periodic payments and a large repayment at the end of the loan is called a *balloon loan.* Because the usual reason for consumer borrowing is to spread the cost of a major purchase over the life of the purchased good, installment loans are much more common for military consumers and will be our primary focus in this section.

The True Interest Rate

Consumers shopping for installment loans should compare three features: the interest rate charged (the annual percentage rate, or APR), the term of the contract, and any prepayment penalties or other fees. The effect of the APR on a loan contract is straightforward: the higher the APR, the higher the monthly payment (for a given term of the loan) and the more total interest will be paid over the life of the loan. The impact of the term of the loan is a bit more subtle. The longer the period over which the installment payments are to be made, the lower the required monthly payments. The total interest paid will be higher, however, because the lender's money is being used longer. In loan contracts, the total amount of interest paid over the life of the loan

58 • PERSONAL FINANCIAL PLANNING

is called the total finance charge, and it is one of the items, along with the APR, that must be disclosed in every loan agreement under the Truth in Lending Act.

Lenders use several different methods to compute the monthly payment on an installment loan. Two loans that appear to be exactly the same (i.e., they are for the same amount, duration, and interest rate) can have very different monthly payments, finance charges, and APRs, depending on how the lender calculates the interest. To protect consumers, the law requires that lenders disclose the APR of the loan. Consumers need only compare the APR to determine which is the least expensive loan.

For example, Table 6-1 illustrates the differences between the "monthly balance" and the "add-on interest" methods of charging interest on a loan for $2,000 at 12 percent interest per year, repaid in twelve equal monthly payments. These two loans sound identical, but they are very different. The monthly balance method amortizes the loan, and it is the "usual" way that loans are repaid. When interest is computed using the monthly balance method, the monthly payments are $177.70 and the APR is 12.0 percent per year. The add-on interest method essentially charges interest on the entire amount borrowed over the whole year, even though some of the principal is being repaid each month. When interest is computed using the add-on interest method, the monthly payments are $186.67, and the APR is 21.3 percent per year.

You might wonder, "Why do consumers need the APR? Anyone could look at these two loans and choose the loan with the lower monthly payments." The example in Table 6-1 is easy because the only difference between the two options is the method used to compute interest. But consumers typically must choose between loans with different durations, different lengths of time until the first payment is due, and any number of other variations. The APR is a standardized calculation that allows consumers to compare the true interest rate for different loans and know which loan has the lowest cost of borrowing.

Table 6-1 shows two different formulas for the APR, and there are many others (one for every type of consumer loan). In what sense, then, is the APR a standardization? In fact, every APR formula is an approximation to the same thing: the true interest cost of the loan. In the days when the Truth in Lending Act was first passed, it was difficult to calculate the true interest cost directly, so these approximation formulas were devised. Today, with financial calculators and spreadsheets, it is easy to do so, but it would be difficult to write the legal language. The bottom line is that all of the APR formulas, as crazy as they may look, are very good approximations of the true interest cost of the loan. Consumers don't have to calculate the APR; they need only compare the APRs that lenders are required by law to reveal to them.

For the most common installment loans (i.e., loans in which interest is computed using the monthly balance method), the monthly payment is determined as illustrated in appendix D. With a careful reading of that section and some practice with a good calculator or home computer, you should be able to compute the monthly payments on these common loans. For the example in Table 6-1, the monthly payment is $177.70, so a total of $2,132.40 will be repaid over the term of the contract. The total finance charge, which is the difference between the amount borrowed and the total repaid, is $132.40.

TABLE 6-1
Comparison of Simple and Add-on Interest
$2,000 @ 12% for 1 Year, 12 Monthly Payments

Monthly Balance Interest Method

Month	Payment	Interest at 1% per month on Outstanding Balance	Principal	Balance Outstanding
Beginning of period				$2,000.00
1	$177.70	$20.00	$157.70	$1,842.30
2	177.70	18.42	159.28	1,682.02
3	177.70	16.83	160.87	1,522.15
4	177.70	15.22	162.48	1,359.67
5	177.70	13.60	164.10	1,195.57
6	177.70	11.96	165.74	1,029.83
7	177.70	10.30	167.40	862.43
8	177.70	8.62	169.08	693.35
9	177.70	6.93	170.77	522.58
10	177.70	5.23	172.47	350.11
11	177.70	3.50	174.20	175.91
12	1767.70	1.79	175.91	0.00
	$2,132.40	$132.40	$2,000.00	$1,103.08*

*Average outstanding balance (sum of last column divided by 12).

$$APR = \frac{\text{Finance charge}}{\text{Average balance}} = \frac{\$132.40}{\$1,103.08} = .12\ (12\%)$$

Add-on Interest Method

Add-on interest = $F = (r \times L) = .12 \times \$2,000 = \$240$
Total to be repaid = $L + (r \times L) = \$2,000 + \$240 = \$2,240$
Monthly payment = Total to be repaid ÷ number of monthly payments (n) = $2,240 ÷ 12 = $186.67

$$APR = \frac{n \times F \times (95T + 9)}{12T \times (T + 1) \times (4L + F)} = .214\ (21.4\%)$$

r = Annual interest rate
n = Number of payments per year (12)
T = Total number of payments over life of loan (12)
F = Total finance charge ($240)
L = Principal amount of loan ($2,000)

60 • PERSONAL FINANCIAL PLANNING

The top half of Table 6-1 provides a good example of an *amortization table*, which gives the payment, interest paid, and principal balance owed after every monthly payment is made. At the end of the first month, you have borrowed $2,000 for one month, and you must pay interest on that at the rate of 12 percent per year. Twelve percent annual interest is 1 percent per month, so you owe $20 (.01% × $2,000) interest after one month. Since you make a monthly payment of $177.70, and you only owe $20 in interest, the remaining $157.70 ($177.70 − $20) goes toward "paying down" your principal, or balance owed. So, after one monthly payment, you owe only $1,842.30 ($2,000 − $157.70), which is your new balance outstanding. In the second month, you pay interest only on the amount that you still owe. Notice how your balance (the column on the right) goes to zero after all twelve monthly payments have been made.

The point of the example in Table 6-1 is not so much to illustrate the arithmetic of calculating loan payments and APRs, but to show how much difference the method of computing interest can make. Do not look only at the advertised interest rate in a loan contract. Take the time to find the APR in the Truth in Lending section. Compare the APR you are offered to typical loan rates reported in the "Money Rates" section of either the *Wall Street Journal* or *Barron's*, or in frequent surveys published in *Money, Consumer Reports,* or *Changing Times*. It often pays to shop around for various loan terms. Interest rates and terms of loans can vary significantly.

Not knowing the market for consumer loans can cost you a lot of money. It is common today for auto loans to offer very low APRs, but as we show in chapter 9, the low-rate loans are often available only if other purchasing conditions are met. As a result, in order to determine whether the offered interest rate is really attractive, identify the costs, if any, of purchasing conditions placed on the loan.

Prepayment Penalties

You should also investigate another important feature of loan contracts: the prepayment penalty. Strangely enough, if you decide you want to pay off your loan in a shorter period than specified in the contract, you may have to pay more interest on the loan than originally stated in the terms. The "sum-of-the-digits" method (the *Rule of 78*) is sometimes used to determine how much of the finance charge originally agreed to will have to be paid if the loan is repaid before maturity.

The sum-of-the-digits method forms a fraction whose denominator is the sum of the digits of the number of payments in the original agreement. For example, for a one-year monthly payment loan, the sum of the digits is $1 + 2 + 3 + 4 + \ldots + 12 = 78$ (which is why this is also called the Rule of 78). The numerator of the fraction is simply the sum of the digits, starting with the highest digit, for the number of payments already made. For example, if you want to pay off the loan after six months, you will have made six payments so the numerator is $12 + 11 + 10 + \ldots + 7 = 57$. The fraction 57/78, or 0.73, determines how much of the finance charge will have to be paid. Since the finance charge in the simple-interest loan of Table 6-1 was $132.40, the sum-of-the-digits fraction says that $96.65 (0.73 × $132.40) will have to be paid, or that $2,096.65 is the total amount due to the lender to prepay the entire loan at this point.

If you were to pay off the simple-interest loan after six months using the Rule of 78, you would have to pay:

Amount due lender	$2,096.65
Payments made (6 × $177.70)	− 1,066.20
Amount still due	$1,030.45

This may seem fair enough, but you should recognize that the sum-of-the-digits method actually overcharges you slightly for interest when you consider how long you have really used the lender's money. To illustrate the amount of the "prepayment penalty" imposed by the sum-of-the-digits method, compare it to the amount you would owe with no prepayment penalty. The standard method to determine the amount owed on a loan is the "amortized" balance. Recall that Table 6-1 was an amortization table that calculated a "balance outstanding" after each payment. Note that the balance after Month 6 is $1,029.83. You had to pay 62 cents more under the Rule of 78. On a one-year $2,000 loan, the difference ($1,030.45 − $1,029.83) using the Rule of 78 is negligible, but for larger amounts and longer-term loans, the difference can amount to a substantial penalty. Look for loans that do not impose prepayment penalties if you think you may want to pay off your loan early.

Collateral

For many loans that consumers use to finance major purchases, the good purchased serves as collateral for the loan. That is, the bank takes a *lien* against the good, so that if repayment is not made as agreed, the bank may repossess the property and sell it for cash. Remember that banks are loaning out their depositors' money and want to have some protection in the event that a borrower fails to repay. Loans can also be collateralized by other property including stocks and bonds, equity in a home, and sometimes even jewelry. Retirement accounts such as an IRA may *not* be used as collateral. In some cases, the bank will insist on taking physical possession of the collateral, as with stock and bond certificates. In other cases, the bank may simply take a lien against the property, which is common when money is loaned against a car or the equity in a home.

Collateralized, or "secured," loans are less risky for banks because they offer some protection in the event the borrower defaults. As a result, the interest rate on a secured loan tends to be lower than for an unsecured, or "signature," loan. The lower interest on secured loans is worth remembering if you want to borrow for some purpose (such as a child's education) where the asset you are financing cannot be used as collateral. It may be worthwhile to use some of your other assets to secure a loan in such cases. You should also consider selling the assets for cash since this may be cheaper than borrowing.

Home-equity Loans

A form of collateralized borrowing that has become quite popular involves second mortgages and lines of credit secured by the borrower's equity in a home. This entails borrowing against the difference between the value of a home as determined by an appraiser and what is still owed to the mortgage holder. Second mortgages and home-equity lines of credit allow homeowners to borrow money at interest rates that are lower than those of normal consumer loans to finance the purchase of durable goods or home improvements by using the equity in the home as collateral.

A 1986 change in the tax law made these loans even more attractive. The law eliminated interest deductions on almost all types of consumer borrowing. The single exception is the home-equity loan. This tax break is a valuable advantage, particularly if you are in the upper income tax brackets. Another advantage of these types of loans is that relatively large amounts of money can be borrowed for long periods of time, often up to fifteen years.

There are several disadvantages of home-equity loans. They can be fairly expensive to set up because the "closing costs" involved in real estate lending can run into several hundreds of dollars. In addition, points (a point is 1 percent of the amount borrowed, paid up front) may be charged on second mortgages, adding further to the cost. Finally, the interest rate charged on a second mortgage will be a few percentage points higher than the going rate on new first mortgages.

If you need to borrow a large amount of money with a reasonably long period to repay, a second mortgage on your home may be a good alternative (an example may be to finance college education costs for children). For smaller amounts and shorter repayment periods, shop carefully for more conventional loans before committing yourself to a second mortgage. You must weigh the tax and interest rate advantages against the sizable up-front closing fees.

Home-equity lines of credit are similar to second mortgages in that the borrowing is secured by the equity in a home and closing costs are involved when the credit line is originally set up. Once the credit line is established, however, borrowers have a great deal of flexibility in the use of the credit available. In most cases, they draw cash against their credit line simply by writing a check and can repay on any schedule that is convenient for them. Borrowers pay interest monthly on the amount of credit they have outstanding, but some institutions make the interest rates fairly attractive. The closing costs and other fees on a home equity line of credit will be lower than on a second mortgage for most banks and lending institutions.

If you have substantial equity in real estate and think that a flexible line of credit would be useful to you because you frequently need to borrow large sums for varying periods of time, you might investigate the home-equity lines of credit being offered by banks and brokers today. Some consumers use home-equity credit lines to finance cars, appliances, educational expenses, and many other needs that have traditionally been financed by conventional bank loans. An obvious potential danger in using your home's equity as a source of funds is that you risk losing your home if you default on your loan obligation.

Sources for Loans

When consumers think of borrowing money, their bank is often the source of credit that first comes to mind. Banks are by no means the only source of consumer credit, however. As we mentioned in chapter 5, the financial sector of the economy is becoming increasingly competitive as different kinds of institutions enter the market for consumer financial services. Therefore, you should also consider as sources of credit those institutions we discussed as possible providers of banking services in general: credit unions, savings and loan associations, and mutual savings banks. Many of these institutions are very consumer oriented and may offer better loan rates than banks in your area. Your stockbroker also will loan you money, using your stocks, bonds, or other qualifying assets as collateral. These so-called margin loans are usually used by aggressive investors to leverage their stock portfolios when they believe stock prices are about to rise, but there is no restriction on their actual use. The rate of interest on broker loans is tied to (usually about 1 percent above) the "broker's call rate," which is a rate of interest that is generally very close to the short-term Treasury bill rate. A loan from your broker may be cheaper than a loan from any other institution. In addition, the repayment terms on loans from brokers are typically flexible: You repay when you want to, but pay interest on the amount borrowed as long as you have it. Finally, if you own permanent life insurance ("whole life"), you can borrow against the cash value of your policy at very attractive rates (see chapter 18 for details). If you already own a whole-life policy with a substantial cash value, this is your best alternative for borrowing small amounts cheaply.

CREDIT AND DEBIT CARDS

One of the most familiar, and certainly most popular, forms of consumer credit offered by banking institutions is the credit card. Banks, credit unions, and thrift institutions usually offer either MasterCard or VISA and sometimes both. Most military credit unions and USAA offer these cards with no annual fee and very low interest rates. Today, bank credit cards are made available to a very broad range of consumers. Through the magic of modern mailing-list technology, you are likely to find in your mailbox an offer to apply for a credit card from a bank that does not even operate in your state. Of course, there are many credit cards other than VISA and MasterCard. Oil companies, major department stores, and financial service conglomerates like Sears (Discover) also offer credit cards. In addition, American Express, Diner's Club, and Carte Blanche offer "travel and entertainment" cards that offer credit but under quite different terms than banks, stores, and oil companies. Most of the long-distance phone companies now offer combination credit-and-calling cards (such as AT&T Universal) that are very convenient for servicemembers.

Additionally, most financial institutions offer automatic teller machine (ATM) cards, or debit cards, that many consumers use along with their credit cards. The debit card is an early sign of the "checkless society" some have predicted for the future, whereby funds may be transferred electronically between consumers and businesses rather than by the traditional method of writing and clearing checks. The debit card is becoming more widely used, as more and more retail and grocery stores have installed the technology with which to automatically debit your checking account when purchasing goods and services. In this section, we discuss the operation of "open credit" arrangements common to credit cards, and the costs and benefits of their use.

The term *credit card* is derived from the nature of the arrangement between the lender—a bank, store, or oil company—and the borrower, the holder of the credit card. When a purchase is made with a credit card, the lender, in effect, makes a loan to the cardholder. The lender agrees to pay the merchant quickly for the goods bought and to bill the cardholder later for the purchase. Credit cards represent preapproved lines of credit, up to a specified limit.

From the point of view of the cardholder, however, the credit card is a very effective substitute for cash or checks in making routine purchases. The insecurity and inconvenience of carrying currency and the uncertainty about the acceptability of personal checks are eliminated, since so many retail establishments (including your post or base exchange) accept, without question, the nationally known credit cards. Use of the credit card allows the cardholder to make a single payment to the bank for all the small purchases made during the month. In that sense, credit cards tend to substitute for checking account balances as well. We can imagine a cardholder buying nearly everything he needs during the month with credit cards and paying them off right after he receives his paycheck. In any case, we know consumers find credit cards very useful, because the volume of credit card usage has surged in the past fifteen years.

Cost of Credit Card Credit

Most credit cards provide credit free as long as the cardholder pays the entire balance of the account within a *grace period*—usually twenty-five days from the end of the monthly billing period. If the cardholder fails to pay off the full amount, however, the lender charges interest on the unpaid balance. Warning: There is a disturbing trend toward doing away with this grace period by a few card issuers. This means that you must check the grace period for any card that you are considering. New laws that require a standardized table of credit terms in promotional pamphlets will make your job easier.

While the convenience and free credit features of credit cards make them potentially useful to everyone, many consumers run up large unpaid balances on their card accounts and continually make sizable interest payments on them. The card issuers make this quite easy by asking that the cardholder make only a minimum monthly payment, which is usually far less than the unpaid balance.

Banks are eager to have cardholders keep unpaid balances outstanding, because the interest rate on these balances is typically much higher than banks earn on their regular loans and investments. In fact, most credit card agreements specify that interest on the unpaid balance will be charged at a rate of 1.5 percent per month, and sometimes even higher. This may seem like a low rate, but consider that if you maintained a $1,000 unpaid balance on your credit card for a year, you would pay more than $195 in interest. Thus the effective annual interest rate exceeds 19.5 percent, which is much higher than you would pay for even an expensive signature loan. Even worse, once the cardholder has run his unpaid balance up to the bank's credit limit, the card is essentially worthless: No more purchases will be approved beyond the credit limit. At that point all that you have is a very expensive loan.

Thus, although credit cards offer great utility to consumers, their misuse costs cardholders many millions of dollars in needless interest expenses. Accumulating credit card debt is an easy trap for an undisciplined consumer and a sure sign that he or she has become dangerously overextended on credit. *We recommend that cardholders plan to pay off their entire balance during each billing cycle.*

Nevertheless, there will be occasions when it will be convenient to pay off a major credit card purchase over a period of several months. Because interest will be charged on these occasions, you should investigate the interest rates and calculation methods used by the various card issuers. The most common interest rate on credit card balances is 1.5 percent per month. In some states the rates are controlled at lower levels, but some issuers charge even higher rates. Many military credit unions have cards with lower rates, and USAA's credit card rate is often one of the lowest rates in the nation. Shopping for the lowest rate is worthwhile, because some institutions are beginning to compete for credit card business on the basis of their lower rates. The magazines referenced at the end of this chapter contain excellent rate-shopping guides on a regular basis.

When comparing cards, keep in mind that you cannot simply compare the interest rates charged on credit cards. Different methods are used by card issuers to determine the *balance* on which they charge interest. As with bank deposits and loans, the method used to calculate the outstanding balance can have an important effect on the total interest expense. The most common method used by card issuers is the "average-daily-balance" (ADB) method, identical to the approach used in savings and checking accounts (see chapter 5). This method applies the daily interest rate to the average of your daily balances during the billing cycle.

Two other methods are frequently used. In the "previous-balance" method, finance charges are levied on the previous due balance as of the beginning of the billing period. The "adjusted-balance" method levies the charge on the amount of the previous balance minus any payments made during the billing period. Thus, the adjusted-balance method results in the lowest finance charge, the previous-balance method in the highest charge, and the ADB method somewhere in between.

You should always read the credit card agreement carefully, however, because some issuers apparently include current new purchases made during the billing period to the ADB. The result is that all new purchases made on an account with a past-due balance are also made at interest (i.e., with no grace period). You should avoid these cards. The balance calculation method must be described on each bill as well as in the agreement.

Credit cards also allow cardholders to get "cash advances" from any bank around the world that services the card. Most cards also allow you to get a cash advance by writing a "check" on your account or using your card in a participating ATM machine. This service can be a real convenience for travelers who run short of cash. The cash advances are assessed a finance charge, however, even when the balance is fully paid within the twenty-five-day grace period. Usually, interest is charged from the day of withdrawal, at the normal credit card rate. Many cards also charge a sizable fee, often 2 percent of the cash advance, in addition to the finance charge. Due to the very high cost of cash advances, you should use this useful service only in emergencies.

Free credit cards are more common today than they were a few years ago. Better-educated consumers have led many financial institutions to offer credit cards with no annual fees and to compete for cardholders in other ways. When banks were deregulated, however, many began to charge at least what it cost them to provide credit card services. Cardholders who always pay off the entire balance generate no interest earnings for the bank, but there are still costs of maintaining the account. The merchants who accept credit cards pay a percentage of each transaction to the issuer, but the income apparently does not cover all costs. As a result, some banks still have an annual fee of $20 to $50 or more for each credit card account. Many banks offer credit cards free with no annual fee for a brief introductory period as a competitive offer to lure new customers. It is common for a credit card issuer to change its terms or rates, and even to change a no-fee card to one with an annual fee. Since there is really no reason to have your credit card issued by your regular bank, feel free to shop for the best deal. There are so many no-fee cards available to servicemembers that you should never pay an annual fee without a very good reason.

Credit card fraud and theft are increasing problems about which cardholders must be aware. Mail-order firms will ship merchandise from telephone orders based on a credit card number. While such services are a real convenience, they do present the danger of some unauthorized person using your credit card number to order goods by phone. Carbon copies of credit slips are routinely stolen and used for this purpose. There is also the risk that a lost or stolen card may be used directly. Cardholders have the responsibility of notifying the issuers of their cards as soon as they realize a card is missing. A number of firms and automobile clubs now offer a service of registering all of a customer's credit card numbers and notifying all the issuers on behalf of the cardholder if the cards are lost or stolen. Be sure to do this, if the service is free.

Occasionally, you will get an offer to buy credit card insurance. There really is little reason to pay for such insurance, because your liability for unauthorized use of your cards is limited to $50, and as a practical matter, few issuers actually attempt to get their cardholders to pay even that. Just make sure that you report any loss within twenty-four hours. Here is an easy way to keep track of your cards in case they are stolen. Right now, and on each birthday, empty the contents of your wallet onto a copy machine and make a copy. This provides a quick and convenient record in case of a loss or theft.

Debit Cards

Debit cards may look like conventional bank credit cards and may even sport the VISA or MasterCard logo, but their purpose is quite different. A debit card is an alternative way for a checking account holder to draw upon his deposits in order to make purchases. When a debit card holder makes a purchase using his card, his checking account is electronically debited (or in some cases, it is debited when the charge slip clears through the bank in a few days). Since use of a debit card affects the balance in the checking account, be very careful to record each transaction in your checkbook ledger. Debit cards are becoming more universally accepted, as many retailers now offer this service in lieu of cash, check, or credit transactions. Unfortunately, they have no "grace period" and none of the protection that credit cards have against fraud under the Fair Credit Billing Act and other protective legislation.

Travel and Entertainment Cards

The travel and entertainment (T&E) cards issued by American Express, Diner's Club, and Carte Blanche are used just like credit cards but are different in a very important way from credit cards such as VISA or MasterCard. Issuers of the T&E cards expect the cards to be used only for the convenience of eliminating cash and check purchases, and not for revolving credit. That means you must pay the full balance when it is due. Failure to use the cards as prescribed may result in very stiff penalties, including interest rates of up to 2 percent per month and probable cancellation of the agreement. These cards should be used only by those who will pay off the entire balance each month.

Since these cards are most useful to business executives who travel and entertain away from home frequently, most military people will not find much extra benefit from having one of them if they already have a conventional bank credit card. Aside from the requirement that the balance be paid in full each month, the annual service or membership charges are rather high ($50 to $75 per year) in relation to the bank credit cards.

Premium Credit Cards

Another credit card service that has been growing in prominence is the premium credit card. "Gold" and sometimes even "Platinum" VISAs, MasterCards, and American Express cards are being marketed as signs that an individual has achieved a high economic standing. The premium cards are usually tied to a large line of credit ($5,000 to $25,000 or more) at a bank and offer a wide variety of other services that may not be of great use to the typical servicemember. The main allure of these cards is their snob appeal, and the primary disadvantage is their high annual cost. It is not uncommon for annual charges to be $50 or more. Although issuing financial institutions may offer expanded services to holders of premium cards, you should ascertain whether the additional services, if used, are worth the extra cost.

It is worth noting that the Fair Credit Billing Act of 1975 permits retailers to offer price discounts of up to 5 percent to customers who pay cash rather than use a credit card. The most extensive use of this legal privilege is found in gasoline retailing. Gas stations often set a lower per-gallon price for customers who pay with cash. In other cases, retailers will not accept credit cards for small purchases of less than about $10. Because retailers pay a fee to the credit card issuer for each transaction, selling small items to credit card holders is not very profitable. You may want to carry enough cash to take advantage of the cash discounts and to facilitate small purchases. You can occasionally negotiate a 1 or 2 percent discount with furniture, appliance, and electronic goods sales managers if you pull out a credit card but then offer to pay instead with cash.

Credit Card Summary

The bottom line on credit cards is that they offer a great deal of convenience and flexibility in paying routine bills, especially when traveling or shopping away from home. But they also can be badly abused. Because they are so readily available, some households have acquired a large number of cards and have used them to pile up even larger debts at the high interest rates the cards charge. Our advice on credit cards is to know yourself and to use them only if you are sure you can control the amount of debt they will allow you to incur. In our experience you will need no more than three different cards: a low-interest card with no annual fee for major purchases or emergencies; a travel and entertainment card, which should be paid off each month; and a debit card issued by your bank, which can be used for everyday cash-free transactions.

Generally, we believe that the cards should not be used as a source of continuous credit because of the high interest costs involved. Cardholders should plan to pay off the entire balance at the end of each and every billing cycle. When shopping for the best credit card, look for institutions that offer free cards with low interest rates; many do. One of the best features of credit cards is that they represent a reserve of purchasing power that can be tapped immediately in an emergency. Ask for a credit limit that is high enough to allow you to finance airline tickets and other emergency expenditures. Credit card credit can be used instead of a large reserve in a savings account, but remember that only the unused portion of your credit line serves as an effective source of reserves. This is another reason to pay off the balance on the card each month.

Advice for Credit Abusers

Like oil and water, credit and some people just do not mix. Through bad luck, bad management, or just lack of willpower, some people either cannot get credit or cannot handle it once they do.

If you cannot get either a VISA or MasterCard, it is probably because your "credit is bad." This could mean about a dozen different things, from having a history of bankruptcy or unpaid bills to just being too young or inexperienced to be offered a credit card. This does not happen much anymore, since issuers are trying hard to get new card customers. If you cannot get a card and you do not have any credit history, then take some measures to build a credit history. Start with an oil company credit card—anyone can get one. Use it and pay it off immediately. Then work your way up to a department store card and eventually to a bank card. Try your own bank or credit union—most military credit unions will start you up with a low credit limit, even if you have no credit history. If all else fails, and you just cannot wait, you can get a "secured" credit card, which is usually very expensive and operates more like a debit card. If you have totally destroyed your credit rating and have exhausted your other options, there are about twenty-five banks that will issue you a card secured by a sizable deposit. If you prove that you can use this for a while, you could "graduate" to a normal credit card. A list of banks with secured cards is available for $4 from Bankcard Holders of America, 560 Herndon Parkway, Herndon, VA 22070, or for $5 from RAM Research's Cardtrak, Box 1700, Frederick, MD 21702.

You may be tempted by an offer (for a fee, of course) from some direct mailer to "check your credit rating." This is something for which you should not have to pay. If you are ever turned down for credit, you can get your credit rating information for free. See point nine in the following section, "Borrowers' Rights."

If you get out of control with high, unpaid credit card balances, you have a serious problem. Each service has trained financial counselors (such as ACS in the Army) to help structure a way out. The only way to fix this problem is to spend less than you earn for a while. Moreover, the sooner you get some help working on your problem, the easier it will be to get out of it. In any case, always keep one credit card paid off in full, so that you can take advantage of the grace period.

BORROWERS' RIGHTS

When considering whether to take advantage of any of the various forms of consumer credit outlined in this chapter, you must be mindful of your legal rights as a borrower. Over the years, the U.S. Congress has passed two major pieces of legislation that protect the borrower's rights: the Consumer Credit Protection Act of 1968 (better known as the Truth in Lending Act) and the Fair Credit Billing Act of 1975. Under these two acts, you, as a borrower, have the following rights:

1. You have the right to know the true interest rate (in APR terms) and total finance charges before signing for any loan.
2. Credit card issuers must advertise the true interest rate (in APR terms) charged on their cards.
3. You must be given at least fourteen days from the postmark on your credit card statement to pay off your balance and avoid paying any interest.
4. When considering your application for a loan or a credit card, a financial institution cannot ignore income from child support, alimony, or a pension.
5. In the event that you purchased goods or services in excess of $50 with your credit card and you are dissatisfied, you have the right to cancel the charges if you

make a genuine effort to settle matters with the seller and the purchase was made in your home state or within 100 miles of your home.

6. In the event that your credit card is used against your will or without your permission (that is, it is stolen or lost), your liability for the unauthorized purchases is limited to $50. If you are able to notify the credit card issuer of the loss or theft of the card before anyone tries to purchase something with it, you will not be liable for any unauthorized purchases.

7. In the event that a debit card is stolen or lost, you must notify the bank within two business days in order to limit your liability to $50. If you fail to do so, you can be liable for the first $500 taken from your account. If sixty-one days pass after the mailing date of your first bank statement showing unauthorized withdrawals, you may be liable for all the money taken from your account.

8. In the event you are applying for a credit card or loan on your own for the first time (in other words, you have no credit record of your own), you have the right to have your spouse's unblemished credit record considered as your own.

9. Should you ever be denied a loan or a credit card, you have the right to be told the specific reasons why you were turned down. You cannot be denied access to what has been reported about you to a credit bureau. If the credit bureau's report was instrumental in your being rejected for a loan or a credit card, you must be provided access to your file at no charge. If you wish to find out what is in your credit record without having been rejected for a credit application, you can contact one or all of the three major credit bureaus: TRW, Equifax, and Trans Union. Any or all may have a file on you, and your report may be accurate at one and inaccurate at another. Therefore, you should check your credit report at all three bureaus. To find out how to get your credit report, call TRW at (214) 235-1200 and Equifax at (800) 685-1111. Write to Trans Union at 25249 Country Club Boulevard, P.O. Box 7000, North Olmsted, OH 44070. TRW's reports are free once a year; Equifax and Trans Union charge $8 per report.

SUGGESTED REFERENCES

Porter, Sylvia. *Sylvia Porter's New Money Book for the 80's,* chap. 16. New York: Avon, 1980.

The following periodicals, available at virtually all military and public libraries, frequently include articles on the latest trends and services in consumer lending:
Money. Published monthly by Time, Inc.
Changing Times. Published monthly by the Kiplinger Washington Editors, Inc.
The Wall Street Journal. Published on business days by Dow Jones, Inc. See in particular the "Your Money Matters" feature.
Consumer Reports. Published monthly by Consumers' Union, Inc.

7

Meeting Medical Expenses

FOR MOST AMERICANS, the escalating costs of medical treatment and care, whether for accidents or sickness, are a major concern. In 1960, about 5 percent of the gross national product was spent on medical care. Today, it accounts for approximately 14 percent—or more than $800 billion annually. That amounts to more than $3,200 for every person in the country. U.S. medical care costs are higher, on a per capita basis, than in any other industrialized country.

Perhaps most alarming is the steadily rising cost of health care: Health-care price increases averaged about 7 percent during the 1980s, which was more than 2 percent higher than the overall rate of inflation for this period. This growth has been at a rate more than double the inflation rate. At current growth rates, Medicare costs will be the largest single component of the federal budget by the year 2000.

Most of us recognize that hospital costs and medical care can easily cost hundreds of dollars a day. We understand that sophisticated medical equipment is costly, and that such things as the intensive care provided in a hospital and the cost of medical malpractice insurance will all be passed on to the consumer of medical services. Despite the prospect of huge medical costs, a great many people today simply do not have adequate medical insurance. Consequently, many Americans still do not receive adequate health care. By the time the need for such coverage occurs, of course, it is too late to find such insurance.

For military personnel, the problem is somewhat different. While we all recognize how quickly a lifetime of savings can be spent on medical care for a catastrophic illness or serious accident, we in the military have a mistaken tendency to assume that all of our medical problems will be taken care of by the government at little or no expense to us. In some cases, that is simply not true.

Although the medical care provided to active-duty servicemembers and their dependents substantially reduces the risk of lost income and out-of-pocket expenses for medical care, it does not entirely eliminate the possibility of drastic financial loss from sickness or accident. This is particularly true if your family lifestyle is critically dependent upon a second income from your nonmilitary spouse to meet mortgage payments, for example.

In this chapter, we will review the entitlement for medical care that servicemembers and their dependents currently have, and then consider how to meet the risk of loss from medical expenses beyond guaranteed coverage. We also will describe recent experiments and trends in the delivery of health care to the dependents of military personnel and military retirees.

UNIFORMED SERVICES HEALTH BENEFITS PROGRAM

The health benefits provided to active-duty personnel, their dependents, retired members of the uniformed services, and the dependents of retired and deceased members of the uniformed services will normally be authorized in uniformed services medical facilities (henceforth called military hospitals). If care is unavailable at a military facility, however, it will be authorized in civilian facilities through the Civilian Health and Medical Program of the Uniformed Services (CHAMPUS).

To receive nonemergency care in service hospitals or to have claims for civilian health care processed by CHAMPUS (discussed later), all patients must be enrolled in the Defense Enrollment Eligibility Reporting System (DEERS), a computerized roster of people eligible to receive health benefits under the Uniformed Services Health Benefits Program. Active-duty servicemembers are automatically enrolled in DEERS. Dependents and retired military personnel must be entered in the DEERS computer data banks at the local military personnel center, not at the military hospital. Dependent children should be enrolled in DEERS as soon as possible following their birth or adoption; a certificate of live birth or a birth certificate may be used to enroll a newborn child.

Active-duty Care

The mandate of military medicine is to preserve the fighting force. Therefore, active-duty servicemembers have first priority for military health care, and their care is provided free of charge. Others are treated on a space-available basis.

Active-duty servicemembers who need emergency medical attention but cannot get to a military hospital will have their bills paid by the government. Nonemergency treatment at civilian facilities requires the permission of authorities at the nearest military hospital. Only if the injury resulted from unauthorized or illegal behavior will the government seek reimbursement for medical expenses it pays for active-duty servicemembers treated at civilian facilities. For instance, a soldier injured and treated while AWOL will receive a bill from the government for any medical expenses.

Care for Retirees and Dependents

Medical benefits and costs will be summarized and discussed in three parts: dependents' medical care in military hospitals, Civilian Health and Medical Program of the Uniformed Services (CHAMPUS), and health benefits for retired members.

Dependents' Medical Care in Military Hospitals
For dependents of active-duty, retired, and deceased servicemembers, and for qualified former spouses, military hospitals provide care on a space-available basis as determined by the local facility commander. The precise services provided are determined by current provisions of law, the capability of the facility involved, and the extent that medical resources and staff are available after providing service to uniformed servicemembers. Because the families of servicemembers often are not located close to a military hospital, and even when they are, such facilities often have limited resources for their primary mission, medical care for dependents at such facilities is not assured. Of course, medical emergencies for dependents are treated immediately at any military hospital.

When nonemergency care cannot be provided to all who are eligible, priority is given to the following:

1. Dependents of active-duty personnel and unremarried widows, widowers, and children of deceased active-duty servicemembers.
2. Retired members and their dependents and dependents of servicemembers who died while retired.
3. Former spouses who meet eligibility criteria.

When staff and facilities are adequate, dependents are eligible for the following care in military hospitals:

- Inpatient care, including services and supplies normally furnished by the hospital.
- Outpatient care and services.
- Drugs for prescriptions written by military hospital or civilian physicians, subject to availability, control procedures, and existing laws.
- Treatment of medical and surgical conditions, nervous and emotional disorders, and contagious illnesses.
- Physical examinations, including hearing examinations and one vision examination each year.
- Maternity and infant care, including normal care and examination of newborn infants and well-baby care.
- Family planning services, supplies, counseling, and guidance.
- Diagnostic tests and services, including laboratory and x-ray examinations.
- Dental care while stationed outside the United States. Within the United States, except for installations specifically authorized to provide routine dental care, this is

limited to emergency dental care; care necessary as an adjunct to medical or surgical treatment of a disease, condition, or injury; diagnostic x rays; and consultant services.
- Government surface or air ambulance service to transport dependents to, from, or between facilities when determined medically necessary by the medical officer in charge.
- Initial issue, fitting, repair, replacement, and adjustment of artificial limbs and eyes.
- Loan of durable equipment such as hospital beds and wheelchairs.
- Orthopedic braces (excluding footwear), crutches, walking irons, elastic stockings, and other orthopedic aids.
- Immunizations.
- Abortions, if necessary to save the life of the mother.

Dependents are *not* eligible for the following types of care in military hospitals:

- Domiciliary or custodial care.
- Prosthetic devices (other than artificial limbs and eyes).
- Hearing aids.
- Orthopedic footwear.
- Spectacles or lenses except in overseas and CONUS locations where authorized by the secretary of defense for sale at government cost.

If a dependent patient requires care beyond the capacity of the military hospital, the facility commander has several options. He may authorize the patient to be transferred—with the patient's consent—to the nearest military hospital where the level of required care is available; he may procure from civilian sources the services or materials required for proper care in the facility; or he may release the patient to a civilian medical provider of the patient's or sponsor's choice. Civilian medical care procured through the military hospital is paid for through government-negotiated contracts. A patient no longer under direct military care may seek civilian care, but payments would then fall under CHAMPUS regulations rather than the supplemental payment arrangement described here.

Normally, there is no charge for outpatient care when dependents receive health benefits in a military hospital. Also, no charge is made for inpatient care of newborn infants while the mother is a patient. For other inpatient care, active-duty families, retirees and their families, and survivors of active-duty servicemembers all pay a small daily fee. In fiscal year 1993, for example, that fee was approximately $9.30 per day for dependents and $4.75 per day for retired officers (enlisted retirees receive inpatient care for free). In some military hospitals, civilian physicians work under contract, and you may be charged a fee for their services. Be sure you understand your potential charges when your dependents are treated in military hospitals by other than active-duty physicians.

CHAMPUS
CHAMPUS—the Civilian Health and Medical Program for the Uniformed Services—is a program wherein the government shares with service families the cost of civilian

health care. CHAMPUS does not cover active-duty servicemembers, only their families. CHAMPUS covers only a portion of your dependents' medical costs; it was never intended that it would provide total coverage. It was created to supplement military health care and operates like a private insurance plan without monthly payments. If you have other medical insurance, you must file that claim first; CHAMPUS will share the remaining costs for care that is covered.

By using the facilities of a military hospital (where available), the families of servicemembers will save money and paperwork. For certain zip codes sufficiently close to military hospitals, these facilities *must* be used rather than civilian hospitals for nonemergency inpatient dependent care. When the military facility cannot provide care, however, active-duty dependents will be given a nonavailability statement and may then use CHAMPUS. CHAMPUS covers care only from certain types of civilian facilities, and this care must be authorized before bills for the services may be shared. A new nonavailability statement must be obtained for each new ailment. Emergency civilian care does not require a statement of nonavailability.

Eligibility for Coverage
CHAMPUS coverage is available to the following five groups:

1. Husbands, wives, and unmarried children of active-duty personnel. Unmarried children up to age twenty-one (twenty-one and over if handicapped and the condition existed prior to the child's twenty-first birthday), and to twenty-three if in school full-time. Divorced spouses are not covered by CHAMPUS except as described below. Children (including stepchildren who are adopted by a servicemember) are still covered by CHAMPUS even if the divorced spouse remarries. A stepchild who was not adopted by the servicemember and leaves the household, however, is no longer covered.

2. Retirees, their spouses, and their unmarried children. However, retirees, survivors, or family members of retirees eligible for Medicare (Part A) are not eligible for CHAMPUS.

3. Unremarried spouses and unmarried children of active-duty or retired servicemembers who died while on active duty or after they retired from the military.

4. Husbands, wives, and unmarried children of reservists who are ordered to active duty for more than thirty days (they are covered only during the reservist's tour).

5. Former spouses of active or retired military personnel who were divorced or received an annulment after at least twenty years of marriage to a servicemember who was on active duty during at least fifteen of those twenty years. There are several other restrictions to this category of eligibility; for example, the former spouse may not be covered by an employer-sponsored health plan and must not have remarried since the divorce or annulment. Contact a health benefits advisor at the nearest military hospital for details.

CHAMPUS Benefits
There are three general categories of CHAMPUS benefits:

1. Civilian outpatient and inpatient care for spouses and children of members of the uniformed services on active duty for more than thirty days.
2. Civilian outpatient and inpatient care for retired members, their spouses and children, and the spouses and children of members who died while on active duty or in a retired status, and certain former spouses.
3. Training, rehabilitation, special education, and institutional care in civilian facilities for spouses and dependents of active-duty members if the dependents are moderately or severely retarded mentally or have a serious physical handicap. Under the Program for the Handicapped, eligibility ends when the sponsor leaves active duty. Surviving spouses and children of servicemembers who die while receiving hostile fire pay or who die from injury or disease while eligible for such pay, if they were receiving such benefits at the time of the member's death, will continue to receive them until they are either twenty-one or their status as dependents ends.

CHAMPUS helps pay most medical bills for inpatient and outpatient care and covers most health care that is medically necessary. The mere fact that treatment is recommended, however, does not mean CHAMPUS will help pay for it. For CHAMPUS to pay for nonemergency medical care, the physician must be fully licensed and accredited, and you must be given a statement of nonavailability by your local military hospital. Check with the health-benefits advisor at your local military hospital to ensure that the care you desire is covered.

To use CHAMPUS benefits, a patient must be enrolled in DEERS CHAMPUS eligibility for service families ends at midnight on the day that the active-duty member is discharged or leaves the service other than through retirement.

Payment for CHAMPUS

Civilian medical facilities that "accept CHAMPUS assignment" charge only the "CHAMPUS allowable charge" for services provided, and they often prepare the CHAMPUS claim for you. *Allowable charges* are the fixed-rate payments that CHAMPUS will pay hospitals for services, based on that service's diagnostic-related group (DRG) category. The health benefits advisor at the nearest military hospital can direct you to the nearest provider that accepts CHAMPUS.

CHAMPUS generally will help pay for any treatment that is proven to be medically necessary for an illness. The amount depends on the status of the dependent's related servicemember: active duty, retired, or deceased. For outpatient care, CHAMPUS will reimburse a percentage of the cost after the beneficiary has paid for expenses up to a specified amount. These amounts, which are called deductibles, are shown in Table 7-1. Table 7-2 summarizes the costs borne by the beneficiary for inpatient and outpatient care.

As noted in Table 7-1, there is no deductible for inpatient care (a hospital stay exceeding twenty-four hours), but the patient must pay an inpatient cost-share. Note that these inpatient charges are for only the hospital stay itself. You will be billed separately by the treating physician and providers of auxiliary services, such as the anesthesiologist. The costs for these services will be shared by the beneficiary using the same formulas as applied to outpatient care.

TABLE 7-1
Annual Deductible Amounts for Outpatient Care

Status	Individual	Family
E-4 and below	$ 50	$150
E-5 and above	$150	$300
Retirees and their surviving dependents	$150	$300

TABLE 7-2
CHAMPUS Costs

Patient Category	Inpatient Care	Outpatient Care
Active-duty dependents	Greater of $9.30/day or $25	20% of allowable charge, after deductible
Retirees, their dependents, survivors, and former spouses	Lesser of 25% of the billed charges or $265 per day	25% of allowable charge, after deductible
Dependent parents, parents-in-law	—Not eligible for CHAMPUS—	

Note: The charges shown are for fiscal year 1993.

To illustrate these cost-sharing rules, we will work through an example. Let us assume that you are a second lieutenant, that one of your dependents undergoes a medical procedure in a civilian clinic, and that the procedure costs $950. If the allowable amount for this procedure is $1000 and this is the first medical cost incurred this year by your family, CHAMPUS would reimburse you $640 (i.e., $640 = [$950 − $150] × .8). Alternatively, if the same dependent had already incurred documented medical costs of $100, then the reimbursement for this procedure would be $720 (i.e., $720 = [$950 − ($150 − $100)] × .8). If your family had incurred documented expenses of $300 or more, you would be reimbursed $760 (i.e., $760 = [$950 − ($300 − $300)] × .8). Finally, if the cost exceeds the allowable charge, you pay the entire amount above the allowable charge. Thus, if the procedure had cost $1200 in this last instance, you would receive $800 from CHAMPUS (i.e., $800 = [$1000 − ($300 − $300)] × .8). You would pay $400 even though you had already incurred costs equal to or greater than the deductible.

Your cost-share under CHAMPUS is capped in each fiscal year. In 1993, the cap, or limit, was $1,000 for active-duty families and $7,500 for all other CHAMPUS recipients. This cap means that CHAMPUS will pay 100 percent of the allowable charge once your cost-share equals the cap. Your cost-share is calculated based on allowable charges, however, and not on actual expenses. Also, you are still responsible for charges above the allowable amount even after you have reached your cap.

If you receive health care from a provider who does not accept CHAMPUS assignment, you must pay the provider directly. You must then file the claims yourself, and CHAMPUS will pay you what it would have paid the provider. If the provider accepts assignment, he or she will file the claim and CHAMPUS will bill you for your cost-share. Also, because local health-care costs often exceed allowable charges, you could easily incur considerable expenses unless you choose a provider who accepts CHAMPUS assignment.

Auxiliary Services and Care for the Handicapped
CHAMPUS will also pay a portion of the costs for a variety of other services, such as mental health, rehabilitation programs, and care for the severely handicapped. The reimbursement provisions vary by circumstance and type of program. A general discussion of the coverage may be found in the official CHAMPUS handbook. Both the handbook and detailed counseling may be obtained from the health-benefits advisor located at your local military hospital.

Retiree Medical Benefits
Retired military personnel and their dependents are eligible for medical care in military hospitals on a space-available basis. For much routine care, filling prescriptions, and so forth, care is usually available and represents a considerable benefit to retirees and their families. For care that is not available at a nearby military hospital, however, retirees and their families may use CHAMPUS once they have obtained the appropriate statement of nonavailability. It is important to recognize two differences in CHAMPUS care for retirees as compared to active-duty dependents: The cost-share is higher, and there is an age restriction.

Dependents of active-duty servicemembers who receive covered outpatient care under CHAMPUS pay 20 percent of the allowable charges after their annual deductible has been paid. For retirees and for surviving spouses and children, the cost-share is 25 percent. The deductible is the same as for active-duty dependents. For inpatient care, retirees and their family members pay substantially more than active-duty dependents—25 percent of the billed charges, or $265 per day, whichever is less. Also, because Americans become eligible for Medicare at age sixty-five, military retirees and their dependents are no longer eligible for CHAMPUS past age sixty-five.

Medical care under Medicare is divided into two parts. Part A provides basic protection against the costs of inpatient hospitalization. Part B coverage is voluntary and provides some protection against medical costs and other expenses not covered under Part A. Part A coverage is paid for from Social Security funds and is provided without charge to anyone sixty-five or older. Part B is voluntary and is paid for by the individual, although it is heavily subsidized by the federal government.

Although retirees and their dependents are still eligible for medical care in military hospitals after age sixty-five, there is no guarantee that this service will be available. With CHAMPUS coverage unavailable after age sixty-five, we recommend enrollment in Part B Medicare at age sixty-five. However, because there are many very large gaps in Medicare coverage that can leave you with enormous medical bills, we also recommend that you purchase private supplemental medical insurance. Group policies are offered at reasonable rates through a number of military associations. We will discuss this type of insurance in more detail in a later section entitled "Supplemental Insurance."

SUMMARY OF MEDICAL BENEFITS

The health benefits available to servicemembers and their dependents are summarized in Table 7-3.

A number of features of the existing health-care system merit your attention. The care actually provided is likely to vary significantly from place to place and from time to time. Your medical needs as an active-duty member will receive prompt and professional care under almost all circumstances. The same may not be true, however, for your spouse and dependents while you remain on active duty, or for you, your spouse, and your eligible dependents following your retirement.

There are occasional shortages and imbalances of trained medical and dental servicemembers throughout military hospitals. Some stateside assignments, such as recruiting, graduate school, or ROTC duty, for example, may not be near any military

TABLE 7-3
Summary of Servicemembers' Health Benefits

Patients	Military Hospitals Outpatient and Inpatient	CHAMPUS Outpatient	Inpatient
Active-duty servicemembers	Yes	No	No
Active-duty families	Yes, space available	Yes	Yes; may need a nonavailability statement
Retirees and their families	Yes, space available	Yes, unless entitled to Medicare	Yes, unless entitled to Medicare
Dependent parents and parents-in-law	Yes, space available	No	No

hospitals. The availability—and capability—of eligible CHAMPUS facilities can vary enormously.

Some overseas assignments may have very small concentrations of military personnel and be located great distances from fully equipped facilities and properly trained medical specialists. When you or your dependents have to rely on outside sources for medical care, the expense can be substantial. In some cases, even where CHAMPUS care is provided, the cost to you and your family can be significant.

DENTAL CARE FOR DEPENDENTS

Eligibility for Coverage

Dental insurance is available through the military from the Uniformed Services Active Duty Dependents Dental Plan (henceforth called DDP) for all DEERS-enrolled spouses and dependent children of active-duty members. The plan covers dependents residing in the fifty states, the District of Columbia, the U.S. Virgin Islands, and Puerto Rico. In April 1993, DDP expanded the treatments it covered and became a comprehensive dental plan. Dependents are automatically enrolled in this extended plan when they are entered into the DEERS system.

Any private practice dentist may provide dental service, but receiving care from a dentist participating in the DDP will probably save you money. DDP is similar in operation to CHAMPUS. If you use a nonparticipating dentist, DDP will reimburse you based on prevailing fees, or what are, in effect, allowable charges. These reimbursements will probably be less than the normal charges of nonparticipating dentists. Also, if you use a participating dentist, you are only required to pay the estimated copayment at the time of treatment, not the full amount. In addition, participating dentists are required to complete and submit the claim forms to DDP at no cost to the patient. Therefore, we recommend that you check with the nearest military health-care advisor for a list of local participating dentists before making your first appointment.

DDP Benefits

Expanded DDP covers most dental services. For preventive care and fillings the coverage is 100 percent and 80 percent, respectively. Coverage for other services varies by procedure, so you should consult your DDP-Delta handbook or your health-care advisor for information on coverage of specific services. By coverage we mean the percentage of the allowable fees that will be reimbursed by DDP. For example, if the coverage for a procedure is 50 percent, DDP will reimburse you for 50 percent of either the actual expense or the prevailing fee, whichever is less. You will pay the total amount by which your dentist's fee exceeds the prevailing fee for that procedure.

Payment for DDP

The monthly premiums for DDP as of September 1993 were $9.65 for one family member and $19.30 for families with two or more members enrolled. You must also pay your cost-share for procedures with less than 100 percent coverage.

Reimbursements under DDP are subject to the following annual limits on how much the plan can pay for any patient's dental services:

Annual Maximum: $1,000 per patient per coverage year for all nonorthodontic services. (The coverage year extends from 1 August to 31 July.)

Lifetime Orthodontic Maximum: $1,200 per patient for all orthodontic services. Costs in excess of these limits will be borne by the servicemember. Also, reimbursement for orthodontic services differs from other dental services. Because orthodontic treatment usually extends over many months, DDP payments are divided into a reimbursement for the initial "banding" or "appliance placement" and monthly progress payments over the duration of treatment. The reimbursement for the initial banding is set at 30 percent of the amount payable by the plan. If orthodontic treatment extends past the month the patient becomes nineteen, progress payments cease as of that month.

Certain dental services are considered medical procedures and are covered under CHAMPUS, not DDP. Therefore, if your dependents require dental care not listed in the DDP-Delta handbook, check with your health-benefits advisor to see if they are covered under CHAMPUS.

SUPPLEMENTAL HEALTH INSURANCE

After evaluating the medical and dental care programs available to you and your dependents at military hospitals and through CHAMPUS, you may wish to supplement these benefits with a commercial health insurance policy. Active-duty personnel with children in school are probably already familiar with various dental and medical insurance policies offered through their schools that provide reimbursement for specific kinds of injuries or risks that children may face traveling to and from and while at school. Many commercial insurance companies offer such policies, and they are often available through associations or groups closely affiliated with active-duty and retired servicemembers.

Why Use Supplemental Care?

Obviously it makes little sense to buy additional insurance for needs that will be met through existing programs to which your family is entitled. But just as obviously, there are some gaps in the medical care paid for by the services. Since the cost of prolonged medical care for a dependent can substantially reduce your family's standard of living, it is wise to consider additional medical coverage, particularly if there is a family history of illness or disease that may require expensive care. In deciding whether to purchase supplemental insurance, you should consider the costs of insurance premiums, the likelihood of future illness in your family, the type of care covered, and the age of your dependents.

For many active-duty servicemembers with a working spouse, health insurance is automatically provided by the civilian employer. In this case, CHAMPUS is required by law to pay only after the private insurance plan pays its share. But most military families are not fortunate enough to have additional civilian health-care insurance. To protect your family from large medical expenses, there are many organizations that issue CHAMPUS supplemental insurance.

Supplemental CHAMPUS insurance pays only after CHAMPUS pays its portion. Coverage varies widely among supplemental insurance plans, as do annual premiums. The annual premiums for inpatient and outpatient care range (in 1993) anywhere from $50 to $200 for an active-duty spouse and $20 to $90 for each child. These plans are provided through various commercial firms and typically have a period, normally six months or one year, for which the cost of care for any preexisting condition will not be reimbursed. Some companies, however, require a two-year wait on preexisting conditions.

Evaluating Supplemental CHAMPUS Insurance

In evaluating the various options offered in supplemental CHAMPUS insurance plans, the first thing to determine is what mix of options is suitable for your particular circumstances. As you compare policies, try to use the same criteria for each one and don't be discouraged when you find that there are many different "packages" offered. The program that costs more may or may not offer additional coverage for your premium dollar.

As with any service or product you purchase, read the terms carefully and do not hesitate to ask questions about specific provisions that you don't understand. The long-term commitment you make to a health insurance program can easily add up to many thousands of dollars over your lifetime. It is worth your time to make the best decision you can when you purchase such coverage, to review that coverage periodically, and to keep informed about new programs.

In addition to analyzing the costs, you should ask yourself the following questions when you evaluate supplemental CHAMPUS insurance:

1. What are the plan's eligibility rules and what are the grounds for termination of the plan?

2. Does the plan pay excess, noncovered charges—charges above what CHAMPUS considers to be reasonable? Several plans pay unlimited excess charges after some initial limit, but most do not.

3. What is the policy on paying for preexisting conditions? Most plans cover an illness that you have had treated within the last twelve months, but only after you

MEETING MEDICAL EXPENSES • 83

have had the policy for twelve months and received no additional treatment. After twenty-four months, most plans will then cover the illness.
 4. Does the plan reimburse you for the CHAMPUS deductible?
 5. If the plan has a deductible, is it in addition to the CHAMPUS deductible?
 6. Will the plan pay the patient's cost-share under CHAMPUS?
 7. What are the limits on hospital stays per year and on the number of outpatient visits? The average for the industry is sixty hospital days per year. There is no standard on outpatient visits—some limit the number to twenty visits per year, while other programs set no limits.
 8. Does the plan limit continuous hospital care?
 9. Does the plan convert to a Medicare supplement? If so, must it be in force as a CHAMPUS supplement for any specified length of time before conversion?
 10. Are the premium payments monthly? Quarterly? Can you charge the premiums to a credit card?
 11. How often and under what conditions can the premiums change?
 12. Does the plan cover the servicemember when he or she retires?
 13. How do premium rates vary with age? Do they vary according to whether you are on active duty or retired from the service?
 14. Does coverage continue for surviving spouses?
 15. What are the membership fees, if any, for the organization that sponsors the plan?
 16. Are there limits, as there are with CHAMPUS, to when a claim can be filed? Most plans require claims to be filed between twelve and twenty-four months after the illness was treated.

As you consider purchase of supplementary insurance, it is also helpful to consult your local CHAMPUS advisor about the coverage that CHAMPUS does and does not provide. Also, if you are retired from the military and have a health-care plan under your current employer, you may not require further insurance.

Addresses and telephone numbers of several of the organizations offering supplemental CHAMPUS insurance are provided after the suggested references at the end of this chapter. Current terms and rates are available directly from these organizations and are also provided in many of the weekly service newspapers and other military publications.

THE EVOLVING SYSTEM FOR MILITARY MEDICINE

In response to rapidly rising medical costs, the Department of Defense has recently chartered a number of studies and experiments to examine ways to reduce its medical expenditures. Most of these studies involve reforms to the CHAMPUS system. Some of these experimental programs may apply to your local area, and at least some parts of them will eventually be adopted throughout the system.

The largest experimental study is the CHAMPUS Reform Initiative (CRI). This study is attempting to learn how a managed-care health program affects costs. CRI allows families of servicemembers and retirees to enroll in CHAMPUS Prime, which essentially makes them members of a health-maintenance organization (HMO), or to take advantage of CHAMPUS Extra, which provides a decrease in copayments if the family uses a health-care provider enrolled in the Prime network. A common feature of these experimental plans is that the beneficiary accepts less latitude in choosing his or her health-care provider in return for lower costs. Although the future shape of the Uniformed Services Health Benefit Program is still unclear, any revision of the current system is likely to include managed care and some reduction in choice.

As of the writing of this book, the future structure of the private sector's medical system is even less clear than the military's. A proposal for substantially altering the makeup of the medical industry is being debated in Congress. For servicemembers, retirees, and their families, the direct impact of these national reforms is likely to be modest. The most significant effects are likely to be on the need for supplemental insurance and on how the military's medical benefits affect retention decisions. If the reforms contain provisions that cap individual liabilities and effectively mandate allowable charges, then the need for supplemental insurance diminishes. If the reforms preclude exclusions for preexisting conditions and all families are guaranteed health insurance, then the military's medical benefits become less important to retention decisions.

SUGGESTED REFERENCES

CHAMPUS Handbook. 6010.46-H. CHAMPUS, Aurora, CO, 80045-6900, July 1992.

DDP-DELTA—Uniformed Services Active Duty Dependents Dental Plan. P.O. Box 269023, Sacramento, CA 95826-9023, revised April 1993.

Helping You Choose a Hospital. American Hospital Assoc., Chicago, IL, 1992.

Gordon, Sol, ed. *Retired Military Almanac.* Washington, DC: Uniformed Services Almanac, Inc. Published annually.

Inlander, Charles B., *150 Ways to be a Savvy Medical Consumer.* Allentown, PA: People's Medical Society, 1992.

Sharff, Lee E., and Sol Gordon, eds. *Uniformed Services Almanac.* Washington, DC: Uniformed Services Almanac, Inc. Published annually.

For additional information about the effects of other health plans on CHAMPUS benefits, contact one of the following:

1. The health-benefits advisor at a military hospital or clinic.
2. The CHAMPUS claims processor for your state.
3. Benefit Services Branch, CHAMPUS, Aurora, CO 80045-6900, (303) 361-3907 or DSN 943-3907.

To resolve problems with DEERS, contact either your military personnel office or DEERS Support Office (DSO), ATTN: FA99, 2511 Garden Road, Suite 260,

Monterey, CA 93940-5387, (800) 334-4162 (California only), (800) 527-5602 (Alaska and Hawaii only), or (800) 538-9552 (all other states).

ORGANIZATIONS PROVIDING CHAMPUS SUPPLEMENTAL HEALTH INSURANCE

Air Force Association 1501 Lee Highway Arlington, VA 22209-1198	(800) 737-3337 in VA (703) 247-5800
Air Force Sergeants Association 400 Locust St. Des Moines, IA 50398	(800) 247-7988
American Military Association Fort Snelling Station, P.O. Box 76 Minneapolis, MN 55440-0076	(800) 562-4076
American Military Retirees Association P.O. Box 2510 Rockville, MD 20852-0510	(800) 638-2610 in MD (301) 816-0045
American Military Society P.O. Box 50282 Washington, DC 20004-0282	(800) 843-2043
Armed Forces Benefit Association AFDBSI, 909 N. Washington St. Alexandria, VA 22314	(800) 776-2264
Army Aviation Association of America Membership Services Inc. 1304 Vincent Pl. McLean, VA 22101	(800) 394-4000
Association of Personal Affairs P.O. Box 3357 Austin, TX 78764	(800) 451-9143
Association of the United States Army 400 Locust St., 8th. Floor Des Moines, IA 50398	(800) 247-7988

Enlisted Association of the National Guard　　　　　　(800) 441-2590
NGAUS Insurance Plans
P.O. Box 907
Minneapolis, MN 55440-0907

U.S. Coast Guard Chief Petty Officers Association　　(800) 424-9883
1255 23rd. St. N.W., Suite 300　　　　　　　　　in DC (202) 457-6820
Washington, DC 20037

Fleet Reserve Association　　　　　　　　　　　　　(800) 322-8717
400 Locust St., 8th Floor
Des Moines, IA 50398

Marine Corps League　　　　　　　　　　　　　　　(800) 394-4000
c/o Membership Services
1304 Vincent Place
McLean, VA 22101

Marine Corps Association　　　　　　　　　　　　　(800) 368-5682
MCA Health Care Plan　　　　　　　　　　　　in DC (202) 393-6600
734 15th. St. N.W., Suite 500
Washington, DC 20005

Military Order of the Purple Heart　　　　　　　　　(800) 394-4000
c/o Membership Services
1304 Vincent Place
McLean, VA 22101

Military Benefit Association　　　　　　　　　　　　(800) 336-0100
P.O. Box 549
Vienna, VA 22183

Military Order of the World Wars　　　　　　　　　(800) 394-4000
c/o Membership Services
1304 Vincent Place
McLean, VA 22101

Mutual of Omaha Insurance Co.　　　　　　　　　　(800) 228-7100
Mutual of Omaha Plaza
Omaha, NE 68175

National Association of the Uniformed Services　　　(800) 843-2043
NAUS Uniservices Insurance Plans
P.O. Box 92560
Washington, DC 20077-7505

MEETING MEDICAL EXPENSES • 87

National Guard Association of the U.S. (800) 328-3323
P.O. Box 907
Minneapolis, MN 55440-9863

National Officers Association (800) 394-4000
1304 Vincent Pl.
McLean VA 22101

Naval Enlisted Reserve Association (800) 394-4000
1255 23rd St. NW, Suite 300
Washington, DC 20037

Navy League (800) 628-9628
5959 S. Staples
Corpus Christi, TX 78413

Naval Reserve Association (800) 424-9883
1255 23rd St. NW, Suite 300 in DC (202) 457-6820
Washington, DC 20037

Non Commissioned Officers Association (800) 662-2620
Membership Services
P.O. Box 105636
Atlanta, GA 30348-5636

Reserve Officers Association (800) 247-7988
400 Locust Street, 8th Floor
Des Moines, IA 50125

Retired Association for the Uniformed Services (800) 638-2610
P.O. Box 2510 in MD (301) 816-0045
Rockville, MD 20852-0510

Society of Military Widows (800) 843-2043
P.O. Box 92560
Washington, DC 20077-7505

The Retired Officers Association (800) 247-2192
TROA Insurance Plans
400 Locust Street, 8th Floor
Des Moines, IA 50398

The Retired Enlisted Association (800) 441-6269
P.O. Box 50584
Washington, DC 20004

The Uniformed Services Association   (800) 394-4000
c/o Membership Services
1304 Vincent Place
McLean, VA 22101

United Services Automobile Association   (800) 292-8556
USAA Life Company   in VA (703) 556-9700
USAA Building
San Antonio, TX 78288

U.S. Army Warrant Officers Association   (800) 424-9883
1255 23rd St. NW, Suite 300   in DC (202) 457-6820
Washington, DC 20037

Also check with your local credit union to see whether it offers CHAMPUS supplemental insurance.

8

Paying Your Taxes

WHILE MILITARY COMPENSATION has some peculiarities that distinguish it from typical civilian pay systems, service personnel are affected as much by federal, state, and local taxes as their civilian peers. For example, certain provisions of the federal tax code make military compensation worth more to the individual than if he were to receive the same level of remuneration in the form of civilian pay. One such provision makes any portion of a servicemember's compensation that is termed an "allowance" exempt from income taxation by all levels of government. Considering the housing (BAQ and VHA) and subsistence (BAS) allowances alone, about one fourth of military compensation is tax exempt. Thus, the tax code, by exempting allowances from taxation, raises the value of military compensation and provides an implicit portion of overall military compensation known as the "tax advantage" component. On the other hand, the remainder of military compensation, those components termed "pay," and any investment or spousal income, are fully taxable by all levels of government. As a result, military people need to be knowledgeable about the tax laws so they can ensure compliance, incorporate tax considerations into their financial planning decisions, and understand the value of their military compensation.

In this chapter we discuss the military member's personal tax responsibilities and the peculiarities of federal, state, and local taxation that apply to servicemembers, and we provide some general tax planning guidance that should be useful in your overall financial plan. The actual specifics of the tax code change from year to year, so we cannot provide definitive guidance about specific provisions in the new 1993 tax laws.

The information provided in this chapter is by necessity general in nature. Each individual family's financial situation is different, and the complexities of the tax law prevent us from giving comprehensive tax preparation guidance here. However, every military installation has a legal affairs office that can offer assistance in tax matters. Also, Army Community Services (ACS) and similar organizations in the other services have forms and, in some instances, personnel who are trained to offer assistance in preparing your tax returns. The VITA (Volunteer Income Tax Assistance) program at each base or post provides unit-level volunteers with limited training to assist with simple tax form preparation and guidance. In addition, the Internal Revenue Service (IRS) maintains local offices around the country. These offices are listed in local telephone books and can be consulted when advice and tax forms are needed. For additional information on the specifics of your tax situation, consult the references listed at the end of this chapter.

PERSONAL TAX RESPONSIBILITIES

Like all Americans, servicemembers are responsible for the payment of their legal tax obligations. While many citizens find reducing their taxes, legally or illegally, to be great sport, military personnel, especially officers and noncommissioned officers (NCOs), have a special professional commitment to integrity and honest dealing that should apply as much in their relationships with the nation's tax collectors as anywhere else. But no taxpayer need surrender more of his hard-earned income to taxes than he is legally obligated. Thus, there is an important distinction between "tax avoidance"—the completely legal studying of the tax laws in search of all the provisions that help minimize the tax owed—and "tax evasion"—lying, concealing income, and other such fraudulent acts that are crimes under the Internal Revenue Code. Although, as military leaders, officers and NCOs have a special responsibility not to evade taxes, they can also benefit as much as other Americans from provisions of the tax law that limit the amount of tax they must pay.

FEDERAL INCOME TAX

Taxes are collected by all levels of government: federal, state, and local. In this section, we will provide an overview of the general provisions of the federal tax code, as federal taxes have the greatest impact on the typical servicemember. The federal income tax structure is extremely complicated. It is based upon the Internal Revenue Code, official rulings, and the decisions of the tax and federal courts. The federal tax computations for the typical servicemember are relatively straightforward, however, and you should probably be able to calculate your federal income tax liability without professional assistance. In addition, you also should be able to determine the tax consequences of potential financial transactions.

All members of the armed forces are subject to the monthly withholding of a portion of their income for taxes. The proportion of your income that is withheld is determined by the number of withholding allowances you claim. The relationship between these allowances and the portion of your income that is withheld is shown in the current income tax withholding tables available at your military finance office or the local IRS office.

You determine the number of allowances that you want to claim when you file a statement (Form W-4) with your finance office. Your W-4 records your marital status and the number of allowances you wish to claim for withholding purposes. That number is important because it affects the amount of tax that will be withheld from your monthly pay. A very rough estimate of the effects of one additional allowance is $25 (in the 15 percent tax bracket) or $50 (in the 28 percent tax bracket) less withheld from your pay each month. The allowances are based on the number of exemptions you expect to claim on your tax return and the income you expect to earn from sources not subject to tax withholding, such as interest income. If you have had more tax withheld during the year than you owe in taxes, you will get a refund from the IRS after you file your return. If too little has been withheld, you will have to send a check for the balance of your tax liability when you file your return. Also, if you significantly underwithhold your taxes during the tax year, you could be required to pay a substantial tax penalty. Specifically, the tax code requires that you pay through withholding at least 100 percent of your previous year's tax liability, or 90 percent of the current year's tax liability. Failure to meet these criteria represents significant underpaying in the eyes of the IRS, and a penalty may be added to your tax bill.

On the other hand, there is good reason not to have too much withheld each month. If you do so, you are in effect extending an interest-free loan to the government—the government holds your excess tax payments all year until you get your refund but pays you no interest for the use of your funds. By filing a new W-4 form, you can adjust the amount of withholding so that it approximately matches the amount of your tax liability. This is a conservative approach. It requires you to estimate your annual federal tax liability from all sources of income during the year and to claim a sufficient number of allowances so that enough tax is withheld to cover your total estimated tax liability for the year. Most servicemembers overwithhold and would benefit from this adjustment.

A more aggressive approach is to have only enough withheld so that you are *sure* you will not be penalized for underpayment during the year. That way, you are able to use or invest the difference between the "conservative" and "aggressive" withholding amounts until you are required to pay your income taxes in full on April 15 of the next year. While this approach offers the potential for additional investment income, it is also somewhat risky. If you fall beneath the minimum required withholding amount, you expose yourself to the risk of a penalty that undoubtedly would exceed the investment return you receive on the amount you underwithheld. Furthermore, to make up the balance of the tax still due and to avoid penalties and interest, you must have sufficient funds to pay your taxes in full on April 15.

Tax Forgiveness

The Internal Revenue Code provides a tax forgiveness provision for any member whose death results from service in a terrorist or military action. This tax forgiveness applies to income not only for the taxable year in which the member dies, but also for any prior year since 1950 that ended on or after the first day served in a combat zone. Furthermore, any tax liability outstanding against such a member at the time of death will be canceled or reduced. Make sure your spouse knows to check out this provision with the legal assistance officer after you are gone by including a note to this effect in the *letter of instruction* that should accompany your will (see chapter 17).

There is also special consideration for military pay earned in a combat zone, such as Operation Desert Storm in 1991. For enlisted members and warrant officers, basic pay received in a combat zone is nontaxable; for officers, the first $500 received monthly is nontaxable.

Filing a Tax Return

All servicemembers must file a tax return with the nearest district office of the IRS responsible for servicing the address used by the member on the tax return. This address is usually the member's temporary residence and not the home of record (or domicile).

Income tax returns and final payments become due on April 15. Military personnel and government employees residing outside the United States and Puerto Rico get an automatic extension until June 15; this also applies if only one spouse is out of the country and files a joint return with the one who is not. This extension only prevents the assessment of penalties for a late filing and payment of tax; interest will be charged on any taxes still unpaid after April 15.

In addition to the automatic extension for persons serving overseas, any individual may apply for an extension to file (IRS Form 4868, available in most libraries, post offices, and legal assistance offices). In these cases, however, the extensions apply only to filing the return; in order to avoid interest and possibly penalties, you must estimate your total tax liability and, on April 15, pay any shortfall between the estimated liability and the amount of tax withheld.

During January of each year, you should receive a withholding statement (Form W-2) from your finance office, documenting your taxable income (i.e., that portion of your military compensation that is subject to taxation), income tax withheld, and Social Security (FICA) tax withheld for the prior calendar year. By using the applicable pay tables, you should verify that your Form W-2 is correct. To verify your taxable income, you must calculate the pay you received in the following categories:

Taxable Military Income
1. Basic pay, including longevity pay. (Note: Enlisted members and warrant officers are not taxed on any military pay received while in a combat zone. Officers may exclude $500 a month if for any part of that month they served in a combat zone. See your legal assistance officer if there is any doubt.)
2. Special pay (Medical, Dental, Veterinary, Foreign and Sea Duty, Proficiency, Diving, Responsibility, Hostile Fire, Nuclear Qualified Officers).
3. Incentive pay for hazardous duty (Flight, Parachute, Demolition, Leprosarium, Thermal Stress, Human Acceleration or Deceleration Tests).
4. Aviation Career Incentive Pay and Continuation Pay.
5. Military retirement pay.
6. Cash awards.

7. Accrued leave and separation pay (except for disability).
8. Armed services academy pay (cadet and midshipman pay).
9. Personal Money Allowances (paid to high-ranking officers).
10. Bonuses (enlistment, reenlistment, overseas extension).
11. The portion of DITY-move incentive payment above 60 percent of the normal cost for moving your allowed weight. (See your local finance office for details.)

The following items are excluded from taxable income and should not be reported on Form W-2:

Nontaxable Military Income
1. Basic Allowance for Quarters (BAQ).
2. Variable Housing Allowance (VHA).
3. Subsistence allowances (BAS).
4. Value of quarters and subsistence received in kind.
5. Overseas cost-of-living allowances (COLAs).
6. Allowances received for uniforms (in kind and gratuity).
7. State bonuses paid for military service.
8. Dividends on veterans insurance.
9. Travel allowances.
10. Family separation allowances.
11. Combat zone pay (when combat zone exclusion applies).
12. Sick pay (after the first thirty days if not combat connected).
13. Forfeiture of pay (to be deducted from basic pay).
14. Detention of pay (taxable when actually paid).
15. Death gratuities.
16. Dislocation Allowances (DLA).
17. Professional education (paid by the U.S. government).
18. Evacuation Allowance.
19. Medical benefits (including dental).
20. Veterans benefits.
21. ROTC allowances.
22. Moving and storage (in kind).
23. Interment Allowance.
24. Group-term life insurance.
25. Medal of Honor pension payments.

In addition to military pay, the following items *are* taxable and should be reported as income on your tax return even though they are not included in the taxable income listed on your W-2 form:

Taxable Other Income
1. Interest received on investments.
2. Dividends.

3. Rental income.
4. Royalties.
5. Alimony. (Note: Alimony is income if received and an adjustment to income if paid out.)
6. Prizes, awards, and gambling winnings.
7. Gains realized on the sale of assets.
8. Spouse's income.
9. Any other nonexempt income.

You will actually compute your taxes using IRS Form 1040, the appropriate tax tables, and supporting schedules. Form 1040 is a single sheet on which you may report your income, withholding taxes, deductions, and exemptions. Supporting schedules are attached as needed. Each year you should receive an accompanying instruction booklet from the IRS along with your tax return forms. If this does not supply the detail you need to complete your tax return, refer to the income tax aids listed in the references at the end of this chapter. If you still have questions, your legal assistance officer, ACS representative, and officials of the IRS stand ready to help you. The location and telephone number of your local IRS office can be found in the local phone book under U.S. Government.

Using IRS Form 1040, you calculate your taxable income for the purposes of determining your income tax liabilities by subtracting itemized deductions and personal exemptions from your adjusted gross income, which is the total of all taxable earnings you received in the various categories of taxable income listed above. One important deduction is interest paid on mortgage debt for up to two homes. This feature is explained in more detail in chapter 11. Instead of itemized deductions, most servicemembers who do not own homes use a standard deduction, reducing their tax liability by a set amount.

Servicemembers (or family members) running a business or earning nonwage income "on the side" will most likely have to report that income on Schedule C and pay a "double" Social Security tax on it (with Schedule SE). As a general rule, if you receive *any* income (except investment or rental income) on which taxes have *not* been withheld, you should check on the likely requirement to report it here. Failure to do so could result in serious tax evasion consequences.

In this section, we have provided an overview of the rules governing federal taxes. Our coverage has not been exhaustive, however, so you should consult a detailed reference document or solicit professional advice if you have any questions regarding an unusual transaction or situation.

STATE AND LOCAL TAXES

As a general rule in the United States, most state and local revenues are raised from property and sales taxes. The largest part of property tax revenues usually goes to support the state's school systems. State sales tax revenues usually provide working funds for state legislatures. Members of the armed forces, like all citizens of the United States, are subject to state taxes unless state laws specifically exempt them from all or part of their tax liabilities while they are in the service. The problem all servicemembers face is knowing which state they are obligated to, and for which taxes.

Domicile and Residence

Before examining state taxes, there are some definitions you must know. Two legal terms define your relationship with a state, territory, or the District of Columbia: *legal residence* (or *domicile*) and *residence*.

Residence is established in a state by residing in that state. Residence involves your physical presence, or the presence of your living quarters from which you may be briefly absent. If you are living in government quarters on a service installation, you are usually a temporary resident of the state in which that installation is located. The term *resident,* for state tax purposes, is *not* the same as that defined here.

Legal residence, which is synonymous with *domicile* and *home of record* for tax purposes, refers to the individual's permanent home for legal purposes and is the basis for determining the jurisdiction to which the servicemember belongs for a number of legal matters. In particular, servicemembers are subject to the tax laws of the state in which their *legal residence* is located.

Generally speaking, a spouse becomes a legal resident of the servicemember's state of domicile (home of record) at the time of marriage. Similarly, your children are legal residents of your state of domicile. It is not necessary that your spouse or children ever reside in your state of domicile for them to become legal residents. For example, if you are born and brought up in Connecticut and enter the service from that state, you might marry a person from Nebraska and have children born in four other states or overseas and never be stationed in or even visit the state of Connecticut. Nevertheless, your family members are legal residents of Connecticut. It is their state of domicile until you establish a new domicile or until they independently establish domiciles.

Everyone has one legal residence (domicile) somewhere, and only one at any given time. This legal residence may be in the state where a person was born—domicile of origin—or it may be a place he or she has chosen—domicile of choice. Once established, legal residence continues until legally changed. One legal residence is not legally abandoned until a new one is established.

Legal residence changes only by a voluntary and positive action. A mere attempt or desire to make a change is not sufficient. As a general rule, to acquire a domicile of choice you must be physically present there with the intention of abandoning the former domicile and remaining in the new one indefinitely (or with no present intention of moving away).

The three conditions—physical presence, abandonment of the old domicile, and intent to remain indefinitely in the new domicile—must be met concurrently. Once a person has established a legal residence in a particular place by being physically present there with the required intent, temporary absence does not cause that legal residence to change. Also, a person whose presence at a place is not through free choice is not required to have a legal residence there merely because of his presence. Thus, servicemembers assigned to a particular post in a particular state do not ordinarily acquire legal residence at that post or even in that state. If, however, a servicemember is physically present at a place and also has a bona fide intent to remain there indefinitely, that place may become his or her legal residence.

In answering the question "What is my legal residence?" servicemembers must consider the facts of their individual cases. No hard and fast rules apply to all cases. Some factors are more important than others, but each can be used as evidence of the servicemember's intent with respect to establishing domicile.

1. Place of birth.
2. Permanent place of abode.
3. Payment of state income taxes or payment of taxes on intangible personal property (this is excellent evidence of legal residence).
4. Registering to vote.
5. Obtaining a driver's license.
6. Voting by absentee ballot (one of the best tests).
7. State from which you entered the military service.
8. Filing with state authorities an approved certificate or other statement indicating legal residence.

Thus, it is possible for you to have a domicile in one state and a temporary residence in another. In fact, most of us in the armed forces are in this position while we are serving inside the United States. The basic rule to remember is this: You do not lose domicile "solely by reason of being absent in compliance with military or naval orders," nor can a new domicile be acquired merely by being physically present.

Some Rules on State Tax Liabilities

Other rules that apply to you and your family members are as follows:

1. Your state of domicile or legal residence may tax your service income and any other income (such as dividends and interest), no matter how or where it is earned.
2. Your state of temporary residence (by virtue of military orders) may tax any income you or your family members derive from working (other than as a servicemember) or investing in that state. Only military pay may not be so taxed by the state of temporary residence.
3. Your state of temporary residence cannot tax your personal property located in the state. Your state of legal residence could, but generally states do not attempt to tax personal property that is not physically located within the state. *Real estate* is a different matter—it is taxed where it is located.

4. You are not required to get state automobile license tags from the state in which you are temporarily assigned to military duty, provided your vehicle bears valid license plates from your state of legal residence or domicile.

5. If you get your state automobile license tags from the state in which you are temporarily residing, you are required to pay only the registration fee. You are not required to pay any additional tax that is levied solely to raise income for the state.

Should You Change Your Legal Residence?

Military personnel can avoid paying state income taxes by establishing their domicile in a state that doesn't have an income tax. As a result, it is not surprising that statistics on the legal residences of military personnel indicate that they are concentrated in these states. A servicemember technically may not, however, alter his or her domicile simply to avoid taxes. As we explained above, in order for a change in domicile to be convincing to state tax authorities, the servicemember must be able to show evidence of his or her intent following separation from the military to return to the new domicile for an indefinite period with no intent to leave. If you are able to provide such evidence without extreme difficulty or large unnecessary expenses, then you should consider doing so. Be judicious in your decision, however, for tax authorities are alert for fraudulent domicile changes. Before acting, you should seek advice at your installation legal affairs office to ensure that your actions represent legal tax avoidance and not tax evasion.

State Taxes

State tax laws change constantly. You should check the latest printing of the *All States Income Tax Guide,* published by the Office of the Judge Advocate General of the Air Force and generally available at your local legal affairs office. In the past decade, as states have become increasingly hard pressed for revenue, they have increased their aggressiveness in the collection of taxes owed. All members of the armed forces are now required to declare their state of legal residence, thus the matching of individual W-2 forms and state of residence is now possible. In addition, state tax is withheld by the military pay system on behalf of a growing number of states. As of 1993, military members who are residents of the following states have state income tax withheld from their pay: Alabama, Arkansas, Colorado, Connecticut, Delaware, District of Columbia, Georgia, Hawaii, Indiana, Iowa, Kansas, Kentucky, Louisiana, Maine, Maryland, Massachusetts, Minnesota, Mississippi, Nebraska, New Mexico, North Carolina, North Dakota, Ohio, Oklahoma, Rhode Island, South Carolina, Utah, Virginia, and Wisconsin. If you are a resident of these states and you pay state tax on your military pay, you may benefit significantly from reduced in-state college tuition and other state benefits. Residents of the following states may have a choice as to whether state income tax is withheld from their pay: Arizona, California, Idaho, New Jersey, New York, Oregon, and Pennsylvania.

Seven states have no income tax: Alaska, Florida, Nevada, South Dakota, Texas, Washington, and Wyoming. If you are a legal resident of one of these states, your income from any source will not be taxed. Twelve other states either do not tax military compensation at all or do not if a military resident of the state is serving outside the state: California, Idaho, Michigan, Missouri, Montana, New Hampshire, New Jersey, New York, Pennsylvania, Tennessee, Vermont, and West Virginia. The remaining states levy some form of tax on military income, but some have exemptions and exclusions that reduce the burden of the state income tax. For the details of the state tax laws in your state of residence, consult the *All States Income Tax Guide*.

The Soldiers' and Sailors' Relief Act prevents states in which nonresident military members are stationed from taxing their military pay, but not taxation of nonmilitary income or the income earned by a family member in the state. Thus, military spouses who work will often have to file "nonresident" state income taxes with the state in which the family is stationed. Since the Act allows servicemembers' states of legal residence to tax their military income, it is possible for many military families to file three tax forms: one for the federal government, one for the servicemember's state of residence (on which the servicemember reports military pay), and a third for the state in which the spouse earns income.

State tax laws can be as complicated as the federal tax code. Seek assistance from your local legal affairs office or from professional tax preparers if you find your filing requirements overwhelming.

Local Taxes

Servicemembers may also be liable for local income taxes levied by town, county, or other local governments in whose jurisdiction their legal residence lies. Generally, you should hear from these local governments about your tax obligations. But it is your responsibility to know about any taxes that you should be paying to a locality. You could find a nasty surprise in the form of a large unpaid back-tax bill when you leave the service and return to your hometown. Contact local government clerks for information on income taxes that may be due while you are on active duty.

RECENT TAX DEVELOPMENTS

The federal tax code has undergone two substantial revisions since 1986. The first revision occurred with the Tax Reform Act of 1986. The most important feature of this act was the elimination of numerous tax brackets in favor of only two: a 15 percent bracket and a 28 percent bracket. Furthermore, the law indexed the income ranges to which these tax rates applied, so inflation would no longer push taxpayers into higher tax brackets. To obtain political support for eliminating tax brackets and lowering the tax rates for upper-middle and high-income earners, the reform process eliminated many tax breaks that had existed under the pre-1986 code. One such provision was that the first 60 percent of capital gains, which was defined as income from investments of duration longer than twelve months, was exempted from taxation. As a result, the maximum effective tax rate on capital gains under the prereform tax code was 20 percent.

In 1990, Congress again revised the tax code by creating tax brackets of 31 and 34 percent. In addition, this revision to the tax code reestablished the special treatment for capital gains by establishing a maximum tax rate of 28 percent on capital gains on assets held for at least one year.

Persistent, large federal budget deficits led to a third round of tax changes in 1993. The 1993 tax law created five tax brackets: 15, 28, 31, 36, and 39.3 percent. The ranges of taxable income to which these rates apply are shown in Table 8-1, which contains the same information as Table 4-5. After 1994, these tax brackets will again be indexed for inflation. In addition, the law specifies that personal exemptions and itemized deductions are phased out for upper-income taxpayers. Also, the new law applies the Medicare portion of Social Security taxes (currently 1.45 percent) to total earnings, whereas prior to this law the Medicare portion only applied to the first $135,000 in income.

The 1986 law also reduced the ability of persons with employer-sponsored pension plans, such as military personnel, to defer taxes by contributing to an Individual Retirement Account (IRA). Prior to the 1986 Tax Reform Act, workers could deduct $2,000 per year from their taxable income by investing this amount in an IRA. After 1987, however, the amount that could be deducted was reduced by $200 for every $1,000 in gross income above $40,000. Taxes on earnings from IRA investments are still deferred for all individuals. There has been some discussion of eliminating this phaseout of the deductibility of IRA contributions or introducing some other tax-advantaged savings plan, but the chances of this happening are not high at this time.

The recent changes to the tax code will create pressures to devise new categories of deductions and other tax loopholes. As marginal tax rates increase, the payoff to

TABLE 8-1
Income Tax Brackets for 1993 and 1994[1]

	Taxable Income Range, Based on Filing Status		
Tax Rate	Joint (Married)	Head of Household	Single
15%	≤ $36,899	≤ $29,599	≤ $22,099
28%	$36,900–89,149	$29,600–76,399	$22,100–53,499
31%	$89,150–139,999	$76,400–127,499	$53,500–114,999
36%	$140,000–249,999	$127,500–249,999	$115,000–249,999
39.3%	≥ $250,000	≥ $250,000	≥ $250,000

[1] These brackets will be adjusted for inflation beginning in 1995.

Source: Omnibus Budget Reconciliation Act of 1993.

these loopholes increases and the temptation for Congress to favor certain portions of the population grows. Thus, we see from recent changes to the tax code that further revisions to the code are likely to occur in the near future. If the recent past is a guide, these changes could have a large impact on many military families. Therefore, it is important that you stay abreast of major changes to the tax code and incorporate any changes that do occur into your financial planning decisions.

SUGGESTED REFERENCES

Internal Revenue Service Publication 17: *Your Federal Income Tax.* Published annually by the IRS. Available free from IRS publications centers. The IRS also publishes numerous other useful booklets on specific tax topics, such as IRS Publication 553, *Highlight of Tax Changes,* and IRS Publication 552, *Recordkeeping for Individuals and List of Tax Publications.*

Numerous personal finance periodicals such as *Changing Times, Money,* and the *Wall Street Journal.*

Tax planning and preparation guides published by the J.K. Lasser Tax Institute, Prentice-Hall, Commerce Clearing House, and accounting firms such as Arthur Young and Price, Waterhouse; available at the beginning of every year in most bookstores. Occasionally reviewed in *Consumer Reports.*

Annual Income Tax Supplement to your service's *Times* paper (e.g., *Army Times, Navy Times*).

Part III

BIG-TICKET ITEMS

9

Buying a Car

IN THE UNITED STATES, an automobile is considered a necessity. Other than your house, your automobile is almost certain to be the largest purchase you will ever make. Transportation is second only to housing in most household budgets. Therefore, making wise decisions when buying a car is an integral part of sound financial planning.

You are faced with a staggering array of vehicles and options from which to choose. Hundreds of models and thousands of option combinations are available. Finance, insurance, and maintenance decisions increase the complexity of your automobile purchase decision. Dealers' and manufacturers' sales incentives, such as rebates, price discounts, cut-rate financing, option bundles, and other enticements, confuse your purchase decision. Many consumers, bewildered by the available choices, make impulse buying decisions. The result is often a vehicle that destroys the household budget without meeting household needs.

This chapter will help you to negotiate the maze of automobile decisions and to devise a systematic plan to guide you through your automobile-purchase choices. If you use the information in this chapter, you should be able to get a good deal on an automobile that meets your needs.

Much additional information is available on each topic covered here. Throughout this chapter, we make reference to useful publications that are readily available in your local library or that can be obtained free of charge by making a phone call. Use these additional resources to supplement the material in this chapter and to aid you in completing your automobile buying plan.

As you approach your automobile purchase, remember that the goal of virtually everyone you meet will be to take as much of your money as possible. While most individuals buy ten to fifteen cars during their lifetime, professional automobile salesmen and loan officers handle thousands of transactions. As professionals, they make their living by getting you to give them your money.

104 • PERSONAL FINANCIAL PLANNING

Almost every decision you make in purchasing a new car will affect the amount you ultimately pay. Selecting options, negotiating the purchase price, determining the trade-in value, and financing and insuring your new car are all opportunities for wily salespeople to separate you from your money. You would be wise to prepare before making one of the largest purchases you will ever make!

GETTING STARTED

How Much Can You Afford?

The first step in your car-buying decision is to determine the amount of your monthly budget to allot to transportation expenses. You should always consider the opportunity cost (see chapter 2) of your purchase decisions. Your household budget is a useful tool to test how increased spending on transportation affects your consumption of other goods. (See chapter 4 for a discussion of household budgets.) The automobile you buy will be the result of many tradeoffs.

It is very important to begin your car-buying process with a solid idea of how much you are willing to spend each month for transportation. Your monthly payments are only a portion of the total monthly cost. Insurance, operating expenses, maintenance, and depreciation add to the total bill. A good rule of thumb is to spend no more than 15 percent of your pretax income for transportation. To estimate your monthly transportation expenses, you must make estimates for the various expenses associated with automobile ownership.

Gather Cost Information

Payments
Automobile payments will be the largest outlay in most transportation budgets. Tables 9-1 through 9-4 show the monthly payments per $1,000 financed at various interest rates for twenty-four, thirty-six, forty-eight, and sixty months. To use these tables, determine the amount you plan to finance after making your down payment. Then, select a payment period shorter than the length of time you expect to own the automobile. Finally, select the interest rate. The amount below the interest rate will be very close to your monthly payments per $1,000 financed. Multiply this number by the amount, in thousands of dollars, you plan to finance. This will give you a very close estimate of your monthly automobile payment. For example, a $15,000 automobile purchase with a 10 percent down payment leaves $13,500 to finance. This amount, financed for four years at a 10 percent interest rate, would result in a monthly payment very close to $342 ($13.5 \times 25.36 = \$342.36$).

As we explained in chapter 6, your monthly payment consists of two components: interest and principal. That is, the bank charges you interest each month, at a stated rate, for the amount of money that you still owe them. The rest of your payment

TABLE 9-1
Monthly Payments (per $1,000) for a 24-Month Loan

Rate	7%	8%	9%	10%	11%	12%	13%	14%	15%
Pmnt	$44.77	$45.22	$45.68	$46.14	$46.61	$47.07	$47.54	$48.01	$48.49

TABLE 9-2
Monthly Payments (per $1,000) for a 36-Month Loan

Rate	7%	8%	9%	10%	11%	12%	13%	14%	15%
Pmnt	$30.88	$31.34	$31.80	$32.27	$32.74	$33.21	$33.69	$34.18	$34.67

TABLE 9-3
Monthly Payments (per $1,000) for a 48-Month Loan

Rate	7%	8%	9%	10%	11%	12%	13%	14%	15%
Pmnt	$23.95	$24.41	$24.89	$25.36	$25.85	$26.33	$26.83	$27.33	$27.83

TABLE 9-4
Monthly Payments (per $1,000) for a 60-Month Loan

Rate	7%	8%	9%	10%	11%	12%	13%	14%	15%
Pmnt	$19.80	$20.28	$20.76	$21.25	$21.74	$22.24	$22.75	$23.27	$23.79

goes to "pay down" the amount of the loan, called the principal balance. The principal portion of the payment is really "paying for the car"; the interest portion is "paying for the loan." This process of paying off the loan is known as amortizing the loan.

Continuing with our example, when you borrow $13,500 from the bank at 10 percent, you have a $342 monthly payment. Calculating the interest portion of that is quite simple—just take the (monthly) interest rate and multiply it by the amount you owe the bank. For the first month, multiply 0.008333 (10 percent annual rate divided by 12 months) by the $13,500 that you borrowed from the bank; you must pay $112.50 in interest. The remaining $230 of your monthly payment is applied toward the principal—it is subtracted from the $13,500 original loan balance, leaving a new balance of $13,280. In the second month, you pay $110.67 (0.008333 times the principle balance of $13,280) in interest, and $231.33 is applied toward the principal. The portion of your payments applied to interest decreases over time, while the portion applied to the principal increases.

Insurance
Insurance costs vary significantly depending on several factors, including the age and driving record of the person insured, the age of the automobile, automobile safety characteristics, insurance coverage limits, use of the automobile, miles driven per year, and automobile location. The USAA Foundation publishes (at no charge) *The Car Guide*, which compares the safety features of most models. This guide helps to identify automobiles that have desirable insurance characteristics, such as passenger safety in accidents, lower damage in accidents, and lower theft rates. Your insurance company will gladly give you quotes on the two or three models you most prefer. You need to determine your insurance costs for different automobiles to estimate accurately your total monthly transportation expenses. A monthly insurance payment of $100 is a realistic estimate for full insurance coverage on a new $15,000 car. The next chapter explains the various types of automobile insurance available.

Operation
Operating expenses, consisting primarily of fuel and oil, will vary significantly depending on the model you choose. The typical automobile owner in the United States drives 1,000 miles each month. Calculate your operating expenses by dividing the number of miles you expect to drive by the miles per gallon (mpg) rating of your automobile. This gives you the number of gallons of fuel you will use each month. Multiply the number of gallons you expect to use monthly by the price you expect to pay per gallon to get an estimate of your monthly operating expenses. For example, if you plan to drive 1,000 miles per month, get twenty-five mpg, and expect to pay $1.50 per gallon for gas, monthly operating expenses would be at least $60 [(1,000 miles ÷ 25 mpg) × $1.50 = $60].

Maintenance
Maintenance expenses include the cost of scheduled maintenance, such as fluid changes, filter changes, and tune-ups. Replacing of worn and damaged parts also adds to maintenance expenses. Maintenance costs vary depending on the items covered under warranty or coverage bought under a separate maintenance contract. For the first two years, the monthly maintenance costs should be very low. Annual maintenance costs during the fifth year are expected to be roughly triple those in the first year. The average maintenance costs over a five-year period are likely to be about $20 per month or more. Actual repair costs, of course, will vary depending on the specific model and on your use of the car. The *Consumer Reports Annual Buying Guide Issue* makes current estimates for average maintenance expenses and provides useful information concerning specific problems with various models.

Depreciation

Depreciation is the decrease in the value of an automobile due to time and use. It is an implicit cost of automobile ownership. Many automobile owners ignore depreciation because they do not write a monthly check to pay for it, but it is one of the largest expenses of automobile ownership nonetheless. Table 9-5 shows an example of how a $15,000 car might depreciate. The owner could sell the car for $8,128 after three years, but after four years he could sell it for only $6,909. In essence, the owner has paid $1,219 to use the car during that year.

While the concept of depreciation is simple to understand, it can be difficult to calculate the actual depreciation in any particular case. There are, essentially, two reasonable ways to account for the depreciation expense of owning a car. The first method is to consider actual cash flows; that is, count your car payments as an expense when paid, and do not count depreciation. The second method is to consider the true economic expense, which would include interest plus depreciation. The interest expense is the interest on the value of the car; in the first year, this is basically just the interest portion of your car payment, plus any interest forgone on your down payment, plus depreciation. (It is *not* correct to add depreciation to the entire car payment because part of the payment goes toward repaying principal.) The second method is preferable, but over a long period both methods produce similar cost estimates. The problem with the first method is that the timing used to "spread out" the purchase price of the car is the length of the car loan, which is simply too short. Notice that the down payment and principal payments (used in method one) total $15,000, or the price of the car; likewise, the total of all depreciation (used in method two) over time is also $15,000. The second method, reflecting the true "cost" of your $15,000 purchase losing its value over time, gives a better indication of the cost of ownership for each period of time.

Depreciation varies considerably across makes and models. New automobiles depreciate much faster than used automobiles; thus, depreciation expenses decrease as

TABLE 9-5
Depreciation Schedule/Resale Value

Automobile Age	Value	% Change	Annual Depreciation
New	$15,000		
One year old	$11,250	25	$3,750
Two years old	$ 9,562	15	$1,688
Three years old	$ 8,128	15	$1,434
Four years old	$ 6,909	15	$1,219
Five years old	$ 5,872	15	$1,037
Total depreciation (years 0–5)			$9,128
Remaining depreciation (years 6–?)			$5,872

automobiles get older. As a rule of thumb, automobiles lose 25 percent of their purchase value in the first year and 15 percent of the remaining value each following year. Table 9-5 provides one example of typical depreciation rates. It shows that a $15,000 automobile depreciates by more than 60 percent in five years. This breaks down to an average monthly depreciation of about $152 per month ($9,128 ÷ 60 = $152.30). Models with excellent maintenance and resale records will generally hold much more of their value than this. The *Kelley Blue Book* is a good source for determining depreciation, as it provides average resale values by model, make, and year.

An often overlooked aspect of depreciation concerns the time during the model year when consumers buy their new car. Base car wholesale prices change little over a model year, which usually run from October 1 to September 30. The used car market, however, bases depreciation on calendar years. Therefore, in 1992, a 1991 automobile bought new in the fall of 1990 will be worth very nearly the same as the same automobile bought late in 1991 (if their mileage and condition are similar). An automobile bought late in a model year depreciates much more rapidly than the same automobile bought early in that model year. You should keep this point in mind, especially if you are considering the purchase of last year's model after new car models have been introduced. Dealers will typically offer sizable discounts on "old"models. If the discount they quote is less than the first year depreciation you calculate, it is no bargain.

Total Expenses

The cost information provided here should enable you to determine the amount of your household budget that you are willing to spend for transportation. You may have other considerations when making your individual purchase decision, such as whether to trade in a used car or the size of the down payment. The following is a rough estimate of average monthly transportation expenses during the first year of ownership, based on the previous estimates; of course, the expenses would change from year to year. The cash flow method and the preferred method of true economic expense are used, as described above.

Explicit Cost (Cash Flow)		*True Economic Cost*	
Payment	$342	Interest	$110
Insurance	100	Insurance	100
Operation	60	Operation	60
Maintenance	10	Maintenance	10
Total cash flow	**$512**	Depreciation	310
		Total cost	**$590**

The economic cost of $590 is fairly close to the explicit cost, using the cash flow method, of $512. The variation is due to the differences in the timing of depreciation and principal payments. As you can see, the big expense in owning a car isn't the operating or even the interest expenses; rather, it is the implicit expense caused by depreciation. As car buyers, we have a tendency to worry too much about gas mileage and not enough about price and resale value.

You can use Tables 9-1 through 9-4 with your different transportation expense estimates to calculate the amount you can afford to finance. Assume the following: Your monthly transportation budget is $385 based on 12.83 percent of a $3,000 pretax income (0.1283% × $3,000 = $385), you have about $2,000 for initial costs, you can finance your car at a 10 percent interest rate, and you earn 6 percent after taxes on your investments. You've made the following expense estimates for the model you want:

Transportation budget	$385
Less foregone interest	$ 10 (= $2,000 × (0.06 ÷ 12))
Less insurance	$ 75
Less operation	$ 60
Less maintenance	$ 10
Maximum payment	**$230**

This leaves you $230 per month for automobile payments. From Table 9-3, you see that it will cost $25.15 for each $1,000 financed over a forty-eight-month period. You can thus afford to finance $9,145.13 [($230 ÷ $25.15) × $1,000 = $9,145.13]. With your $2,000, you can make a 10 percent down payment and finance the remaining 90 percent. You could afford a car that retails for about $10,161 ($9,145.13 ÷ 0.90 = $10,161.26). Your estimated 10 percent down payment would be $1,016 ($10,161.25 × 0.10 = $1,016.13). Remember, taxes and registration will cost another $1,000 or so in most cases. In this example, you would need about $2,016 to buy a new $10,200 car. Your actual expenses will vary somewhat from this example. Therefore, it is extremely important for you to do your homework before going automobile shopping.

FINANCING

You should make arrangements to finance your automobile before you begin to shop. Arranging your financing in advance serves a threefold purpose. First, it helps you to determine the price range in which you can reasonably afford to shop. Second, it gives you more control over your purchase decision. You will have a financing alternative rather than being dependent on the financing arrangements offered by the automobile dealer. Finally, you will be able to recognize a good deal if the dealer offers one.

In this section, we will examine the common methods of financing an automobile purchase. Chapter 6 contains a more general discussion of consumer loans and credit.

Loans

Financing sources often have loan terms that obscure the actual cost of borrowing money. When shopping for financing, your actual cost of borrowing money is an important consideration. By law, all lenders must provide you with a rate of interest based on a standardized calculation. This rate of interest is the annual percentage rate (APR). Keep your eye on the APR. Without making your own detailed calculations, it is the most useful method of comparing the cost of different loans.

Financing your automobile purchase involves several decisions. You must decide the source of the loan, the amount to borrow, the duration of the loan, and the interest rate. Your decisions in each of these areas will affect your credit costs, both in the total interest you will pay and in the amount of your monthly payments. Careful evaluation of various sources of auto loans will help you reduce credit costs while making monthly payments that fit your family's budget. Note also that interest paid on automobile loans is no longer tax deductible, thus adding to the cost of a loan and making your decision even more important.

Most lending institutions finance new cars for thirty-six or forty-eight months. Sixty-month financing is also available on some expensive or very durable automobiles. Most lenders finance used cars for twenty-four months and only occasionally for thirty-six months. You should never finance your loan for a period longer than you plan to keep the automobile. Many car owners are making payments on cars that they could not sell for enough money to pay off their loan balances.

One thing to keep in mind is that the longer the duration of the loan you take, the more you will pay for it. This is true for two reasons. First, a longer duration means the principal is generating interest payments for a longer time. Second, lending institutions typically charge a higher interest rate for longer-duration loans. Consider the following example. You want to borrow $10,000 of your new automobile purchase. After shopping around, the best deal you can find is a bank that offers the following loan schedule: thirty-six months at 8 percent, forty-eight months at 10 percent, sixty months at 12 percent. Your payments under the various terms are compared below.

Loan Duration	36 mo.	48 mo.	60 mo.
Monthly payments	$ 313	$ 254	$ 222
Total principal payments	$10,000	$10,000	$10,000
Total interest payments	$ 1,281	$ 2,174	$ 3,347
Total payment to bank	$11,281	$12,174	$13,347

As you can see, your monthly payments are smaller, but you end up paying the bank an additional $2,066 in interest for the privilege of stretching out the payments from thirty-six to sixty months.

You should shop for automobile financing as diligently as you shop for your automobile. If you ignore financing alternatives, you can easily squander the money you saved through careful research on dealer cost information and through skillful negotiations.

Self-financing

We congratulate you if you have saved enough to pay cash for your new car. Even though you plan to pay cash for your new car, there is still a financing cost of sorts. This financing cost is the opportunity cost (forgone interest) of the money you spend. If your money was in a money market account earning 7.5 percent interest, and your marginal tax rate is 15 percent, your opportunity cost (financing cost) is 6.375 percent [$0.07 \times (1 - 0.15)$]. Self-financing is an excellent method of buying an automobile; it is very difficult to get a consumer loan at a lower rate of interest than the opportunity cost of your investments. Self-financing is an even better method if you have the discipline to pay yourself back. To do this, you should calculate payments that include both principal and interest. Select a reasonable loan period and make monthly payments back to your savings.

Collateralized Loans

Another method of financing your automobile purchase is a collateralized loan. To get a collateralized loan, you use something of more value than the loan as security. Then, if you are unable to make your payments, the lending institution keeps the item you used to secure your loan. As an example, you can frequently use your savings account as security for an automobile loan. Most banks will loan you money against your savings account for about 2 percent above the interest rate they are paying you. You should understand that you do not have the use of your savings while it serves as collateral for a loan. Therefore, it would be unwise to use your emergency fund as collateral for a car loan. If you have enough equity in your house, you can frequently borrow against this equity for an automobile purchase. This type of loan has the added benefit that the interest you pay is tax deductible. Be aware, however, that if you default on a collateralized loan, you lose the collateral. This could be your house!

Borrowing from a Bank or Credit Union

Your bank and your credit union are potentially excellent sources from which to secure automobile financing for several reasons. First, your credit institutions should treat you, their customer, with courtesy. Second, they are more likely to explain your credit options in detail. Third, they can provide you with detailed value estimates (wholesale and retail) for both your used car and the new car you plan to buy. You should apply to your bank or credit union for an automobile loan at least seven days before you begin to shop for your automobile. This allows them adequate time to process your loan application and will ensure that the money is ready when you need it.

An important dimension of your financing decision is the duration of your loan. In chapter 6 we discussed amortization, which is the process of repaying an installment loan. The longer the loan period, the slower the loan is amortized. Because automobiles depreciate very rapidly when they are new, cars may depreciate faster than a long-term loan is amortized. As a result, it is possible for you receive less in a trade-in (or from insurance if your car is stolen or destroyed) than the outstanding balance on your loan.

For example, assume you borrow $10,000 for forty-eight months at 10 percent interest to purchase an auto, but you have a wreck after one year and the car is totaled. On average, the car would have been worth $7,500 after one year, and you could expect the insurance company to pay you that amount. The principal balance on the loan, however, would be $7,830.18, so you would have to write the bank a check for $330.18 to clear the loan. If you had financed the car for only thirty-six months, then the remaining principle would be only $6,992.57. The check from the insurance company would allow you to pay off the loan and still apply $507.43 toward a new car. The lesson here is that in addition to costing you less in interest over the period, loans of shorter duration reduce the risk of having the value of your asset fall below the loan principal.

SELECTING AN AUTOMOBILE

After determining your monthly transportation budget, you can omit automobiles that are too expensive. A good strategy is to reduce your transportation alternatives to two or three before you become influenced by salesmen's pitches, showroom glitter, and that new car smell.

Your Transportation Requirements

Your most important transportation decisions revolve around function, economy, comfort, and style. You should select your automobile based not only on your current needs, but also on your projected needs while you expect to own the vehicle. Allow for possible relocation and changes in family size. The previous discussion of new car depreciation shows that it is very expensive to sell a new car after only a year or two.

Comparative analysis is a useful technique for comparing the overall benefit of several automobiles with different features and for analyzing your purchase decision in advance. A simple but effective comparative analysis technique is to create a simple table listing the automobile features important to you. Table 9-6 identifies several features that are important to many buyers and illustrates a possible range of weights across features. The USAA Automobile Pricing/Auto Purchase Service (800-531-8905) offers a free brochure, *How to Buy a Car*, that identifies functional areas many drivers find important. Evaluate your three final candidates with regard to each feature, and rank-order them (3 to 1 from best to worst). Multiply the rank by the weight and record the result on the chart. Sum the column for each candidate. The model with the highest sum is the one that comes closest to meeting your overall transportation requirements.

TABLE 9-6
Comparative Analysis

Feature/Characteristic	Weight	Car A	Car B	Car C
Matches functional needs	3			
Depreciation history	2			
Fuel efficiency	2			
Insurance costs	1			
Model maintenance history	1			
Manufacturer reputation	1			
Comfort	2			
Handling	1			
Performance	1			
Style	1			
Safety record	3			
Low price	3			
Total				

The nice thing about this method is that it forces you to compare the characteristics of your top three models. You should set up your own comparative analysis system by determining and weighing the characteristics that are important to you. The key is to set up and use a comparative analysis that reflects your personal automobile preferences. Remember: Analyze your automobile needs before you begin to shop. Your analysis will help you navigate through myriad automobile choices and to select the one that best satisfies your transportation desires.

Optional Equipment

Carefully selecting optional equipment for your new automobile helps ensure that the automobile meets your functional, economical, comfort, and style needs. You should decide what options are important to you before you ever visit a dealer's lot. Options increase the cost, utility, style, and resale value of an automobile. Your most important option choices include engine, transmission, air conditioning, power brakes, and power steering. An automatic transmission and air conditioning add to the resale value of an automobile. Thus, you will be able to recoup some of your cost when you sell the vehicle. Air bags and security alarms will decrease your insurance cost. Other options do little to enhance the utility, style, or resale value of your automobile. The more options your automobile has, the more likely it will require frequent minor repairs due to its increased complexity. Today, 90 percent of the cars sold in the United States have automatic transmissions, and 75 percent have air conditioning, power brakes, power steering, steel-belted radial-ply tires, and stereos. The following simple guidelines can help you make your option selections:

- Select only the options you want. Make your option decisions before you visit a dealer.
- Consider options that increase convenience, durability, and resale value. Avoid extravagant options that increase the cost and complexity of your car without providing tangible benefits.
- Shop for a model that includes most of the options you want as standard equipment. This will decrease your overall cost because dealers have a higher markup on options.
- Consider waiting for a "special order" car that has only the options you want. An overloaded model on the dealer's lot may be available immediately, but it will cost you more money.
- Be aware of dealer-installed options. Dealer-installed air conditioning is almost always inferior in quality to factory-installed air conditioning. Options such as fabric protection, paint protection, and rust protection are available from independent sources at a fraction of the cost you will pay a dealer, and in some cases, their application could harm the car. Dealer markup for these options, including both material and labor, is often in the hundreds of percent.
- Factory warranties are rarely a bargain.

BUYING A NEW CAR

Buying from a Dealer

Do your homework if you plan to buy from an automobile dealer. Know exactly what model you want and which options. Research the dealer cost for both the base price of the model and the options you want. Have a financing plan. Shop several dealers so that you are more likely to get a fair deal.

There are several advantages in buying from a dealer instead of ordering the car from the factory. First, there is very little time delay in getting the car you want. If it is not on their lot, most dealers can locate the car you want and execute a dealer trade within a couple of days. Second, you can see and thoroughly inspect the actual vehicle that you will be getting. Third, the dealer from which you buy your automobile is likely to be more responsive to any maintenance problems that result after you buy your car. There are a couple of significant disadvantages to buying from a dealer, however. First, it is very possible that the available car that most closely meets your needs will have many undesired, costly options. Second, you will be dealing with professionals whose job it is to turn your money into their profit. Buying from a dealership without preparing is like opening a vein before swimming with sharks. You need to know which car you want and how much you are willing to pay for it before you start negotiating with a dealer.

You can also factory-order a new car from a dealer. Dealers would much rather sell you a car off of their lot, however, because it is costing them money in interest. Dealers make a profit immediately when they sell you a car. An advantage of ordering your new car from a dealer is that you get and pay only for the options you want. A disadvantage is that you will have to wait from four to six weeks for delivery. Also, you cannot inspect the car before you sign a purchase contract.

Dealer Cost versus Retail Cost

Dealer cost is the amount that a dealer pays the factory for an automobile plus gas, oil, advertising, and floor plan. Floor plan is the interest (probably about 1 percent per month) dealers pay banks on the money they use to purchase vehicles displayed on their lots.

The difference between dealer cost and sticker price is dealer profit. You can determine dealer cost by reviewing a new copy of *Edmund's New Car Prices* at your library. This publication provides separate profit estimates for the base car and options. For example, the profit (as a percentage of price) on the base car might be 15 percent. The percentage of profit on the options might be 17.5 percent. On an average $15,000 car, the cost breakdown of the retail price might be as follows (ignoring floor plan, a cost that varies with time):

Dealer cost of base car	$10,646
Dealer profit on base car	1,879
Dealer cost of options	1,650
Dealer profit on options	350
Gas, oil, advertising	100
Freight	375
Retail price	**$15,000**

Here the dealer profit is $2,229. Let's see how you can estimate dealer cost from a sticker price of $15,000. Subtract the cost of gas, oil, advertising, and freight ($15,000 − $100 − $375 = $14,525). This gives you the retail price of the car including options. You can split this amount into the base price of the car and the total cost of the options. Here the "sticker" shows that the base price of the car was $12,525 and the total price of the options was $2,000. Profit on the base car is 15 percent. Thus, the dealer cost is 85 percent of retail, or $10,646 ($12,525 × 0.15 = $10,646). The profit on options is 17.5 percent. Thus, dealer cost is 82.5 percent on the options, or $1,650 ($2,000 × 0.825 = $1,650). The retail price of the car plus options minus the dealer cost for the car plus options leaves a dealer profit of $2,229 ($14,525 − $10,646 − $350 = $2,229). Your goal when negotiating your new car purchase is to reduce the amount of dealer profit as much as possible. The dealer's goal when he sells you a new car is to make dealer profit as large as possible.

Taxes and tags will add another $1,000 or so to the purchase price. This amount, with a down payment of 10 percent, or $1,500, will result in an initial cash outlay of about $2,500 for a $15,000 car.

Using an Automobile Pricing/Buying Service

If, like many Americans, you find the process of buying a new car difficult, expensive, and aggravating, a buying service will reduce the time and energy you spend searching for a car and perhaps save you a considerable amount of money. Buying services allow you to order exactly the car you want equipped with only the options you want. You will pay the service a predetermined fee above dealer cost; with some models the fee is a fixed dollar amount and with others it is a percentage above the dealer cost. In our example, we'll use a predetermined fee of 1.5 percent above dealer cost on the base car and options. The result is that you save over $2,000, as calculated below:

Dealer cost of base car	$10,646
Dealer cost of options	$ 1,650
Total wholesale cost	$12,296
1.5% of wholesale cost	$ 184
Gas, oil, advertising	$ 100
Freight	$ 375
Your cost	**$12,955**

If you don't mind negotiating with dealers, then you might investigate an auto pricing service. Most auto pricing services will provide you with detailed cost information on particular models, usually for less than $10 per model. Normally it takes two to four weeks to process your specific request. Also, they may offer to buy your car for you and to have it delivered to a local participating dealer. The USAA Auto Pricing/Buying Service provides both services, and regional services are available in many areas. Pricing services are worthwhile if only to estimate accurately the wholesale cost of an automobile to the dealer. This information will help you determine how much you are willing to pay a dealer for a particular car.

Your cost estimate using a pricing service will not include a manufacturer's rebate to dealers called "holdback." Holdback is an additional 3 to 4 percent profit built into the wholesale price (dealer cost) of domestic automobiles. Manufacturers rebate this percentage to dealers periodically based on total volume. Remember, dealer profit is a percentage above dealer cost. Holdback is a part of "dealer cost." Holdback in our continuing example would range from $369 to $492 in additional profit to the dealer. This additional 3 to 4 percent profit gives dealers pricing flexibility that most automobile shoppers do not recognize even if they know the dealer's wholesale cost.

Dealing with a Dealer

If you decide to purchase your car from a dealer, there are several things you must be concerned about and familiar with before you see the dealer. From the moment you set foot on the lot or in the showroom, you will undergo a battle of wits and several stages of negotiations with the dealer.

Negotiating with a dealer will be a matter of your personality style. There are any number of books and guides that will help you in developing your negotiating plan. Additionally, there are some things you can do to enhance your position before the negotiations begin. Timing, for example, is a significant indirect negotiating tool.

There are times when dealers are more susceptible to making good deals than others. Dealers typically have monthly and quarterly sales targets. Frequently, salesmen have bonuses tied to these targets and will be more susceptible near the end of the period. Dealers are also more likely to make a good deal when business is slow. More customers shop for cars on weekends than during the week; therefore, midweek may be a better time to shop than on weekends. Weather also affects the number of customers. You are more likely to get a good deal when rain or snow keeps most shoppers away. Winter is simply not a time when most customers shop for cars. This makes it an ideal time for the bargain hunter.

Seasonality is also important, and automobile dealers are more likely to offer deals during and after the Christmas season for several reasons. There are fewer automobile customers during the holiday season because people are spending money for other things and do not have the cash available for down payments. Dealerships also are trying to cut year-end inventory for tax purposes.

How do you know if you are getting a good deal from a dealer? Do your homework. You should use a pricing/buying service (discussed above) to determine the actual dealer cost of the car you want and to get a price quote. If a dealer cannot beat the buying service price, you may not be getting a good deal. You are getting a very good deal from a dealer if his price is within a couple of hundred dollars of the pricing service quote.

Only human imagination limits the techniques automobile salesmen use to sell cars. Dealerships train their salesmen to pass you off to another salesman or the sales manager if they cannot sell you a car. You will usually negotiate your deal with a salesman, and then he will try to get you into the closing room. There, the closer, whose specialty is writing sales contracts, will write up the deal. Sometimes, the closer will intentionally manipulate the cost, trade-in, down payment, and financing numbers to confuse the customer. Customer confusion equals dealer profit. Once the purchase order is written, the closer will try to add unnecessary, high-profit options, fabric protection, rustproofing, floor mats, dealer warranties, and even insurance. The closer must then present the purchase order to the sales manager for his approval and signature. Passing you off from person to person reduces your resistance to buying and creates confusion. Each person in the process tries to sell you additional options you do not want, change the terms of the deal, and get more money from you. Remember, these professionals have closed hundreds of sales transactions.

Many car dealerships are honest businesses with an ethical sales force. You must watch for the ones that are not. Salesmen have, on occasion, sold cars that were similar, but not the same, as the ones test-driven by customers. Some unscrupulous dealerships may misplace your car keys so you have to stay there longer. On occasion, dealerships have substituted inferior dealer-installed options for factory-installed options.

The point of this section is to help you understand that you are dealing with experienced professionals who are adept at turning your money into dealer profit.

The following are some general guidelines that will be helpful if you decide to negotiate your new car purchase with a dealer.

- Know what model automobile and what options you want, and have your financing prearranged, before you go to a dealer's lot with the intention of buying.
- Let the dealer know you are a serious buyer. You should be ready to buy a car if you get the deal you want. Say to him, "I will buy a car today if you have the car and deal I want."
- Keep the four major parts of the automobile purchase transaction separate. It is too confusing to discuss your trade-in, down payment, and financing while you are trying to negotiate the purchase price of a new car. Tell the salesman, "We can discuss my trade-in and financing when we have agreed on the total sale price."
- If necessary, let the salesman know that you have done your homework. Tell him, "I know your cost for this car." When you confront a salesman with this information, he will almost always try to convince you that your information is outdated or incorrect. Do not allow him to convince you that you are wrong. Your cost estimate will be very close. Besides, you can always buy your new car from the buying service that provided you with the price quote.
- If you do not get the deal you want, tell the salesman that you think you can get a better deal by shopping around. Salesmen hate to hear those words. Record the terms of the deal offered on the back of the salesman's business card.
- After you have negotiated a satisfactory deal with a salesman, do not allow him or another dealer representative to reopen negotiations.
- Make sure that the purchase contract or sales order lists exactly the car and options you want and that it stipulates that no dealer-installed equipment will be substituted for factory-installed options.
- If you order your car from the factory, make sure that the sales contract states in writing that the order is contingent on timely delivery within four to six weeks.
- Do not sign a purchase order or sales contract that has blank spaces. Write "N/A" in blank spaces before signing.
- Do not sign a sales contract or purchase agreement unless you have read every word. Question the salesman on any point that you do not fully understand. Remember, confusion on your part almost certainly means more dealer profit.
- Make sure that the sales manager or an officer of the dealership signs the purchase order or sales contract. Many dealerships will not honor a contract signed by a salesman.
- Domestic cars include dealer preparation charges in the basic list price. Dealer preparation charges for imported cars are separate from the list price. Make sure that the purchase order or sales contract is clear if there is a separate charge for dealer preparation. Watch out for extra dealer preparation charges and for unwanted dealer-installed options. Dealers sometimes charge customers for dealer preparations that they did not perform and attempt to add high-profit, dealer-installed options to purchase orders or sales contracts.

- Make sure your purchase order or sales contract records your deposit. The contract should have a stipulation that the deposit is refundable if the dealership does not meet the terms of the contract.
- If you have a trade-in, be sure that the purchase order or sales contract records its value.
- Any verbal promises from the salesman must be explicitly written on the purchase order or sales contract if you expect the dealership to honor it.

ALTERNATIVES TO BUYING A NEW CAR

Used Cars

Should you consider a used car rather than a new car? If you are unwilling to make a large down payment or large monthly payments, a used car may be for you. You have no doubt noticed that in most cases new cars are much more expensive to own and operate than used cars. There are basic expense tradeoffs between new and used cars. Depreciation and insurance are more expensive for newer cars; maintenance is more expensive for older, higher-mileage cars. Consider your maintenance aptitude and your tolerance for car trouble when making this decision. Table 9-7 illustrates these tradeoffs, but it does not account for the inconvenience or major repairs that a used car may entail.

If you're considering buying a used car, you should compare the costs of new and used cars by constructing a table similar to Table 9-7. Estimate the depreciation and operating costs using the techniques previously described in this chapter. Insurance costs will decline as the appraised value of the automobile declines. (Chapter 10 contains a full explanation of auto insurance.) Contact your insurance company to obtain more precise estimates. For these comparisons, annual interest costs should be based on the market value of the auto each year, presuming that you are financing a purchase of that magnitude. For example, if you borrow at 10 percent, the interest cost for the first year is $1,500 (0.10 × $15,000). The interest cost for the

TABLE 9-7
Typical Automobile Operating Costs
(Based on a New Purchase Price of $15,000 and Borrowing at 10%)

	1st Year	2nd Year	3rd Year	4th Year	5th Year
Depreciation	$3,750	$1,688	$1,434	$1,219	$1,037
Insurance	1,200	1,100	1000	900	800
Interest costs	1,500	1,125	956	813	691
Operation	720	720	720	720	720
Maintenance	80	110	190	240	280
Total costs	$7,250	$4,743	**$4,300**	$3,892	$3,528

second year is $1,125 (0.10 × $11,250 [$15,000 less $3,750, or 25 percent depreciation the first year]).

To estimate the cost for a used car, simply use the column that represents the age of the used car. For the example shown in the table, a three-year-old car would have annual costs of about $4,300. The annual operating expenses for a three-year-old car are 69 percent ($4,300 ÷ $5,750 = 0.69, or 69 percent) of those for a similar new car. Differences of this magnitude between the costs of owning new and used cars are typical.

Determine the kind of used car you want. Know your price range and decide where you want to buy your car. The primary advantage of owning a carefully selected used car is that it will be much cheaper to own and operate than a new car. You can save the significant cost of depreciation associated with new cars if you buy a two- or three-year-old car and avoid the expensive major repairs associated with older cars by keeping the two- to three-year-old car for only three or four years. This potentially large savings has an increased risk in that the car may break down at an inopportune time and require unexpected, expensive repairs. When considering a used car, you should determine the repair history for similarly equipped cars of that model year. The *Consumer Reports Annual Buying Guide* provides this information for most models. Information is also available on models that are prone to serious mechanical problems and require higher than average repair costs. *Motor Trend* magazine is also an excellent source of information (most libraries have back issues). The few minutes you take to review a detailed, professional analysis of the automobile you plan to buy will be time well spent. Price guides such as the *Kelley Blue Book* and the *NADA Official Used Car Guide* are also available in most libraries. Both provide you with average wholesale and retail value estimates. These guides will also provide you with information to make adjustments for high or low mileage and the options on the car. There is no substitute for a mechanical inspection by a trained mechanic to help you determine the value of a used car.

Good used cars are available at fair prices, but you must search carefully. Purchasing a used car from a private owner may allow you to buy a good car at less than retail. You will almost certainly pay near retail for a used car you buy from a new car dealer, but you may get a limited warranty. Selling only quality used cars and providing warranties helps preserve their reputations. New car dealers also have maintenance departments and probably have performed some minor repairs. You are likely to find the worst selection of used cars at a dealer that specializes in only used cars. This is where new car dealers dispose of their worst used cars. Used car dealers may not have very good maintenance facilities, probably will not provide a warranty, and probably will charge you a retail price.

The following are several generalizations about the expenses of owning and operating a used car:

- Never buy a used car unless you get a mechanical inspection by a mechanic whom you pay. The mechanic's written list of mechanical deficiencies will ensure that you know what problems your target vehicle has. Armed with this information, you should be able to negotiate a reduced price for the used car roughly equal to required repairs.

Buying a car with impending repairs is just like paying more for the car. You should have a mechanical inspection done only on cars you have inspected and want to buy. Mechanical inspections rarely cost more than $50, and the mechanical inspection will almost always save you money.
• Several studies confirm that total costs of a three-year-old car are about two thirds the costs of owning a comparable new car during its first year of operation.
• If you plan to own your car for only two or three years, a new car will be significantly more expensive to operate than a used car because of the rapid depreciation that occurs in the first two years of ownership.
• A used car ceases to be economical when major repairs become likely each year. This is likely to occur after the fourth or fifth year.

Leasing

Leasing an automobile is very similar to renting it on a long-term basis. You will normally pay a deposit equal to the first and last monthly payment. Depending on the terms of the lease, you are responsible for all scheduled maintenance during the lease period. Most leases have a stipulation stating the maximum number of miles the lessor allows during the lease period. If you exceed the limit, you must pay a monetary penalty of perhaps 15 cents per mile. You may also purchase an option, for a few hundred dollars, to buy the leased vehicle for a predetermined price when the lease expires. This type of lease is an "open-ended" lease; a lease without this option is a "closed-ended" lease.

Closed-ended leases are those for which you have no financial responsibilities other than scheduled maintenance and monthly payments. At the end of the lease, you return the automobile to the leasing company. The leasing company charges you a higher monthly payment because the automobile you return may be worth less than they calculated. Most leases written today are closed-ended leases.

Open-ended lease payments are cheaper because you guarantee the value of the automobile at the end of the lease. If the car you turn in is worth less than estimated in the terms of your lease, you pay the difference. Normally, the difference is no more than three months' payments. If the car is worth more than the lessor expected, the leasing company will pay you the difference. The leasing company determines the automobile's value at the end of the lease, however. Do not expect a check.

There are three advantages to leasing an automobile. First, the security payment when leasing is probably lower than the down payment when buying. Second, the monthly lease payment is almost always lower than the monthly payment you would have if you bought the same car because the lease company will still own the vehicle when your contract expires. Third, the lease transaction itself is relatively simple. Moreover, because consumer interest is no longer a tax deduction, leasing is less impractical than it used to be. The most significant disadvantage is that over the long run, leasing will invariably be more expensive than buying the same car because the lease arrangement always includes a profit for the lease company.

The best leases amount to a loan (of the difference between the price of the new car and the predetermined end-of-lease value) at an interest rate between 12 and 17 percent. If you can obtain financing at an interest rate below this range, you will generally be better off doing so and not leasing.

You should remember two important things when considering an automobile lease. First, leases are legally binding contracts. You cannot simply return a leased vehicle to the company and be done with it. As with all legally binding contracts, read and understand every word before signing it. Second, if you lease a "lemon," the leasing company probably will not take it back. You have little legal recourse if the car has continuous maintenance problems, because you do not own the vehicle.

DISPOSING OF YOUR OLD VEHICLE

For most people, disposing of a used car is an integral part of buying a new one. If you own an old car, you have essentially three choices concerning its disposition: You can trade it in on a new car to offset part of the down payment, you can sell it outright to a used car dealer, or you can sell it to a private party.

The main advantage of trading in your used car is convenience. You drive to the dealership in your old car and drive away in a new car. The main disadvantage is that a trade-in confuses the negotiation process by making it more difficult to determine how much you are actually paying for your new car.

The chief advantage of selling your used car to a used car dealer is again convenience. There is a used car dealer somewhere who will buy your car at some price no matter what the condition. The main disadvantage of this option is that you will rarely get more than minimum wholesale value. Even if you do not sell your car to a used car dealer, it is a good idea to get a price quote from one. This will give you an idea of the minimum trade-in value you should accept.

The advantage of selling your used car to a private party is that you will probably be able to sell it for a higher price that is somewhere between the car's wholesale and retail value. The main disadvantage is the inconvenience of dealing with the advertising and the actual sales transaction. You will probably get many calls from people who only want to look. If you decide to sell your used car yourself, you should develop some screening criteria to determine over the phone which buyers are serious. Another disadvantage is that you are unlikely to sell your car on exactly the same day as you pick up your new one. This results in either no transportation or excess transportation for a period, and it may cause a financing problem if you plan to use the proceeds from the sale as a down payment on your new car.

Whatever method you use to dispose of your old car, there are several steps you should take to ensure that you receive top dollar.

- Thoroughly clean your used car from bumper to bumper. Steam clean the engine and undercarriage, and scrub the wheels and tires. Shampoo the carpet and vacuum

the trunk. Touch up chipped paint. Wash and wax all painted surfaces, polish the chrome, and clean the windows.
- Change the oil and bring all fluids up to the recommended level. Replace all burned-out bulbs. Check the air pressure in the tires, including the spare. Correctly mount the spare tire and jack in the trunk.
- Tighten every screw, nut, or bolt that you can find. Lubricate all moving parts such as hinges.
- Clean every piece of junk out of the glove compartment and trunk. Leave only the owner's manual in the glove compartment.
- Locate your title and check the procedures for transferring automobile ownership in your area.

If you decide to sell the car yourself, put a For Sale sign in the window. Make sure that the car is in a place where lots of potential buyers can see it. Put many notices on bulletin boards and include pull-tabs with your phone number. Use electronic bulletin boards if available. Advertise in your local free paper and in the classified section of your local newspaper. In your advertisement, clearly describe your car, especially its better features. Be sure to include your asking price in all advertisements and do all advertising simultaneously. State the times you prefer to receive calls, and be available when people want to inspect your car.

HOW LONG SHOULD YOU KEEP YOUR CAR?

You should keep your car until it is no longer economical to do so. The question is how to determine whether it is economical. You need to be able to determine the cost per mile per month for operating your automobile, and you will need records of your automobile expenses and the number of miles you drive each month.

Keep records of the maintenance performed (and the expense of such maintenance) on your automobile. You should maintain your car according to the manufacturer's scheduled maintenance recommendations. Calculate the monthly expense to maintain your automobile from your maintenance records. Your maintenance and repair records are essential in determining whether your car is still economical to operate.

When to trade in your vehicle is a personal decision. If you maintain accurate maintenance records and calculate the values shown in Table 9-7, you will know the cost of owning and operating your car and whether it is rising or falling. The decision to replace your vehicle should depend in part on a comparison between these costs and the costs that you estimate for a newer model. This comparison, together with your valuation of the convenience and added satisfaction of owning a newer car, should allow you to make an informed decision. If owning a newer vehicle is worth the added costs, then it is time to trade in your car.

A final word about maintaining your car. Good maintenance habits have other benefits and make economic sense. Fulfilling scheduled maintenance requirements will ensure that you fulfill the terms of your warranty. Frequent changing of fluids and filters prevents costly maintenance problems and prolongs the life of your car. Your maintenance record will help you sell your car, because it is of major interest to used car buyers.

SUGGESTED REFERENCES

The following references may be available from your library, credit union, or insurance agent:

The Car Guide. Safety information published by the USAA Foundation.
Consumer Reports Annual Buying Guide. Used car repair information.
Edmund's New Car Prices. Dealer profit information on new cars and options.
Kelley Blue Book. Used car wholesale and retail prices.
NADA Official Used Car Guide. Used car wholesale and retail prices.

The following periodicals often provide information relevant to purchasing an automobile:

Changing Times. Specific model information and comparisons.
Consumer Reports. Especially the April issue.
Motor Trend. Specific model information and comparisons.

10

Automobile Insurance

AN UNFORTUNATE CHARACTERISTIC of the automobile is its ability to inflict injury on other individuals and to destroy or damage property. As the owner or operator of a motor vehicle, you assume responsibility for compensating anyone injured. Most automobile owners cannot afford such payments from their own resources, so automobile liability insurance provides protection against major losses. Almost all states require liability insurance.

The purpose of this chapter is to provide general information about automobile insurance and normative guidelines to help you make an educated insurance decision. We offer money-saving hints (not at the expense of security) along the way. At the end of the chapter we provide a checklist to assist you in your decision.

WHAT IS AUTOMOBILE INSURANCE?

An automobile insurance policy contains contractual agreements that protect you from a collection of risks. Each type of risk corresponds to a specific type of coverage, each with its own premium. The sum of all premiums is the total premium for your policy. You have a great deal of control over your premiums. You can alter the amounts of coverage as well as the deductible (where applicable). As a general rule, the lower the coverage, the lower the premium; however, premiums do *not* increase in proportion to the increase in coverage. For example, increasing liability coverage from $10,000 to $25,000, a 150 percent increase, may only increase your premium by 10 percent. The premium-coverage tradeoff is important. Your primary goal is to ensure that you are adequately protected. Your secondary goal is to find a policy that provides the necessary protection at the lowest cost.

Automobile Insurance Is a Major Budget Category

Automobile insurance is expensive, and it is getting more expensive each year. This is due, in part, to the rapid increase in the costs of medical care as well as an increase in personal-injury lawsuits. Also fueling the rapid rise is the fact that as premiums increase, more people choose to "save" money by not insuring their automobile or by underinsuring. This creates a vicious circle in which we all lose.

Your Car Influences Your Insurance Premium

Since your automobile insurance premium is a major budget expenditure, we recommend that you consider the insurance costs for the car you buy. Car models have different claims records. A car with a good claims record can earn you a significant discount on insurance coverage. Understandably, high-performance sports cars are naturals for high premiums, while station wagons and "family" cars are naturals for low premiums. Also, "safe" cars are sure bets for lower premiums. Safety features such as antilock brakes and air bags cost money, but they may reduce your insurance premium enough to justify their purchase on purely economic grounds; the added lifesaving protection you get could be a "free" bonus. Check with your insurance company before purchasing an automobile to determine if the car merits a discount or a surcharge. Officers can contact USAA to get a copy of *The Car Guide*, which provides safety and claims information for automobiles and light trucks (see references at the end of this chapter). You can also obtain this information from *Consumer Reports*, *Consumer Reports Buying Guide*, and *Motor Trend* magazine.

Shop Around for an Insurance Company

Automobile insurance is an important decision for the average household. You should shop around as carefully for a "good" insurance company as you did for the car you bought. Prices differ so much among companies that it would be unwise not to do some comparative shopping. Doing so, and letting your insurance agent know you are doing so, gives you some leverage in the process.

As you shop around, do not be fooled by extremely low premiums offered by little-known and potentially "shady" companies. Well-known companies are generally well known for good reasons. You want your insurance company to be there when you file a claim. If you move often, you want an insurance company that will cover you as you move from state to state. The company you choose should have experience in the insurance industry. When you compare coverage, make sure you compare similar policies. Take good notes on the specifics and prices of each type of coverage, using the checklist provided at the end of the chapter. *Consumer Reports* magazine occasionally rates automobile insurance companies for their cost and service records.

Understand How the Insurance Company Evaluates You as a Risk

An insurance company evaluates you as a risk in order to determine what premium to charge. They consider your driving record and history of traffic violations (your recent record and history carry greater weight); the year, make, and model of your car; your use of the car; annual mileage; and your age and gender. The company then assigns you to a risk tier: standard, nonstandard, or preferred (some companies may have more or fewer tiers). Some companies reject all high-risk groups outright.

Once they assign you to a tier, the insurance company may further evaluate you as a risk. Some of the very same factors used to place you into a tier are considered again. The company may also consider marital status, location of the car, number of cars insured, other operators and their records, and applicable discounts such as that for antilock brakes. Each insurance company makes a value judgment about who and what they will insure.

By understanding how an insurance company evaluates you, you can strive to lower your premiums by improving any rating criteria within your control. A good driving record is a must. You may consider the cost of a few speeding tickets as the fines you pay, but speeding could cost you thousands of dollars due to higher insurance premiums. If you do not need to use your car to commute to and from work, then don't use it, and save on the premiums. Notice who is listed as the principal driver. If the car is truly a second family car driven by all, list the family member with the best driving record as the principal driver. Whatever you do, however be honest. You can get into serious trouble if you provide false information just to save a few dollars.

THE INSURANCE POLICY: EXPLANATIONS AND RECOMMENDATIONS

The typical automobile insurance policy consists of five basic types of coverage: liability, medical payments, collision, comprehensive, and uninsured motorist. An assortment of optional coverage is also available. The following is an outline of the types of coverage available to you as well as recommendations on each type of coverage. You must temper the recommendations with your own attitudes toward risk.

Liability Coverage

The insurance company pays others for injuries and property damage caused by you, or someone using your car with your permission, as a result of driving negligently. Liability coverage, mandatory in forty-seven states, is the most expensive type of coverage and the most necessary. Individuals injured in an automobile accident often seek compensation for personal injury through the courts. You risk losing current and future assets if you fail to carry adequate liability insurance. Liability coverage is the *last* place you want to skimp. There are two types of liability coverage: bodily injury and property damage.

Bodily Injury Coverage

Bodily injury (BI) coverage covers the medical expenses and associated litigation fees for losses resulting from injury or death in an accident in which you were at fault. Losses can result from medical bills, lost wages, and pain and suffering. Court awards for pain and suffering can be enough to ruin you financially if you are underinsured. You will probably be taken to court if you cause an accident that results in personal injury or death. This is why liability premiums are so high.

There are two types of bodily injury coverage: split-limit (or multiple-limit) and single-limit.

Split-limit Coverage

Split-limit BI coverage pays a maximum amount to each person injured in an accident, subject to a maximum limit per accident. For example, $100,000/$300,000 coverage means that the insurance company will pay up to $100,000 to each person injured, but no more than $300,000 per accident. If a single individual suffers damages of $150,000, the insurance policy would cover only $100,000 of the damages. If you injure six people in an accident, the company would be liable for up to $300,000 worth of damages.

Single-limit Coverage

Single-limit BI coverage pays a maximum single amount per accident, regardless of the number of individuals injured. For example, if you carry a policy with $300,000 bodily injury coverage, one injured person could claim up to $300,000 from your insurance company.

Most states prescribe minimum limits for liability coverage. The typical amount is $25,000/$50,000, a meager sum given our litigious society. A number of states have no-fault laws. This means that an injured party will receive compensation from his or her own insurance company. Since you receive compensation for your injuries, the need for litigation decreases. This should decrease your insurance premiums.

Property Damage Coverage

Property damage (PD) coverage pays the costs of damage to someone else's property. Damage is most often to another car, but coverage includes other types of property. The average state minimums are around $10,000—not enough to cover the cost of a typical new car.

Liability Recommendations

1. Buy as much liability coverage as you can afford. Increasing liability coverage does not raise your premium proportionately. Even if you increase coverage from $50,000 to $300,000 (a 500 percent increase), your premium might only increase by 25 percent.

2. Carry no less than $100,000/$300,000 (split-limit) or $300,000 (single-limit) coverage.

3. Follow recommendations 1 and 2 even if you live in a no-fault state.

4. If you own a home and/or assets worth more than $300,000, consider an umbrella policy that will provide even more protection (see chapter 12).
5. Carry at least $50,000 property damage coverage.
6. Obtain insurance that covers *any* car you legally drive, even if it is a rented or borrowed vehicle.

Medical Payments Coverage

Medical payments coverage pays the medical expenses of individuals injured in your car. This coverage is normally optional in states without no-fault laws and ranges from $1,000 to $100,000 per person.

Most people already have medical and hospital insurance of some sort and may choose to forgo this duplicate coverage. Military families have hospital benefits, but remember that all passengers may not be immediate family members. A small amount of additional coverage may make sense, because medical payments coverage often includes a funeral benefit.

States with no-fault laws may require you to carry personal injury protection (PIP) coverage. This is a more comprehensive form of medical payments coverage that covers medical bills, lost wages, and some funeral expenses for injuries to you or any passenger regardless of who is at fault. Some states require a minimum amount of PIP, usually around $10,000, but amounts vary by state.

Medical Payments Recommendations

1. Purchase a minimum of $5,000 in medical payments coverage even if you have a good health insurance policy for yourself and your family. This will help cover any medical expenses for non–family members.
2. If your state requires PIP, purchase $10,000 coverage (or the state minimum if it exceeds $10,000).
3. If your state requires PIP coverage and your state's no-fault rules allow you to "coordinate benefits" with your health insurance policy, do so; you may be able to save a significant amount of the PIP premium. By coordinating benefits you position your health insurance policy as the "primary" policy. In other words, you would seek reimbursement from your health insurance company before applying to your auto insurer.
4. Obtain insurance that covers you if you are injured while using someone else's car.

Collision Coverage

Collision coverage pays for physical damage to your car regardless of who caused the damage. It accounts for approximately 30 percent of the total insurance premium on a new car and carries a deductible (an amount you must pay before the coverage becomes effective). You choose the size of the deductible, which normally ranges from $50 to $1,000; the higher the deductible, the lower the premium. Increasing your deductible from $200 to $500 or $1,000 can save you anywhere from 25 percent to 40 percent on your premium. You can bank the savings in an interest-bearing investment and use the savings to pay the deductible if you have an accident. Insurance is too expensive to file claims for small losses. A higher deductible removes the temptation to claim small losses, but remember that you must report all accidents to your insurer.

The *Kelley Blue Book* value of your car (which you can get from your insurance company or bank) is the maximum insurance settlement possible on your car. For cars with a low resale value, collision coverage is a waste of money. For cars that are four to five years old, the decision to carry collision coverage depends on the risk you are willing to bear. You should seriously consider dropping collision coverage on low-value cars that are six years old or older. If you borrowed to purchase your vehicle, the "owner" (your bank or financial institution) may require collision coverage because they hold the title.

Collision Recommendations

1. Carry collision on cars with substantial "blue book" value, but choose the highest deductible you can afford.
2. Drop collision coverage altogether on old, low-value cars.
3. If you financed your vehicle, check with your financial institution before canceling your collision insurance.

Comprehensive Coverage

Comprehensive coverage reimburses you for damage caused by mishaps other than a crash, including vandalism, theft, falling objects, flooding, glass breakage, and collisions with animals. It carries a deductible that normally ranges from $50 to $1,000; for a little extra premium, you can get full glass damage coverage with no deductible.

Comprehensive Recommendations

1. Choose the highest deductible you can afford.
2. Cancel coverage on cars with low resale value.
3. If you financed your vehicle, check with your financial institution before canceling your comprehensive insurance.

Uninsured Motorist Coverage

Uninsured motorist coverage (UIM) protects you and your passengers from uninsured motorists and hit-and-run drivers and is especially important in states without no-fault laws. UIM coverage reimburses you for bodily injury or death in accidents where the uninsured motorist is liable. It covers payments for medical expenses, losses due to permanent disability or death, loss of income, and any other damages entitled by state law. It does not reimburse you for property damages.

Minimum coverage offered by insurance companies normally coincides with state minimums required for liability coverage. Although UIM is a normal part of every insurance policy, you may generally elect to reject it. You must do so in writing, however. UIM premiums are on the rise because increasing numbers of drivers violate state laws and do not carry insurance. Therefore, the probability of having an accident with an uninsured motorist rises, which forces premiums up.

There is a newer category of coverage called *underinsured motorist coverage (UNM)*. UNM coverage applies to settlements when you have an accident with another driver who is at fault but whose insurance coverage limits are unable to compensate you for your damages. UNM coverage kicks in where the other party's coverage stops. You can buy coverage limits similar to those available for liability. UNM coverage may be a separate coverage with its own premium or it may be part of the UIM coverage. State law determines what constitutes a UNM loss and under what conditions you will receive payment.

UIM/UNM Recommendations

1. Carry UIM in an amount comparable with your bodily injury liability coverage.
2. Carry UIM coverage unless you are in a state with outstanding no-fault laws or you have an excellent medical insurance policy for yourself and your family.
3. Check with your insurance company to determine if your UIM coverage includes UNM coverage; if not, ask for it.
4. Check to see if UNM coverage pays only if your policy exceeds the liability coverage of the underinsured motorist, or if it pays for damages in excess (up to your limit) of the underinsured motorist's coverage.
5. Check with your insurance company each time you move to determine the requirements of your new state.

Rental Car Coverage

Before renting an automobile, see if your insurance company provides coverage. Coverage usually extends to any automobile you temporarily drive, but check to make sure. Your company may not cover renting classic automobiles or other expensive models. Also make sure you have adequate coverage for the state where you are renting, since mandatory coverage amounts vary substantially from state to state. If you damage a rental vehicle, the rental company usually charges you for the rental revenue they lose while repairing the vehicle.

Rental Car Recommendations

1. Make sure your auto insurance applies to rental cars, to include any rental revenue you may owe.
2. Check with your credit card company to see if your card covers the collision damage on a rental car when you pay with their card. If it does, then do not carry rental car insurance and always rent with that credit card.
3. When in doubt, purchase the rental car insurance.

Leased Automobile Coverage

Leasing an automobile is becoming a popular alternative to purchasing. Insurance coverage for your leased vehicle is similar to insurance for a vehicle you own, with one major exception. If your leased vehicle is stolen or totaled, most leasing companies consider this an early termination. You will generally owe the lessor more than your insurance company allows, due to depreciation of the leased vehicle. You should consider carrying "gap insurance" or "total loss protection" to cover the difference between what your insurance company would normally pay and the amount you would actually owe to the lessor.

Optional Coverage

Many optional coverages duplicate protection you already have from other sources. One way to save money is to avoid purchasing unnecessary options. There are many options, but we will discuss only the more prominent ones. If you have adequate personal property, health, and life insurance policies, you can reject any options related to these risk categories. If you need more life insurance, buy more life insurance; do not sign up for limited life insurance on your automobile insurance policy.

Rental Reimbursement
The insurance company pays a certain amount per day, for a specified number of days, toward the renting of a car while yours is being repaired after an accident. Reimbursement is normally up to $30 a day. If you own more than one car, or if alternate transportation means are available (company car, local mass transit), do not select this coverage.

Towing and Labor Coverage
The insurance company pays the cost of towing your car to a repair shop and pays for any immediate labor involved. If you are a member of an auto club that already provides this service, you should not select this coverage. Also, read the fine print. Be sure you understand the limits of the towing arrangement and exactly what labor costs are reimbursable.

AUTOMOBILE INSURANCE CHECKLIST

This checklist provides you with a list of most possible coverage categories as well as other areas of importance when shopping for insurance. Use this list to construct a spreadsheet for comparing insurance companies.

COVERAGE   **COST**

State-required minimums

    Bodily injury liability:
    Property damage liability:
    Personal injury protection:
    Uninsured motorist:
    Other:

Desired levels of coverage

    Bodily injury liability:
    Property damage liability:
    Personal injury protection:
    Uninsured motorist:
    Underinsured motorist:
    Medical payments:
    Collision:
        a. $100 deductible:
        b. $250 deductible:
        c. $500 deductible:
    Comprehensive:
        a. $ 50 deductible:
        b. $100 deductible:
        c. $250 deductible:
        d. $500 deductible:
    Towing and labor:
    Rental reimbursement:

Miscellaneous charges

    Membership fee:
    Others:

AUTOMOBILE INSURANCE CHECKLIST
(continued)

COVERAGE   **COST**

Service Record

    Claims:
        Average handling time:
        Bureaucratic red tape:
        Settlement over disagreements on dollar amounts:
        In-house estimate service or number of estimates required:
        Assignment of fault:
        Value of car:
    Billing:
    Agent availability:
        Toll-free number:
    Accident forgiveness program:
        After how many years?
    Changing coverage:
    Rate increases:
    Explanation of protection benefits:
    Will you be dropped?
        Cancellation standards:
        Nonrenewal standards:
        What moves you into higher risk tiers?
        What brings you down from higher risk tiers?
    Are rental cars also covered?

Special Discounts

    Annual mileage:
    Antitheft:
        Active devices:
        Passive devices:
        Military post:
        Etched windows:
        Other:
    Antilock brakes:
    Air bag:
    Automatic seat belts:
    Children at military academies:
    Children away at school:
    Children on active military duty:
    Certified driver education:

AUTOMOBILE INSURANCE CHECKLIST
(continued)

COVERAGE   **COST**

Special Discounts (continued)

    Good driver:
    Good student:
    Multicar:
    Multipolicy:
    Nonsmoker:
    Professional (doctor, lawyer):
    Senior driver:

Record with state agencies

    Department of Insurance
    Department of Consumer Affairs

Recommendations from family and friends

SUGGESTED REFERENCES

The following references are available from the USAA Foundation, telephone (800) 531-8857 or -8080.

    Auto Insurance: Getting the Best Value
    Automobile Insurance
    Encompassing Your Insurance Needs
    The USAA Car Guide

Additional References:

    Consumer Reports
    Consumer Reports Buying Guide
    Motor Trend Magazine

11

Housing

ONE OF THE most important decisions military families make during a permanent-change-of-station (PCS) move is where to live at the new duty station. In recent years, the Department of Defense has eased the strain of moves on families with such policies as permissive temporary duty (TDY) for house-hunting trips. Nevertheless, this major question must still be answered every three or four years: "Where should we live?"

There are three basic options: Military families can live in quarters provided by the government; they can rent housing on the local economy; or they can buy a house. The factors that influence this decision are not entirely financially motivated, but the choice is often constrained by finances.

This chapter discusses some of the housing problems faced by military families and suggests a way of analyzing housing alternatives. Because determining where you live is ultimately a personal decision, our guidelines must be adapted to fit your particular situation. This chapter provides an outline of the primary considerations for most military families in selecting their housing.

THE GENERAL APPROACH

The first step is to determine whether there is any choice to make. Depending on the post to which you are being assigned, you may find one of two extremes: You may be required to live on post, or you may be forced to live off post because no government quarters are available. Check with the local housing office at your new duty station. They will have the most current information.

If you are not required to live in government quarters, then your family must make a decision. Start by making a "wish list" of desirable housing attributes. List your objectives in order of importance: low maintenance costs, closeness to community facilities, a good school system, low taxes, convenient public transportation, a quiet neighborhood, and so on. To make an informed housing decision, you must first understand your family's needs and preferences.

Next, get an idea of the alternatives available. Ask the housing office of your gaining command about the availability of housing, both government provided and on the local economy. If you are going overseas, your options will probably be limited to government quarters or renting on the local economy. Likely sources of information include your sponsor, the local chamber of commerce, a local newspaper (particularly the Sunday edition), real estate agents, and friends stationed at your new location.

Now, determine your housing budget. You must consider your VHA and BAQ allowances, but don't stop there. Most American homeowners budget 30 to 35 percent of their after-tax household income toward their mortgage. VHA plus BAQ will often be significantly less than that amount. The amount that you decide is appropriate will depend on the amounts you must budget for transportation, entertainment, investment, maintenance, and other budget categories. Refer to chapter 4 for help with the budgeting process.

At this point you are ready to compare the housing budget against the available alternatives. First, consider the civilian versus government options. Comparing the local rental market to what is available on post should be rather straightforward. The local housing office should have information on items like square footage of quarters, number of bedrooms and bathrooms, and appliances; this will allow an easy comparison with local rentals. To live in government quarters is essentially to rent from the government, and to pay your BAQ and VHA for rent plus utilities. Usually the local rental market will give you greater variety to choose from, but often at additional costs. In weighing your decision, make sure you properly evaluate costs of commuting (both time and gas) and costs of utilities, which together are minimal when living in government quarters. Consider nonfinancial aspects of the choice as well, such as your ability to choose neighbors, your sense of security in the neighborhood, the flexibility of departure dates due to military necessity, responsiveness of maintenance workers, and many other considerations.

Comparing the rental versus purchase decision is a bit more complicated but starts with the same considerations of desired housing attributes and nonfinancial factors. The latter part of this chapter deals with these aspects in detail.

Following this general approach, you can accommodate your housing needs. However, you must have detailed knowledge of each of your options in order to make an accurate assessment. The sections that follow provide an outline of the data you need to gather, the places to look for it, and how to incorporate this information into your decision process. Because the civilian versus government quarters option has already been fully discussed, the remainder of the chapter is devoted to the rent versus buy decision for off-post housing.

RENTING

Some people think money spent on rent is "lost money"—you pay the rent and at the end of the contracted period you have nothing. This view is incorrect. Rent is payment for the purchase of housing services. These services may also be acquired through the purchase of a house, which implicitly combines the acquisition of housing services with an investment decision.

The decision to rent should be made after a careful review of total costs and family goals. As we mentioned above, owning your home almost always costs more each month than renting an equivalent dwelling. Many families decide to buy in the expectation that they will make money when they sell the home, in effect earning a return on the extra spending. You should be aware, however, that homeowners do not always make money when they sell, due to the risk inherent in real estate investments. Further, you may decide to rent in order to use possible savings toward other financial obligations.

Generally, renting a dwelling is more advantageous than buying that type of dwelling if the following conditions hold:

1. You do not have the cash for the down payment and the closing costs required when you buy (or you do not wish to tie up your liquid reserves in a home for three or four years).
2. You don't want to incur a large mortgage debt.
3. You want lighter responsibilities regarding housing and do not wish to concern yourself and your family with the worries caused by taxes, utilities, maintenance, insurance, need to resell, and so forth.
4. You prefer to spend a larger portion of your income on other priorities, such as cars, travel, or entertainment.
5. You anticipate being at your new station for only a few years, or you do not believe local housing prices will rise during the period you anticipate owning the house.
6. You desire the amenities (swimming pool, tennis courts) readily available in some rental units.
8. You are not familiar with the area or do not think it is an attractive place to own property.

Checklist for Renters

At the end of this chapter we present a checklist for buyers. Much of the investigation a buyer should perform is also applicable to a renter, particularly the topics listed under Neighborhood. In addition, renters should be sure that they and their landlords agree *in writing* to the following details:

1. Who pays for utilities (water, gas, oil, electricity, cable, garbage collection)?
2. Who pays for the repairs that become necessary?
3. Is the rent fixed or can it be suddenly increased after you have moved in?
4. Do you have the right to sublet?

5. To what extent are you liable for damages to the dwelling or surrounding property?
6. Is a deposit required, what does it cover, how and when will you get it back, and do you accrue interest on it?
7. Who pays for taxes and the insurance covering damage to the dwelling? What are the limits?
8. Are children, pets, pianos, waterbeds, child-care providers allowed?
9. Can you alter the dwelling? If so, do the improvements (added cabinets, toolshed) become the landlord's property, and will the landlord reimburse you for repairs and improvements?
10. Does the lease give the landlord unrestricted access to the property at any time?
11. Can the landlord put the property on continual public exhibition to prospective renters or buyers? (You should try to limit this to thirty days before you vacate.)
12. What is the role of the real estate agent, if applicable, and who pays the fees?
13. Are there any "special fees," such as a health board fee when you vacate and have owned a pet, a cleaning fee, a general maintenance fee, a renter's fee, a security guard fee, a community assessment fee, a delivery fee, or a sidewalk fee?
14. What are the parking, guest, and storage restrictions? Are there fees attached to these restrictions?
15. Who specifically owns the dwelling, and what is that person's address and telephone number? Who is his legal representative? (If nothing else, this question shows that you have an interest in the proper management of the dwelling and should help to minimize potential "shady" actions by the landlord.)
16. What type of renter restrictions—age, marital status, income, race, and occupation—are there? Because of the antidiscrimination laws, this question may have to be asked in a number of different ways in order to get a true picture.
17. What are the restrictions on appliances? Do you have to use existing appliances such as washer, dryer, and refrigerator, or can you bring in your own? How do any future purchases or repairs of appliances by your landlord affect your rent?
18. Is there an additional cost for storage facilities?
19. Are there any restrictions in the use of utilities? (Some landlords can control the amount of heat and hot water to a specific dwelling.)
20. How much notice must be given before moving, and are there any financial penalties?
21. Finally, is a military clause included in your contract releasing you from your lease in the event of transfer or other reason? A servicemember should never sign a lease unless it includes a military clause such as the following example:

> In the event the Tenant or spouse is or hereafter becomes a member of the United States Armed Forces, the Tenant may terminate this lease on thirty days' written notice to the Landlord in any of the following events:

      a.   If the Tenant or spouse received permanent-change-of-station orders to depart from the area where the premises are located.
      b.   If the Tenant or spouse is relieved from active duty.
      c.   If the Tenant or spouse has leased the property prior to arrival in the area and the orders are changed to a different area prior to occupancy of the property.
      d.   If the Tenant or spouse is assigned government quarters.

Rents due will be prorated if departure occurs during the middle of a month.

Be sure all the rental details are in writing; do not rely on verbal promises. In addition, it is wise to check with former tenants or other people living in the neighborhood about the landlord's reputation. Calls to the local chamber of commerce, Realtors Association, and the consumer affairs office may save you some future headaches. The required visit to your station housing office will also help you identify questionable landlords. Finally, before you sign the lease, and (even better) before agreeing to terms verbally, you may take a draft of the lease document to your legal assistance officer for review. This is a free, yet valuable, service.

In summary, if the cost of owning a house in your new location is beyond the limits you can or wish to spend each month, renting may be your best alternative. Even if you do have the financial resources, if you anticipate that the appreciation of homes in your new locale will not be sufficient to offset the closing costs associated with ownership (discussed in the next section) and provide a reasonable return on your down payment, renting may be for you. Definitely keep this last point in mind: Home values can go down as well as up.

Renting provides the most flexible alternative if government quarters are not available or do not meet the housing goals of your family. Especially if you expect a four-year tour of duty, renting for a year provides a good opportunity to learn about the area firsthand before committing yourself to buying. Do not avoid renting because you feel compelled to buy in order to benefit from recent appreciation. These areas may be in for a decline, similar to those experienced by the northeastern real estate market in the late 1980s and early 1990s. Quick profits in real estate are unlikely. Buying a home requires a significant investment of time, effort, and careful financial analysis.

BUYING

A home is the biggest single purchase most people make in a lifetime, so a great deal of thought and effort should precede any decision to buy. The information in this section will prove to be very helpful in deciding whether buying is the right decision for you and your family. If you buy, this chapter will also explain the process to you.

Real estate agents expect to sell a house to a buyer after showing them houses for an average of four days. Their motivation is to get as large a commission as possible in the shortest possible time period. They often will encourage you to make compromises on your goals or expectations with respect to price. For this reason, it is critical that you and your family determine beforehand how much house you can afford and what housing attributes you desire. It is helpful to prioritize your needs and wants in advance so that you can make prudent adjustments if necessary.

How Much House Can I Afford?

Early in the home-buying process, it is important to get a realistic sense of how much house you can afford. An acre of land, a two-car garage, and a Jacuzzi in the master bedroom sound wonderful, but can you really afford them? The worksheet in Table 11-1 provides a simple method for estimating how much you can afford to spend on a house based on the amount of money you wish to budget for monthly housing expenses.

First, figure your ability to make a down payment. Total your liquid assets and liabilities, and deduct an amount for an emergency cash fund (about two months' income) from the difference. What remains is the amount of money you have available for a down payment and closing costs.*

Next, examine the monthly home ownership expenses to see what you can afford in the way of a monthly mortgage payment. From your monthly budget (see chapter 4), find the amount you can afford or desire to spend on housing each month. (If you received advance pay for the move, remember to decrease your monthly income by the amount to repay the government.) From this amount, subtract the necessary expenses associated with home ownership. (Property tax and utilities figures are available from your real estate agent. Your insurance company can provide insurance costs. You or a reputable repair contractor can make estimates on maintenance costs.) The monthly amount that remains is the amount you can afford to pay in mortgage payments (principal plus interest).

Now you are ready to calculate the most expensive house you can afford. Using the current interest rate available for a thirty-year, fixed-rate mortgage, read down that column in Table 11-2. Find the number closest to the amount you calculated for principal and interest. Read across that row to the leftmost column to find the largest mortgage you can afford to repay. For example; if you calculated $850 per month available for principal and interest in Table 11-1, and interest rates are approximately 8.5 percent, then you could afford to repay a mortgage of $110,000. This is the largest mortgage that you can afford, not the most expensive house. Subtract 5 to 8 percent of the mortgage amount as an estimate of the closing costs, then add back in the amount available for a down payment and closing costs that you calculated above. The result is the maximum house price you can afford. Continuing our example, if you assumed

---

* Closing costs, which are fees for inspections, legal work, and so on, are explained in a subsequent section of this chapter.

TABLE 11-1
Worksheet — How Much House Can I Afford?

Liquid assets	
Cash	_____
Savings	_____
Stocks	_____
Bonds	_____
Mutual funds	_____
Life ins. cash value	_____
Other	_____
TOTAL ASSETS	_____
Liabilities	
Credit card balances	_____
Loans	_____
Other debts	_____
TOTAL LIABILITIES	− _____
Emergency fund	− _____
Total available for down payment and closing costs	= _____
Monthly budget for housing	− _____
Monthly home ownership expenses	
Maintenance	_____
Insurance	_____
Property taxes	_____
Utilities	_____
Other	_____
TOTAL EXPENSES	− _____
Amount remaining for monthly mortgage payment (principal & interest)	= _____
Max. mortgage loan amount (see Table 11-2)	= _____
Closing costs (estimate 5 to 8% of max. mortgage)	− _____
Amount available for down payment plus closing costs	+ _____
HOUSE PRICE You Can Afford	= _____

that closing costs will amount to approximately 6 percent of the mortgage amount, you would estimate the costs to be $6,600 ($110,000 x .06). If your analysis of your costs and liabilities in Table 11-1 showed you had $20,000 available for a down payment and closing costs, you could afford to purchase a house costing no more than $123,400. You would then compare this figure with home prices in your area to see if you can satisfy your housing desires.

Using this method, you will have a financially sound estimate of the home you can afford based on your actual budget. Banks, however, do not follow the same approach and may tell you that you can afford much more or less than you calculated. To get an idea of a bank's typical calculation for mortgage amounts, do the following:

1. Take the figure you have for your total gross monthly income (before taxes, allotments, and deductions) from your budget and multiply this amount by 0.28 (28 percent). This is the amount a bank or mortgage company will allow for your mortgage payment (by mortgage payment we always mean the principal, interest, taxes, and insurance).

2. Next, compute the total amount of your other monthly debt payments, including car loans, credit card payments, and child support or alimony payments. Add this figure to the figure you calculated in paragraph one. This combined total should not exceed 36 percent of your total gross monthly income. If it does, you may have to reduce the mortgage payment accordingly.

The fact that your numbers and the bank's numbers may disagree does not mean that you have wasted your time. Your figures represent your own financial situation and budget priorities. The bank's figures are based on historical probabilities of default. Trust your own figures and do not be tempted into signing a large mortgage simply because a bank offers it to you. If a bank offers you a lesser amount than you think you would like, however, consider shopping around for other lenders, readjusting your housing priorities, or reconsidering the rental option.

Finding the Right Home to Buy

Once you have determined the maximum house price you can afford, you can start your search for the right home. Use the buyer's checklist at the end of this chapter to establish your priorities. Your first decision is whether to look for a house on your own or use the services of a real estate broker. If you are very familiar with the local area, have a good idea of what you are looking for, have a long lead time, and are familiar with real estate laws and the house-buying procedure, you may do well conducting the search on your own.

Most people believe that houses that are not listed with a real estate agent (that is, those offered for sale by owners) are cheaper, since the real estate commission will not be included in the sale price. (This assumes that sellers decide how much they want for their homes and add the amount of the commission to the desired price.)

TABLE 11-2
Monthly Principal and Interest Payments on a 30-Year Mortgage

AMOUNT MORTGAGED	\\\\ INTEREST RATE												
	6.0%	6.5%	7.0%	7.5%	8.0%	8.5%	9.0%	9.5%	10.0%	10.5%	11.0%	11.5%	12.0%
$50,000	$300	$316	$333	$350	$367	$384	$402	$420	$439	$457	$476	$495	$514
$60,000	$360	$379	$399	$420	$440	$461	$483	$505	$527	$549	$571	$594	$617
$70,000	$420	$442	$466	$489	$514	$538	$563	$589	$614	$640	$667	$693	$720
$80,000	$480	$506	$532	$559	$587	$615	$644	$673	$702	$732	$762	$792	$823
$90,000	$540	$569	$599	$629	$660	$692	$724	$757	$790	$823	$857	$891	$926
$100,000	$600	$632	$665	$699	$734	$769	$805	$841	$878	$915	$952	$990	$1,029
$110,000	$660	$695	$732	$769	$807	$846	$885	$925	$965	$1,006	$1,048	$1,089	$1,131
$120,000	$719	$758	$798	$839	$881	$923	$966	$1,009	$1,053	$1,098	$1,143	$1,188	$1,234
$130,000	$779	$822	$865	$909	$954	$1,000	$1,046	$1,093	$1,141	$1,189	$1,238	$1,287	$1,337
$140,000	$839	$885	$931	$979	$1,027	$1,076	$1,126	$1,177	$1,229	$1,281	$1,333	$1,386	$1,440
$150,000	$899	$948	$998	$1,049	$1,101	$1,153	$1,207	$1,261	$1,316	$1,372	$1,428	$1,485	$1,543
$160,000	$959	$1,011	$1,064	$1,119	$1,174	$1,230	$1,287	$1,345	$1,404	$1,464	$1,524	$1,584	$1,646
$170,000	$1,019	$1,075	$1,131	$1,189	$1,247	$1,307	$1,368	$1,429	$1,492	$1,555	$1,619	$1,683	$1,749
$180,000	$1,079	$1,138	$1,198	$1,259	$1,321	$1,384	$1,448	$1,514	$1,580	$1,647	$1,714	$1,783	$1,852
$190,000	$1,139	$1,201	$1,264	$1,329	$1,394	$1,461	$1,529	$1,598	$1,667	$1,738	$1,809	$1,882	$1,954
$200,000	$1,199	$1,264	$1,331	$1,398	$1,468	$1,538	$1,609	$1,682	$1,755	$1,829	$1,905	$1,981	$2,057
$210,000	$1,259	$1,327	$1,397	$1,468	$1,541	$1,615	$1,690	$1,766	$1,843	$1,921	$2,000	$2,080	$2,160
$220,000	$1,319	$1,391	$1,464	$1,538	$1,614	$1,692	$1,770	$1,850	$1,931	$2,012	$2,095	$2,179	$2,263
$230,000	$1,379	$1,454	$1,530	$1,608	$1,688	$1,769	$1,851	$1,934	$2,018	$2,104	$2,190	$2,278	$2,366
$240,000	$1,439	$1,517	$1,597	$1,678	$1,761	$1,845	$1,931	$2,018	$2,106	$2,195	$2,286	$2,377	$2,469

Going alone does not guarantee that you will save money, however. If the house is listed by an agent and you want to buy it, the price you pay will include the commission whether you use the services of an agent or not. (As we discuss later, the seller actually pays the commission from the proceeds of the sale.)

On the other hand, if you are not familiar with your new area, and time is of the essence, you may want to provide a listing of your housing needs to real estate agents and let them compile a group of homes that meet your criteria. You may want to tell the real estate agent that you want a house costing about 90 percent of the maximum you can afford. Whatever price you tell the broker will most likely become the least expensive house they will show you. After all, they get paid a percentage of the sale price, so the more expensive the house, the better it is for them, even if it may not be better for you.

During normal economic times, when there is no backlog of loan applications and inspection appointments, you should plan to visit your new station sixty to ninety days before your anticipated relocation date. If necessary, use the permissive TDY allowance (authorized to servicemembers just about to PCS for the purpose of locating housing at a new duty station). Also, certain expenses associated with your move, including house- and apartment-hunting trips, are deductible from your income taxes as a moving-related expense if you itemize deductions. These expenses are deductible only up to a certain amount during the year of your move, but any excess can be added to the purchase price of your house (called the basis for tax purposes), reducing the amount of capital gain tax you owe in the future if you sell the house for more than you pay for it.

When you make your house-hunting trip, take a few items with you. A street map will help orient you to the local area and to the location of the house in relation to schools, fire department, shopping, transportation, and your new job. Obviously, you should have a pen and paper. Experienced house hunters often use paper outlined in a matrix fashion, with the features they want (garage, bedrooms, and so on) listed vertically and the houses listed horizontally. Keeping this information on one or two sheets of paper makes comparison easier when decision time arrives.

Before you leave home, measure any oversize furniture. With this information and a tape measure, you will be able to determine if it will fit in a prospective house. A flashlight will be handy for looking into areas such as cellars, crawl spaces, and attics.

Although you will probably want to employ the services of an inspector for the house you ultimately choose, in your early searching you can note obvious and critical flaws. To check the electrical system, carry a night light and plug it into several outlets in different rooms in the house. If the light does not work in every outlet, you can anticipate electrical problems.

After you look at five or six houses, many of the features start to blend together. As an aid to your memory, in addition to the matrix outline, it may be a good idea to carry an instant camera during your trip. Two or three pictures of key features of each house will prove invaluable as you make a final decision at the end of a long and tiring search.

When viewing a home, try to visit during bright daylight hours. During times of limited visibility, or at the end of a tiring day, your imagination may turn the "handyman fixer-up" special into your dream house. Always go back to view the house one more time before you make a final decision. Also, if the house is not vacant, ask to move furniture to see the condition of walls and floors, particularly if the furniture looks out of place.

The Role of the Real Estate Agent

In the past, the process of listing a house with a Multiple Listing Service (MLS) made any real estate agent who showed the house a subagent of the listing company. This meant that the real estate agent always worked for the seller and never for the buyer. This system is currently evolving to one in which you will be able to choose to work with a buyer's agent (i.e., an agent who works for you and must represent your interests) or a seller's agent (i.e., an agent who represents the seller even though the agent is showing you a number of houses). Which type of agent you should choose will depend on your circumstances and the stipulations of the local laws governing these relationships. Whatever relationship you choose to establish, however, you should clearly understand whom "your" agent represents and what that implies.

A buyer's agent has the fiduciary responsibility to represent the buyer. This normally means that the agent must show all properties that may meet the buyer's needs, including properties being sold by owners and other properties not listed in the MLS. Moreover, the agent will be expected to offer advice on the value of property and on your negotiations with the seller and/or his agent. The sticking point in using a buyer's agent is the source of the agent's compensation. Compensation options include an hourly rate, a fixed or flat fee, a percentage of the sales price, or in the case of houses listed in the MLS, a portion of the commission fees paid by the seller to the listing agency. The use of any of the first three compensation options may increase your purchase costs for houses listed with a real estate agency because the seller is obligated to pay a set commission to the listing agency. Also, be aware that the Department of Veterans Affairs will not permit you to include any sales fees you pay to a buyer's agent as part of the acquisition cost when determining the mortgage amount that it will insure.

If the real estate agent with whom you are working is a seller's agent, the agent works for the seller, not you. The seller is considered to be the "client" and the buyer is the "customer." The seller agrees to list property with a firm that serves as the seller's agent to market the property. In return for finding a buyer, the agent receives a commission from the seller. The services offered are of considerable benefit to both the seller and the buyer—just remember that the agent is working for the seller first. If you reveal privileged information to a seller's agent (for example, how much higher you are willing to bid on a home), the agent is required by law to pass this information along to the seller. Simply ignoring this warning could turn out to be (monetarily) the most costly mistake you ever make.

What attributes should you be looking for in a real estate agent of either type?

First of all, the agent should be well acquainted with the local real estate market. The ability to understand your family's needs and know which properties in the area fit them is essential. In addition to being able to provide an independent check on your estimate of what you can afford to buy, the real estate agent should be familiar with different types of mortgages available. Check the qualifications of your real estate agent. Not all agents are professional Realtors. The professionals normally are members of the National Association of Realtors, meeting certain qualifications and abiding by a code of ethics.

Probably the best means of finding an agent is to ask for referrals from friends or associates in the area. A satisfied customer is usually the best reference. You want an agent who will take the time to learn your family's needs and show you as many properties as necessary to meet those needs. If you cannot find any word-of-mouth testimonials, contact the local Board of Realtors and ask for the names of former Realtors of the Year or, if you are seeking a buyer's agent, for the names of real estate firms that offer such services. Realtors of the Year make good candidates because they are individuals who have distinguished themselves professionally or have demonstrated support for the community through civic activity. You might also consider visiting an open house hosted by a real estate agency. This will give you an opportunity to meet several Realtors and evaluate their abilities to make you feel comfortable during this time-consuming and emotionally draining period.

Support services offered by real estate firms might include computerized mortgage search capabilities and access to the local MLS. The mortgage search support can make the administrative hassles of applying for your mortgage easier, but it does not guarantee the lowest mortgage rate available. Mortgages are like any other commodity—you should always comparison-shop. The MLS is a computerized network with a complete listing of all homes offered for sale in the area through the agents who use the service. It does not include homes for sale by owners, or by sellers requesting an exclusive office listing, or homes offered by real estate firms that are not members of the MLS. Using the MLS, the broker can quickly identify listed houses that meet your family's need.

A better understanding of how real estate firms earn their commission will give you additional insight into the home-buying process. The firm that handles the sale receives a commission of approximately 6 percent (the actual commission is negotiated) of the selling price of the house, if the firm both lists (secures the client and places the property on the market) *and* sells the property. If the sale is by an agent from another firm, the commission is usually split fifty-fifty between the two firms. This explains why an agent will probably initially show you properties listed by the agent's own firm. If you note this trend and the houses are not compatible with your needs, let the agent know. If you suspect you are not getting a complete picture of all the homes available in your area, find another agent.

The commission system also raises issues of dual agency when using a buyer's agent. Even if you hire a buyer's agent, that agent must act as a seller's agent for any properties listed with the agent's firm. In these cases, the agent faces the dilemma of dual agency—the obligation to simultaneously serve the interests of both the buyer and the seller. When this situation arises, the agent is obligated to declare his or her dual agency. You then have the choice of allowing the agent to serve in this capacity or of finding a buyer's agent from another firm.

We must reiterate the importance of understanding the role the agent plays in the process of buying a home and how that role varies with the type of agent. A buyer's agent is your representative, and a seller's agent is the seller's. *Never* tell a seller's agent you will probably pay higher than your first offer or any subsequent offers. Seller's agents are required by law, at the risk of losing their license, to pass such information on to the seller. Wait until the seller refuses your offer before you volunteer that you are willing to spend more, no matter how comfortable you feel with the seller's agent. The law and the profit motive are both on the agent's side—the more you pay, the more money the agent earns in commission.

Which type of agent should you use? At this time, seller's agents are more prevalent and, therefore, easier to find. Also, with a seller's agent you don't have to include agent fees when estimating closing costs—the seller's agent's fee is paid by the seller. However, a seller's agent will not be working for you. As a rule, the less experience you have with purchasing a house and the less familiar you are with an area, the greater is the value of hiring a buyer's agent.

More about Closing Costs

In addition to a down payment—normally 5 to 20 percent of the purchase price—prospective home buyers will encounter other expenses. These expenses, commonly referred to as closing costs, range from a bank's loan application fee to an attorney's fee for information about the zoning of the property. A brief description of these costs, and estimates of each based on a $100,000 house, follow; more expensive homes will have higher closing costs. (Note: Certain costs can be negotiated. Always inquire as to whether negotiation is possible.)

Appraisal
To ensure you are paying a fair market price for property, lending institutions require an appraisal of the property by a third party. The appraisal is usually based on what comparable houses have sold for recently, the current cost to build the same type of house, or the capitalized value of the rental income that the house produces. (The capitalization rate is a multiple of the annual rent. For example, if comparable houses rent for $10,000 per year and sell for $100,000, then their capitalization rate is 10. Using the capitalization rate is a quick way to get a rough estimate of the value of the house.) Even though you pay for the appraisal, the lender requiring it probably will give you a copy only if you ask for it. So ask for it. The price ranges from $150 to $300.

Attorney's Fee (Lender's)
Financial lenders will likely require you to pay for the services of the attorney who presides over the closing proceedings, looking out for the mortgage lender's interest. Fees will be based on the price of the house and usually range from $400 to $800.

Attorney's Fee (Yours)
In addition to the lender's attorney, you will probably need an attorney to handle sticky phases of the purchase, such as the purchase-and-sale agreement and closing. Your attorney will coordinate all required activities associated with your house purchase, including preparing and reviewing contracts, filing necessary documents with local government agencies, and negotiating on your behalf with the seller or seller's attorney. A typical fee range would be $300 to $600.

House Inspection
A good house inspection can help you avoid a "lemon" and may aid in negotiating a lower price. The inspector will make sure you are aware of structural flaws in the property. Areas of concern for older homes include the condition of the roof, gutters and drain spouts, water pipes, furnaces, water heater, central climate control unit, storm windows, insulation, and electrical wiring. Recommendations from a real estate agent (they want your business again when you sell, so they have a long-term interest) or friends about a reputable inspector are crucial, particularly if the property is old. Some inspectors may be part of a professional organization. Call the American Society of Home Inspectors in Arlington, Virginia, for information on members servicing your area. These inspectors are certified by examination, which helps establish their credibility. You can expect to pay between $100 and $300. Note that this inspection is only for structural flaws, *not* appearance flaws (e.g., the walls need a good coat of paint). You should ask the engineering firm conducting the inspection what their policy will be if you discover a major structural flaw that they missed—who is liable to fix the damage.

A good inspection is well worth the money. Make sure that you are present and take copious notes, since the inspector can "teach" you things about the arcane points of the home's infrastructure, such as the furnace, utility systems, gutters, and so on. This analysis can be the basis for your "to do" list after purchase. Ask plenty of questions, and you will get an inexpensive but effective education.

House (Homeowners') Insurance
If an outstanding mortgage will be held on your house, the lender will require that you provide proof of insurance, in the form of a receipt for the premium for the first year's coverage, at the closing. Most lenders have working relationships with particular insurance companies. Consider them, but be certain to do comparison shopping. Since the property purchase will usually consist of land and a structure (house), you do not need to insure for the entire purchase price. If the house is destroyed by some peril, the land and usually the foundation of the house are still intact. A general rule of thumb is to insure for 80 percent of the replacement value of your home.

Firms that specifically offer policies to servicemembers price their policies competitively and provide outstanding service. The cost of coverage varies but generally ranges from $400 to $700 per year. The next chapter covers homeowners' insurance in depth.

Loan Application Fee

A loan application fee or origination fee is a nonrefundable fee paid to the lending institution to cover the costs of processing the loan application. It discourages "casual shoppers" from applying for loans without being serious about the purchase. The typical range is $100 to $300, or often 1 percent of the loan amount.

Points

Mortgage lenders want to make loans that will be repaid on time. To help ensure that a borrower can afford to make the mortgage payments, lenders often adopt the rules of thumb that the mortgage payment must be less than 28 percent of gross income or that all debts must be less than 36 percent of gross income. To reduce the payments and allow more families to qualify as good risks, lenders will offer to charge a lower interest rate on the loan if the borrower pays an advance interest charge, called points, to make up the difference. A point is 1 percent of the face amount of the loan. For example, a two-point fee on a $150,000 loan results in a charge of $3,000 that is included in the closing costs.

At times, the rate of interest that lenders can charge on FHA, VA, and conventional financing is lower than the yield that they could earn in other investments in the market. Here again, the lender will charge points to make up the difference.

Because the IRS recognizes points as an interest charge, all "reasonable and usual" points paid to secure a mortgage are fully deductible from income for tax purposes in the year you purchase your house. However, points paid to refinance your house must be deducted over the life of the loan.

Even though they are tax deductible, points raise the effective interest rate of your mortgage about the quoted rate. You must analyze the after-tax cash flow to determine whether a loan with points is better than a loan without points.

Private Mortgage Insurance

Private mortgage insurance (PMI) is designed to protect the mortgage holder against possible default by the homeowner. It is generally required by all lenders when a buyer pays less than 20 percent of the house purchase price as a down payment; however, it is not required for VA mortgages. Typical costs are $600 to $900 at closing plus $25 to $30 each month. PMI is *not* mortgage *life* insurance, which is a life insurance policy that pays the outstanding balance of the mortgage in the event of death. Before buying mortgage life insurance, check with your current life insurance carrier to see if your mortgage balance is already covered.

Survey

To make sure you are buying the land area you think you are buying, lenders usually require a current survey. A new survey is expensive and sometimes not needed. During negotiations with the seller, inquire about the date of the last survey and ask for a copy. You can have it updated for a fraction of the cost of a new one. The cost for a full survey will range from $200 to $400; for an update, the cost will be $100 to $200.

Title Search and Insurance

Title insurance is a contract with a company that agrees to provide compensation up to the face amount of the policy against losses stemming from defects or failure in the title by which real estate ownership is founded. The company researches by going back to the original owner of the real property and compiles a history to date, making sure no hidden flaws are in the deeds. This is a single-premium insurance policy, paid at closing and generally in the $500 to $800 range. It is normally a good idea to purchase an optional *owner's* policy, in addition to the required *lender's* policy. This is discussed further in the next chapter.

Miscellaneous

Other costs you may incur, depending on the location, include mortgage tax (varies by region and price), recording fees ($30 to $75), pest inspection ($100 to $200), water purity and pressure test if the property has a well and is not on city water ($75 to $100), radon and lead hazard testing ($25 to $100), and prepaid interest and property taxes for the period between closing and the end of the month.

Sources of Money for a Down Payment and Closing Costs

The median price of a new home built in the United States in 1990 exceeded $100,000; half of the new houses cost less and half cost more. The closing costs identified in the previous section, combined with a 20 percent down payment, mean you would need about $25,000 in liquid assets to move into a house. Fortunately, servicemembers are eligible to participate in government-backed VA and FHA loan programs. But even when the down payment is reduced to 5 percent, or $5,000, you still need about $10,000 to buy a $100,000 house.

If you do not have the necessary funds readily available, you may want to investigate the following sources.

Your Individual Retirement Account

Under certain circumstances, it may be advisable to use funds previously deposited into an IRA to bridge the gap. Be sure to work into your calculations the fact that removing funds from a pre-1987 or deductible IRA account before age fifty-nine and a half will result in a penalty of 10 percent of the amount withdrawn. Also, you will have to pay ordinary income tax on the money as well. (Remember, you deducted your IRA deposits from your income in the year of deposit and thus never paid taxes on that income.) If, however, you have a nondeductible IRA, established during tax year 1987 or later, to which you made nondeductible contributions, you may withdraw contributions and pay penalties and taxes only on the portion of the withdrawal that has not already been taxed, such as accrued interest, dividends, or capital gains. (IRAs are discussed more fully in chapters 8 and 13.)

Carefully analyze your housing choice before using this option, since you will never be able to replace the tax-free compounding funds you withdraw from your

IRA. But if you have identified your dream house or if you anticipate the house will appreciate in value greater than the after-tax and penalty cost of early withdrawals from pre-1987 IRAs, it might not be a bad idea. In any case, this is an expensive source of funds, and you should give careful consideration before using it.

Generous Parents
If your parents are able to assist you financially, they may be another source of funds. Under current tax laws, each parent can give both you and your spouse up to $10,000 each year without incurring a gift tax. This could be an excellent means to start distributing estate assets at a time when an heir really needs the assistance.

Increase Personal Exemptions
After you buy a home, your tax liability will probably decrease because of increased deductions for interest and real estate expenses. With this in mind, you should consider increasing the number of exemptions you claim for tax withholding purposes. Instead of receiving a larger refund each April, thus giving the government an interest-free loan, you can receive a larger after-tax paycheck each month. This will increase your cash flow to meet higher housing expenses. See your local finance office for instructions on completing a new W-4 form.

Advance Pay
Another source of money for down payments is available to military members who undergo a permanent change of station (PCS). Each time a servicemember undergoes a PCS, a total of three months' advance pay is authorized (one month is authorized at the departing duty station and two months at the new duty station) to help offset moving expenses. If you anticipate buying a home, you may want to take advantage of this interest-free loan to augment your down payment fund. Repayment is normally made over a twelve-month period, but the repayment period can be extended to twenty-four months in some instances. Your finance office will assist you in filing the proper request. If you plan to consider this option, remember to prepare for the drop in monthly income while you are repaying the advance.

Equity Sharing
Equity sharing is another means for parents, other family members, or friends to help someone purchase a home. By providing all or a portion of the down payment, the "investor" (person providing the money) can share in the tax advantages that accrue to homeowners as well as any future appreciation. The resulting benefits and costs of home ownership can be divided up many ways. This can be a worry-free way to invest, since the investor will probably have more confidence in a co-owner who is a family member. Even so, it is wise to seek knowledgeable legal counsel to prepare documents outlining such an agreement.

Cash Value of Life Insurance Policy
Many whole-life policies allow the policyholder to borrow the cash value built up in the policy. As we discuss in chapter 18, this may be a good source for cash if you

already have whole-life insurance. If you do not, however, we recommend that you do not get such a policy.

Negotiate with the Seller

Most sellers are eager to sell their homes and will consider all reasonable attempts by a buyer to make the deal go through. If you find the home of your dreams but are unable to immediately pull together all the necessary financial resources, you may consider asking the owner about renting the property with an option to buy in the future. The seller may set a higher selling price for the property or charge above-market rents. This would compensate him for the risk he is taking that you may not actually go through with the deal, in which case he would have to go through the process of marketing his home again.

FINANCING YOUR PURCHASE

If you have to borrow a portion of the purchase price of your house (as virtually all home buyers must), then you have to decide the size of your down payment, the type of mortgage loan to use, and the length of the repayment period. Each of these facets is a fairly complex decision by itself. This section provides a brief sketch of how to examine these choices and also gives some general recommendations.

Down Payment Size

For most military families, the size of the down payment is constrained by lender requirements and the amount of available assets. They don't really have a choice. If your assets exceed the required down payment, however, you must decide whether and by how much your down payment will exceed the minimum. When making this decision, you should realize that if you make a down payment above the minimum, you are choosing to invest in your house. You should, therefore, base this decision on whether such an investment provides a better after-tax return than the alternative investments available to you. The return implicitly earned by your down payment is the after-tax interest rate you would pay on the additional mortgage amount. Given this return, you must decide what portion of your investment portfolio to place in your house. Chapters 13 and14 describe how to analyze your options when constructing your overall investment portfolio.

Types of Mortgages

Unless you pay cash or make special arrangements with the seller, you will need a mortgage loan to finance your house. The most common mortgages today are fixed-rate and variable-rate (also known as adjustable-rate) loans. Make sure you understand the basic features of each before selecting a loan. If it is practical, you might also want to establish a banking relationship with a potential mortgage lender so that in times of heavy demand for loans, you will have priority. This normally occurs when mortgage interest rates decline significantly, thus allowing more potential buyers to qualify for loans.

You should also understand that many lenders make a large portion of their profits from fees associated with making loans. Lenders usually bundle or package their loans and sell these loans to investors, earning a fee of about three-eighths of 1 percent of the outstanding balance, or $375 for a $100,000 loan. The Federal National Mortgage Association, commonly referred to as Fannie Mae (FNMA), and other investor organizations support the mortgage market by purchasing mortgages from local lenders and thereby replenishing their supply of loanable funds. This is common practice, and you should not be concerned if your lender intends to sell your mortgage.

Fixed-rate Mortgage

A loan with a fixed interest rate requires the borrower to make a monthly payment that does not change over the period of the loan. This payment includes interest on the loan and a partial reduction of principal. As the loan is amortized over time, the interest portion of the monthly payment decreases and the amount applied to repaying the principal increases so that the entire loan is paid off at the end of the agreed-upon period. At the buyer's option, an escrow payment, which is a prorated portion of the annual taxes and insurance charges, may be included in the monthly payment, but then changes in taxes and insurance costs will cause the monthly payment to change.

This type of mortgage is ideal for purchasers who have a stable income and want predictable housing costs. Since the lender is taking the risk of forgoing higher future interest rates, fixed-rate mortgages are always provided at higher interest rates than comparable adjustable-rate mortgages. If you plan on keeping your mortgage at least five years and you feel comfortable with the rate and the fixed monthly payment, this may be your best choice. As we discuss later, you have the option to refinance the mortgage if rates decline.

Adjustable- or Variable-rate Mortgage

Adjustable-rate mortgages (ARMs) differ from fixed-rate mortgages in that the interest rate charged on the outstanding balance of the loan can change at intervals determined at the beginning of the loan. Changes in adjustable-rate mortgage interest rates are generally tied to changes in some financial index. The index is normally an average of national interest rates or of rates offered by banks in the area. The ARM interest rate will include a premium over the index rate to compensate the lender for the default risk in the loan. A typical specification for an ARM interest rate might be "the index of Treasury securities, adjusted to a constant maturity of one year, plus two percentage points."

Because your payments are adjusted according to interest rate changes in the economy, the lender shifts a large element of risk (interest rate risk) to the mortgage borrower. Therefore, the initial interest rates on an ARM are lower than for comparable fixed-rate loans. Many purchasers who cannot qualify for a fixed-rate loan, with its higher monthly payments, can qualify for an adjustable-rate mortgage. Be certain, however, that you will be able to meet possibly higher payments if you are forced to own the house longer than planned and interest rates rise in the interim.

Military families can benefit from many other aspects of ARMs. As frequent movers, they can benefit from the low interest charges on ARMs in the early years. Some ARMs are convertible, which includes an option to replace the adjustable rate with a fixed rate after a specified period of time. In addition, most ARMs are assumable. This means that a buyer can take over the payments on an existing loan and thereby reduce the financing costs.* Overall, these features of ARMs make them ideal for many military homeowners. Before deciding, however, buyers should be fully aware of the following characteristics of ARMs.

The ARM has three important aspects to understand: adjustment periods, adjustment indexes, and adjustment caps. The adjustment period is the length of time between adjustments to the interest rate charged on the ARM. As the borrower, you generally will be able to choose adjustment periods ranging from six months to three years. Mortgages with the shortest adjustment periods will have the lowest initial rates and the fewest points, since the short adjustment period makes them less risky to the lender. Adjustment indexes are standard, commonly reported interest rates that will determine your interest rate. Some common indices are the constant maturity indices of six-month, one-year, three-year, and five-year Treasury securities and the Federal Home Loan Bank Board Cost of Funds index. If you think rates will increase, use a long-term index (such as the Treasury index), since they adjust more slowly; if you think they will decrease, choose a shorter-term index (such as the Cost of Funds index). Make sure the index used by the lender is computed by an independent source and is published regularly in papers such as the *Wall Street Journal*. The final interest rate you will pay is based on the index value plus a premium, which ranges from one to three percentage points. If the constant maturity index for one-year Treasury securities is 5 percent and the lender adds a 2 percent premium, your interest rate would adjust to 7 percent at the beginning of the new adjustment period.

The last aspect of the ARM to understand is the cap. Most loans have a cap on the amount the interest rate can increase each adjustment period (usually 2 percent) and over the life of the loan (usually 6 percent). So a one-year adjustable loan with an initial 7 percent rate could increase only to 9 percent at the end of the first adjustment period and to 13 percent over the life of the loan.

Interest rates vary over time, so ARMs are somewhat risky. However, over the last seven years, ARMs have saved borrowers much in interest payments. Since interest rates were stable and ARMs offered low initial rates, short-term homeowners benefited greatly. The following chart illustrates this experience for a $100,000 loan.

---

* Usually, the only assumable fixed-rate loans are loans backed by the government, such as VA loans. Keep in mind, however, that if you allow someone to assume your VA loan, you may not obtain another VA loan until that mortgage is repaid.

ARM vs. 30 Year Fixed-Rate Loan

	1986	1987	1988	1989	1990	1991	1992
ARM rate	8%	10%	10%	10.375%	11.125%	10.5%	8.875%
Interest paid	$7,970	$9,889	$9,825	$10,122	$10,777	$10,093	$8,442
30-year fixed rate	10.25%	10.25%	10.25%	10.25%	10.25%	10.25%	10.25%
Interest paid	$10,226	$10,169	$10,106	$10,037	$9,960	$9,784	$9,780
Savings from ARM	$2,256	$280	$281	$(85)	$(817)	$(219)	$1,338

These figures are taken from the USAA pamphlet *Finding and Financing a Home*. The ARM rate is based on 11th District Cost of Funds Index with an annual cap of 2 percent.

Be careful of options available for some ARMs that guarantee that your monthly payments will remain constant over the term of the loan regardless of the direction and amount of the change in the index. This option can lead to negative amortization whereby the amount you owe grows instead of declines. In this configuration, the ARM resembles a normal fixed-rate mortgage. If interest rates increase, however, you actually *add* to the amount you owe the lender. In effect, you are borrowing funds from the lender in order to keep your payments constant. This can happen if the interest due for one month exceeds the amount of the agreed-upon monthly payment. In effect, you stretch the length of the loan beyond the originally stated term. Also, if you sell your house, the increased loan balance can actually cause you to owe *more* money at closing.

Mortgage Costs

When you compare the costs of available loans, be sure you consider all the costs involved. Ask each prospective lender to provide you with a written statement of the following information:

    Preliminary fees $_____
        (appraisal, credit investigation, etc.)
    Down payment   _____
    Closing costs   _____
        (title search, legal fees, points, etc.)

    Total initial costs $_____

    Monthly mortgage payment   _____
    Escrow payments for taxes   _____
    Escrow payments for home insurance   _____
    Other escrow charges   _____

    Total monthly payments $_____

Be sure the costs are fully itemized, complete, and in writing. Under a national law called RESPA, the lender is *required* to provide a projected Uniform Settlement Sheet, which details all these charges and more. This information must be available to you at least twenty-four hours prior to closing. Ask for it, and make sure you review it and understand each of the entries.

Another Alternative: Seller Financing

Seller financing can be used as a second mortgage to close a deal or as a means to finance the entire transaction. Under proper conditions, this can be beneficial for both the seller and the buyer. The buyer saves on many of the closing costs previously mentioned and often borrows the money from the seller at a below-market interest rate. The seller's benefits are also substantial. First, sellers who provide financing often find it easier to sell their property for the price they want. Further, although the interest rate to the seller may be less than a bank would charge, it may be more than the seller could earn in a certificate of deposit or a money market account.

Although the seller-financed mortgage is not a very liquid asset for the seller, the risk is not too great as long as the value of the property does not decline. The seller-financier is protected because the house is collateral for the loan; if the buyer does not make payments, ownership reverts to the seller. Another possible benefit to the seller is the ability to defer taxes on a portion of the capital gain. In an installment sale, the proceeds from the sale are reportable for tax purposes in the year they are received. This spreads the capital gain from the house sale over the life of the mortgage, as the payments of the gain are received.

Types of Mortgage Assistance

There are three major means of securing a mortgage, each normally referred to as a particular type of loan: the conventional loan, the Department of Veterans Affairs (VA) guaranteed loan, and the Federal Housing Administration (FHA) insured loan. Before you purchase a house, you should fully investigate the availability and net cost of each method. The best one to use depends on a number of factors, including prevailing interest rates, your long-range plans for buying homes in the future, the willingness of lenders and sellers to deal with government bureaucracies, and your potential risk as seen by the lender. You should, of course, keep in mind that the following information is based on laws and regulations that are subject to change and, in some cases, also subject to local conditions.

Conventional Loan

A conventional loan is a financial agreement between you and a lender in which there is no outside agency insuring repayment of any portion of the loan. If you seek a conventional loan, you will offer two kinds of security: the mortgaged property and your own credit or investment worth. The great majority of single-family homes are financed with conventional loans. In this type of loan, a financial institution lends its own money and takes the entire risk of loss. As a result, conventional loans are usually limited to 95 percent of the appraised value. What this means to you is a relatively large down payment. Also, the rate of interest on a conventional loan tends to be higher than an FHA-insured or VA-guaranteed loan because the lender is assuming the majority of the risk.

VA Loan

The Department of Veterans Affairs offers a home loan guarantee program that has many advantages for veterans, active-duty servicemembers, and reservists. The principle advantages are lower interest rates, negotiable points, and smaller down payments. Other advantages include long maturities, limits on costs, required inspections, and no prepayment penalties. The loan guarantee is a valuable benefit available to most servicemembers.

Eligibility for loan guarantees remains quite simple, with a general requirement of 181 days of "other than dishonorable" service since 1940. Active-duty servicemembers can use their benefit more than once, as long as they fully terminate their previous VA loan liability before reapplying. Veterans and eligible reservists may use their benefit only once after active-duty service. Eligibility is not subject to an expiration date except in the case of reservists, who must apply before 28 October 1999.

As of 28 October 1992, several important changes were incorporated into the familiar "GI Loan" program of the last few decades. The first concerns the size of the entitlement. For loans that are less than $56,250, the VA will guarantee $22,500 of the mortgage in the case of default by the borrower. For loans between $56,250 and $144,000, the VA will guarantee $36,000 of the mortgage. For loans that exceed $144,000, the VA will guarantee $46,000 of the mortgage. "Manufactured" or prefabricated homes are limited to a $20,000 guarantee. The VA no longer establishes a maximum loan amount; however, the loan amount may not exceed the "reasonable value" of the home and property. The VA will require an appraisal of the property to ensure compliance with this stipulation.

Whatever the price of your home, the VA guarantee is very valuable to you. Since the government is guaranteeing a substantial amount of your mortgage, the VA greatly reduces the risk of the loan to the lender. This reduction in risk should cause the lender to charge lower interest rates and points and to require a smaller down payment than it would for a conventional mortgage. Under new VA rules, each of these items is negotiable between the lender and the seller. The VA will review the conditions of the mortgage agreement to safeguard the soldier or veteran but will not stipulate them. Therefore, it is your responsibility to get the best deal possible. Shop around! Adjustable-rate mortgages are now guaranteed also. In order for the VA to offer its guarantee, these ARMs are subject to annual caps of 1 percent and 5 percent over the life of the loan.

Another major change to the VA program concerns points. Prior to 1992, the VA required the seller, not the veteran, to pay all points. This provision was not truly enforceable, however, because the price of the home was negotiable. The new law reflects this by allowing the veteran borrower to negotiate payment of points with the seller. Either party may pay the points or split payment between them. But the veteran still may not add the points to the loan amount. Therefore, you should include who pays this large out-of-pocket expense when you negotiate the sale agreement.

The VA charges a "funding fee" for its services based on the loan category and a percentage of the loan. The 1993 fee structure is shown below:

Loan Category	% on Veterans Loan	% on Reservists Loan
Home loan w/ 5% or less down or refinance/home improv.	1.25	2.00
Home loan w/ 5% to 10% down	0.75	1.50
Home loan w/ 10% or more down	0.50	1.25
Manufactured homes	1.00	1.00
Interest rate reduction loan	0.50	0.50

If you believe that you are eligible for a VA-guaranteed loan, you should submit a VA Form 26-1880, "Request for Determination of Eligibility," with the required documents to the VA to obtain a VA Certificate of Eligibility. This certificate must be shown to the lender before a VA-guaranteed loan can be arranged, so you should obtain your certificate at once even if you are not actively looking for a house.

The steps in arranging a VA-guaranteed loan are as follows:

1. Find the property suitable to your needs. Make your final decision to buy only if you are sure the price is right, the house is right, and you are completely satisfied in all respects.

2. Apply to a lending institution (such as a bank, savings and loan association, insurance company, or mortgage company) that makes the type of loan you wish to obtain.

3. Present your plan to the lender with your Certificate of Eligibility. Lenders generally have the forms and other necessary papers for applying for a VA loan. If your lender turns you down, see another one. The fact that one lender is not interested in making this particular type of loan does not mean that all other potential lenders will also turn you down.

4. If the lender accepts your application, the VA, at the request of the lender, arranges for an appraisal of the property and also determines if the property meets acceptable standards of good construction. The appraisal cannot indicate whether the purchase is wise or unwise, or what the resale value may be at some future time. In addition, because valuations vary across appraisers, the VA-appraised value could differ from that made by another appraiser hired by you, the FHA, or the lender.

5. As the result of the appraisal, the VA will forward to the lender a Certificate of Reasonable Value. At this point, if the lender decides to make the loan, it will notify you that it has approved the loan if it has "automatic" approval authority from VA.

If it does not have approval authority, the lender will send the paperwork—loan application, credit report, employment verification, copy of the executed sales contract, and so on—to the VA for approval.

6. The lender closes the loan and sends a report of the closing to the VA.

Overall, the VA home loan guarantee is an excellent benefit that can assist you in your home purchase. Aside from the financial benefits outlined above, the VA safeguards veterans from unscrupulous lenders, sellers, and builders through a variety of measures. It inspects and appraises all properties, monitors any unfair actions of lenders and suspends violators from VA participation, and requires a one-year warranty on new homes. The VA also limits the chargeable fees on mortgages, allows early prepayment without penalty, and encourages forbearance by lenders if a borrower experiences financial difficulties. Before you get a mortgage, consult with the VA by calling (800) 827-1000. Get a copy of *Federal Benefits for Veterans and Dependents* and VA Pamphlets 26-4 and 26-5.

FHA Loan

An FHA-insured loan is a private loan underwritten by the Federal Housing Administration. Like the VA mortgage program, the FHA does not actually loan the money but insures the lending institution (bank, savings and loan, insurance company, or mortgage company) against default by the borrower. The reduction in risk passes through to the borrower in the form of lower rates. In addition, the FHA makes stipulations about certain aspects of down payments and closing costs to assist the borrower.

The FHA will insure mortgages up to certain maximum amounts:

One-family home	$151,725
Two-family home	$194,100
Three-family home	$234,600
Four-family home	$291,600
Condominium	$151,700

The FHA adopted several new rules for administering their mortgage program in 1992. Most of the changes increased the up-front costs to the borrower. An important change concerns the exclusion of closing costs in the mortgage amount. Formerly, closing costs could be included in the financed amount. Now, the only significant cost that can be financed is the Mortgage Insurance Premium (MIP). This premium, 3 percent of the value of the loan, is the cost of the FHA loan to the borrower. Required down payments are still comparatively low, however, at 2.25 percent of the value of the property plus some closing costs. The total amount due at closing is the sum of the down payment and the normal closing costs.

Other changes include the ability to purchase multifamily dwellings and the ability to use the FHA benefit to refinance or rehabilitate a home. For refinancing, the down payment increases to 15 percent of the home value plus closing costs.

Although the FHA tightened its mortgage program, it is still quite attractive. By insuring the lender, the FHA program allows the borrower to purchase a home with much less cash up front than a conventional mortgage. You should compare the FHA and VA loan programs when researching mortgage options. Also, if you have used your VA-loan eligibility, then the FHA program offers another source for obtaining a guaranteed mortgage.

Selecting the Length of Your Mortgage

There are two standard lengths for mortgages, fifteen and thirty years, from which you must choose. The better length for you will depend on a number of factors, so a simple formula is impossible. The following paragraphs, however, describe the issues and provide suggestions on how to think about them.

Because you use the lender's money for half the time and because the lender is exposed to the risk of default or, in the case of conventional mortgages, unanticipated inflation for fifteen fewer years, fifteen-year mortgages are usually available at lower interest rates than thirty-year mortgages. One can typically find them for 0.10 to 0.50 percentage points (sometimes referred to as 10 to 50 basis points) lower. In spite of the lower interest rates, monthly payments for fifteen-year mortgages are generally larger because the entire loan must be repaid in half the time. The lower monthly premium associated with thirty-year mortgages is, in fact, the main advantage of the longer repayment period for a young family on a tight budget.

From a purely financial viewpoint, a shorter repayment period is generally the better choice. A longer repayment period would be superior if you could reinvest the difference between the premiums for fifteen- and thirty-year mortgages during the first fifteen years and pay off the remaining balance on the thirty-year mortgage with something left over. Calculation of the necessary return on your investment of this difference requires a careful cash-flow analysis. Because the interest component of mortgage payments is tax deductible while the return on alternative investments is taxed, the analysis must use after-tax cash flows. Simulations for a variety of mortgage interest rates and marginal tax rates suggest that the return on your alternate investment must exceed the interest rate on your mortgage for you to prefer the thirty-year repayment period on financial grounds. To obtain such a return on average, you would have to invest in an asset much riskier than your house, such as a stock fund (see chapter 13), making the alternative an inferior investment for a typical investor. Thus, from a purely financial standpoint, a shorter repayment period is generally superior. But if you are contemplating this choice and are making your decision on a purely financial basis, you should perform a detailed analysis of the present value of your after-tax cash flows before making your decision.

In summary, a fifteen-year repayment period is generally financially superior to a thirty-year period. The main attraction of a thirty-year mortgage is its lower monthly payment, which allows you to buy a more expensive house. Since this feature usually dominates other considerations, the thirty-year mortgage is the common (and valid) choice. Thus, if your personal financial circumstances permit you to buy the house you desire and finance it with a fifteen-year mortgage, then you probably should do so. If this is not possible, then the thirty-year mortgage is appropriate for you.

Paying Off Your Mortgage Early

Some homeowners wonder if they should pay off their mortgage after an unexpected windfall, like an inheritance, makes it possible to do so. The basic issues in this decision are similar to determining the length of your mortgage—paying off your mortgage early is analogous to choosing a shorter-term loan, while not paying it early is like choosing a longer term. There are some differences, though. Most important, the prevailing interest rates will have changed since you got your mortgage.

From a financial viewpoint, you want to determine where the inheritance will earn the greatest after-tax return. If interest rates have increased since you initially financed your house, you are borrowing money inexpensively through your mortgage, and you are more likely to be able to earn a higher return elsewhere. In such circumstances, you probably should invest elsewhere rather than retire your mortgage. Conversely, if interest rates have fallen, your mortgage is an expensive loan, and your alternative investments are less attractive. Now, you might want to retire the mortgage.

Another factor you should consider is that equity in your house is not very liquid. There are only two ways to use this capital for other purposes: sell your house or take out a home-equity-backed loan. Therefore, if you anticipate the need for another loan in the not-too-distant future, you might want to invest the inheritance, and then use it instead of borrowing and having to pay interest and loan-application fees.

Finally, there is a certain peace of mind that comes from owning your house completely. If that is important to you, you might want to retire the mortgage.

Refinancing Your Mortgage

Homeowners unfortunate enough to purchase their homes when interest rates are high are not necessarily stuck with those high rates forever. Refinancing your mortgage is a valuable option. In practice this means securing a new loan and repaying the old mortgage. This option may be attractive to homeowners with fixed-rate as well as variable-rate mortgages. Those with fixed-rate mortgages could lower their payments and pay less interest. As previously discussed, variable-rate loans are set based on adding a premium to an index of market interest rates. If market interest rates decline in general, then it is likely that the index, and thus the variable interest rate, will decline as well. Under these circumstances, you may be wondering why a homeowner with a variable-rate mortgage would want to refinance. Some home buyers take variable-rate mortgages not because they prefer the uncertainty about their future monthly payments, but because the interest rate they were offered was more attractive than that available on fixed-rate loans. However, when interest rates decline and fixed-rate mortgages become available at more reasonable rates, some homeowners may want to have the peace of mind that a low fixed-rate mortgage offers. Also, just as the rise in an ARM is capped for each adjustment period, the decline is also capped.

Despite the advantages of possible lower monthly payments with a refinanced loan, don't rush to do it without considering all the consequences. The initial out-of-pocket expenses can be quite substantial. Generally, you will be required to pay many of the same closing costs you faced when you initially purchased your home: appraisal, title search, loan application fee, and points. Also, your current mortgage may specify prepayment penalties.

A general rule of thumb is that if current interest rates are at least two percentage points below your present rate, it may pay to refinance. Depending on the particular circumstances, the actual minimum differential required to produce a net savings may be smaller or larger than 2 percent, but this rule is a useful indicator of when it pays to examine this option.

You should also consider the length of time you plan to own the house: Will you have time to recoup the expenses of new closing costs from lower monthly payments? To find out, do this simple calculation:

1. Estimate the total closing costs associated with securing a new loan (5 to 8 percent of the outstanding balance on the old mortgage).
2. Determine the monthly difference between your old and new loan payments.
3. Divide the monthly savings into the total cost of refinancing.

This gives you the number of months you would need to remain in your current home to break even. For example, if your estimated closing costs are $5,000 and your monthly savings from a lower interest rate are $100, you would need to remain in the house more than four years before you would realize a net savings ($5,000 ÷ by $100 = 50 months, or 4.2 years). We've ignored interest on the $5,000 here, so the calculated number is actually too low—you would have to maintain ownership with the new loan for more than five years to make it worthwhile.

If you are determined to refinance and you do not have adequate liquid assets to pay for the associated costs, you still may be able to refinance. If you have accrued enough equity in the property (either from your down payment plus monthly payments or from appreciating property value, or both), you can finance the associated refinancing charges. For example, assume your current mortgage is $75,000 and you face $5,000 in refinancing costs. If your home is worth at least $100,000, you would be able to borrow $80,000 ($75,000 to pay off the old mortgage and $5,000 to cover refinance charges). Although your monthly payment will be a little higher, you can still save money in the long run if the interest rate differential is sufficient.

A 1985 IRS ruling has made refinancing a little less appealing. Before the ruling, all charges for points paid during the refinancing of your house were deductible during the tax year when the new loan was taken. Now, however, the taxpayer must spread the deductions for points over the life of the loan. For example, if you paid three points in a thirty-year loan for $90,000, your out-of-pocket cost for points would be $2,700 (0.03 × $90,000). Instead of deducting the entire $2,700 during the tax year you refinance, your annual deduction is $90 per year ($2,700 ÷ by 30 years). (As stated earlier, this ruling did not change your ability to deduct the entire amount in the first year when you initially buy your house.)

One final strategy to save money in this area is possible. Ask the holder of your existing mortgage to renegotiate the interest rate. He may not go as low as the current market rate, but he may be willing to split the difference. This kind of deal is beneficial for both: The lender keeps you as a customer at a higher rate than current market rates, and the borrower saves on closing costs. If your loan has been packaged and sold to investors, however, you are out of luck; loans that have been packaged for resale cannot be renegotiated.

One related opportunity that may help you is a little-known program called VA Rate Reduction Refinancing. If you have a high-rate VA or commercial loan and rates have fallen, you can use this program to refinance the loan through a mortgage service company to obtain a lower-rate VA mortgage. Because the new loan can include the closing costs, you may be able to reduce your monthly mortgage payment without incurring any out-of-pocket expenses. However, the rate you get under this program won't be as low as the market rate.

TAX CONSIDERATIONS FOR HOMEOWNERS

To promote realization of the American dream of home ownership, the tax laws are structured so that nonhomeowners subsidize homeowners. Certain expenses associated with home ownership are deductible for tax purposes and thus reduce the amount of income taxes that homeowners pay. Servicemember homeowners with mortgages enjoy an unusual advantage: They receive tax-free quarters allowances to pay interest expenses, which are themselves tax deductible. Although this benefit has come under congressional attack in recent years, it has not yet been eliminated. As demands to balance the federal budget and reduce defense expenditures continue, however, this use of a tax-free allowance to pay for a tax-deductible expense may again become a target of critics.

Tax deductions for homeowners begin during the search for a new home. All servicemembers who relocate and incur expenses beyond their reimbursements for house-hunting trips, moving household goods, travel, and temporary living expenses are entitled to an adjustment to income for the difference. In other words, you can reduce your taxable income by the amount of your out-of-pocket expenses—another reason to keep good records. The amount of the adjustment is limited, but home buyers get other benefits. Any excess expenses not deductible for tax purposes in the year a house is purchased can be added to the basis price of your home, which reduces the tax paid on any gain when you sell the house.

Of course, the primary tax advantage is that all the interest paid on a mortgage loan is deductible from your income when computing your federal, state, and local income taxes. Other advantages include the following:

1. Deduction of all points paid to secure a mortgage.
2. Deduction of property taxes.
3. Deduction of mortgage prepayment penalties.
4. A deferral of capital gains taxes on the sale of a house if you buy a home within two years (four years for active-duty military) that is more expensive than the one you sell.
5. A once-in-a-lifetime exclusion from capital gains of up to $125,000 from the sale of a house if you are fifty-five or older and have lived in the house as a principal residence for three of the last five years. Married couples can take advantage of this benefit even if only one spouse meets both requirements.

The tax advantages of home ownership are significant, and they should be thoroughly analyzed before you make your housing decision. (See the section on renting versus buying, later in this chapter.)

SELLING YOUR HOUSE

If you are required to relocate after purchasing your home, you will be faced with the decision of whether to rent your home (and become a landlord) or to sell it. For more information about leaving your equity in your home and renting, see chapter 15, which deals with real estate investments. If you decide to sell, you also have to decide what price to ask, whether to use a broker, and whether to use seller financing.

Should You Use an Agent?

Before hiring an agent, you must decide what type of listing agreement you want to enter. Your choices are as follows:

1. *Exclusive Right to Sell.* The listing broker receives a commission if an offer for the house is accepted at any time during the listing period, regardless of who is responsible for locating the buyer and arranging the sale. The problem here is the need to pick a good agent who will aggressively market your house. At a minimum, your house should appear in the Multiple Listing Service so that agents from other brokerages can serve as subagents for the broker with whom you listed and earn a commission by selling your house.
2. *Exclusive Agency Listing.* The agent you hire is the only agent who may earn a commission for selling your house during the listing period. You are free to sell the property yourself and save on the commission. The problem here is that your house may not be listed in the Multiple Listing Service and thus not get the widest possible exposure to potential buyers.
3. *Open Listing.* You give the agent the right to sell your house, but you retain the right to sign contracts with other agents or sell the property yourself without pay-

ing a commission. This arrangement gives your agent little incentive to spend money to aggressively market your house.

Of course, you could attempt to sell the home without the services of an agent. The ultimate concern is which choice will give you a larger net amount: selling the house yourself and avoiding the commission, or using the professional marketing expertise of a real estate agent. After reviewing the agent's duties outlined below, decide if you have the time and temperament to accomplish them yourself.

If you decide to use a broker, you can expect that person to do the following:

1. Suggest the most cost-effective ways to improve the property appearance.
2. Price your house at market value based on recent sales. (This is a market analysis, not an appraisal.)
3. Screen buyers.
4. Schedule appointments with qualified buyers.
5. Help arrange financing.
6. Facilitate contract and closing procedures.

Whichever option you choose, remember that the commission is negotiable. A higher commission may cause the agent to work harder, but it leaves you with less after the sale. Also, it might be a good idea to sign a short contract at first, perhaps for two or three months, and closely monitor how aggressively the agent markets your home with open houses, newspaper advertisements, and so on. An agent's skill and resources can result in quick, efficient, and profitable sales, but not all agents are created equal. Do not renew a contract with an agent who is not working hard for you. Be aware that an agent will not want to bend on any of these points, so you must be an able negotiator to get a listing contract that best serves you and not the broker.

Should You Sell It Yourself?

If market conditions are good and you have the skill and time, you may decide to sell your house without the help of an agent. If you choose this option, you should take care to do the following:

1. Screen potential buyers over the telephone. Do not grant appointments without first ascertaining how serious they are about buying. You can waste a great deal of time showing your home to casual shoppers.
2. Price your house realistically. This is difficult. If the price is too high, you may discourage potential buyers, and your property will stay on the market longer. On the other hand, if you underprice, it probably will sell quickly, but you will be "leaving money on the table." To avoid this, keep track of the sale of comparable houses in your area and hire an appraiser to value your home (if the appraisal supports your asking price, use it during negotiations to convince potential buyers that they are getting a

good deal). You might also request a periodic market analysis (which is free) from a real estate agent.

3. Present your home in the best possible light. Keep it immaculately clean, always tidy, surrounded by well-groomed and edged lawns and shrubs. Take the time to freshen faded paint, replace dying shrubs, and make all other cosmetic repairs. Well-presented homes generally sell first and often command the best prices.

What about negotiating? If you are selling your own house, the buyer will probably assume that your price is more negotiable because you are not paying an agent's commission. You might consider setting a price that has room for negotiation, and then increasing it by 3 percent. If the price is fair, don't lower it before first receiving an offer from a buyer. If the buyer asks if you will take a lower price, repeat the asking price and suggest that the potential buyer make an offer. If you show your hand first, you will have less leverage as the negotiations continue.

When negotiating with a potential buyer, it may be a good idea not to have your spouse with you. Having an excuse to leave the negotiating table to consult with someone is a powerful negotiating tool. The buyer may feel he is more powerful than you—since you do not have the ability to make decisions—and will probably let his guard down and be less careful about what he says. If you are not married, say you need to consult with a friend, financial advisor, or lawyer.

If you are remaining in the same area and planning to buy a new home, include a contingency clause in your contract that makes the sale of your current home contingent on finding a new home. You must weigh the tradeoff here. You might discourage some potential buyers with this restriction; on the other hand, you could conceivably end up with no place to live. Another way around this problem is to make the purchase of the new house contingent on selling your current residence at satisfactory terms. But this reduces the strength of your negotiating position and could result in your accepting less for your home than you would have received under normal conditions.

RENT VERSUS BUY: A QUANTITATIVE ANALYSIS

Because all owners of real property are allowed itemized deductions for real estate taxes and interest expenses and because they may sell their property for more than they paid for it, a direct comparison of rental costs and mortgage payments is not appropriate. The homeowner's tax advantages and potential capital gains provide tangible financial benefits that must be explicitly considered in a quantitative rent-versus-buy analysis. Let's look at an example.

Capt. Stan Smith and his wife, Mary, a school counselor, have one child and a combined family income of $50,000. Like many military families, the Smiths cannot now itemize their tax deductions; they don't own a home and don't have enough other deductions to make itemizing worthwhile. After reviewing their tax records, however, they find that they had tax-deductible expenses of $3,400 in the previous year; if they bought a home, they would have sufficient deductions to itemize, and this $3,400 amount could become tax deductible as well.

The Smiths are considering buying a house for $100,000. They want to compare the financial effects of buying to renting a comparable house for $800 a month. If they buy, they plan to allot $10,000 for a down payment and $4,500 for closing costs from a money market mutual fund, now paying 4 percent interest. The first year's property taxes are estimated to be $1,800, the interest on a 8.5 percent, thirty-year loan of $90,000 would be $7,624, and the amortization of principal would be $680 for the first year. The Smiths made the following calculations for the effects of home ownership on their taxes:

	Rental	Purchase
Taxable income	$50,000	$50,000
*Interest on MMF	$580	
Standard deduction	($5,700)	
Itemized deductions		($3,400)
Interest expense deduction		($8,970)
Real estate taxes		($1,800)
Net taxable income	$44,880	$37,176
Taxable income reduction, purchase:		($7,704)
× Marginal tax rate (1993)		× 28%
Tax savings due to purchase:		($2,157)

*Interest forgone if you had purchased = 0.04 × $14,500 = $580

The Smiths save $2,157 in taxes annually by purchasing, as compared with renting. Then they incorporated that tax savings into an overall cash-flow summary shown in Table 11-3.

In this example, it is cheaper for the Smiths to buy than to live in a rented home. We do not mean to suggest that this will always be the case. In fact, many homeowners suffer negative cash flow as compared with their rental alternative but choose to buy anyway because they simply prefer to have their own home or because they expect to turn a profit when they sell the property.

A complete analysis of the rent-versus-buy decision should include the expected capital gain (or loss) as well as the monthly cash flows. If you are interested in making the more complete financial analysis that includes the effect of a change in your house's resale value, refer to chapter 15, where we discuss real estate as an investment. Our simple example in this chapter can easily be fit into the analysis we illustrate there. Be aware, though, that some of the tax benefits of being a landlord (such as deducting depreciation) are not available to homeowners who occupy their own property.

TABLE 11-3
Rent vs. Buy Cash-flow Summary

Homeowner (costs) or benefits	
Interest[a]	($7,624)
Real estate taxes	($1,800)
Insurance differences[b]	?
Maintenance	($500)
Utilities[b]	?
Transportation cost difference[b]	?
Forgone interest	($580)
Tax savings	$2,157
Net cost of home ownership	($8,347)
Rental cost avoided[c]	$9,600
Net benefit (cost) of home ownership[d]	$1,253

[a] Note that the $680 principal or equity payment portion (of your total mortgage payments) is not included. You paid it, but at the same time your ownership in the home went up by the same amount.
[b] Include this expense if the comparison is between government quarters and buying a house in the local area, or if your rental is closer or provides utilities.
[c] For individuals making comparisons to living in government quarters, use the sum of your BAQ and VHA as rental cost.
[d] Does not include potential gain from property appreciation.

A CHECKLIST FOR HOME BUYERS

We close this chapter with an amended Department of Veterans Affairs checklist for prospective home buyers.

CHARACTERISTICS OF PROPERTY (proposed or existing construction)

NEIGHBORHOOD. Carefully take into account each of the following:

- Convenience of transportation.
- Location of stores.
- Location of schools.
- Absence of excessive traffic noise.
- Absence of unpleasant sights and odors.
- Availability of play areas for children.
- Fire and police protection and garbage collection.
- Residential usage safeguarded by adequate zoning.
- Community taxes and assessments.

LOT. Consider each of the following to determine whether the lot is sufficiently large and properly improved:

- Size of front yard.
- Size of rear and side yards.
- Walks providing access to front and service entrances.
- Drive providing easy access to garage.
- Lot draining satisfactorily.
- Lawn and landscaping satisfactory.
- Septic tank (if any) in good operating condition.

EXTERIOR DETAILS

- Porches.
- Terraces.
- Garage.
- Gutters.
- Storm sash.
- Weatherstripping.
- Screens.
- Breezeway.

INTERIOR DETAILS. Does the house provide what your family needs?

- Acceptable cost of heating and utilities (check and double check this).
- Rooms large enough to accommodate desired furniture.
- Dining space sufficiently large.
- At least one closet in each bedroom.
- At least one coat closet and one linen closet.
- Convenient access to bathroom.
- Sufficient and convenient storage space.
- Kitchen well arranged and equipped.
- Laundry space ample and well located.
- Windows provide sufficient light and air.
- Sufficient number of electrical outlets.

CONDITION OF EXISTING CONSTRUCTION

EXTERIOR CONSTRUCTION. Inspect to see that the following appear to be in acceptable condition:

- Wood porch floors and steps.
- Windows, doors, and screens.
- Gutters and wood cornice.

- Wood siding.
- Mortar joints.
- Roofing.
- Chimneys.
- Paint on exterior woodwork.
- General design and architecture.

INTERIOR CONSTRUCTION. Check to ensure the following:

- Plaster is free of excessive cracks.
- Plaster is free of stains caused by leaking.
- Door locks are in operating condition.
- Windows move freely.
- Fireplace works properly.
- Basement is dry and will resist moisture penetration.
- Mechanical equipment and electrical wiring and switches adequate and in operating condition.
- Type of heating equipment is suitable.
- There is adequate insulation in walls, floor, ceiling, or roof.
- Floors are level and without cracks.
- These appear to be in acceptable condition:
  —Wood floor finish.
  —Linoleum floors.
  —Sink top.
  —Kitchen range.
  —Bathroom tile and papering.
  —Exposed joists and beams.

To be *sure* the house is a good buy, get expert advice on the condition of existing construction, paying special attention to the following items.

- The basement will stay dry after heavy rains.
- The foundations are sound.
- There has been no termite or other pest damage.
- The title is free, clear, and unencumbered.

SUGGESTED REFERENCES

U.S. General Services Administration, Consumer Information Booklets:

Consumer Handbook on Adjustable Rate Mortgages
A Consumer's Guide to Mortgage Lock-in
A Consumer's Guide to Mortgage Refinancing

Guide to Single Family Home Mortgage Insurance
Home Buyer's Vocabulary
The Mortgage Money Guide, Wise Home Buying
Several pamphlets on home safety and repair

USAA booklet:
Finding and Financing a Home

Internal Revenue Service Publications:

Pub. 523, *Selling Your Home*
Pub. 530, *Tax Information for First-Time Homeowners*
Pub. 534, *Depreciation*

Department of Veterans Affairs Publications:

VA Pamphlet 26-4, *VA Guaranteed Home Loans for Veterans*
VA Pamphlet 26-5, *Pointers for the Veteran Homeowner*
VA Pamphlet 26-6, *To the Home Buying Veteran*

12

Protecting Your Wealth with Insurance

SAVING AND INVESTING to achieve your financial goals isn't always easy. Neither is keeping what you've already got. Your assets can be lost by accidental damage or theft, or you could be held liable for large monetary damages in a civil lawsuit. Reducing the risk of potential loss with insurance can be expensive. You will need to balance the amount of risk you are willing to assume against the cost of eliminating it with insurance. The purpose of this chapter is to provide general information on homeowners', property, and liability insurance, and to present guidelines to help you determine the right amount and type of coverages to select. At the end of the chapter we provide a checklist to assist you in your decision.

HOMEOWNERS' INSURANCE

If you own a home, you will want to insure both real property (i.e., the structure itself) and personal property against loss. Home insurance policies cover both types. Homeowners' insurance (or related policies for renters) is a must for every family that owns a home. Although 95 percent of all homeowners are covered by homeowners' insurance, according to David Klein, an insurance expert from the Hartford Insurance Group, only about 70 percent of the population is properly insured.

There are two important decisions you must make: what policy to choose and how much coverage to get. Before you can decide on either, however, you must understand what the various policies cover and what each type of coverage offers. You need to consider four factors when comparing coverages:

1. What property is covered?
2. What perils (types of loss or damage) are covered?
3. To what extent will you be reimbursed for losses?
4. How much does the insurance cost?

Types of Homeowners' Policies

A home and its contents are exposed to direct damage by a tremendous number of perils, such as fire, flood, theft, loss, lawsuits, and breakage or other damage. Insurance is a way to transfer the financial risk of these perils to the insurance company. Although you cannot insure against all types of risk (for example, you cannot insure against a fall in the price of your home), many risks are insurable. There are many different homeowners' policies available to cover the amount of risk that best suits your needs.

The term "homeowners' insurance" is to some extent a misnomer. The standard homeowners' policy can cover just about everything you own. It can provide protection against personal liability and property loss, and sometimes it even covers medical bills.

There are six basic types of homeowners' insurance: HO-1, HO-2, and HO-3 for the typical home; HO-4 for renters; HO-6 for units or condominiums; and HO-8 for older homes. Each type offers two basic coverages or protection plans: property protection and liability protection. Additional coverages are often included.

Property protection reimburses you for losses or damages to your house and/or its contents. The amount of protection required is usually figured by computing the replacement cost of your house. Coverage for personal property is usually set at 50 percent of the home's replacement cost. There are, however, limits to specific types of property—for example, silverware is limited to $2,500 and jewelry to $1,000 in many theft policies. Such limits do not apply to fire loss.

Personal liability protection protects you against liability from injury or damage to others that may have been caused by you or a family member. It also protects against accidents involving others that happen in or around your home, and in some cases, while you or a family member are away from home. The protection extends to legal fees, and you need not be at fault in the case of injury for the limited medical coverage to apply.

Additional protection can include coverage of expenses in the event your home is rendered uninhabitable, coverage for lost or stolen credit cards, coverage for items taken off your person in a robbery, coverage for new locks in your home should you lose your keys, and much more.

The range of possible coverage is enormous. Policies differ in the types of perils covered as well as the degree of protection offered. Table 12-1 describes each type in detail. Coverages for HO-1 and HO-8 are not shown. While HO-1 offers basic protection and is the most limited, it is written only in rare instances. HO-2 is generally the lowest level of coverage offered and is the basis for comparison of other coverages. HO-3 offers the most extensive coverage and is the most common policy written because it costs about 5 percent more than HO-2 coverage but insures against a much broader set of risks. All policies exclude floods and earthquakes (which may be insured separately), war, and nuclear contamination. Your policy will specify the perils against which you are insured, as well as exclusions, which are risks that are not covered.

TABLE 12–1
Standard Types of Home Insurance Coverage

Policy Type	House and Attached Structures	Detached Structures	Personal Property	Additional Living	Trees and Shrubs
HO–2 Broad	Up to 100% of replacement cost	10% of house amount	50% of house amount	20% of house amount	5% of house amount, $500 maximum
HO–3 Special	Same as HO–2	Same as HO–2	Same as HO–2	Same as HO–2	Same as HO–2
HO–4 Renters	Additions and alterations, up to 10% of personal property	Not applicable	$4,000 minimum	20% of personal property,	10% of personal property, $500 maximum per item
HO–6 Condominium	$1,000 on additions and alterations	Not applicable	$4,000 minimum	40% of personal property	10% of personal property, $500 maximum per item

How Much Coverage Do I Need?

Now that you are familiar with the types of coverage available, you must determine how much coverage you need in order to adequately protect your home, its contents, and your liability.

Covering Your Home

The most important factor in determining your coverage is the value of your home. You should base your decision on your home's *replacement* value—the cost of rebuilding the same structure in the same location. Replacement value and *market* value are two entirely different concepts. Market value is simply the price a buyer is willing to pay for your home. It includes the value of the land and many intangibles (location, quality of schools, and so on). Replacement value does not include land value, and it varies over time, depending on things such as wage rates and the cost of building materials.

You can determine the replacement value of your home by estimating the cost based on construction costs in your area, asking the insurance company to calculate the replacement cost, or hiring an independent appraiser.

You generally do not need to insure for 100 percent of the replacement value of your home, because the probability of total loss of your home is very low. For example, even a severe fire will not destroy your house's foundation. For this reason, your mortgage lender will only require that you obtain about 80 percent coverage. If a home with a replacement value of $150,000 is covered for $120,000 (80 percent), the insurance company will reimburse the homeowner for losses up to a total of $120,000. Although you may be able to insure for less than 80 percent of the replacement value, some insurance companies do not fully reimburse you for partial losses if your coverage is less than 80 percent of replacement value. Be sure to understand the nature of your coverage and how the insurance company will reimburse you as the size of your loss varies.

For example, let's assume that you had a fire in your garage that totally destroyed the garage and adjacent kitchen and that the cost of repair is $25,000. If you have 80 percent coverage (of your $150,000 house), the insurance company will reimburse you the full $25,000. If you had only 70 percent protection, however, the insurance company might divide your actual 70 percent coverage by the 80 percent "required" coverage to determine its level of reimbursement in the event of a partial loss (70 ÷ 80 = 87.5% of $25,000, or $21,875).

Another thing to keep in mind is that the replacement value you determine for your home when you first take out your policy is only valid at that point in time. Given the general tendency for construction costs to rise, the replacement value of your home increases over time. So 80 percent today may be something less than 80 percent tomorrow. If your insurance company offers a *replacement cost endorsement option,* you can shift the responsibility for keeping the replacement cost coverage up to at least 80 percent from you to your insurance company (for a premium, of course). If you subscribe to this option, your insurance company will most likely require that you insure for 100 percent of the replacement value they determine. Although the replacement cost guarantee itself may not cost much more, the fact that you must insure for 100 percent of replacement value may increase costs by 10 percent of the base premium or much more.

Unique Older Homes

The "replacement value rule" is not applicable to unique older homes (Victorian homes, stucco homes, and so on) for which replacement either is not feasible or is prohibitively expensive. Given the structural problems commonly associated with older homes (e.g., bad pipes, poor wiring), the risks that typical HO-2 policies insure against are the accidents most likely to occur in older homes. To insure at 80 percent or higher of replacement cost, however, may be too expensive using an HO-2 policy. A more affordable alternative is an HO-8 policy that limits coverage to some portion of the full market value of your home (discounting the land).

Personal Property

Most policies reimburse content losses up to 50 percent of the amount of insurance on the home itself. Content insurance comes with a deductible, typically $100 to $250. Your premiums go down as your deductible goes up. The default value of the loss is determined on an "actual cash value" basis (actual cost minus depreciation). So, when filing a claim based on actual cash value, you probably will be reimbursed for the item in an amount that you would expect to be able to purchase a similar item in a garage sale, or perhaps a bit more. You can, however, customize your homeowners' policy to better suit your needs. One way is to purchase a replacement cost insurance rider to enable you to replace a loss with equipment of comparable value at current prices.

You must be aware of the limits of your coverage by type of item—both the dollar limit and the causes of loss that the insurance company recognizes as reimbursable. See the "Special Limits of Liability" section of the policy you are considering to get this information. For example, coverage of jewelry is often limited to $1,000. This means that if your $10,000 ring is stolen, you will get only $1,000 from your homeowners' policy. Moreover, your policy most likely will not cover you for mysterious losses.

If you need more coverage on uniquely valued items, you can take out extra insurance with a personal articles floater or rider. These are simply endorsements attached to your base policy specifying the amount of additional coverage you have purchased and the specific item for which it was purchased.

An alternative method for securing additional personal property coverage is to purchase it through personal property insurance. If you need more coverage than is offered by your basic homeowners' policy, therefore, compare the cost of obtaining the additional coverage you desire through riders to your homeowners' policy with the cost of obtaining that same additional coverage through a personal property insurer.

Recommendations

1. Insure your home at no less than 80 percent of its replacement cost.
2. Maintain a detailed room-by-room inventory of all major items contained in your home. Include model numbers, serial numbers, date of purchase, and purchase

price of all major items. Supplement your written inventory with a picture and/or video inventory. You will find this well worth your time in the event of a loss and when comparison shopping for insurance. Keep this record in a safe place *away from* your house.

3. Review your inventory annually; however, add major items as soon as you purchase or receive them.

4. Review your policy annually to ensure that you are covered for at least 80 percent of *current* replacement cost.

5. Reevaluate your policy whenever there is a major change in the value of your home or its contents—major remodeling, additions to the structure, major purchase of new furniture or jewelry, and so on.

6. If your insurance company offers replacement cost endorsement, include it in your policy if you desire to avoid the hassle of always checking to make sure you are still within the 80 percent standard coverage.

7. If the standard content coverage is inadequate, determine whether the coverage limits of your policy can be increased to suit your needs, and whether it is less costly to take out a separate (additional) personal-property policy. In any event, you should consider a policy that covers the replacement cost of the contents.

8. Carry the largest deductible you think you could afford in the event of a loss.

9. Whether or not you are satisfied with your insurance company, shop for your policy every two or three years to ensure that your firm is still competitive.

10. Reappraise your valuables every three years.

Additional Insurance Requirements

Flood Insurance

Damage caused by floods is not covered by homeowners' policies. If you live in a community susceptible to flooding, and your community participates in the National Flood Insurance Program, you can obtain flood insurance through the Federal Emergency Management Agency (FEMA). Flood insurance will cover your home for up to $185,000 in structural damage and up to $60,000 in content loss. Premiums vary with risk of flooding and are government subsidized. For details about the program, call FEMA at (800) 638-6620. We recommend that you carry flood insurance if you live in an area susceptible to flooding.

Title Insurance

There are two types of title insurance: one protects your lender, the other protects you. The lender requires you to pay for a policy to protect them at settlement. You are not protected against a defective title unless you purchase a separate policy for yourself. "What could be wrong with the title?" you ask. A lawyer or lender will tell you any number of horror stories. For example, a previous owner may have had thousands of dollars in unpaid traffic tickets, and the state may have put a lien against his or her property. If the lien against the property is not noted until after the property is transferred, you would be liable for the unpaid tickets. It is better for an insurance company to deal with these rare but costly surprises. Once you've paid the mandatory fee for the lender's title insurance, you'll find that the cost of an additional owner's policy (for yourself) may be roughly the price of a case of beer. Also, it's a one-time cost, not an annual one. We strongly recommend that you purchase an owner's title insurance policy when buying real property.

Mortgage Life Insurance
Mortgage Life insurance (or credit life insurance) pays off the remaining balance on your mortgage in the event of your death or the death of your spouse. The premium is added to your mortgage payment. This is normally a very expensive form of life insurance, usually three times and in some cases about ten times more expensive than term life insurance coverage for the mortgage or loan amount. We recommend that you have adequate life insurance and *avoid* mortgage life insurance. (See chapter 18 on life insurance.)

Earthquake Insurance
Basic homeowners' policies do not insure against damage caused by earthquakes. Therefore, we recommend that you consider adding earthquake insurance to your homeowners' policy if you live in an earthquake-prone area. In major disasters, the federal government has generally provided some level of assistance to the owners of damaged homes, usually in the form of subsidized loans. As a result, many experts debate the need for this insurance. You will have to balance the cost of purchasing private insurance against your family's tolerance for risk and the degree to which you expect the government to respond rapidly and generously in the event of an emergency.

Now That You're Informed, What Should You Do?

All homeowners' policies are not the same, nor do all typical policies cost about the same. As with all insurance, the first rule is to shop around. When you shop for insurance, make sure you are comparing apples with apples. Because there are so many options, this is not as easy as it sounds.

There are hundreds of companies that provide homeowners' and related insurance. Two that are very popular among servicemembers are USAA and Armed Forces Insurance, but many other firms can serve your needs. Always get more than one quotation. See appendix A for the names, addresses, and telephone numbers of firms catering to the military.

For more detailed information, order a copy of the *Buyer's Guide to Insurance: What Companies Won't Tell You,* published by the National Insurance Consumers Organization. Send a check or money order for $3 along with a self-addressed, stamped, business-size envelope to NICO, 121 North Payne Street, Alexandria, VA 22314.

INSURANCE FOR OTHER CIRCUMSTANCES

Insuring Your Rental Property

Military families often purchase a home and rent it out once they make a PCS move. Since they still own the home, they are responsible for insuring it. It is very important to check with your insurance company to determine what your homeowners' policy coverage protects once you move, and for how long that protection is in force. Also, verify whether it matters if your home is vacant or not.

You should normally replace your homeowners' policy with a fire policy, which provides coverage for the dwelling itself and damage to personal property in the event of the perils named in the policy. It does not cover theft of personal property and furnishings left in the dwelling. Make sure your tenants understand that they are responsible for arranging for their own renters' insurance to cover their personal property. To protect against theft, you can obtain a separate policy that covers the contents, if any, that belong to you. The fire policy may be extended to provide personal liability protection on request. However, if you have a homeowner's policy for your current home or a personal liability policy is already in force, liability coverage can be extended from that policy to the rental property.

Renters' Insurance

A renter has no vested interest in the building itself, and he or she often (but wrongly) assumes that losses sustained from fire or theft are covered by the landlord's policy. Renters are provided little or no protection from the landlord's policy. Renters' insurance can provide contents, liability, and off-premises-theft coverage. Policies usually cover additional living expenses (those above your normal monthly rent) in the event your rental unit is rendered uninhabitable and you are forced to live in a hotel or other temporary lodging facility.

Insurance in Government Quarters

If you live in government quarters, you are "covered" by government insurance. Such coverage, however, is normally limited to personal property damaged in or stolen from your quarters, and the coverage limits are sometimes ridiculously low. The insurance provided by the government is very limited, especially when it comes to personal liability protection. You would be wise to take out specific insurance policies for personal property and personal liability protection or purchase a renters' policy that covers both categories of risk. Such a policy can provide protection wherever your tour of duty takes you.

LIABILITY PROTECTION AND UMBRELLA POLICIES

Most homeowners' policies offer $100,000 liability coverage as a minimum, and your automobile-insurance policy will usually include liability coverage. Given our litigious society, the amount of coverage in these policies is usually inadequate. The need to protect your home and the physical things you own is readily apparent to you; however, protecting your future income is not so obvious. Because liability judgments can include some portion of all your future income to someone you injure, you could lose not only everything you own today, but also a substantial portion of your future earnings. It is, therefore, imperative that you maintain adequate liability coverage.

We recommend that you carry at least $300,000 worth of liability coverage. If the limits available under your homeowners' and automobile policies are not adequate, consider an umbrella policy for $1 million of coverage or more.

Automobile and homeowners' policies provide only limited personal liability insurance. An umbrella policy picks up where your existing coverage leaves off and goes to whatever limit you select, normally the $1 million to $5 million range. Coverage extends well beyond damages assessed for physical injury. An umbrella policy covers judgments for injuries on your property, unintentional libel or slander, catastrophic automobile accidents that exceed your policy limit, sickness or disease, shock, defamation of character, mental anguish, wrongful entry, malicious prosecution, wrongful eviction, and more. Compensation for defense costs and court costs is also included.

Such extensive liability coverage may seem ludicrous at first, but judgments in the $500,000 range and higher are common. Lawsuits are not at all rare if you own a home and are even more common if you rent your property. One mistake can ruin your financial future. All of your assets, current and future, are in the hands of the court. If your dog seriously injures a child or the postal deliverer slips on your porch and suffers an injury, you could be facing a major lawsuit. Even if you are found not liable, the cost of defending yourself can be substantial.

You must assess your total liability potential and compare it to the coverage provided by your homeowners' and automobile policies. First, determine your asset base—anything you own that is cash or could be converted to cash, including an assessment of your future earnings. Compare your asset base with your "exposure"—the amount of driving you do, the number and ages of others insured on your policy, any recreational vehicles you or your family operate, your status in the community, the judicial environment in which you live, and so on. Identify the liability limits on your basic insurance policies; if a probable lawsuit could "wipe you out," consider an umbrella policy. In most cases, you would be well served with the additional protection.

Although umbrella policies do protect against a broad set of risks, their coverage does have limits. In general, there are categories of losses that carry a deductible, and personal liability losses that are either uninsurable or normally covered under a different type of policy are not covered. Most exclusions under basic policies are not covered by the umbrella policy.

The insurance company providing the umbrella policy will normally specify minimum limits on your primary insurance policies. Also, the company might require that all your primary policies be with them. The cost can be quite low—a million-dollar policy may be offered for as little as $125 per year.

HOMEOWNERS' CHECKLIST

This checklist is provided to assist you in your insurance decision. Use it to set up a worksheet for comparing insurance companies. We suggest you compare no fewer than three companies when making your decision. Make sure all quotes are for the same *type* of insurance.

Initial Worksheet
1. Replacement value of home (not land) $ _____
2. Percentage of #1 you wish to insure: _____ %
3. Dollar value of desired insurance (#2 x #1): $ _____
4. Estimated replacement value of contents: $ _____

Compare the Following:

1. Cost of $_____ (see line 3 above) worth of insurance on home.
   a. With $250 deductible:
   b. With $500 deductible:
   c. With $1,000 deductible:

(A fairly standard deductible is $250. As you decrease your deductible, your premium goes up!)

2. Cost of a replacement cost endorsement on the house.

3. Content coverage:
   a. Is it available for replacement value of contents? At what additional cost?
   b. Are the limits suitable to my needs?
   c. If not, are floater policies available by item type?
      (1) Types and limits of floater policies I will need.
      (2) Cost of each policy.

4. If too many content floaters are required, is separate personal property insurance available? Cost?

5. If a discount ("teaser") subscriber rate is offered, will the premium get renewed at the "normal" rate? If so, what are the normal rates?

6. Is the insurance company able to meet my other insurance needs? If so, do they offer multipolicy discounts?//
7. What are the discounts available for the following:
    a. Smoke alarms?   d. Burglar alarms?
    b. Dead bolts?   e. Age of home?
    c. Fire extinguishers?   f. Other?

Part IV

BUILDING YOUR NEST EGG

13

Investing in Financial Assets

WHEN WE THINK of investing, financial assets are normally what we have in mind—stocks, bonds, certificates of deposit. In broad terms, there are two major categories of financial assets, and their key features are quite different. The first group includes all types of *debt* instruments for which the "investor" loans money to a financial intermediary, such as a bank, or to a government or corporation in return for a specified interest rate for a fixed period of time, at which point the principal (the amount loaned) is returned. We often call debt instruments "fixed-income assets" because the repayment schedule, which is income from the investor's perspective, is fixed. The second group includes various *equity* instruments through which the investor buys a stake in the company's profits. In equity investments, no interest rate is specified in advance. The amount the investor earns (or loses!) depends on how the company performs over time. As a general rule, financial markets will "price" assets according to their riskiness. Financial assets with higher returns also have higher risk, while assets with lower returns have lower risk.

DEBT INSTRUMENTS

Checking Accounts

Banking laws permit many types of checking accounts to pay interest. You may not think of your checking account as a debt instrument, but in fact it is very much like one. You lend your money to the bank, and they agree to pay you a specified amount of interest on it. Checking accounts are nearly perfectly liquid; that is, the funds stored there are very easy and inexpensive to exchange for other things. Additionally, negotiable order of withdrawal (NOW) and super-NOW accounts are technically savings accounts against which checks can be drawn. They are offered by banks and savings and loan associations, and in practice they are essentially the same as a checking account. The NOW account is an attractive vehicle if your account balance is consistently over the minimum required by your bank.

Credit unions offer share draft accounts, which are also interest-bearing checking accounts. Many military installations have credit unions, and you should investigate the services they offer. A share draft account can enable you to earn interest on part of your checking account money.

Savings Accounts

Many financial institutions—commercial banks, credit unions, and savings and loan associations—offer various types of savings accounts. Regular passbook accounts pay interest at an advertised rate from the date of deposit to the date of withdrawal in many banks. Other savings accounts, particularly money market savings accounts, may pay higher interest, with an interest rate that varies according to market conditions.

You should recognize that banks use different methods to compound interest. You can lose interest in some accounts by taking your money out just before the end of the compounding period. This is particularly true of many credit unions. In other accounts, you earn interest each day your money is on deposit regardless of when you withdraw it. Because these variations affect your effective return, you should carefully investigate the compounding policies of banks in your area before you open an account. You should also be sure your bank is insured by the Federal Deposit Insurance Corporation (FDIC), which currently guarantees the safety of deposits up to $100,000.

Certificates of Deposit

Banks, savings and loans, and credit unions also offer certificates of deposit (CDs). The major distinction from a savings account is that a CD requires you to "lock up" your money for a certain period and, therefore, is not suitable for emergency funds. Of course, you can always get your money before the CD matures if you really need it, but you will forfeit interest, depending on how your CD penalizes early withdrawals. CDs can be a useful means to accumulate money for longer-term goals. Again, be sure to check very carefully the conditions attached to the CD and the compounding method.

CDs have varying maturities, typically from a single week to eight years, and they usually have a minimum deposit requirement, typically $500 to $1,000. Normally, you receive higher interest on your money by agreeing to leave it on deposit for longer periods of time. For example, in early 1993, six-month CDs were available at interest rates averaging 3.7 percent, while five-year CDs paid 6.25 percent. This is not always the case, however. Long-term yields are occasionally lower than short-term rates.

One of the most important aspects of a CD you need to check is the early withdrawal penalty. Banks talk about "substantial penalties for early withdrawal," but in practice, some banks levy much smaller penalties than others. A small early withdrawal penalty is valuable, because it allows you to get your money out of a CD at low cost if you need it or if interest rates go up. This may allow you to earn the higher interest that CDs pay in relation to savings accounts on a portion of your emergency funds and other short-term savings. In addition, it allows you to trade up at low cost to a higher-yielding CD if interest rates rise after you have purchased a CD.

To see how this attractive feature of CDs works, suppose you put $5,000 in a four-year CD at 5 percent interest, compounded annually. At the end of four years, you would have $6,078. Now suppose that after one year, rates on new CDs rise to 7 percent. At the end of that year, your CD deposit would be worth $5,250 ($5,000 × (1 + 0.05)). You would like to withdraw your money from the 5 percent CD and put it into a new three-year, 7 percent CD, but you know that the bank is going to impose a penalty if you do. How bad is the penalty? Many banks levy a penalty equal to three to six months' interest on the CD you are cashing in. At 5 percent interest, a three-month penalty on a $5,000 withdrawal is about $63. So you could get about $5,187 out of your 5 percent CD even after paying the penalty. If you put $5,187 into a new three-year CD at 7 percent, you would have $6,354 in three years, $276 more than the $6,078 you would have received if you'd stayed with the original CD.

Some banks will reduce the interest credited on your CD to the passbook savings rate for the entire period you have owned the CD in addition to levying a forfeiture of interest for some period. You just have to read the fine print.

Shopping for the highest-rate CDs is actually quite easy—periodicals such as *Barron's* and *Money* rate the top-yielding CDs in every issue. Try to find CDs that combine high yields with lenient early withdrawal penalties. The best CDs offer an attractive means to save for future goals: They let you lock in high rates of interest when they are available and trade up to even better rates if they subsequently are offered. No other savings vehicle offers this feature. As we will see, bonds that are traded on secondary markets can be sold before maturity without any penalty, but their value in the market fluctuates with changes in interest rates. CDs can offer yields that approach government bond returns but with less risk.

U.S. Government Savings Bonds

Many small investors buy U.S. savings bonds, which are sold at a 50 percent discount from their face value. The face value itself really doesn't signify any particular maturity value, because the interest rate is variable. Series EE bonds pay interest based on average market-based rates. Specifically, people who hold bonds for at least five years get the higher of two interest rates: a guaranteed minimum 4 percent (it is 6 percent on bonds bought before March 1993, and 7.5 percent on bonds purchased before November 1986) or a market-based return adjusted every six months to be 85 percent of the recent return on five-year Treasury obligations. For example, in early 1993, the

EE bond interest rate was 6 percent. The interest earned on savings bonds is exempt from state and local income taxes but not federal income tax. Because EE bonds do not actually pay periodic interest, all tax on the rising value of the bonds is due when they are redeemed. You may elect instead to pay tax on the accumulated interest from year to year if you desire. Bonds held by a child with few other taxable assets, or held by any child over fourteen, will usually benefit from this treatment. See any tax guide for the mechanics and the pros and cons of this option.

Also, Series EE bonds now carry a complex and lengthy set of special provisions that, if carefully followed, can help pay for your child's college education. Here's the good deal: Interest earned in redeeming Series EE bonds bought from 1990 on are tax exempt if higher-education costs in the redemption year exceed principal and interest received. But note the many restrictions. The bonds must be registered in the name of someone at least twenty-four years of age when the original purchase is made. This person is considered the owner of the bond. College costs must be for the bond owner or the owner's spouse or dependent. (Note: These bonds can be purchased by anyone, but must be registered as explained above.) Tuition and fees, but not room and board, are eligible costs. Costs offset by scholarships and employer aid aren't eligible either. Also, if married, the owner will have to file a joint tax return in the redemption year.

The tax benefit is available only to people who meet certain income restrictions in the year the bond is redeemed. In 1992, the full benefit was available only to married couples filing joint returns with a modified adjusted gross income up to $66,200 and to single filers with incomes up to $44,150. A partial benefit was available to joint filers with 1992 incomes up to $96,200 and to single filers with income up to $59,150. The caps are indexed to rise with inflation. These limits allow most servicemembers to participate.

These rules may require you to make a key decision. Should savings bonds you purchase go into your name or your child's name? The answer depends on what you assume your financial status will be at the time your children will require college funding. If you do decide to buy them in your children's names, be sure to use their Social Security numbers, and not yours, or you will have tax problems when they are redeemed.

An important thing to remember about your U.S. savings bonds is that if any are lost, stolen, mutilated, or destroyed, they will be replaced free of charge by the U.S. Treasury. To report such a case, use application form PD-1048, which is available at most banks. It's still a good idea to record the bond numbers and put the list in a separate location; this makes the bonds much easier to trace to you.

Treasury Bills, Notes, and Bonds

Treasury bills, notes, and bonds are debt instruments that differ from savings bonds in that their return is not guaranteed and they are negotiable, meaning they can be bought and sold by private investors (savings bonds can be redeemed only by "reselling" them to the government). Major financial centers have active markets in bonds, notes, and bills, and savings invested in them are fairly liquid. There are, however, some drawbacks. They are riskier than simply having money in a bank account. Also, they cannot be bought without some kind of service charge or commission unless you arrange to buy newly issued obligations directly from one of the twelve Federal Reserve banks.

You can buy these bills, notes, and bonds from the nearest Federal Reserve bank by calling the bank to find out when the next issue will be available, then sending in a cashier's check for the full amount with a letter of instruction. However, the Federal Reserve establishes a minimum purchase that varies between $1,000 and $10,000, depending on the instrument, so most servicemembers would probably ask their bank or broker to buy government bonds for them. Consider the charges for this service when you calculate your yield.

Even though government bonds carry no risk of default, they have important elements of risk. The government will keep its promise stated in the bond to pay all principal and interest when due. The government does not, however, make any promises regarding the value of those dollars when you get them. If there is unanticipated inflation while you own government bonds (or any other bonds or CDs, for that matter), you will lose purchasing power even if you don't lose money. And, of course, there is price risk during the entire period you hold the bond. Bond prices change constantly with market interest rates, so that the price at which you can sell your bond (and therefore the value of your investment) changes from day to day. Many investors have been disappointed after confusing default risk (against which government bonds protect you) with price risk (against which they cannot protect you). The formulas in appendix D describe how bond prices vary inversely with the discount rate (or yield). The price of the bond is simply the discounted value of the cash flow it provides.

Treasury bills are short-term obligations of the government that mature within one year. These are normally not suitable for small investors, because the minimum denomination is $10,000. Treasury notes are intermediate-term obligations of the government that mature within one to ten years. Interest is paid semiannually. Notes are often quite attractive to small investors because their minimum denominations are small ($1,000 to $5,000). Treasury bonds are long-term obligations of the government that may have maturities as long as thirty years. Again, the minimum denomination is $1,000. Many brokers push "zero-coupon bonds," which are much like savings bonds in that you buy them at a discount and collect no "interest" until maturity. They have by far the highest level of price risk.

For savers who take the time and interest to manage their savings funds actively, federal government obligations can frequently provide higher rates of return than savings accounts and CDs. The risk of default is negligible since they are backed by the full faith and credit of the United States. The government bond market is very active, making it easy to buy and sell bonds, and price and yield information is available daily in major newspapers. (Bond prices are quoted as a percentage of face value. If your $1,000 face-value bond is quoted at 90, that means its market value, what you could sell it for, is $900.) Interest earned on Treasury obligations is not taxed by state or local governments. But remember that banks don't charge a broker's fee for CDs or savings accounts. Therefore, you should compare the return net of taxes and broker's fees before you choose between the various debt instruments.

U.S. Government Agency Securities

Many agencies established by Congress also issue debt instruments (bonds). Their securities are not guaranteed by the government, but it is unlikely that the government would allow them to default because it supervises them and is often a part owner. Because of their slightly poorer guarantee, these bonds pay a higher yield than those of the Treasury. The Federal National Mortgage Association (FNMA; the bonds are known as Fannie Maes), the Government National Mortgage Association (GNMA, or Ginnie Mae), the Tennessee Valley Authority (TVA), the Export-Import Bank, Federal Land Banks, and others issue such bonds. Interest earned on these obligations is taxable by federal and often by state and local governments. Be particularly careful when buying GNMAs. These bonds are backed by pooled mortgages and are the most popular of the agency securities. Brokers and fund salesmen like to push GNMAs because of their high stated yields. But because mortgage owners have the option to prepay their mortgages when rates fall, the return on most GNMA funds fall well short of their advertised yields. They are still a good investment—just incredibly oversold and misunderstood.

Municipal Bonds

Municipal bonds are the obligations of state and local governments, and their interest payments often are exempt from federal taxes and sometimes from state and local taxes, too. Partly because of their tax-exempt status, municipal bonds usually pay lower interest rates than taxable bonds, so they are not normally attractive to investors with low marginal tax rates. (Your marginal tax rate is the percentage of any *additional* income that would go to taxes and not the average tax rate on all income. If you are in the 28 percent bracket, you pay 28 percent of any increase in income to the government and keep only 72 percent.) For a taxpayer in the 28 percent bracket, the tax-exempt yield on a 6 percent municipal would be the equivalent of a 8.33 percent taxable yield. Yields higher than that are normally available on taxable bonds. Therefore, small investors with low marginal tax rates cannot really benefit from investing in municipal bonds. Moreover, the market for municipal bonds is much less liquid than either government or corporate bonds. Thus, these bonds are not appropriate investments for most military investors.

Corporate Bonds

Corporate bonds generally offer a higher return than savings accounts. They are not redeemable before maturity but may be resold in secondary financial markets, potentially at a profit or loss. There are two major classifications. Secured bonds are guaranteed by a mortgage on the company's property, much like a mortgage on a home. Unsecured bonds, called debentures, are backed by the general credit of the company, similar to a signature or unsecured loan.

Both types of bond promise to pay a specified sum at maturity and interest at a fixed rate regularly until then. The principal and interest are usually payable before the dividends on the borrowing company's stock. If the company goes bankrupt, bondholders have a claim on assets ahead of the stockholders, but the company may still default on its debt. In addition to default risk, corporate bondholders also face price risk caused by changes in the market rate of return. Corporate bonds may be bought from a broker, or indirectly through bond mutual funds (see the next chapter).

EQUITY ASSETS

One of the great American dreams is to get rich quick, and many people try to do that on Wall Street. Between 1982 and 1993, the Dow Jones Industrial Average has gone from below 800 to over 3,400. This represents a compounded annual return of 14 percent—very good, but certainly not the get-rich scheme the media would have us believe. And you would have had to have guessed the exact time of the market peak (in 1993) and bottom (in 1982) to get that return—something almost no one can do. In fact, had you bought a five-year or longer certificate of deposit at your local bank in 1982, you also would have earned solid double-digit returns—and at a fraction of the risk.

Investing in stocks need not be mysterious. As in all investments, there are risks and there are corresponding expected rewards. Anyone considering investing in the stock market must first do a bit of homework on those risks and rewards, for the most likely way to lose money in stocks, as in any investment, is through ignorance. We hope to provide a starting point for that homework and also to dispel a few myths along the way.

Historically, stocks have outperformed both short- and long-term bonds by a wide margin. Over the past sixty-five years, the average real return on stocks has been about 7 percent per year over inflation. Over the same time period, government long-term bonds have returned between 1 and 2 percent on average per year; corporate long-term bonds have only a slightly higher average real return. For the "safest" investments—U.S. Treasury bills—the real rate of return has been about zero. Apparently, rates of return on the safest, shortest-term bond investments are only adequate to compensate for inflation but not large enough to provide an after-inflation rate of return.

We conclude that short-term bonds and savings accounts are appropriate for storing purchasing power for short periods of time, such as when consumers save for a new car in a year or two or when they keep emergency reserves in a money market mutual fund. However, these very safe investments will probably not provide a real return after inflation over a longer period of time. (This is especially true when taxes on interest are considered.) In order to earn a positive real return after inflation, investors must accept some of the risks involved in long-term bond and stock investing.

It is important to understand that when we say stocks earn on average 7 percent above inflation, we do not mean to imply that stocks will have a return 7 percent above inflation every year. Quite the contrary; rates of return on stocks vary considerably from year to year. In some years, stocks return much more than inflation; in other years, they decrease in value considerably. That is why stocks are a risky means to save for short-term goals. In the past, the up years in the stock market have been sufficiently good to compensate for the down years and to provide a rate of return about 7 percent higher than inflation. Unfortunately, there is no riskless way to earn a rate of return substantially above the rate of inflation over the long term. Investors have to accept some risk to earn positive real returns.

For uninformed investors, investing in the stock market approaches the mystical. The odd vocabulary, the need to go through a broker, the sense that it is not an "even" playing field, well-publicized abuses—all seem to work against the individual investor. However, the average investor can, with careful homework, a tolerance for risk, and patience, earn greater returns in the stock market over time than in most other investments. This is not to say that small investors should invest *directly* in individual stocks. We recommend that most small investors start with *mutual funds,* a way to "pool" your investment with others that is covered at length in the next chapter.

What Is Stock?

The first thing you need to know about the stock market, or any investment for that matter, is the actual investment product. A share of stock represents a part of the equity capital of a publicly held company. This means that a private company decided to allow the public to be part owners of the firm and sold shares of ownership through a stock offering. If a company has one million shares of outstanding stock, then owning one share means that you own one one-millionth of that company.

So why would a company "sell out" to the public? Usually because the company has plans (and needs money) for growth and expansion, and its bankers feel that borrowing the money might create too heavy a debt burden. The company looks for "partners" to finance this growth, and taps the public markets for these funds. Another reason for selling stock is that the founders of the company may want to realize some of their investment without selling the entire firm. William Gates, the founder of Microsoft (the computer software company), took his company "public" in the 1980s for this very reason.

A unique aspect of a publicly held company—a company in which the stock is traded on public markets—is that ownership and management of the company are separated. Management, as an agent for the stockholders, is responsible for maximizing the stockholders' share value through the firm's growth and profitability. Yet, one might ask, who is really serving the interests of the stockholders? Management decides on everything from the direction of the company to the compensation of the top executives. How does the shareholder have any voice in the process? Through the board of directors. Usually a group of business experts from both outside and inside the company's management, the board acts as the voice of the shareholder-owners and conducts board meetings to ensure that the interests of the shareholders are being met. Shareholders usually have the right to elect board members.

Each shareholder is entitled to his or her proportionate share of all the earnings—that is, the profits—generated by the company. This is where the stock gets its true value. As a shareholder in that firm, you are entitled to a proportional share of this and all future years' earnings (after paying interest to the bondholders). However, these earnings may or may not be distributed to shareholders as dividends. Periodically, the board convenes to decide how much of the earnings will be paid out to the shareholders in the form of dividends and how much will be plowed back into the company to finance future growth. This is a critical decision that reflects a careful balancing act between the present cash needs of the shareholders and the future potential of the company. For instance, had McDonald's paid out all its earnings in dividends in the early 1960s, its shareholders might well have sacrificed that company's enormous growth.

Different industries pay out varying percentages of their earnings as dividends. Electrical utilities, for instance, traditionally pay out most of their earnings, as they have relatively less need for expansion. Emerging growth firms, on the other hand, have many opportunities for expansion and thus tend to pay lower dividends or none at all.

One of the advantages of owning stock is the ease of trading it. A glance at the newspaper, a call to a broker, and you can instantly buy or sell most stocks listed on the organized exchanges. Note, however, that you are not buying stock from the company but from another owner of the shares who has decided to sell. When a company first brings its shares to the market, this is an initial public offering, or "new issue." Only when buying a new issue are you supplying capital directly to the company.

Immediately after (and often before!) the initial public offering, shares begin trading on the exchanges as investors call up their brokers to buy or sell. They are then said to be trading on the secondary market—the market among investors—as opposed to the primary market, that between the company and the initial purchasers of the shares. Although company management is not directly involved in trading the shares after that point, it remains responsible to the owners of those shares and is quite concerned about the value of the shares in the secondary market.

Making Money in the Market

By now you should sense that the major factor in stock prices is the earnings potential, or profitability, of a company. The value of a company, and hence a share of its stock, is equivalent to today's assessment of the value of all future earnings paid out by that company. The secondary market is an auction market where prospective buyers of stock, represented by brokers, meet with the sellers of stock, represented by other brokers, to agree on the price.

If a company were to announce a major advancement in its product line, one that could double the earnings of the company in years to come, a seller of stock would certainly expect a higher price than before the announcement. The buyer, on the other hand, would be willing to pay a higher price. Thus, we would expect to see the price of a share of stock climb immediately after a major announcement of this sort. Conversely, should a company announce bad news, we would expect to see the price of the stock go down.

We will discuss the market as a whole later in this chapter, but bear in mind that the fundamental cause for stock price fluctuations is the changing projection of future earnings. In addition, as explained in appendix D, falling interest rates, all other things being equal, cause the prices of stocks to go up; rising interest rates, other things equal, cause stock prices to decline.

There are two components of the returns from a share of stock: dividends and the price appreciation. We can express this equation as follows:

$$\text{Total return in percent} = \frac{\text{Dividends} + \text{Increase in Share price}}{\text{Share price}}$$

To be competitive in the market, therefore, a company must generate either high dividend returns or high share price appreciation. The board of directors decides dividends, based on earnings performance and need of funds for expansion; the market decides appreciation, based on expected future performance.

The 1986 tax reforms repealed the long-term capital gains deduction so that all capital gains and dividends are now taxed at the ordinary income tax rate. It is still true, however, that capital gains are not recognized as income until they are "realized"—that is, when stock is sold for more than its original purchase price. Hence, dividends are received and taxed annually, but capital gains are taxed only when stock is actually sold. Net capital losses are subtracted from taxable income, but allowable losses are capped at $3,000 per year, with unused losses carried forward to subsequent years.

Investment Advice

If you were to ask most investors how they decide which stocks to buy, the responses would range from mystical to hysterical. In general, most investors rely on three sources: stockbrokers, the media, and friends. Unfortunately, none of them have any "secret insights" to advise you on which are the best companies. You should also cast a suspicious eye over stock recommendations in newspapers, unless you're the only person with a subscription. *USA Today's* "Money" section covers stocks and virtually always recommends a "buy." At a rate of two per day, they could recommend the entire New York Stock Exchange within three years. The recommendations of friends and acquaintances should, obviously, be acted upon with care. Stockbrokers and other professionals in the business may be good sources of information but should not be considered infallible, nor do they possess special "inside information."

Stockbrokers are paid for generating trading activity, not for picking stocks, so don't be afraid to ask questions before setting up an account.

1. "How many other accounts do you handle?" Too many, and you may get lost in the shuffle, especially if you are one of the smaller accounts.
2. "How long have you been a stockbroker?" Often, new accounts are handed over to new stockbrokers. Try to meet an established stockbroker.
3. "May I speak to some of your other clients?" This is perhaps the best thing to do. It is the only way to get a reasonably reliable feel for this person's ability to give you good advice. If he won't refer you to any of his other clients, find a different broker.

Consider whether you should even be using a broker at all. If you don't feel confident in your stock selections without advice from a broker, you may be better off investing in mutual funds (discussed in the next chapter), thereby using managers with demonstrable performance records to make such decisions for you.

Discount Brokers

Consider using a discount broker if you make your own investment decisions. Discounters achieve substantial cost savings by hiring no analysts and dealing with customers through salaried employees rather than commissioned brokers. Thus, they cannot provide you with any guidance, but they do pass along most of their savings to you in substantially lower commissions when you trade. Discounters provide the same service you get from conventional brokers with regard to trading execution and documentation, record keeping, and securities safekeeping. The following table compares approximate 1993 commission charges for buying or selling shares of a $30 stock among several discount brokers and Merrill Lynch, the largest conventional broker:

Broker	Phone	Number of Shares		
		100	300	500
Pacific Brokerage Services	(800) 421-8395	$ 25	$ 25	$ 25
Charles Schwab & Company	(800) 435-4000	50	94	114
Muriel Siebert & Company	(800) 872-0711	45	77	91
Waterhouse Securities	(800) 934-4443	35	51	79
Merrill Lynch	(800) 637-7455	85	204	292

Analyzing Stocks

If you are a serious investor who wants to invest directly in stocks, it is almost a requirement that you do some research yourself. Stock research comes in two forms: technical and fundamental analysis. Technical analysis is concerned less with the stock and its earnings and more with its trading history. Technical analysts, or technicians, claim to be able to spot trends and patterns in trading that mere mortals such as ourselves are unable to recognize. They use arcane terms like "head-and-shoulder formations" and "resistance levels" and assert their ability to predict future price movements from historical patterns. There is certainly sufficient skepticism among teachers and practitioners of finance as to whether there is any truth to their unproven claims. In fact, one of the most respected voices on the subject of financial markets, Professor Burton Malkiel of Princeton, claims that prices on Wall Street are a "random walk," meaning that no information from the past can help predict future price changes. Yet the technicians persist, and usually offer an opinion apart from the more earthbound analysts, the fundamentalists.

Fundamental analysis is the process of developing a business evaluation of a company, specifically its earning ability in foreseeable future years. All available information about a company is incorporated into earnings projections. Once that information is gathered, the analyst then discounts those projections back to a fair present value of the stock. If the analyst's projections show that the stock is underpriced, it is rated as a buy; if the stock is overvalued, the recommendation is to sell.

One popular fundamental analysis process consists of four elements: *economic* analysis, *industry* analysis, *company* analysis, and *pricing* analysis. Each of the levels of analysis is a go/no-go screen; only companies that pass the screen are further analyzed. Once the last screens are complete, the analyst has a list of stocks considered for purchase.

The first level, economic analysis, is a macroeconomic assessment of the economy as a whole. The stock market, after all, is merely a reflection of the U.S. economy. It stands to reason that the market will do well in strong economies and poorly in weak economies. If the future macroeconomic outlook is for stable or falling inflation, lower future interest rates, and healthy economic growth, the climate for stock investments is positive. In fact, the best time to buy stocks is during recessions, just before other investors begin to anticipate renewed growth in the economy.

Further analysis focuses on the performance of specific industries within the current economic environment. Certain industries lead recoveries and business expansions, while others lag. If you anticipate a business recovery, industries such as electronics, metals, automobile suppliers, and the like should be considered. In the latter phase of the recovery, industries such as automobile manufacturers, consumer goods, and recreation and leisure goods should be evaluated.

The purpose of the next level, company analysis, is not to identify the winners but to screen out the losers. In every industry, no matter how strong the economy is or how "right" that particular industry is, some companies are better, some are worse. Fundamental analysts use several tools here, such as company visits and ratio analysis (a technique by which key indicators of a company's financial health are compared against specific industry benchmarks). A detailed discussion of company analysis is beyond the scope of this book. If you want to learn more about financial analysis of individual companies, consult a good text in managerial finance; see the references at the end of this chapter for suggestions.

The final level of analysis is a pricing analysis of the individual stock. It doesn't matter if IBM, for instance, passes all your screens and is considered the finest corporation in the world. If the stock is too expensive, it's not a good buy. Pricing analysis estimates a reasonable price for a share of stock and compares it to the current market price. If the current market price is less than or equal to your "fair" price, it's worth buying. If it drastically exceeds your "fair" price, let it pass. Then, among all the stocks rated as "buys," select one or more that compete well against the others.

The problem with the approach described above is that it is difficult to execute. Individual investors are not trained to make these types of assessments. This work is too time-consuming to accomplish, and the payoffs to the research are minimal unless you have an enormous investment portfolio. Perhaps even more important, most of this research is *already* incorporated into the current price of the stock. By the time an investor researches and reacts to positive information on a stock, the price gains from that information have already been taken by a professional trader. In the terminology of finance experts, markets have a tendency to be *efficient*. This means that the "fair" price for a stock at any given time is simply its current market price, which has already reacted to any available information. Even if markets are not efficient, professional money managers and traders are likely to snap up the bargains long before you even notice them.

An Alternative Approach

Although the top-down approach described above is the most widely used and discussed stock-picking method for professionals, many consistently successful investors attack the problem from the opposite direction—a "bottom-up" approach. In *One Up on Wall Street,* successful former mutual fund manager Peter Lynch states that any good management team with a decent product can do well in business. With the bottom-up approach, most of your analytical effort concentrates on specific individual companies in a search for good managers to trust with your money. A much smaller amount of time goes into industry analysis; the reasoning again is that good people will make good money regardless of the nature of their business. Finally, many bottom-up practitioners take pride in doing virtually no macroeconomic analysis. Believing that broad cyclical moves in the economy are difficult if not impossible to predict, they feel more confident searching within the market for good relative values among individual stocks. Noticing good products and good managers *before* the Wall Street traders do is perhaps the only way that the individual investor can "compete" in an already overanalyzed market.

The purpose of fundamental analysis, it should be reiterated, is to give the investor a sense of what a particular share of stock is worth and how that stock stacks up against alternative investments. A careful analysis of a particular company can reveal insights and observations not seen by the casual investor. It allows the investor to be proactive in dealing with stockbrokers, rather than blindly accepting the unseen analysis of the broker's firm. It is an inexact science, but if performed carefully the process will help you earn at least the fair returns of the market even if you're not lucky enough to surpass them. However, unless you are committed to acquiring skills

DEBT/EQUITY ASSETS

There are a wide variety of financial assets that combine a fixed-return with equity. The rules concerning the fixed-return and equity features are often complicated and vary with each asset. As a result, the investor should take great care when purchasing these assets. Two of the most popular types are convertible bonds and exchangeable bonds. A convertible bond is a corporate bond that can be *converted* at the option of the holder into common stock of the *same* corporation. An exchangeable bond is like a convertible bond except that the bond can be *exchanged* for common stock of a *different* corporation. In both cases, the conversion from a bond to a stock occurs at a predetermined price. The advantage of these types of assets is that they offer the safety and fixed income of a bond with some of the potential for large gains that you would enjoy as a stockholder. The market recognizes this advantage. As a result, these assets often sell at a premium over both their bond and conversion values. Before these assets are purchased, a careful analysis is necessary to determine if their unique features are worth the additional premium.

COMMODITY SPECULATION

One prominent member of a leading brokerage house concluded that more than 98 percent of those small investors who enter the commodity markets "lose their shirts." He went on to marvel that there were always more people ready and eager to take the losers' places.

A major attraction of the commodity market is the chance to "make a killing" with a small stake by using *margin*. Margin allows a small investor (with perhaps around $1,000 to invest) to control a large commodity contract (tens of thousands of dollars). For example, $800 on an 8 percent margin contract will allow you to control $10,000 worth of a commodity. Assume, for illustration, a speculation in a standard contract of 60,000 pounds of soybean oil. If the price goes up only 1 cent per pound, you make $600 on your margin deposit (ignoring brokerage expenses).

What risks do you run?

1. What if the price should drop? If it is a 1 cent drop, your margin is practically wiped out, plus you owe the broker fees and will have to replace your margin deposit.

2. Not all commodities are traded actively at all times. To control the wild gyrations in commodity prices somewhat, the exchanges impose limits on the price movements that can occur in a single trading day. Soybean oil prices, for example, can go up or down only 1 cent per day before trading ceases for the day.

(Continued from previous page: that go well beyond this brief introduction, such as a careful study of a managerial finance textbook, the best vehicle for making equity investments may well be mutual funds, which are the subject of the next chapter.)

Suppose you suddenly hear that a bumper crop of soybeans will be harvested and you call your broker to sell. Let us assume you are very lucky. Of 350 people who place hurried orders to sell, you are in the first 5 percent; in fact, you are number 16 in a list containing the other 349 sell orders. Except now the buyers also know that the price will fall and will not buy. As a result only five buyers (who desperately need soybean oil) buy before the price drops the full 1 cent and trading stops. The next day only another five buy, the price drops 1 cent again, and trading stops. The third day is a repeat performance. Finally, on the fourth day, you (in the lucky top 4 or 5 percent), sell your contract. In the meantime you have lost sleep and $600 per day plus fees and commissions. You can get "locked out" of the market like this and lose control over the extent of your losses.

3.   At this point you may say, "Why sell at all? I will just wait until the price goes up again." Unfortunately, another difference between stocks and commodities must now be noted. All commodity contracts come due on a certain date. You must sell the contract before that date—unless you really want to have 60,000 pounds of soybean oil delivered to your local warehouse in your name in a tank car. If that should occur, you would of course have to pay the full $10,000 or the value of the commodity plus shipping and storing expenses! Even if you had a contract with a due date some time off and did not sell, you would still have to cover your $600 losses per day during the price drops.

All our discussion of commodity speculation so far has assumed that you are "buying long"—that is, you have obligated yourself to buy the commodity at the agreed price. This means you make money when the price goes up and lose when the price goes down. You could just as well "sell short," or obligate yourself to deliver the commodity for the agreed price. This way you win when the price drops and lose when it goes up. You can bet either way on commodity price movements (and most active stocks too for that matter), and you make money if you guess correctly. You lose if the price moves against you. Unlike stocks, though, commodities are a "zero-sum game." There is a short position held by an investor for every long position, so everyone's gains and losses offset in total.

One final point on commodities. You don't have to employ all the leverage available to you. You can choose to control fewer contracts than the maximum allowed with the money you put up. This would reduce your risk. It would also, of course, reduce your potential profit. For example, you might pay the full price in cash for a Canadian Maple Leaf gold bullion coin (around $385 in 1993). While this is a "commodity speculation," many people would see the purchase as a fairly conservative investment.

BEWARE OF SCAMS

Countless investors, eager for quick gains, get lured into fraudulent scams. The North American Securities Administration Association estimates that annual U.S. investment fraud totals $40 billion. You can avoid becoming a victim by recognizing a few telltale signs of a scam:

1. Unsolicited telephone calls. Beware of persistent salespeople on the phone promising quick profits. Just tell them you don't like to discuss business at home, and politely but quickly hang up.
2. High-pressure tactics. Chief among these is a sense of urgency that the salesperson will try to make you feel (for example, "We have only a few shares left in inventory at this low price, and they're going fast," or, "Better buy now before this news hits the street").
3. Too good to be true. This is the most reliable of all tip-offs. Every scam will be described as a deal offering huge profits at little risk. The only people who are giving away something for nothing are the poor souls who fall for these fish stories and invest their hard-earned dollars. Financial markets will "price" risk so that assets with higher average returns will also have higher risk. In other words, if something sounds too good to be true, it probably is.

If you are offered an investment that seems questionable, just say no!

TAX AVOIDANCE FOR SMALL INVESTORS

While the tax reforms of 1986 have generally reduced the tax rates most Americans face, some significant changes were also made that affect the taxation of investment returns. The most important are the loss of special tax treatment for capital gains, the restrictions on the use of Individual Retirement Accounts (IRAs), and the new rules on tax exemption of municipal bonds. You need to be aware of the tax laws because taxation can greatly affect the actual rate of return you earn. You want to use tax-exempt and tax-deferred investments when they offer you a higher rate of return, but don't buy an investment simply because of its tax status. Do the arithmetic and make sure it is better for you than a fully taxable alternative.

The arithmetic to which we refer involves comparing the after-tax rate of return on a fully taxable investment with the return on tax-exempt or tax-deferred investments. A simple method for obtaining the after-tax return is to multiply the taxable rate of return by one minus the marginal rate at which it will be taxed. Don't forget about state income taxes. For example, if your federal income tax bracket is 28 percent and your state income tax bracket is 7 percent, you pay 28 cents of every dollar of extra income you earn to the federal government and (almost) 7 cents of every extra dollar you earn to the state government. So if you can earn 8 percent on a fully taxable investment, you get to keep approximately 5.20 percent $[0.08 \times (1 - 0.28 - 0.07)]$ after taxes. In this case, it would be wise to use a tax-exempt investment only if you could find one that paid more than 5.20 percent. (Many municipal bonds issued by states are not taxable to citizens of that state, while fully taxable interest is often taxed by states. So if you purchase a municipal bond from another state, and its interest is taxable in your state, you will have to compare the after-tax return of the fully taxable bond to the after-tax return of the municipal bond.)

For investments that offer tax deferral until a later time, the comparison is a bit more complicated. Normally, when the tax law allows deferral of taxes, it will specify that all the returns will be fully taxable at some later time, usually after age fifty-nine. With tax deferral, the government "lends" you the current taxes for reinvestment without charging you interest. The practical effect of tax deferral is that you earn a higher compound rate of return, so your investment grows more rapidly. Thus, tax-deferred investments offer excellent ways to save for long-term goals. IRA accounts, annuity contracts, and cash-value policies sold by insurance companies have been among the most popular means to earn tax-deferred interest.

Tax deferral is certainly a valuable tax benefit. For example, if you earn 5 percent on a taxable savings account and you pay 28 percent of your earnings to the federal government (and you live in a state with no income tax), your after-tax rate of return is only 3.6 percent (0.05 × 0.72). A $10,000 investment earning an effective rate of interest of 3.6 percent would be worth $20,285 in twenty years. If you could defer the tax on the 5 percent earnings, however, your money would grow at 5 percent and you would have $26,532 after twenty years. Of course, in a tax-deferred investment, you will owe taxes on all the accumulated interest ($16,532) when you take the money out in twenty years. But even if you pay the 28 percent tax on that amount, you will still have $21,903 left, more than you would have with the fully taxable asset.

Two points are important about tax deferral. First, the higher the rate of taxable return you can earn, the more valuable it is to be able to defer taxes on it. For example, if you used 10 percent in place of 5 percent in the previous example, the tax-deferred advantage is more than $10,000 after twenty years. Second, tax deferral becomes more valuable as tax rates rise, as they have under the 1993 tax changes.

Under current federal tax laws, you may deduct an IRA contribution of up to $2,000 from your current taxable income if your income is $40,000 or less for couples filing jointly, or $25,000 for an individual tax return. The allowable deduction is reduced by $200 for each $1,000 that taxable incomes rises above these levels. Thus, no deductions are possible for single taxpayers who earn more than $35,000, or for couples who earn more than $50,000.

You may contribute more than $2,000 to your IRA in any year, and the additional contribution will earn tax-deferred interest, but it cannot be deducted from current income for tax purposes. When you withdraw funds from your IRA, you pay taxes only on income that was not taxed previously. That is, you will owe taxes on the contributions for which you took a deduction and on all accumulated interest, but not on any additional contributions you made above the deductible amount. Therefore, you must maintain careful records showing which contributions were tax deductible and which were not. In fact, this process is simplified by maintaining separate IRA accounts for tax-deductible and non-tax-deductible contributions.

Congress clearly intends tax-deferred investments to be used only for long-term goals, such as saving for retirement. For IRAs and deferred annuity contracts, the law stipulates that substantial penalties, normally 10 percent of the tax-deferred return, will be imposed if you make any withdrawals before you are fifty-nine and a half. And, of course, you will pay the tax you owe on the deferred earnings at that time, too. The law does allow penalty-free withdrawals if you become disabled before retirement age, but for most people, the invested funds are pretty well locked up for a long time.

The length of time you need to leave your funds in your IRA before the benefit of tax deferrability outweighs the penalty depends on your tax rate, your return on the investment, and whether you can deduct the contributions from current income. With a 28 percent tax bracket, a 10 percent return, and a fully deductible contribution, you will earn a higher return in an IRA, even with the penalty, if you leave your funds in the IRA for at least six years. If you cannot deduct the contribution, then you must leave the funds in the IRA for eleven years to break even after the penalty. Therefore, it is best to use a tax-deferred investment only if you are sure you will not need the money for a number of years.

Prior to 1986, 60 percent of capital gains (profits realized when an asset such as stock or real estate is sold) on assets owned for more than six months was excluded from taxation. Because stocks and real estate typically derive much of their return from capital gains, this provision favored these investments. Part of the rationale for this exclusion was that it gave investors some additional incentive to invest in risky assets, and it was partial protection for investors so that they would not pay taxes on the purely inflationary portion of the capital gain. Now, however, the full amount of capital gains income must be claimed for tax purposes. This may change again in the near future, although no one yet knows quite how or when. But even with the less generous treatment of capital gains, stocks and other risky assets still typically provide higher rates of return than safer investments over long periods. Therefore, these assets remain appropriate investments for long-term goals.

SUMMARY OF FINANCIAL INVESTING

Over the long term, returns for investors in bonds consistently exceed those of savings accounts, and returns on stocks exceed bond returns. However, bonds are riskier than savings accounts, and stocks are riskier than bonds. All investors must evaluate their tolerance for risk and invest accordingly. Those who blindly avoid bonds and stocks (and the mutual funds that invest in them) on the basis of risk aversion also give up the opportunity to earn the higher returns needed to keep ahead of taxes and inflation. Wisely selected and patiently held equity investments can help you reach your long-term goals—those financial needs ten or more years away. Use bonds and certificates of deposit to meet nearer-term specific financial needs, and limit your risk by matching bond maturities with the date you need the funds. Savings accounts and money market mutual funds are appropriate for emergency reserves and very short-term goals. Focus on after-tax returns, and examine investment alternatives that allow you to legally defer or avoid taxes. Quite frankly, we see no reason to recommend highly risky investments such as leveraged commodity futures and some other extremely volatile investment vehicles not discussed here to the small investor. The evidence suggests that with such investments, your broker will make a good living at your expense. Finally, if you decide to invest in stocks or bonds, we recommend that you consider using mutual funds as the vehicle for implementing your investment strategy.

TIPS ON SAVING AND INVESTING

While no chapter on investing in financial assets can cover this complex area completely, the information we provided should give you an idea of the investment media available. As you research various ways to invest and plan for your future needs, you may find it useful to keep in mind some tips on saving and investing.

1. Set financial goals based on your future consumption needs.
2. Begin saving now and save a minimum amount each month. Your future goals will be expensive. Plan your spending to avoid major changes in your living standard when the future arrives. Compound interest is an amazingly powerful force, but it requires time to work.
3. Beware of mob psychology in investment decisions. Greed, unrealistic expectations of gain, and ignorance can spell disaster for an investment program. Investigate "hot tips" carefully and regard even the conventional wisdom with skepticism. Remember: In order to have a reasonable expectation of larger gains, you must accept higher risks of loss. There is no free lunch.
4. Diversify your holdings. Use a variety of investment media to meet your goals. A well-balanced savings plan should include short-term savings, investment in stocks and bonds, and, frequently, real estate.
5. Shop around for reliable brokers, insurance agents, or other professionals. Use their knowledge to your advantage, but beware of high fees.
6. Inform yourself. Know your personal finances and understand your investment options. If you educate yourself, you won't be misled by sellers of financial services you don't need.
7. Keep records of your investment performance for tax purposes and to assess your progress toward your goals.
8. Use available legal methods of tax avoidance and tax deferral to increase your after-tax return.

Your financial planning will be successful if you set out your goals, honestly evaluate your willingness to save and invest, and then take the actions necessary to achieve those goals.

SUGGESTED REFERENCES

Brealy, Richard A. *An Introduction to Risk and Return from Common Stocks,* 2d ed. Cambridge, MA: The MIT Press, 1987. An excellent introduction to the basic concepts of investing.

Edleson, Michael E. *Value Averaging.* A lively guide to a simple and effective investment strategy.

Gitman, L. J., and M. D. Joehnk. *Fundamentals of Investing,* 3rd ed. New York: Harper & Row, 1988.

Lynch, Peter. *One Up on Wall Street.* New York: Penguin Books, 1990. Currently available in most bookstores.

The Outlook. Standard and Poors, Inc., 25 Broadway, New York, NY 10004. Published weekly and available in many libraries.

Schell, Lawrence D., and Charles W. Haley. *Introduction to Financial Management.* New York: McGraw-Hill, 1991.

Train, John. The *Money Masters.* New York: Harper and Row, 1980. An entertaining analysis of the techniques used by nine great investors.

———. *Preserving Capital and Making It Grow.* New York: Clarkson N. Potter, 1983. A very readable overview of investment strategy for long-term goals.

ValueLine Investment Survey. ValueLine, SE 44th Street, New York, NY 10017. Available by subscription and in many libraries.

14

Buying Mutual Funds

MANY SERVICEMEMBERS LACK the time or the knowledge necessary to invest directly in stocks, bonds, and other securities. Mutual funds offer the means to indirectly invest in many types of securities without the need to spend hours each week analyzing your investments. This chapter will give you the necessary information to invest in mutual funds on your own.

MUTUAL FUND BASICS

Mutual funds are investment companies that invest pools of money from many individual investors. When you buy a mutual fund, you are really hiring an investment management team. This management team takes your money, along with thousands of other investors' money, and buys stocks, bonds, or other securities according to the fund's stated investment objectives. The management team makes all the decisions regarding when to buy and sell a particular security. This frees up time for you, the individual investor.

Not only do you get a management team to make your investing decisions, you also get a diversified portfolio by investing as little as $1. Suppose you decide to invest $1 in Twentieth Century Growth Fund, which has no minimum investment. For simplicity, let's say that the fund owns equal amounts of fifty different stocks. As a result, you would now own 2 cents ($1/50$ of your dollar) worth of each stock. Even if one stock went completely bankrupt, you would only lose 2 percent (or 2 cents) of your investment. The risk of losing all your money is therefore decreased dramatically compared to your alternative of buying just one stock with your dollar. To achieve a reasonable level of diversification when investing in stocks directly, you would need to buy at least 100 shares (to reduce transaction costs) of twenty different stocks. If the average share price of the stocks you bought was $25, you would need at least

$50,000. You can get the same level of diversification (risk reduction) in a mutual fund with only $1. For most of us, then, mutual funds are our only choice if we want a diversified portfolio.

Mutual funds also enable you to buy securities you would otherwise not be able to buy. For instance, who has $100,000 to buy a jumbo CD or piece of commercial paper, or $10,000 to buy a Treasury bill? Few people in the military do. But we all have a few dollars we could invest in a money market mutual fund, which buys those securities.

Mutual funds provide these advantages and more. For a servicemember who wants to invest his money in a diversified, managed portfolio without committing a lot of time, mutual funds are the way to go.

MUTUAL FUND FEES

Obviously, mutual funds will not manage your money for free. You will have to pay for the convenience they provide, but as a wise investor you can reduce these fees tremendously through good research before you buy a fund. Three types of fees you need to be aware of are commissions to buy and sell the fund (called loads), yearly management fees, and so-called 12b-1 fees.

Load versus No-load Funds

There are two types of loads: front-end loads (sales commissions) and back-end loads (redemption fees). By law, mutual funds can charge a sales commission of up to 8.5 percent of your investment. If you invest $1,000 in a mutual fund with an 8.5 percent front-end load, then only $915 goes into the fund, while $85 goes to the salesman who sold you the fund and possibly to the fund's underwriters. In reality, however, you are paying a commission of 9.3 percent ($85 ÷ $915 = 9.3%); you pay $85 to get an actual investment of $915, *not* $1,000. This means you would have to get a return of 9.3 percent on your mutual fund before you even break even on your initial investment of $1,000!

The most expensive type of front-end-loaded funds you can buy is the so-called *contractual* mutual fund like Fidelity Destiny, Summit Investors, First Investors, Security Action, and others. Insurance agents, commissioned financial planners, and other mutual fund peddlers prefer to sell you this kind of fund because the salesman's compensation is so much more lucrative than with other load funds. Contractual mutual funds obligate you to invest a set number of dollars every month over a ten- to twenty-year time frame. This "contract" is not generally a legal obligation, and you can get out of it whenever you wish. The bad thing about contractual plans is that they charge "up front" in the first year the majority of the total sales commission for your expected investments over the full life of the plan (8.5 percent of anticipated investments). This means that 50 percent or more of your first year's investments go into the salesman's pocket, and not into your account. As a result, the total effective present value of the sales commission you pay can be as high as 13 percent. On a "little" $100-a-month, twenty-year contract plan, this is roughly equivalent to writing a check to the salesman right now for almost $2,000 commission. Worse yet, if you want to get out before the end of your "contract," you may lose up to 40 percent of your initial investment, because the up-front commissions are nonrefundable after your grace period (usually eighteen months) expires (see "A Dumb Way to Buy Mutual Funds," *Changing Times,* March 1989, pp. 59–63). Salesmen armed with more than an ounce of persuasion, a bag of tricks, and years of experience are quite skilled at making these plans look attractive to the unsophisticated investor. Avoid these types of funds.

Even if a mutual fund does not have a front-end load, you may have to pay a commission (usually 2 to 6 percent) to *sell* your fund shares. Commissions paid at the time of sale are called a back-end load or redemption fee. Funds commonly impose redemption fees to discourage short-term investing or market timing (switching in and out of a fund to make short-term profits). Redemption fees are not prominently advertised, so you need to read the fund's *prospectus* carefully to see if the fund has any. Some funds have "declining" redemption fees that start out high and then decline to a very low fee (or none at all) after you've held the shares several years. If the redemption fees apply only to money invested for six months or less, then you should not be concerned with them if you are a long-term investor.

Considering the fact that loads buy you nothing and simply reduce your return, should you ever buy a load fund? Do load funds outperform no-load funds, which charge no commissions to buy and sell them? Looking at all the available evidence, there is no study that has shown that load funds consistently outperform no-load funds. Remember that the load fee does not pay for superior research or better management. It simply compensates the salesman for selling you the shares. Based on the evidence, you should buy a load fund only if you are willing to pay someone to pick a mutual fund for you. The simple example in Table 14-1 shows the difference a load can have on your return. You invest $100 each month for five years in each of three mutual funds: a no-load fund, an 8.5 percent load fund, and a typical fifteen-year contract fund. Assuming the returns are 12 percent per year and management fees are

TABLE 14-1
Comparison of Net Returns in Load and No-load Funds
(Assuming a Steady 12% Rate of Return)

Fund	Monthly Investment	Total Value Net of Load	After 5 Years
No-load	$100.00	$100.00	$8,167
8.5% load	$100.00	$ 91.50	$7,473
Contract	$100.00	$ 50.00 (1 year) $ 97.50 (4 years)	$6,992

zero for each fund, your earnings in a no-load fund over the five-year time frame would exceed those of a load fund by about $700 and exceed those of the contract fund by about $1,200 (which is a full year's worth of investment contributions). If you are willing to invest a little time to pick your own fund, then no-load mutual funds are the way to go. This chapter will give you the knowledge you need to pick a fund yourself and avoid loads.

Management Fees

In order to pay the management team that guides the fund's operations, all mutual funds (load and no-load) charge *management fees*. These fees come out of the fund's assets and income; thus, the greater the fees, the less your net return. For example, a fund with a yearly return before management fees of 15 percent and management fees of 2 percent will return only 13 percent to you. Fund management fees generally range from .5 percent to 2 percent a year, with most of the larger funds charging under 1 percent. You will never write a check for these fees—they are deducted internally by the fund managers from the fund's total pool of assets gradually over the course of a year. This is confusing for most beginning investors, and this confusion makes it easy for some load-fund salesmen to imply that no-load funds are, in a sense, charging a load because of the management fee. Remember that *all* funds charge a management fee, even load funds.

12b-1 Fees

In 1980, the Securities Exchange Commission (SEC) adopted Rule 12b-1 under the 1940 Investment Company Act, which allows mutual funds to use their assets to finance sales-related expenses. Asset-based sales charges, or "12b-1 fees," permit a fund advisor to pay for distribution costs, including commissions to salesmen and distribution and advertising expenses to promote the fund to prospective shareholders. Funds without 12b-1 fees market their shares directly, primarily through advertising, with investment advisors or principal underwriters paying distribution expenses out of their own profits. Until July 1993, 12b-1 plans with fees as high as 1.25 percent were quite popular with fund promoters because they allowed the fund to advertise itself as "no-load" while still paying ample commissions to salesmen out of investors' pockets. Moreover, fund promoters could circumvent existing maximum sales charge rules by adopting 12b-1 plans, either separately or in combination with front- or back-end sales loads. This allowed them to effectively charge investors more for distribution than could have been charged as a front-end sales load under existing maximum sales charge rules. Starting in July 1993, the SEC prohibited the sale of mutual-fund shares that have an asset-based sales charge in excess of .75 percent of a fund's average annual net assets. Furthermore, under these new rules, funds may not be described as "no-load" if they have asset-based sales charges of more than .25 percent of average annual net assets. Even though this recent change prevents mutual funds that charge 12b-1 fees greater than .25 percent of average net assets from masking load charges, you should read the mutual fund prospectus carefully to check for *any* 12b-1 fees. 12b-1 fees are misleading in that they appear quite small in comparison with typical front-end loads but are actually very large. Since they are charged each and every year, their long-term effect on returns is quite substantial compared to the one-time charge of a front-end load. For example, a 12b-1 load of .75 percent has the same effect as nearly a 4 percent front-end load if you were to hold the fund for five years. Over longer periods, even the smallest 12b-1 fees seriously degrade an investor's return.

MUTUAL FUND PRICES

As a mutual fund investor, you are concerned with two prices: the price per share when you buy the fund (offer price) and the price per share when you sell the fund (net asset value, or NAV). The NAV is simply the market value per share of the fund's assets on a given day minus the liabilities (debts) per share. Most large newspapers such as the *New York Times* and the *Wall Street Journal* contain daily mutual fund price quotations. An example of a mutual fund quotation is shown here.

	NAV	Offer Price	NAV Change
Templeton Group:			
Income	10.05	10.52	–.01
World	15.95	17.43	+.03
Bull & Bear Group:			
Capital Growth	6.90	NL	....
High Yield	7.83	NL	+.07

The Templeton Group is a "family" of load funds. The load is the difference between the offer price and the NAV. If you were to buy and sell the Templeton World Fund on the day above, you would pay a price of $17.43 per share to buy it and receive only $15.95 per share if you sold it. The load, then, equals $1.48 a share ($17.43 – $15.95). To calculate the percent load, simply divide the load by the offer price. For Templeton World, the percent load would then equal 8.5 percent ($1.48 ÷ $17.43), which is the maximum that can be charged by law. Note, however, that the true effective load is really 9.3 percent ($1.48 ÷ $15.95), as only $15.95 of your money is actually invested and the other $1.48 is just a commission markup that primarily goes into the salesman's pockets. The "NAV change" is the dollar change in the NAV from the previous day. Since Templeton World went up by 3 cents a share from the previous day, the previous day's NAV must have been $15.92 ($15.95 – 0.03).

The Bull & Bear Group is a family of no-load funds. These type of funds are easy to distinguish from load funds because of the "NL" in the offer-price column. You buy and sell no-load fund shares at the NAV. That means if you were to buy Bull & Bear Capital Growth, you would pay $6.90 per share and no commission. If you were to sell it, you would also sell it for $6.90 per share on that day. The dots in the NAV Change column for Bull & Bear Capital Growth Fund mean that the NAV did not change from the previous day.

Unfortunately, you cannot assume that the fund charges no load just because there is an "NL" in the offer-price column. It is true that the "NL" fund charges no front-end load. But the fund may charge a redemption fee when you sell your shares, or it may charge annual 12b-1 fees. In our example above, Bull & Bear Capital Growth Fund actually charges a rather large, 1 percent 12b-1 fee. To find out, read the fund's prospectus; these fees will be (by law) clearly stated and not hard to find.

TYPES OF MUTUAL FUNDS

All mutual funds can be further classified as either *closed-end* or *open-end*. *Closed-end* mutual funds are not found in the mutual fund price quotation section in the newspaper; their shares are sold on stock exchanges, just like normal stocks. They have a fixed number of shares outstanding, and the mutual fund does not normally buy or sell fund shares. Instead, fund shares are bought and sold between investors on the stock market. An investor who buys or sells closed-end funds must pay a brokerage commission just like someone who buys or sells stocks. The share price of a closed-end mutual fund is dependent not only on the current market value of the assets it owns, but also on the supply of and demand for the fund's shares on the market. Most closed-end mutual funds trade below the NAV of the fund (this is called trading at a discount). If the fund becomes popular, then the fund's price on the market may exceed the NAV. An example is the Taiwan Fund, which has traded at a premium of 100 percent over its NAV. The current prices of closed-end funds can be found in your newspaper's stock pages. As a general rule, favor closed-end funds that trade at a discount to their NAV, but don't expect that the discount will disappear soon. Realize that you risk a loss in your share price due not only to a decrease in the value of the fund's assets but also to a possible decrease in demand for the fund's shares on the market.

The second major category of mutual funds is *open-end* funds. These are the most common type, with over 3,000 to choose from, compared with about 100 closed-end funds. In contrast to closed-end funds, open-end fund shares can be bought or sold only from the mutual fund itself or through its salesmen. Open-end fund shares do not trade on the stock market like closed-end funds. An open-end fund will sell as many shares as investors demand and must redeem (buy back) investors' shares whenever investors want to sell them. The share price of an open-end fund is purely dependent on the net asset value of the securities in its portfolio (and any load, if applicable). Thus, unlike closed-end funds, open-end funds' share prices are not directly affected by the supply and demand for their shares, but by the supply and demand for the securities in their portfolio. This chapter will focus primarily on open-end mutual funds. They are more convenient and generally favored by small investors over closed-end funds, and even over direct investment in individual stocks.

Categories of Open-end Mutual Funds

Mutual funds can also be classified by their investment mix, as stated in their prospectuses. Funds can be generally grouped into six categories: money market, stock (equity), bond, combination stock and bond, foreign, and real asset. Figure 14-2 ranks the funds from least risky (money market funds) to most risky (real asset funds). These categories encompass at least six typical investment *objectives,* ranging from capital preservation to aggressive growth, as shown in the accompanying illustration.

Money Market Mutual Funds
Money market mutual funds invest in short-term, fixed-income securities such as Treasury bills and CDs. Because these funds invest only in short-term securities, there is little asset price or default risk with them. Though they are not federally insured, over the last twenty years only a few money market mutual funds have experienced a loss; these losses were minor and were generally "made good" by the fund manager, so that no investor lost money. Therefore, you should not experience a loss in a money market fund, and they are the most conservative types of mutual funds to buy.

These funds provide returns based on the returns on the securities in which they invest. Therefore, the returns on money-market funds vary as short-term interest rates vary in the economy. However, the yields of money market mutual funds are usually much greater than what you could get in a bank savings account or even a bank money market deposit account. Also, unlike other funds, the shares of money market funds are set at $1, so returns are provided by issuing new shares and not through changes in share price. Most newspapers print the latest seven-day average yields on money market funds once or twice a week (see the *Wall Street Journal* every Tuesday and Thursday).

Money market funds are an excellent place to put your emergency savings and savings intended for short-term goals (less than a year). Most money market mutual funds offer free check writing (for checks greater than a certain minimum amount, usually $500), telephone wire redemption services, and electronic fund transfers to or from your bank account. That makes money market funds among the most liquid of all mutual funds. Getting your cash out in time of need could not be much easier.

Money market mutual funds can be classified into three categories: general money market, U.S. government, and tax exempt. *General* money market funds invest in securities such as jumbo CDs (over $100,000), commercial paper, and Treasury bills. This type offers the highest yield of any money market fund. *U.S. government* money market funds invest only in U.S. government securities, such as Treasury bills. They are considered safer, but the yield is also less, to reflect the reduced risk. Finally,

FIGURE 14-2
Mutual Fund Categories and Risk

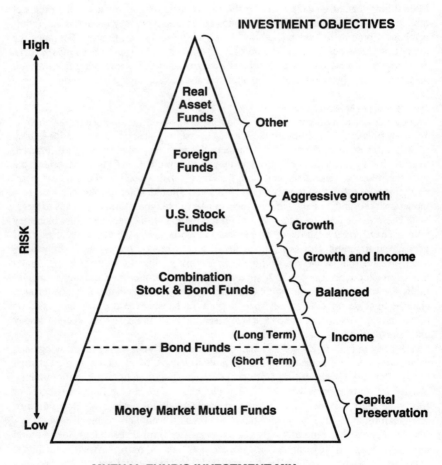

tax-exempt money market mutual funds invest in short-term municipal securities that are exempt from federal income taxes and may be exempt from state and local income taxes as well. Because of the decreased yield in tax-exempt funds, only individuals in the highest tax bracket should put money into them. To calculate the taxable equivalent yield on tax-exempt money market funds, simply divide the tax-exempt yield by one minus your marginal tax rate, which is the tax rate applied to the last dollar you earn (see chapter 8 for a discussion of current tax brackets).

Stock Mutual Funds

Stock or equity mutual funds can be broken into six categories, based on the fund's objectives, from least risky to most risky: income, growth and income, index, growth, aggressive growth, and specialized or sector. *Income* stock funds invest primarily in high-dividend-paying stocks and are the least risky type of stock fund. *Growth and income* stock funds invest not only in high-dividend-paying stocks but also in those stocks that pay few dividends and have high potential for capital gains (increases in share price due to increased earnings potential). The objective of *index* funds is to invest in a basket of stocks equal to a broad market index (e.g., the S&P 500) in order to get the same return as the market. Because of the low need for active management, index funds have the lowest expense ratios of any stock funds. *Growth* stock funds seek primarily capital appreciation and are not concerned with dividends. *Aggressive growth* funds have the same objective as growth funds, but they invest in more speculative stocks and seek rapid appreciation of capital. Finally, *specialized,* or *sector,* stock funds are the most risky of all stock funds because of the concentration of their stocks in one industry. Because they are not as diversified as the other stock funds, they carry greater risk. Sector funds tend to be the big winners—but also the big losers. Sector funds also have quite high expense ratios; therefore, they are not the best bet for the small or beginning investor.

Bond Mutual Funds

There are four main types of bond funds: high-yield, investment grade, U.S. government, and municipal. *High-yield* bond funds invest in so-called junk bonds. "Junk" is a popular catch-all term referring to all bonds with low safety ratings, or with no rating, from the major bond-rating agencies. Such bonds pay higher yields because they carry greater risk of default. *Investment grade* (normal) bond funds invest in higher-quality but lower-yielding corporate bonds. U.S. Treasury bonds make up the majority of the portfolios of *U.S. government* bond funds. Finally, *municipal* bond funds seek to obtain tax-free income by investing in fixed-income securities of states, cities, and other localities. As with most municipal securities, they are free from federal income tax and sometimes free from state and local income tax. Bond fund prices, like those of stock funds, are not fixed. They vary with the market value of the securities the fund owns. An important relationship to keep in mind for bond funds is that market interest rates and bond prices vary *inversely.* If interest rates rise, bond prices will fall, and so will your bond fund's share price. Also, be aware that the longer the average maturity of your fund's bond portfolio, the more volatile (or risky) the fund's returns will be.

Combination Stock and Bond Mutual Funds

Mutual funds that invest in a combination of stocks and bonds are also common and include asset allocation, balanced, and income funds. *Asset allocation* funds make active moves among a wide range of securities, including stocks, bonds, CDs, and Treasury bills. Their goal is to gain a high return by switching between securities when economic conditions and their forecasts supposedly warrant it. As a result, they seek to become the only mutual fund you need because they make the decision on whether you should be in bonds or stocks and how much money should be in each. Obviously, because these funds attempt to achieve higher yields by timing the market, their returns tend to be more volatile than other combination funds. *Balanced* funds seek to maintain fixed percentages of stocks and bonds in their portfolios. They do not try to time the market like asset allocation funds attempt to do. Because of their diversity, they generally have lower risk than most stock funds. *Income* funds seek current income through high-dividend-paying stocks as well as bonds.

Foreign Mutual Funds

Foreign mutual funds invest primarily in securities of countries other than the United States. Three types are prevalent: international, global, and single-country funds. *International* funds buy non-U.S. securities, usually in a very wide range of countries but sometimes in just one geographic region, such as the Pacific rim. *Global* funds buy both U.S. and non-U.S. securities. *Single-country* funds buy securities from only one country; an example is the Japan Fund. The majority of single-country funds are closed-end. Most foreign mutual funds invest only in stocks. Be aware that when you buy foreign mutual funds, you are taking on an additional risk called *exchange rate risk*. That means your return on the foreign fund will be affected not only by the return on the securities the fund bought, but also by changes in the foreign exchange rate between the dollar and the other country's currency. If the dollar appreciates versus the foreign currency, then it will take more foreign money to buy one dollar. So when your fund's returns are exchanged into dollars, you will receive fewer dollars per unit of foreign currency than before, and your return in dollars will be less than the return the securities provided when measured in terms of their home currency. By the same token, if the dollar depreciates and becomes worth less in terms of the foreign currency, then foreign money will buy more dollars and your return will increase.

Real Asset Mutual Funds

The last type of mutual funds, real asset funds, are among the most specialized of all funds. The two most popular types of real asset funds invest in precious metals and real estate. *Precious metals* funds primarily invest in gold or stocks of companies that mine gold. Gold is usually viewed as an inflation hedge because its price often increases when inflation heats up. There are also mutual funds that invest in real estate primarily through buying shares of real estate investment trusts. Again, these are highly specialized investments and therefore carry greater risk. Neither of these types of funds (or international funds, for that matter) is meant to be held as your only investment asset. By themselves, they provide highly volatile returns that well outweigh their expected rewards. But holding a small amount of these "inflation-hedge" funds as a portion of a well-balanced investment portfolio can actually enhance your investment performance by *reducing* the risk of your total portfolio. Therefore, a beginning investor might want to put a small share, about 10 to 15 percent, of his or her investment assets into these specialized types of funds.

BUYING AND SELLING MUTUAL FUNDS

With over three thousand mutual funds to choose from, it is easy to feel overwhelmed. This section will help you narrow the field and provide you with some knowledge about buying and selling funds and measuring returns.

Selecting a Mutual Fund

There are ten steps in the mutual fund selection process:

1. Formulate your financial goals and investment objectives.
2. Match each investment objective with a general fund category.
3. Based on your risk preference, pick a specific type of fund within the general category.
4. Decide whether you want a load or a no-load fund.
5. Drop funds with no proven management record.
6. Drop undiversified funds unless they meet a specific goal.
7. Drop high-expense funds. Check for other fees and hidden loads.
8. Drop fund(s) with the lowest risk-adjusted long-run returns.
9. Drop funds with high portfolio turnover rates.
10. Order prospectuses from the remaining funds and review them. Pick the fund that offers the services you desire.

Step One—Goals. The process of selecting a mutual fund begins with stating your financial goals and investment objectives. Chapter 1 can help you with the process of formulating your goals and objectives. Once you have identified goals and objectives, you can then begin to match them with a general fund category. For example, assume you have a financial goal of buying a $15,000 car in four years. Your investment objective may be to invest $250 per month in an investment with an expected annual return of 10 percent in order to come up with the $15,000 you need four years from now (appendix D explains how to do these simple calculations).

Step Two—Fund Category. Once you know your goals, you need to decide which mix of the six categories of mutual funds previously discussed best matches your investment objectives. The type of fund category you choose will depend in part upon your investment horizon, or the time frame over which you plan to invest, because the

TABLE 14-3
Mutual Fund Worksheet

Fund name:					
Objective:			Telephone #:		
Minimum investment:			Toll free?		
Minimum add'l invest:			Phone exchange allowed?		
Additional fund services:					
Fund Management and Performance					
# of securities held:			Risk level:		
# of industries:			Risk-adjusted rating:		
Annual Total Returns during the Previous Five Years					
Year	19	19	19	19	19
This fund					
Index					
T-bill rate					
Fund Expenses					
Front-end load:			Portfolio turnover (%):		
Redemption fee:			Management fee:		
Expense ratio:			12b-1 fee:		
Income and Tax Considerations					
Income yield:		Income distribution date:		Capital gains distribution date:	
Tax exempt interest:		Federal?		State & local?	

horizon length affects the relative risk of the various funds. For example, stock funds are less risky the longer your horizon. Any need you may have for steady income and whether you need to maintain purchasing power will also factor into your choice of a fund category. You should also consider your own personal income tax situation as well. In general, savings for short-term goals of less than one year should be invested in money market mutual funds. Money going toward medium-range goals of one to five years should be invested in short-term bond funds, combination stock and bond funds, or conservative stock funds. Finally, a mix of stock funds, foreign funds, and real asset funds may be used to satisfy long-range goals of greater than five years. For example, you might choose to invest the $250 per month for your car goal in a bond fund.

Step Three—Type of Fund. Having picked one of the six categories of mutual funds, you have greatly narrowed the field of mutual funds from which to choose. The next step is to pick which type of fund within the general category best matches your tolerance for risk and your financial objectives. You decide the level of risk you can tolerate and measure that against a fund's objective and portfolio holdings. Your own financial goals and objectives should match those of the fund you choose. For the car example, you have several types of bond funds to choose from: high yield, investment grade, U.S. government, and municipal. If you have a high tolerance for risk, then you might want to choose a high-yield bond fund. On the other hand, if you are very risk averse, then perhaps a U.S. government bond fund would be best. We will assume that you are risk averse and therefore choose to invest your car savings in a U.S. government bond fund. An even more risk-averse investor might be wise to limit the selection to a fund concentrating in short-term government notes.

Step Four—Load. Now that you have narrowed the field of mutual funds to one specific type, you must determine whether you want a load or a no-load fund. If you do not have the time or the desire to go through the process of selecting a specific fund and you can afford paying a sizable sales load, then you may want to go to a broker or financial planner who will recommend a load fund of the type you desire. For those of you who choose this path, the selection process has just ended. For those who want to invest in a no-load fund, you will need to proceed through the remaining selection criteria. In our example, you would have to decide on the specific no-load, U.S. government bond fund in which to invest.

Get Information Resources: From here on, you will need access to a good information source on mutual funds. There is a list of many commonly used mutual fund information resources at the end of this chapter. *Forbes, Money,* and *Business Week* provide good low-cost information. You may also want to order or buy at your local bookstore one of the mutual fund almanacs such as *Donoghue's* or the *Individual Investor's Guide to No-Load Mutual Funds* (published by the American Association of Individual Investors [AAII]). These have more complete data than any of the magazines. Your local library may have many of these resources available at no charge.

AAII, as well as others, also sells computerized mutual fund updates that facilitate screening and ranking mutual funds. These screening and sorting programs may be purchased by mail directly from the companies or organizations that produce them. Information on how to order the programs is provided in advertisements that appear in the magazines listed above.

Step Five—Record. You will now want to narrow the field of no-load U.S. government bond funds to a reasonable number. Since mutual funds have been around for a long time and there are many proven funds, you need not invest in newly started funds. Check to see which funds have established long-standing performance records. Also, make sure that the manager of the proven fund has been with the fund for at least the last three years. The fund's return may look great, but if the manager who earned those returns has since left, there is no guarantee the new manager will be just as good.

To compare the remaining funds, you may use a worksheet similar to the one shown in Table 14-3. Fill in any areas on the worksheet that you can. Any blanks may be filled in once you have narrowed the field further and called to obtain each fund's prospectus.

Step Six—Diversification. The next area to evaluate is the diversity of a mutual fund's portfolio. This is especially important with stock mutual funds. As a general rule, a mutual fund should have at least twenty substantially different securities in order to reduce its level of what financial experts call "diversifiable risk" to a minimum. The *Individual Investor's Guide to No-Load Mutual Funds* grades each fund's diversification.

Step Seven—Expenses. Unless a fund has consistently earned spectacular returns, you should drop it if it has a high annual expense ratio. The Securities and Exchange Commission requires all funds to include a *fee table* in their prospectus that will include the "ratio of expenses to net assets" for the fund. This should include the administrative expenses, management fee, and any 12b-1 charges imposed by the fund. Drop all money market funds with expense ratios of greater than .75 percent a year. The lowest-expense money market fund has an expense ratio of .33 percent a year as of this writing. Bond funds with expense ratios of greater than 1 percent a year should be dropped. Finally, all other types of funds with annual expense ratios of greater than 1.5 percent should not be considered further, as they either are inefficient or charge too much in fees. Also, be wary of funds whose management is partially absorbing expenses temporarily. If the fund ceases that practice, you will see their annual expense ratio go up.

In checking the expense ratio, you should also see if the fund has any 12b-1 fees. These fees are levied in addition to the fund's yearly management fees. Because 12b-1 fees cut into a fund's return, you should avoid funds that use them unless the fund offers a high risk-adjusted return or very low expenses to compensate for the 12b-1 charges. The investor in our example would now be down to less than a half dozen bond funds from which to choose.

Step Eight—Return. You should now look at each fund's performance. If you could predict the future, you would want the fund with the highest risk-adjusted return. Return needs to be adjusted for risk; otherwise, you might buy a high-return fund that also has unacceptably high risk (see the discussion on the risk-reward relationship in chapter 2). The easiest way to evaluate a fund's risk-adjusted past return is to look in *Forbes, Money, Business Week,* or *Changing Times* at their risk-adjusted ratings for each fund. *Forbes* gives each fund two grades based on its performance relative to other funds in its group during up and down markets. You can get a feel for the riskiness of each fund by looking at its performance grade in down markets. The lower the grade, the higher the risk of loss if the economy experiences a recession. *Money* does the same thing for the top performers in each fund category but goes one step further and ranks each fund based on its risk-adjusted return as well (where the risk-adjusted return equals the fund's excess return over the Treasury bill rate divided by the standard deviation of the fund's returns). *Business Week* also ranks funds on their risk-adjusted returns, but it ranks them based on the number of times each fund has failed to beat the Treasury bill rate over the last five years. The lower the ranking, the higher the risk of loss will be. Finally, *Changing Times* gives each fund a risk rating based on the variation of its returns over the last five years. One or all of these measures should be used to evaluate the risk-adjusted returns of the funds you are considering. Remember, though, that these historical guidelines cannot actually predict the best performers in the future.

You should also enter on your worksheet each fund's returns for each of the last five years (these come from the fund's prospectus). These returns should be compared with a market index (such as the S&P 500 index for stock funds and the Merrill Lynch bond index for bond funds) and with the rate you could have received on Treasury bills each year. Those funds with returns in excess of the index and Treasury bill rate are preferable. Eliminate those funds that have unacceptably low risk-adjusted returns.

Step Nine—Turnover. Of the remaining funds with the highest risk-adjusted return, you should look at each fund's portfolio turnover rate. These figures can be found in *Business Week, Money,* and the *Individual Investor's Guide,* among other places. A portfolio turnover ratio of 100 percent a year means that the fund normally holds securities one year before selling them. A higher rate means that they hold securities less than one year on the average. The average fund portfolio turnover rate is around 100 percent a year, but it varies widely by fund type. Studies have shown that funds with high portfolio turnover rates have lower returns when compared with similar type funds that have slower portfolio turnover. This is due, in part, to the fact that high portfolio turnover results in greater brokerage costs. Drop any funds with portfolio turnover rates that seem unusually high relative to the group of funds you are still considering.

Step Ten—Order Prospectuses and Choose. At this point, you are ready to order prospectuses from the remaining funds. When you receive a prospectus, review it carefully. The Securities and Exchange Commission currently requires that all mutual funds provide potential investors with a copy of the fund's prospectus. Although the SEC is expected to change this rule and permit mutual fund companies to sell funds directly through newspaper and magazines advertisements to investors who haven't yet seen a prospectus, unless you are sophisticated investor familiar with the fund advertised, you should first order and read the prospectus before sending any money. The purpose of the prospectus is to provide complete disclosure of information about the fund. The SEC dictates what information must be included. A statement that advises investors to "read the prospectus carefully before you invest or send money" must appear on the cover. The prospectus must also summarize fund fees and expenses and disclose whether the fund is a load or no-load fund. You should find a hypothetical example of the effect of fees on earnings over one-, five-, and ten-year periods. The prospectus will also publish a per-share result table, which is like a condensed financial statement. It will show earnings in dividends and capital gains distributions on one share for each year indicated. It will also show the rise or fall in value of that share during the year. The prospectus specifies the fund's required initial investment amount and minimum subsequent investment amounts. As you study the prospectus, determine how the fund calculates its total return and yield, its investment objective, the principle risks associated with investing in the fund, and practical information about services the fund offers. Finally, if all else is equal among the remaining funds, you should look at the services the fund provides. These services may include an 800 number, check writing, systematic investment or withdrawal, wire redemption, electronic funds transfer, telephone conversion privileges to other funds within the fund group, automatic reinvestment of capital gains and dividends, and retirement plans. Choose the fund that offers the services you desire at the lowest cost.

Now you are ready to decide how to invest your money in the fund you have chosen.

Mutual Fund Investment Strategies

Lump-sum investing, dollar cost averaging, and value averaging are three of many possible investment strategies. Using the *lump-sum* approach, you simply invest all your money for the year or your entire goal at once. This strategy presumes that you already have a nest egg ready to invest. A variant of this strategy is the "market timing," lump-sum strategy. Under this strategy, you attempt to time your lump-sum investments so they occur when market conditions are most favorable. Thus, this variant presumes that you have liquid assets ready to invest and that you are able to time the market. That means you know how to buy low and sell high. Discerning the time when stock or bond prices have reached an extreme level is easier said than done. Empirical studies show that few professional money managers have the ability to consistently time the market. Thus, if you take the lump-sum approach, many finance experts recommend that you use a simple "buy-and-hold" strategy and avoid trying to time the market. It sounds boring and simple, but it takes discipline to avoid the "follow-the-herd" mentality that turns so many new investors into financial lemmings.

You may not yet have accumulated a sizable amount of money to invest, or you may be uncomfortable taking an investment plunge with all your money at once. One simple way to reduce the risk of placing too much into a mutual fund when the price is at its high is to *dollar cost average*. Dollar cost averaging simply involves investing a constant dollar amount each month into a mutual fund. Dollar cost averaging enables you to pay less per share than the actual average share price. This happens because your investment of a constant dollar amount buys more shares when the price is low and fewer shares when the price is high. Because of this feature, you will earn a positive return even if you sell your shares at a price per share equal to the average price per share you paid. Table 14-4 illustrates the mechanics of dollar cost averaging using $100 per month for twelve months in three different market scenarios.

Most mutual funds offer systematic investment plans whereby they take the constant amount out of your checking or savings account once every month. That makes dollar cost averaging a simple and convenient strategy. Most mutual funds also reduce or waive the minimum initial investment if you start a systematic investment plan. So if you don't have enough money to meet that minimum initial investment, check to see if you can get around it by initiating a systematic investment plan.

Another investment strategy you may want to consider is called *value averaging*. With value averaging you seek to increase the total *value* of your mutual fund by a set amount each month, as opposed to investing a set amount each month. In a nutshell, this strategy is like combining dollar cost averaging with a "side fund" for regularly placing your investment gains or from which you can replace your investment losses. For instance, assume your goal was to see the value of your fund account increase by $100 each month. If the current value of your fund account is $800 (200 shares times $4 a share), then you want it to rise to $900 in value next month. Next month rolls around and the share price is still $4; that means you need to purchase $100 worth of shares to bring the account value up to $900. In this case it is just like dollar cost averaging. What if instead the share price had risen to $5? Your account would then be worth $1,000 (200 shares times $5 a share). In that case you would not have to invest anything that month to bring the value of the shares up to the target of $900. In fact, you could actually *sell* $100 worth of the fund; but doing so may incur a tax liability, so you might be better to just "hang on to" the excess value until next month, when the value target increases to $1,000. With value averaging, the amount you invest each month depends on what happens to the share price. The idea behind the strategy is to force you to buy low and give you signals as to how to sell high, without any need for market-timing expertise. The average cost per share with value averaging will be less than with dollar cost averaging. Since this strategy involves other potential complications, readers interested in implementing it should see the related reference (Edleson) listed at the end of this chapter.

Tracking Your Mutual Fund's Performance

The SEC requires that mutual fund companies provide shareholders with annual and semiannual reports. These reports provide up-to-date financial information. You can

TABLE 14-4
DOLLAR COST AVERAGING

Amount Invested	Rising Market		Declining Market		Fluctuating Market	
	Price Paid for Each Share	Number of Shares Bought	Price Paid for Each Share	Number of Shares Bought	Price Paid for Each Share	Number of Shares Bought
$100	10.00	10.00	10.00	10.00	10.00	10.00
$100	10.45	9.57	9.55	10.47	9.25	10.81
$100	10.90	9.17	9.10	10.99	10.25	9.76
$100	11.35	8.81	8.65	11.56	10.70	9.35
$100	11.80	8.47	8.20	12.20	9.95	10.05
$100	12.25	8.16	7.75	12.90	10.20	9.80
$100	12.70	7.87	7.30	13.70	9.45	10.58
$100	13.15	7.60	6.85	14.60	9.80	10.20
$100	13.60	7.35	6.40	15.62	9.55	10.47
$100	14.05	7.12	5.95	16.81	10.30	9.71
$100	14.50	6.90	5.50	18.18	10.15	9.85
$100	14.95	6.69	5.05	19.80	10.00	10.00
Sum $1,200		97.73		166.83		120.59
Average Share Cost[1]	$12.28		$7.19		$9.95	
Average Share Price[2]	$12.47		$7.53		$9.97	

Notes
[1] Average Share Cost = Total Dollars Invested ÷ Total Shares Purchased
[2] Average Share Price = Sum of Price Paid per Share Column ÷ 12

also get additional information such as a summary of portfolio holdings and Statement of Additional Information (SAI). You can easily monitor a fund's net asset value (NAV) by checking the financial pages of the daily newspaper. As mentioned above, most large newspapers contain daily mutual fund price quotations. In addition to listing mutual fund NAVs, the *Wall Street Journal* reports total return information for various time periods and ranks funds against others with the same investment objectives. Table 14-5 shows an excerpt from the *Wall Street Journal*'s Mutual Fund Quotations.

Table 14-5 lists the sponsoring company's name or "family" first. Funds within the family appear in alphabetical order below. A *p* after the fund's name indicates that the fund charges marketing and distribution costs or 12b-1 fees. An *r* after the fund's name indicates that the fund charges a redemption fee or back-end load. A *t* indicates that both *r* and *p* apply. An *x* indicates that the fund just went ex-dividend, which means it just distributed dividend earnings to its shareholders, and an *e* indicates ex-distribution, which means it just distributed capital-gains earnings to shareholders.

The next column lists fund objectives by category. These are based on classifications developed by Lipper Analytical Services, Inc. Investors in the Bull & Bear Group family of funds, for example, have a choice between a growth and income fund (G&I), a sector fund (SEC) (gold in this case), a world bond fund (WBD), a general U.S. taxable bond fund (BND), a municipal bond fund (GLM), a capital appreciation fund (CAP), and a global stock fund (WOR).

As explained above, net asset value (NAV) is the daily price of one share of the fund. The next column is the offer price. An NL in this column means that the fund does not charge a sales commission. A load fund that is front loaded would have an offer price higher than the NAV. An offer price equal to the NAV indicates that the fund charges no up-front fee but may charge a fee when you sell. Also, by definition, funds with 12b-1 fees greater than .25 percent would be loaded even though an NL may appear in the offer-price column.

The next column, NAV change, indicates the difference between the listed NAV quote and the previous day's quote. For example, the Bull & Bear Gold Fund's quoted NAV per share of 14.13 is 66 cents higher than the previous day's NAV.

The total return columns reflect each listed fund's performance over various time periods. Performance calculations are in percent and assume reinvestment of all distributions. Sales charges are not reflected. A *k* means that the quote was recalculated by Lipper Analytical using updated data. The *Wall Street Journal* publishes a year-to-date (YTD) calculation daily. Other results ranging from four weeks to five years are offered on specific days during the week. Table 14-5 reports four-week and one-year returns.

The last column, R, is the *Wall Street Journal*'s ranking based upon the longest time period listed each day. Funds are ranked against other funds with the same investment objectives. An A means the fund is ranked in the top 20 percent; B means

TABLE 14-5
MUTUAL FUND QUOTATIONS

	Inv. Obj.	NAV	Offer Price	NAV Chg	YTD	—Total Return— 4wks	1 yr	R
Bull & Bear Gp:								
FNCI p	G&I	18.12	NL	−0.14	+3.2	−0.8	+3.2	E
Gold p	SEC	14.13	NL	+0.66	+42.3	+17.2	+29.5	B
GlbInc p	WBD	19.19	NL	+0.01	+9.2	+2.2	+18.7	A
GovtSec p	BND	15.28	NL	−0.05	+4.9k	+1.2k	+12.5k	D
MuniInc p	GLM	17.50	NL	−0.03	+4.1k	+0.5k	+11.2k	E
SpEq p	CAP	24.18	NL	−0.37	−2.8	−2.1	+16.4	A
USOvs p	WOR	7.93	NL	−0.04	+4.5	+1.4	+3.4	E

the fund is in the next 20 percent; C, the next 20 percent; D, the next 20 percent; and E, the bottom 20 percent.

Tracking your fund's performance is as important as deciding which fund to invest in. You will want to monitor your fund's performance over time. If a fund's performance doesn't live up to your expectations, you may want to switch funds. Once you decide to switch funds or when you reach your investment objective, you will have to sell your shares.

Selling Your Mutual Fund Shares

Having used one of the above investment strategies to buy a mutual fund's shares, the question is when to sell them. One potential answer is that you should sell your fund shares when you need the money for your financial goal. In the car example, you would sell the shares of your U.S. government bond fund after four years to buy your new car. Another reason to sell your fund shares might be if your objectives for the money change. If you decide to save your car money for retirement and live with your clunker, then you might think about switching the money in your bond fund to a growth stock fund. Another reason to sell your fund may be if the fund changes portfolio managers and the star manager goes to work elsewhere. Follow the fund's performance over the next year to see how the new manager does.

The performance of your fund may be another reason to sell. If the risk-adjusted return does not match your expectations or is way below returns of funds with similar objectives, then it might be wise to sell your shares and invest elsewhere. Be patient and disciplined. It's best not to sell in disgust just because your fund or the market has a bad quarter or even a bad year. Even the best funds have periods of subpar performance. Always focus on the long-term record. Another danger here is selling out at market bottoms, missing the "ride" back up to the top, and then buying in (too late) back at the market peak. This is common with inexperienced and undisciplined investors and is a behavior you should try hard to avoid.

Should an investor try to "time the market" by attempting to follow the economic cycle and adjusting which mutual funds to invest in accordingly? Probably not. Our economy is affected to a large extent by random events that, by definition, cannot be predicted. Experts who spend their whole lives analyzing the economy have trouble accurately predicting what will happen next. Studies of investment newsletters that claim to be able to time the market show that few (no more than would be expected by random chance) are able to beat the return of a buy-and-hold strategy. The major results of attempting to time the market are more taxes, increased transactions costs, reduced returns, and ulcers.

MUTUAL FUND RETURNS

You've picked your mutual fund and held it for a while; now you need to measure your return. Unless you invest a lump sum of money on January 1, the published return figures will not be the return that you experience. Someone who invests his money at any other time or dollar cost averages will have a completely different return than those published in the leading newspapers and magazines. To know your true annual return requires knowledge of the sources of return as well as the methods of calculating your return.

Sources of Mutual Fund Return

Your mutual fund return may come from three sources: dividends, capital gains distributions, and changes in the share price of your fund. When a mutual fund earns dividends or interest on its securities, it passes those along to you, the shareholder, in the form of dividends. If a mutual fund sells some of its securities for more than it paid for them, it must pass that profit along to the shareholder in the form of capital gains distributions. Finally, if you sell your fund shares for more than you paid for them, you will earn a profit (or capital gain) on those shares. However, it is also possible that you could have a loss on the shares by selling them for less than you paid. Your total return on the mutual fund includes profits or losses from all three sources. Of course, if you paid a load, this will also reduce your return.

Measures of Mutual Fund Return

If the return stated in the information resources is not your return, then how do you calculate it? What follows is a simple equation you can use to calculate your approximate annual return (AAR). It works better for short periods of time and is really just meant to give you a rough idea of how you've done.

$$AAR = \frac{(D + C + E - B) \div n}{(E + B) \div 2}$$

Where: D = Total dividends received per share
C = Total capital gains distributions per share
E = Ending price per share of the fund
B = Beginning price per share of the fund
n = Number of years you owned the fund

For a more exact calculation of how you've done, you can use the IRR (internal rate of return) feature of any computer spreadsheet software and most financial calculators. You just list, month by month, all cash flows into or out of the fund, including its *current value* as a positive entry in the last period. Be careful not to double-count reinvested dividends (which are not a cash flow at all). The answer you get will be your monthly rate of return; multiply it by twelve or, more correctly, annualize it using the methods shown in appendix D to get your annual rate of return on your fund investment.

TAX AND OTHER CONSIDERATIONS

Many investors have a hard time understanding the various distributions that mutual funds pay out and their tax implications. As stated above, mutual funds are required to pass along net investment earnings and realized capital gains (actual profits) to the investor. If the NAV of a fund is $6 per share, and then it makes a 70 cent dividend payment or distribution to the shareholder, the price, or NAV, of the mutual fund falls immediately by the amount of the distribution to $5.30 per share. The distribution is then taxable. These distributions create two common problems for investors.

First, you can incur a needless tax liability by purchasing shares of a fund just before it makes a large distribution. The investor buying the example fund just mentioned would have to pay tax on the 70 cent per share distribution, even though the value of his holdings has not changed. Check the distribution dates with the fund before you invest; it's best to wait until just after the distribution date to send in your money.

The second problem results from the reinvestment option that most investors use, whereby these distributions are directly reinvested into shares of the mutual fund. Many investors mistakenly pay tax *twice* on the reinvested shares by not adjusting the tax basis on those shares when they later sell them. Since our investor has already had to pay tax on the reinvested shares bought with the 70 cent distribution above and has had to reinvest those funds by buying "new" shares at $5.30 each, the investor's *cost basis* for this mutual fund should go up by the amount of the distribution. It's easy to forget this small point and pay taxes again on the same shares when they are sold; to make matters worse, the IRS has a hard time "catching" this mistake, which costs investors a sizable amount in taxes that should have never been paid.

This last problem brings up an important caution for investors in mutual fund shares—*good recordkeeping is crucial!* Many investors pay too much in taxes when they later sell mutual fund shares because they did not keep all the records of purchase that their fund sent them. You should keep a record of every purchase made (especially reinvestments) and all dividend, distribution, and sales proceeds received for as long as you own any shares in that fund, and then a few more years to satisfy the IRS.

SUMMARY

Mutual funds offer the individual investor many advantages, but they also have some disadvantages. In concluding this chapter on mutual funds, let's take a look at each.

Advantages

The advantages of mutual funds are numerous. Here are just a few. Mutual funds enable you to diversify your investment money with as little as $1. Diversification equates to reduced risk, or a higher reward-to-risk ratio. Mutual funds also offer convenience. They are easy to invest in and require little time once selected. Investing in mutual funds can involve very low transaction charges. When compared with buying individual securities, the time, commissions, and other money saved by investing in mutual funds can be substantial. Buying a mutual fund means buying a professional management team. You leave the buy and sell decisions up to them and chart their progress. By going through mutual funds, you obtain the choice and capability to invest in securities you may not otherwise have had the necessary resources to purchase individually. The low initial investment for most mutual funds makes them very attractive for the investor with limited finances. They are also very liquid in that you can sell your shares back to the fund whenever you wish. Mutual funds may enable you to invest your money with fewer commissions than you otherwise could. Finally, mutual funds offer services such as dividend and capital gain reinvestment and automatic investment and withdrawal that are hard to find elsewhere.

Disadvantages

The disadvantages of mutual funds are not as numerous as the advantages, but they are still worth considering. Mutual funds give you little control over individual stocks, as you have no say over when your mutual fund buys and sells securities or what securities it buys and sells. This leads to possible adverse tax consequences as well, since you may receive capital gains distributions at a time when your other income has increased. You may then be bumped into a higher marginal tax bracket. The final disadvantage is that you may end up spending quite a bit in fees, possibly much more than if you had invested directly in the securities. Buying a fund with high loads, high management fees, and high 12b-1 fees will start you (and maybe keep you) way behind the investor who puts his money directly into stocks or bonds. You must do your homework to keep the fees and expenses low. Weigh the advantages against the disadvantages before investing in a mutual fund.

SUGGESTED REFERENCES

The Individual Investor's Guide to No-Load Mutual Funds. Chicago: International Publishing, 1994. Published every June.
Donoghue, William. *Donoghue's Mutual Funds Almanac.* Published yearly.
Edleson, Michael E. *Value Averaging: The Safe and Easy Strategy for Higher Investment Returns.* Chicago: International Publishing, 1991.
Investment Company Institute. *1994 Mutual Fund Fact Book.* Published yearly.
United Mutual Fund Selector. Usually on library reserve.
Wiesenberger Investment Companies Service. Usually on library reserve.

The following periodicals, available at virtually all military and public libraries, frequently include articles on investing in mutual funds and fund performance histories and comparisons:

Forbes. First issue in September.
Money. August issue and throughout the year.
Changing Times. September issue and throughout the year.
Barron's. January issue and quarterly reports.
The Wall Street Journal. Throughout the year and quarterly.
Business Week. Last two issues in February.
Financial World. First issue in February.
Consumer's Digest. March/April issue.
Consumer Reports. Occasional rankings; see index at end of each issue.

The following publications are also useful, but probably are not available in libraries:
Schabacker's Mutual Fund Quarterly Performance Review
Morningstar's Mutual Fund Values
Morningstar's Mutual Fund Sourcebook
Mutual Fund Investment Newsletters:
Fund Kinetics
Growth Fund Guide
Mutual Fund Forecaster
Mutual Fund Strategist
The No-Load Fund Investor
Schabacker's Mutual Fund Investing
Zweig Bond Fund Timer
Donoghue's Moneyletter

15

Investing in Real Assets

WE SPEND MOST of our lives earning income. We work, save, and invest, and the result is a flow of income that sustains our families. The last two chapters discussed investments in financial assets. There is another type of asset, real assets, that we can add to our portfolio of investments. Unlike financial assets, real assets are tangible goods that we can see, touch, and smell, such as houses, antiques, collectibles, and precious metals. Like financial assets, they can be bought and then resold, hopefully for a profit.

Real assets, especially investments in rental property, can be very risky. Vacancy rates and property taxes vary by location, and with many communities under financial pressure, property taxes may increase in the near future. Resale values will depend on many local factors that affect the supply of and demand for houses. If recent experience teaches us anything, it is that real asset prices, including house prices, can both rise and fall. Most important to keep in mind, investments in real assets can be very illiquid, so the investor bears the additional risk of not being able to sell quickly.

Most of the people who successfully invest in real assets are professional, not personal, investors. They are real estate developers who know the local market extremely well, who own several properties, and who structure real estate deals so that they risk very little of their own equity in any single property. Or they are college professors who understand commodity markets very well. If you want to invest in real assets, understand that such people are your competition.

The target audience for this book, in our opinion, would achieve substantially better success by investing in mutual funds, supplemented with some carefully chosen stocks and bonds, than with real assets. Still, for some investors, real assets can be a valuable addition to their portfolio, especially as a hedge against inflation. If you think you might be an investor for whom real assets are attractive investments, you need to understand the essentials before you invest; read on.

DIRECT REAL ESTATE INVESTMENT

Direct real estate investment means buying houses, condominiums, apartments, offices, or land to rent out or sell to others. The potential rewards from successful investment can be substantial and come in many forms: cash flow from rental income, tax benefits to property owners, capital appreciation in the value of the property, or a potential retirement home.

A thorough appraisal of a potential real estate investment requires financial analysis as well as consideration of critical factors not easily captured in financial terms. Some key aspects of real estate that must be considered during your analysis are the long-term nature of the investment, the limited liquidity of property, and the effects of a continuously changing economic and political environment (e.g., tax laws, inflation, interest rates, business cycle, etc.). Success depends on understanding how economic and social forces can affect your return on investments in this area. Therefore, careful analysis must include checking the sensitivity of your results to the assumptions and forecasts you made along the way.

Financial Analysis: Cash Flow

Understanding the financial implications of any real estate investment involves identifying all the sources of revenues and all the operating expenses. A spreadsheet program, such as Lotus 1-2-3, Excel, or Quattro Pro, will assist you in setting up the basic information and doing "what if" analyses to test the sensitivity of your results. Also, many Shareware programs are now available to help you in analyzing your property. The numerical examples that follow discuss the potential purchase of a four-plex apartment financed with a thirty-year, fixed-rate, 8.5 percent, $200,000 mortgage. A four-plex consists of two floors with two apartments on each floor. We will assume rent of $700 per month per apartment. Table 15-1 is a projected income statement for the four-plex. An explanation of each item in the income statement follows.

Gross Rental Income
Gross rental income represents the total annual cash proceeds (the monthly rent times twelve months) you expect to earn from the property assuming 100 percent occupancy. To determine the expected monthly rent, find out the current market rental income for property that is comparable in size, construction quality, amenities, and location. Sources for this information include local papers, inquiries to landlords, friends, and real estate agents. You should also include a rent escalator clause for leases of more than one year to protect against the rising costs of operating the property. This can be based on the rate of inflation or the expected percentage increase in operating costs, especially property taxes.

Other Income
Other income refers to other sources of income that the property may provide. For example, you might consider providing laundry facilities on the premises of the four-

TABLE 15-1
Projected Annual Income Statement: Four-plex Apartment

Gross rental income (@100% occupancy)	$33,600	
Other income (laundry, vending machines, etc.)	$0	
Less: Vacancy allowance	($3,360)	
Gross revenues		$30,240
Operating expenses:		
Mortgage principal & interest	$18,454	
Property taxes	$3,500	
Insurance	$1,500	
Utilities	$1,500	
Repairs & maintenance	$1,000	
Association dues (condos)	$0	
Replacement reserve	$500	
Management expenses	$3,360	
Other	$0	
Total operating expenses		$29,814
Pretax Operating Cash Flow		$426

plex. By charging residents for use of the facilities, you could create an additional source of revenue.

Vacancy Allowance
Vacancy allowance refers to the annual amount of gross rental income that you will not receive due to vacancy or to rent in arrears. Determine the normal vacancy rate for your area by checking with real estate agents, other landlords, and local planning boards. Initially, assume at least a 10 to 15 percent vacancy rate to test the sensitivity of the investment to market conditions.

Operating Expenses
Not all of the operating expenses we list will be applicable to all properties. However, you must carefully identify those associated with your property in order to estimate correctly the cash flow from the investment. Because operating expenses have a significant impact on the profitability of any real estate investment, you must forecast them accurately prior to investing and control them carefully following the purchase.

Mortgage Principal and Interest
The annual mortgage expense represents the "amortized" annual repayment of the amount you borrowed from a financial institution to purchase the property.

Amortization refers to the gradual reduction of the total amount remaining to be repaid (the principal). For fixed-rate mortgages, the monthly total payments will be constant, so multiply by twelve to get the annual payment. During the early years of the loan, the great majority of your payments will be for interest charges with only a small amount reducing the principal. Later, the payment will be applied mostly to principal and less to interest. Look at both fixed- and variable-rate mortgages when doing your sensitivity analysis. (Refer to chapter 11 for a discussion of fixed- and variable-rate mortgages.) Closing costs can be substantial but, as a one-time expense, should be analyzed by adding them to the purchase price.

Property Taxes
Changes in property taxes may affect your return significantly and are a major source of uncertainty. Check with the real estate agent or local tax assessor for current and anticipated future tax rates. As mentioned above, you may want to consider including a tax escalator clause in your lease.

Insurance
Insurance cost is based on several factors, including property value and the distance from the nearest fire station. An estimate of the cost can be obtained easily from an insurance company. You may want to reduce your annual cost of insurance by raising the deductible amount. It is important, however, to ensure that your deductible is not unreasonable and that coverage is adequate, covering all potential risks including liability. Be sure to read chapter 12 so you are familiar with the various forms of insurance you will need, particularly "umbrella" coverage for catastrophic lawsuits.

Utilities
Expenses such as heating fuel, electricity, and so forth, that are not paid by the tenant must be forecast. In most cases, the tenant should pay the utilities so that they have incentives to be efficient.

Repairs and Maintenance
Expenses associated with plumbing, heating, roof, glass, doors, and carpentry repairs and lawn maintenance are included under repairs and maintenance.

Association Dues
Association dues are applicable for condominium and town house owners.

Replacement Reserve
The replacement reserve allowance provides for the periodic replacement of items that are subject to physical deterioration, such as carpets, paint, and mechanical equipment. If you invest in older property, this could be quite substantial.

Management Expenses
Allow at least 10 percent of the rent if you plan to hire someone to manage the property. This expense can rise as high as 40 percent of annual income for properties in

short-term rental markets such as ski condominiums, beach homes, and other vacation properties. These higher fees are due to the much higher advertising, reservations, cleaning, and turnover inspection costs associated with short-term rentals.

Other

Any other expense not mentioned above that will affect the profitability of the property (e.g., advertising or tax preparation service) should also be listed.

Pretax Operating Cash Flow

The pretax operating cash flow figure represents the difference between operating revenues and operating expenses. A negative pretax cash flow indicates that you are paying additional money each year to own this "investment." Unless you desire tax losses (discussed later), there is no financial reason to hold such an asset. Only nonfinancial reasons would cause you to accept the negative cash flow. A condo at a ski resort that you would like to use in retirement is one possible example. More often, though, the operating cash flow should be positive, constituting the first benefit of real estate investment. If you have a negative pretax operating cash flow, the after-tax numbers may be better. Even so, try to negotiate a much lower purchase price. Indeed, you can use your estimated negative cash flow as leverage in your negotiations. (Please note that the term "operating cash flow" normally excludes loan payments. We include loan costs in our definition to capture all out-of-pocket expenses that affect the family's cash flow.)

Financial Analysis: Tax Effects

The income tax consequences from real estate investments provide another benefit to the owner. The rental income from real estate used for investment purposes is fully taxable. However, you can deduct all expenses incurred in earning that income. (In contrast, a homeowner can deduct only property taxes and interest on the mortgage.) To determine income taxes due on an investment property, begin with the pretax operating cash flow and make the following adjustments. Table 15-2 provides an example.

Replacement Reserve

Add back the amount initially deducted for reserves to the operating cash flow. These funds were not actually spent but only set aside for future use; therefore, they are not tax deductible. When you spend the reserve on repairs and maintenance, the operating cash flow decreases and your taxes will be reduced as a result.

Mortgage Principal and Interest

For the purposes of calculating your income taxes, you need to adjust your calculation of the cash flow because only the interest portion of your mortgage payment is tax deductible. To accomplish this adjustment, add your total payment back in and then subtract the interest portion. This amount can be found on the amortization schedule provided by your mortgage company. (You can also determine the interest portion of

TABLE 15-2
Cash Flow Analysis: Tax Effects

	1994	1995	1996	1997
Operating cash flow	$426	$694	$967	$1,240
Plus replacement reserve	$500	$500	$500	$500
Plus mortgage principal & interest	$18,454	$18,454	$18,454	$18,454
Less mortgage interest	($16,942)	($16,808)	($16,663)	($16,505)
Less depreciation	($6,182)	($6,182)	($6,182)	($6,182)
Taxable Income	($3,744)	($3,342)	($2,924)	($2,493)
Marginal tax rate	28%	28%	28%	28%
Taxes	**($1,048)**	**($936)**	**($819)**	**($698)**

your payments by developing a mortgage spreadsheet on your personal computer using spreadsheet software or specific real estate software.) Simply total the interest portion of your mortgage payments for as many months as you have owned the property during that year, and subtract that amount from the sum of your pretax operating cash flow and your annual mortgage payment (principal + interest). The reduction of taxable income by the amount of your interest payments is a major tax benefit of real estate ownership.

Depreciation

The concept of depreciation recognizes that most man-made property loses value over time due to wear and tear. Real estate is one of the very few types of man-made property that generally does not lose value over time. In fact, well-maintained real estate can increase in value over the long run. Nevertheless, tax regulations allow owners of income-producing assets to deduct a portion of the assets' cost each year. When determining the depreciable base value of a property, you must first subtract the value of the land; it does not qualify as a depreciable asset. The value of the apartment in our example can be separated into $52,222 for the land and $170,000 for the building. The depreciable base value of the property would be $170,000. This amount would be divided by the number of years allowed to depreciate real estate (currently 27 1/2 years for residential rental property and 31 1/2 years for commercial property) for an annual tax deduction of $6,182. Alternatively, use the Internal Revenue Service's Modified Accelerated Cost Recovery System Tables (MACRS). It may sound imposing, but it is actually quite a simple means of calculating the depreciation expense. It is found in IRS Publication 527, *Residential Rental Property,* and Publication 534, *Depreciation.* Certain components of the property, such as appliances, may be depreciated over a shorter period. The MACRS has rates for depreciating those items as well. Since the depreciation deduction does not actually require cash outlays, it is a major source of tax benefits from real estate ventures. You enjoy the potential appreciation of your property, and you also generate a tax shelter.

Taxable Income

Adding the replacement reserve and the mortgage principal and interest and subtracting the mortgage interest and depreciation expenses gives the taxable income. If the taxable income is negative, you can use it to offset income from other investments as well as ordinary income. Under the Tax Reform Act of 1986, however, the amount of tax losses that can be applied to reduce other taxable income is limited. The rules are fairly complex, but taxpayers with gross adjusted incomes less than $100,000 are limited to a $25,000 real estate loss (to "shield" other income), or no loss at all if you do not "actively participate" in the management of the property. To ensure that you can demonstrate your active participation, be sure to keep records of all communications with management companies and tenants to prove that you made all major decisions regarding the property. To ensure compliance with the tax code, read the IRS's Publication 527, *Residential Rental Property*, or consult a tax expert.

Income Taxes

To determine the actual taxes owed, multiply the net taxable income, derived from the above adjustments, by your marginal tax rate (see chapter 8).

After-tax Cash Flow

To determine the after-tax cash flow (ATCF), subtract income taxes from the pretax operating cash flow of Table 15-1. See Table 15-3. Note that if your taxable income from this investment is negative, your after-tax cash flow will be larger than your pretax cash flow.

Should your ATCF be negative, you will be paying out more to own the property than you receive in rent, tax refunds, and other income. Some investors willingly accept negative ATCF on their real estate investments because they believe the potential appreciation of the property will generate a substantial capital gain in the future. Others accept a negative ATCF in order to own the property for some future personal reasons. In this case, the real asset is *not* a financial "investment."

If you are considering an investment that generates a negative ATCF, make sure you can afford the lower standard of living during the time you wait for the property to appreciate in value or until you occupy it. Also, if you are basing your decision on anticipated appreciation, you should be very confident of your forecast that substantial appreciation will occur. Otherwise, you would be wise to place funds in some other investment.

Net Present Value Analysis

To make a complete analysis of your real estate venture, compute the after-tax cash flow for each year you anticipate owning the property. Table 15-3 shows these calculations for a four-year holding period. For this example, it assumes that the rental income increases 1 percent per year. This forecast is uncertain at best. However, careful research and consideration of similar properties will reduce the uncertainty. Alternatively, complete the calculations in Table 15-1 for a few years using several different assumptions about the growth in rental income, the vacancy rate, maintenance costs, and so on. Then test the sensitivity of your key assumptions to varying conditions. For example, if you initially assume a vacancy rate of 10 percent, calculate what happens to the after-tax cash flow if you double the vacancy rate. If you get a substantially negative cash flow, you should closely evaluate your ability to subsidize the property with income from other sources. Test other key assumptions such as income and operating expenses. Also beware of possible "rent control" legislation that will reduce the growth of future rents.

You must include the down payment and the closing costs in your analysis. Here we assume a 10 percent down payment on a purchase price of $222,222 (the $200,000 mortgage is 90 percent of the purchase price) and closing costs of $6,000. If you will incur an early withdrawal penalty when you sell other assets to pay for either of these items, you need to include these penalties as well.

Now that you have the after-tax cash flows for each of the years of ownership, you must calculate the net resale value of your property. See Table 15-4. The first step is to forecast a rate of appreciation over the period for which you expect to own the property. If property in your area has been appreciating significantly, try to identify the factors driving this appreciation. Will these factors continue to cause property values to rise in the future? If so, will your property benefit? If you really have no knowledge base, then a relatively safe method would be to look up the long-term government bond interest rate and use half of that as your conservative estimate. Realize, though, that real estate values are regional and very cyclical phenomena, difficult even for the experts to predict. Over thirty years or so, prices are likely to increase at or above the inflation rate; however, over a four-year period, almost anything could hap-

TABLE 15-3
After-tax Cash Flow (ATCF)

	NOW	1994	1995	1996	1997
Operating cash flow					
(from Table 15-1)		$426	$694	$967	$1,240
Less taxes (Table 15-2)		($1,048)	($936)	($819)	($698)
After-tax optg cash flows		$1,474	$1,630	$1,786	$1,938
Down payment (@ 10%)	$22,222				
Closing costs (see chap. 11)	$6,000				
Equity at resale					
(see Table 15-4)					$23,263
Annual cash flows	−$28,222	$1,474	$1,630	$1,786	$25,201

pen. Use your informed judgment about the rate of appreciation to estimate the amount for which you expect to sell the property. Our example assumes a 2 percent nominal appreciation rate.

Next, you must calculate the taxes you expect to pay on the capital gain. Subtract selling costs, usually about 7 percent of the sales price, from the forecast resale price to get the net proceeds. To calculate the amount of capital gains (or losses), you must subtract the tax basis, which is equal to the purchase price minus the total depreciation allowance you have taken on the property since you bought it, from the net proceeds. This result is the taxable capital gain (or loss). Multiply this amount by your marginal tax rate to get the taxes payable or, in the event of a loss, the reduction in your income taxes owed from all sources of income.

Having calculated the taxes that you will owe, you can now determine how much equity you will have after the investment is sold and taxes are paid. Subtract the selling expenses, the outstanding balance on the mortgage, and the taxes owed from the forecast resale price. Enter the result in Table 15-3 in the year you intend to sell the property.

The net present value (NPV) of your investment property is a calculation that compares this real asset investment with your next-best alternative of similar risk. Appendix D outlines the method under the heading "Present Value." The net present value rule is very simple: *If the NPV is positive, then invest in this real asset.* This conclusion implies that you are earning a greater return on this investment than on your next-best alternative investment of similar risk. The place to incorporate consideration of your next-best alternative investment is in your choice of the discount factor. You should set the discount factor equal to the rate of return you expect to receive on the next-best alternative investment of similar risk. Because mortgaged investment property is highly leveraged, it is quite risky. We use a 20 percent discount rate in our example, but there is no set rule.

In the example in Table 15-3, the net present value is –$12,675. To determine this value, we discounted the annual cash flows at 20% using the following formula:

$$NPV = -\$28{,}222 + (\$1{,}474 \div (1.20)^1) + (\$1{,}630 \div (1.20)^2) + (\$1{,}786 \div (1.20)^3) + (\$25{,}201 \div (1.20)^4) = -\$12{,}675.$$

Because the NPV in this example is negative, we should not buy the property. As long as our assumptions are accurate, this investment would make $12,675 less over its life than our next-best investment of equal risk.

As always, you should determine whether the result is sensitive to your assumptions. The NPV is very sensitive to the assumed discount rate, so it is especially important to explore how changes in this variable affect your result. If you are using a spreadsheet or a financial calculator, you might also calculate the internal rate of return (IRR). The IRR is the discount rate that would make the NPV equal to zero. If the IRR is considerably larger than the rate of return you expect to receive on your next-best alternative investment of similar risk, then you can be fairly confident that

TABLE 15-4
Projected Equity Value at Resale (1997)

Tax calculation:	
Forecast resale price	$240,540
(@ 2% annual appreciation)	
Less selling expenses @ 7%	− $16,837
Less tax basis (purchase price − depreciation)	− $197,494
Taxable gain (or loss)	= $26,209
Marginal tax rate	× 28%
Taxes payable (or reduced)	= **$7,338**

Equity calculation:	
Forecast resale price	$240,540
Less selling expenses	− $16,837
Less mortgage balance	− $193,102
Less taxes	− $7,338
Equity after taxes	**= $23,263**

the NPV is positive and this investment is a good one. In our example, the IRR is about 2 percent, which is much smaller than our discount factor of 20 percent.

The outcome of the net present value analysis will also be very sensitive to the net resale value (or more accurately, your projected after-tax equity value) of the property. Therefore, use several scenarios when calculating this value to determine if your investment is too dependent on optimistic assumptions in Table 15-4.

Investment Choices

Residential Properties

Residential properties are familiar to anyone who has owned a house and probably are a good place for the first-time real estate investor to start.

When you shop for rental properties, look for the largest number of units you can afford (duplex, triplex, four-plex). The more units you have, the larger your rental income stream will be and the lower your per-unit operating costs. For example, the insurance premium for a duplex normally will not be twice the amount for a single-family house. Having more units also reduces the vacancy risk and therefore improves the cash flow. Many servicemembers get their start by buying a duplex and living in half while renting out the other half, and then eventually renting out both halves. This is a wise approach, as you "break yourself in" to the real estate business gradually and will get to know your property and the tenants.

One increasingly viable means of buying investment property in some areas is through auction. Many economically depressed areas offer hundreds of properties for sale by auction each week, including properties from savings and loan bailouts sold by the Resolution Trust Corporation (RTC). Check the real-estate section of your local Sunday newspaper or ask a broker.

Small investors should probably avoid commercial property. Office buildings, shopping centers, and raw land might have a greater profit potential, but they are also riskier. Successful investment in this type of property requires greater skill, experience, and tolerance of risk.

Vacation Properties
Many military families will buy a vacation property as an investment as well as a place to vacation with their families. Much of the previous discussion applies as well to properties in resort or vacation areas. Attractively, rental income is usually much higher per week or month. Finding a property with the most months of possible income is therefore quite important. Year-round resorts are one possibility, as well as ski and golf resorts. Note that there are strict tax rules about how much you may use the property yourself during a year and still claim it as an income-producing investment. Only income properties can be depreciated and have expenses deducted for tax purposes. Typically, you cannot use the property more than two weeks per year and still claim it as an income-producing property. In doing the financial analysis of a vacation home, you must scrutinize each area, because the popularity of resort areas changes more frequently than well-established residential areas. An example of a cash flow analysis for a vacation property appears on the next two pages.

Time-sharing Properties
Resort time-sharing provides a method of dividing up property such as hotels, apartments, condominiums, recreational vehicle parks, and houseboats and selling the individual living units for specified lengths of time each year.

There are two basic legal formats from which to choose. The *right-to-use* format provides a contractual right to occupy a living unit for one week a year for a specific term of twenty to forty years. The buyer pays for the entire period in advance, and at the end of the contract all ownership rights are terminated unless the contract contains a renewal clause or a right to buy. The *fee-simple* format provides the buyer a fee ownership in the unit purchased. The buyer owns the living unit for one week a year in perpetuity. This transaction will be handled much the same way as a normal real estate purchase, with delivery of a recordable deed that conveys the time-share interest.

Keep in mind that once you have this long-term right to use a resort, you will also have a long-term commitment to its maintenance, repair, refurbishing, and management. These fees can increase drastically over time and are often glossed over during the sales pitch.

Many states have adopted time-share regulations in the form of consumer protection and disclosure requirements. Be alert, however, that the marketing presentations

CASH FLOW ANALYSIS OF A RESORT PROPERTY INVESTMENT

The following example is an analysis of a purchase of a ski condominium in a popular ski and golf resort. The purchase price is $47,000. Note that the final decision rests in part on the analysis of the tax shields provided by a year of losses. These losses can reduce your taxable income only if you are an "active participant" in the management of your property. Also, the final NPV is negative, indicating that we should not purchase the property. The internal rate of return is naturally less than the 20 percent used to discount the cash flows for the NPV and tells us that we are not doing as well as our next-best alternative investment.

Be very careful before you run out and sign a mortgage based on an analysis such as this. For example, a small positive NPV of say, $100, would be insignificant for an investment of this size. A knowledgeable investor would be indifferent concerning such a small NPV. Perform a sensitivity test by testing your numbers against different scenarios of vacancies, taxes, fees, repairs, and the like. This analysis is very sensitive to the rate of appreciation that you assume in your calculation of the resale value. Slight changes in your assumptions can greatly affect the NPV. Also, consider the nonfinancial aspects of ownership when deciding on close calls.

Projected Income Statement: Vacation Ski Condo

Gross rental income	$10,150	
Other income	$0	
Less: Vacancy allowance of 15%	$1,522	
Gross revenues		$8,628
Less operating expenses (not including mortgage expense)		
Property tax	$710	
Insurance	$150	
Utilities	$400	
Repairs & maint.	$200	
Association dues	$2,172	
Replacement res.	$200	
Management expenses	$0	
Other	$0	
Total operating expenses		$3,832
Operating cash flow		$4,796
Less mortgage expense		$3,813
Cash flow before taxes		$982

Cash Flow Analysis: Tax Effects

	1994	1995	1996	1997	1998
Operating cash flow (assuming 3% growth)	$4,796	$4,939	$5,088	$5,240	$5,397
Plus replacement reserve	$200	$200	$200	$200	$200
Less interest	$3,477	$3,448	$3,417	$3,383	$3,346
Less depreciation	$1,709	$1,709	$1,709	$1,709	$1,709
Taxable income (loss)	($154)	$18	$198	$384	$578
Marginal tax rate	28%	28%	28%	28%	28%
Taxes (tax savings)	($53)	($5)	$45	$97	$152

Projected equity value at resale (Year 5)

Tax calculation:

Forecast sale price (@4% apprec/yr)	$57,183
Less selling expenses (@7%)	$4,003
Less tax basis (sale pr. – deprec.)	$38,455
Taxable gain	$18,728
Tax rate	28%
Taxes payable	$5,244

Equity calculation:

Forecast sale price	$57,183
Less selling expenses	$4,003
Less mortgage balance	$45,006
Less taxes	$5,244
Equity after taxes	$2,905

After-tax cash flow (ATCF)

	Now	1994	1995	1996	1997	1998
Operating cash flow		$4,796	$4,739	$5,088	$5,249	$5,397
Less mortgage expense		$3,813	$3,813	$3,813	$3,813	$3,813
Less taxes		($53)	($5)	$45	$97	$152
After-tax cash flow		$1,036	$1,131	$1,230	$1,330	$1,432
Down payment (@10%)	($4,700)					
Closing costs (@5%)	($2,350)					
Equity at resale					$2,905	
Annual cash flows	($7,050)	$1,036	$1,131	$1,230	$1,330	$4,337
Present value of cash flows @20%	($7,050)	$863	$785	$712	$641	$1,743
Net present value of condo	($2,306)					
INTERNAL RATE OF RETURN	7%					

to entice you into buying are handled by experienced salespeople. The major selling point will be that for a fraction of the cost of a hotel room year after year, you can own the unit for a certain period of time each year. The seller will manage the property and provide for clerk and maid service, laundry service, and so forth for an additional cost. If you do not plan to visit the same location each year, the seller will inform you about exchange networks. For another fee, you can trade units with other time-share owners in various locations around the world.

Due to high-pressure sales tactics, a number of states have enacted mandatory "cooling-off" periods of five days during which a buyer can cancel his or her contract. Don't buy today just because the purchase price will supposedly be increasing tomorrow. Be firm and disciplined. You would do well to take plenty of time in deciding how this investment fits in with your vacation plans. Do you want to commit $15,000 to $40,000 for something that may not be desirable every year? Will you be able to rent the unit if you don't use it? Will the developer continue to have the same incentive to oversee things as carefully as it did during the sales period? Spend some time talking to existing purchasers to see whether they would buy again. Finally, have all the paperwork reviewed by an attorney before signing away your hard-earned cash.

If you are considering investing in this type of real estate with the prospect of selling later at a profit, be aware that such units are the first to decline in price during a recession, since people take fewer vacations. Likewise, when the economic recovery appears, they will probably be the last to recover. Don't make the mistake of buying at the top and selling at the bottom. Conversely, though, you can actually strike some remarkable deals during rough economic times with owners who need to sell their time-shares. The network for this is not terribly well developed, but thorough research will certainly turn up both good and bad opportunities.

Being a Landlord

Being a landlord offers one method of reducing your cash operating expenses. Rather than hiring a manager or real estate agent, you can perform the management and maintenance duties yourself. This burden will be light if you take care in selecting your tenants. Most property managers won't be as motivated to do as thorough a job as you would. Of course, if you are located far from your property, you may have no choice but to hire a manager.

Whether or not you manage the property yourself, set and enforce strict standards. Establish a security deposit of one month's rent in advance, along with a last-month rent deposit (you may be required to pay interest on these). Gather detailed information about potential tenants through an application form and formal interviews. Take the time to call their former landlord. Spend the funds necessary to perform a credit check at a local credit bureau. Also, make sure you are aware of local antidiscrimination laws and eviction laws, and all other legal landlord-tenant guidelines.

Prepare a lease outlining the agreements reached with your tenant. Leases of one year in length or more must be in writing. Otherwise, a month-to-month lease implies that either party can back out of the agreement with thirty days' notice. Set up a preoccupancy inspection with your tenant and have it formalized with a signed inspection report. When the tenant moves, inspect the premises again to determine whether any monetary assessments should be made for damages. This procedure, plus the prospect of not receiving a refund of the security deposit, may motivate your tenants to take care of the property.

INDIRECT REAL ESTATE INVESTMENT

If you are convinced your portfolio should include real estate but you don't have the opportunity or time to invest directly and manage a property, other options are available. Generally, these options include real estate partnerships and real estate investment trusts. Equity sharing (see chapter 11) is another means of investing in real estate.

Partnerships

Partnerships provide a means for people with common goals to combine their resources and make investments that would be beyond the resources of any one individual. Partnerships also spread the risk of a venture among many people.

Partnerships are either general or limited. A *general* partnership requires that all partners contribute some form of consideration to the partnership and that they all participate in the management. Consequently, all partners are potentially liable for debts incurred by the partnership. Your own personal assets can be seized to satisfy debts incurred by the partnership. With this in mind, be very careful in the selection of your general partners. They should be well known to you and completely worthy of your trust. Make sure that you find partners who have similar goals and attitudes toward risk, since they will have the authority to make unilateral binding decisions. A note of caution: Good friends do not always make good financial partners.

The more common *limited* partnership, as the name implies, limits the liability of limited partners. The limited partners provide the bulk of the investment capital and have minimal management responsibility. They share in the profits and losses, but their financial liability is limited to the amount of their investment.

Before investing in a limited partnership, one should thoroughly research the past records of the general partners, read the prospectus that described the investment, and check court records for any legal complaints brought against the partnership.

Under the Tax Reform Act of 1986, all capital gains will be taxed at ordinary income rates. The tax law also limits the ability of "passive" investors, those not actively involved in the management of real estate investments, to use excess deductions generated by their passive investments to offset other income. As a result, the real estate limited partnerships today are designed to provide current income and/or capital gains.

Real Estate Investment Trusts

A real estate investment trust (REIT) represents a type of investment company, or mutual fund, that raises funds by borrowing or by selling shares of stock to the public and then investing the funds in a portfolio of real estate investments. The shares of REITs are traded on the NYSE and AMEX stock markets and the over-the-counter markets. Like mutual funds, REITs pay out substantially all the income they earn to their shareholders, and they may be an excellent method to participate in the income and capital gains potential with the assistance of a professionally managed portfolio of real estate properties. You can also enjoy some tax benefits by placing your shares in an Individual Retirement Account (IRA), Keogh plan, or any other tax-deferment instrument.

There are three types of REITs: *equity* REITs, which invest in properties such as shopping centers, hotels, apartments, and office buildings; *mortgage* REITs, which make both construction and mortgage loans to real estate investors; and *hybrid* REITs, which invest in both categories.

Each REIT has specific investment objectives. As with any investment, you must investigate each REIT thoroughly—including types of properties and/or loans, financial status, track record, and future plans. A broker or one of the many stock investment guides will start you in the right direction.

A similar type of investment is a sort of hybrid of REITs and limited partnerships and is known as a master limited partnership (MLP). MLPs are fairly new, and the tax laws regarding them are currently in flux. They are very large partnerships whose shares are traded much like REITs and must be bought through a broker.

SOME FINAL COMMENTS ON REAL ESTATE INVESTMENT

Never overlook the riskiness of real estate investment. Since there is potentially a tremendous capital gain in a savvy investment, there is also the possibility of drastic losses. The primary risk is that the value of the property may fall. Also, unexpected vacancies, irresponsible tenants, and large repair bills increase the riskiness of the investment. But some real estate, in conjunction with a well-crafted investment portfolio of financial assets, can actually reduce overall portfolio risk, particularly during times of inflation. Always bear in mind, though, the illiquidity of this type of investment. Before you make that initial down payment, do your homework and the financial analysis suggested. Also, beware of any get-rich-quick schemes. Be skeptical. However, if the potential returns are high in light of the risks you have outlined, do not hesitate to seriously consider an investment in real estate. Even in times of negative press reviews, good bargains can be found if you do your homework.

OTHER REAL ASSETS

A pair of enlisted man's trousers from the Civil War sold for $10,000 and a Union officer's pair of swords sold for $15,000 in the 1993 militaria market. In 1986, a first edition of Karl Marx's *Communist Manifesto* published in 1847 sold at an auction in London for almost $40,000. A factory-sealed copy of the Beatles' record "Yesterday, Today, and Tomorrow" sold in California for $2,000. These are just a few examples of "real assets"—tangible items of property that can be seen, felt, held, or collected.

The categories of tangible assets include precious metals, such as gold, silver, and platinum; common metals, such as copper and zinc; and precious gems, such as diamonds, rubies, and emeralds. Collectibles cover everything from stamps, coins, and comic books to antiques, works of art, and Oriental carpets. For each of these special groups—and for literally hundreds of others ranging from buttons to sheet music to depression glass to beer cans—there exists a devoted clientele of buyers and sellers who create a market. The common characteristic of collectibles that creates such a potentially lucrative market is scarcity.

Although most collectors pursue their hobby for enjoyment, many collectibles have become important parts of a diversified portfolio of assets. Particularly in times of high inflation, tangible assets such as precious metals and certain collectibles can offer much greater real returns than their stock or bond counterparts. Collectors who carefully invested in certain collectibles in the '80s and '90s often outperformed the traditional financial asset investor.

Analysis of Real Assets

The only tangible source of return for real assets (other than real estate) occurs in the form of appreciation of value. However, other aspects of real assets make them potentially useful investment tools.

The first advantage is that they can be a hedge against inflation. Since the appreciation of their value is dependent purely on the supply and demand in the market, inflation will not erode their capital gain. Remember that stocks and especially fixed return bonds will pay some income and appreciation over time. In the case of the bond, the fixed payments suffer an erosion in value by inflation.

A second advantage of real assets lies in their diversification potential. As with any investment program, placing all your resources in one company or one type of investment is likely to increase your risk of loss. By including some real assets along with the financial assets that are likely to dominate your investment plan, you may actually reduce the overall risk of your portfolio.

Still a third advantage of real assets is the enjoyment the owner derives from ownership, sometimes referred to as "psychic income." Although not a financial reward, beautiful antiques on display in your home may be a source of great pride. A "classic" auto gives enjoyment through use or at car shows. Collectors of a variety of goods simply enjoy collecting.

Balanced against the advantages of investing in real assets are some equally noteworthy disadvantages. These assets tend to be illiquid. They are not easily converted into cash. A financial asset such as a U.S. savings bond can easily be converted into cash at any bank. A valuable coin or a first-edition book, on the other hand, cannot easily be sold except to another collector or dealer. Often public auction is the best way to sell many real assets, but that can be a very time-consuming process. The auctioneer will appraise the item, list it in a catalog for sale, mail or deliver catalogs to prospective buyers, conduct the sale, and then settle the accounts for consignors and buyers. This process may take months and not yield the "true" value of your asset.

A second disadvantage of real assets involves the dealers and middlemen who buy and sell such items. Often they have high markups, which the buyer must pay. It is the buyer's responsibility to know what a fair price should be. Not all auction houses are equally reputable, and not all sellers are totally honest or even knowledgeable. Those that are both and belong to appropriate professional and trade organizations often have invested a great deal of time and money of their own to develop their expertise and reputations. Buyers and sellers both should recognize that the professional services they provide are not free.

Still a third disadvantage of real assets as an investment is that they provide no current income. A savings account or a certificate of deposit will pay some periodic interest. A bond will have a coupon rate that the investor will receive on a semiannual basis. Other financial assets, such as stocks, will pay dividends in many cases. But a real asset normally generates no income and will not yield any return until it is actually sold.

Thus, real assets should "round out" your investment plan and never be the basis for your entire portfolio.

Types of Real Assets

While the advantages and disadvantages apply in greater or lesser degree to all real assets, the range and variety of possible investments within this broad group makes sweeping generalizations hazardous. The most important aspect of your decision to invest in a particular asset must be personal knowledge. You are better off if you take the time to become thoroughly knowledgeable about the area of interest or to pay a professional whom you trust to represent your best interests. Each specific area has its own unique pitfalls and opportunities.

Precious Metals
Gold, silver, and platinum attract the most attention of all precious metals and are often recommended as part of an investor's portfolio. They are highly speculative and are usually favored as a traditional hedge during periods of inflation and political/financial uncertainty. In the 1990s they experienced tremendous price volatility; this has clearly shown the risk as well as the potential profit from investing in this area. For example, gold peaked at over $400 an ounce in 1990 but sold for less than $330 an ounce in 1993.

You can purchase gold, silver, and platinum in a variety of forms—bars or ingots, coins, jewelry, bullion, mining company stocks and mutual funds, and futures contracts. Transaction costs and storage costs will vary with each type of investment.

Jewelry will cost more than the value of the precious metal it contains simply because of the workmanship involved in crafting each piece. Poor resale makes jewelry a generally poor choice as a pure investment. But then, you don't get the enjoyment of wearing most of your other assets!

Gold coins, such as the Canadian Maple Leaf, the American Eagle, the Chinese Panda, and the Australian Koala also sell for a premium above the value of their gold content. The difference reflects what the issuing government must spend to mint and distribute the coin, as well as the relative preference of consumers. Premiums charged for one-ounce and ten-ounce bars are lower than for coins, but the owner may have to pay for "assaying" expenses that partially offset the savings. (Also, some coins have a guaranteed value as currency below which their value may not fall.)

Rather than buy gold or any precious metal directly in any form, you can invest by purchasing mining stocks, mutual funds that invest in several mines, or even options and futures contracts. At this point, you are really trading in financial rather than real assets since you will not take physical possession of the asset.

Collectibles

As stated above, collectibles comprise a broad range of items sought after for their beauty, scarcity, and age. The 1970s and 1980s have brought lucrative gains to those owning expensive paintings, rare automobiles, baseball cards, and some fine military collectibles (particularly U.S. Civil War items).

In particular, for many investors, stamp collecting turned out to be more than a hobby during the speculative fever of the late 1970s. A set of the Graf Zeppelin airmail stamps issued in 1930 rose in value more than fourfold in less than a year. Then from a high of $8,500—for a set of three stamps that cost only $4.55 at the post office when they were issued—the price plummeted back below $3,000. Many long-time collectors were amazed at the prices paid as newcomers flocked to the "hobby." Experienced collectors were not surprised to see the market return to levels consistent with the long-term trends for stamp values after the speculative bubble burst.

The danger with buying popular collectibles as an investment is that the inexperienced player hoping for a quick gain can easily be taken by those with experience and knowledge in the particular area. For someone who has a keen interest in the subject, investing first in knowledge leads to buying wisely later. For the uninformed, overspending and regret are more likely to be the case.

SOME FINAL COMMENTS ON REAL ASSETS

If you are considering adding real assets to your investment strategy, honestly evaluate your goals and tolerance for risk. Include this method of diversification in your investment plan only if you understand what you are buying. Recognize that some real assets are not very liquid and transaction costs can be expensive. For most people, real assets (other than real estate) should be no more than 10 percent of their investment portfolio, serving primarily as a hedge against inflation. Because of the extreme volatility of real-asset prices, they are inappropriate for use except as a portion of a portfolio intended for long-term goals.

SUGGESTED REFERENCES

Wurtzeback, C., and M. Miles. *Modern Real Estates.* New York: John Wiley and Sons, Inc., 1991.

Part V

PLANNING FOR RETIREMENT AND LATER

16

Military Retirement Benefits

BECAUSE THE PROFESSION of arms requires considerable energy and stamina, national policymakers have long provided a generous retirement plan for career soldiers, sailors, and airmen. Originally intended to provide for those who had spent their entire productive lives in service to their country, the military retirement plan now also serves a vital role in personnel policy. Because it is a generous plan, it encourages early retirement, thus ensuring that the servicemembers on active duty are youthful, energetic, and able to measure up to the physical demands of modern combat.

There are three ways to retire from the armed forces. The most common is retirement for *length of service*. You may retire after twenty years of active service, and, in most cases, you *must* retire after thirty years of active service. The second way is retirement for *age*. Because comparatively few people are in this category, and because pay and benefit calculations are exactly the same as for length-of-service retirees, we will consider these retirees to be the same as length-of-service retirees. Finally, you can retire for *disability* if you suffer a physical or mental disability that is rated at 30 percent or higher.

This chapter, organized into four sections, will help you to understand your basic entitlements as a retired member of the armed forces. The first section covers retirement pay for length-of-service retirees; the second section covers retirement pay for disabled retirees; the third section considers the effect on your retirement pay of taking a second "retirement job" with the government; and the last section briefly covers other benefits for retired military members.

This chapter will not answer every possible question. You should refer additional inquiries to the finance and accounting office nearest you, or you may call your servicing finance center for information. For the most complete and detailed information, refer to the regulation your service publishes on the subject, e.g. Army Reg. 37-104-1 "Payment of Retired Pay to Members and Former Members of the Army."

RETIREMENT PAY FOR LENGTH-OF-SERVICE RETIREES

The retired pay you receive depends upon the length of service and the rank achieved before retirement. Congressional concern over the cost of military retirement, about $12 billion in 1993 alone, has led to several changes to retirement plans. As a result, there are three different ways to calculate your retired pay for the first year of your retirement. The method you should use depends on the date you entered the service. To determine when you entered the service, look at any one of your Leave and Earnings Statements. The middle block on the top line, labeled "PAY DATE," contains six numbers. The first two numbers represent the year, the second two the month, and the last two the day on which you entered the service. For example, 810606 means that you entered service on 6 June 1981. Officers who had an ROTC scholarship or who graduated from a service academy use the date of that scholarship instead of the Pay Date to determine which retirement system applies to them. So, for example, an officer with a Pay Date of 810606, but who began a two-year ROTC scholarship on 1 September 1979, uses the 1979 date.

If you entered service before 8 September 1980, then you are covered by System 1. If you entered service between 8 September 1980 and 31 July 1986, your retirement pay is calculated using System 2. If you entered service on or after 1 August 1986, then use System 3. The method for calculating your first retirement paycheck is described below.

In all three systems for calculating length-of-service retirement pay, your retirement pay is subject to income tax. If you choose, the government will withhold some portion of your pay.

System 1: Entered Service prior to 8 September 1980

Under this system your retirement pay is computed at 2.5 percent of your base pay at retirement multiplied by the number of years you served, with an upper limit of 75 percent. For example, an O-5 who retires on the twentieth anniversary of her entry into the service will receive 50 percent (2.5% × 20) of the base pay of an O-5 "over twenty" from the pay table current at the time of retirement. An E-7 retiring after twenty-three years of service will receive 57.5 percent (2.5% × 23) of the base pay of an E-7 "over twenty-two" (there is no seniority pay raise for twenty-three years). Those who serve more than thirty years will not receive more than 75 percent of their base pay. See Table 16-1 for a sample calculation.

There is one exception to this rule. Your retirement pay is subject to a time-in-grade "lock-in" provision. Enlisted servicemembers who accept promotion to a higher grade must serve two years in that grade before they are eligible to retire. Thus, an E-7 who accepts a promotion to E-8 at nineteen years of service is not eligible to retire until after he has completed twenty-one years of service. Officers have a three-year "lock-in" if they accept promotion, but there is an important difference. Officers can retire within that three-year period, but if they do, they retire at the next lower grade. Future legislation may dilute the effect of this provision.

MILITARY RETIREMENT BENEFITS • 255

TABLE 16-1
Retirement Pay under the Three Retirement Systems

For an O-5 retiring in June 1993 at 20 years of service:

Base pay:	18th Year	$3,806.70 (over 16, FY 91 pay table)
	19th Year	$4,193.70 (over 18, FY 92 pay table)
	20th Year	$4,348.80 (over 18, FY 93 pay table)
	Final	$4,480.80 (over 20, FY 93 pay table)

	System 1	System 2[a]	System 3[a]
Years served	20	20	20
Percent of base pay	50%[b]	50%	40%[e]
Base pay for purposes of retired pay	$4,480.80[c]	$4,116.40[d] (high 3)	$4,116.40[d] (high 3)
Monthly retired pay[f]	$2,240.40	$2,058.20	$1,646.56[g]

For an E-7 retiring in June 1993 at 23 years of service:

Base pay:	21st Year	$1,949.10 (over 20, FY 91 pay table)
	22nd Year	$2,031.00 (over 20, FY 92 pay table)
	23rd Year	$2,247.30 (over 22, FY 93 pay table)
	Final	$2,247.30 (over 22, FY 93 pay table)

	System 1	System 2[a]	System 3[a]
Years served	23	23	23
Percent of base pay	57.5%[b]	57.5%	50.5%[e]
Base pay for purposes of retired pay	$2,247.30[c]	$2,075.80[d]	$2,075.80[d]
Monthly retired pay[f]	$1,292.20	$1,193.58	$1,048.28[g]

Notes
[a] Illustrative only. No one under System 2 or 3 is eligible for normal retirement in June 1993.
[b] Years of service × 2.5%.
[c] Base pay in final month.
[d] Average of "high three" base pays = (B1 + B2 + B3) divided by 3.
[e] 40 + (years of service over 20) × 3.5%.
[f] Rounded down to the next lowest whole dollar.
[g] At age 62, pay is recalculated as if under system 2.

System 2: Entered Service between 8 September 1980 and 31 July 1986

Concern over the rising costs of military retirement led Congress to modify the retirement system in 1980. If you entered service between 8 September 1980 and 31 July 1986 (that is, Pay Date 800908–860731, including both end dates), calculate the percentage (of base pay) that you will receive exactly as before. In System 2, however, that percentage is applied to the average of the base pay over the last three years of service instead of to the base pay at retirement.

For example, consider an O-5 who retired on his twentieth anniversary of service in June 1993 under System 2. Suppose that he was promoted to that grade before seventeen years in service so that, even with the lock-in, he can retire at the grade of O-5. During his eighteenth year of service he is paid as an O-5 over sixteen, because the seniority raise doesn't come until the eighteenth year is completed. During the next two years of service, he is paid as an O-5 over eighteen. For retirement purposes, he receives a percentage of the average of these "high-three" base pays (see Table 16-1).

System 3: Entered Service on or after 1 August 1986

In 1986, Congress took further action to contain the rising costs of military retirement. Those entering service on or after 1 August 1986 still use the "high-three" average base pay for determining their retirement benefits, but they calculate the percentage of that average base pay differently.

Persons who retire at twenty years of service can do so with 40 percent of their "high-three" average base pay, so that each of the first twenty years earns 2 percent per year. Every year of service after twenty earns an additional 3.5 percent per year in retirement benefits. For example, an E-7 retiring at twenty-three years of service would earn 50.5 percent (2% × 20 plus 3.5% × 3) of his "high-three" average base pay. As before, retirement pay is capped at 75 percent of base pay at thirty years of service, and the same lock-in provisions apply.

This change is intended to discourage early retirement. Under current law, retired servicemembers are restored to the "System 2" level of benefits when they reach sixty-two years of age. That means that the retired E-7 will be returned to 57.5 percent (2.5% × 23) of his "high-three" average base pay when he turns sixty-two. See Table 16-1 for a sample calculation.

Cost-of-Living Increases

Retirement pay is indexed to the Consumer Price Index (CPI) to ensure that its purchasing power is not eroded by inflation. Under Systems 1 and 2, the benefits are fully indexed to the CPI. That means that if the CPI increases by 5 percent, the benefit should increase by 5 percent. Under System 3, the benefit is partially indexed at one percentage point less than the CPI increase. If the CPI increases by 5 percent, retirement pay will increase by 4 percent. Indexation occurs on December 1 each year, so retirees get a cost-of-living pay raise in their December paycheck.

Although currently the benefit is fully indexed under Systems 1 and 2, Congress has the authority to index the benefits by less than the full amount of the increase in the CPI. With the changes to the military retirement plan enacted in 1986, we believe that Congress has signaled its intent to index the benefits under Systems 1 and 2 less than fully. In fact, in every year since 1984, Congress has increased current retirement pay by approximately 1 percent less than the increase in the CPI. It seems clear that Congress intends to continue this practice in the future. This means that the purchasing power of your retirement pay will decrease by 1 percent per year. This type of *CPI-minus-1* indexation is a common practice in pension plans. It does, however, have one very important implication: *Every servicemember must have some sort of personal savings plan to augment his or her retirement pay from the military.* That is the subject of a major portion of this book.

DISABILITY RETIRED PAY

Permanent Disability

When a servicemember becomes unfit to perform the duties of office because of a permanent physical or mental disability, he or she is eligible for disability retirement from the military. Medical authorities will rate the disability using a standard Department of Veterans Affairs rating schedule. Disabilities of 30 percent or greater qualify for retirement. A line of duty (LOD) investigation is also required. There are two alternative methods for calculating your disability retirement pay—the length-of-service method and the percent-disability method—and you should select the one most favorable to you. Each has slightly different consequences for taxation. Your disability retired pay, using the length-of-service method, is determined according to the following formula: Pay = monthly basic pay x years of service × 2.5%. Using the percent-disability method, the retirement pay is given by the following formula: Pay = monthly basic pay × percent disability.

Table 16-2 contains sample calculations. Note that in the example the O-3 finds it in his interest to take the percent-disability pay, while the E-8 prefers the length-of-service calculation. In general, the fewer years of service you have and the greater your disability, the more likely it is that you will choose the percent-disability method.

These formulas are affected by the date on which you entered service. If you entered before 8 September 1980, you use your full basic pay at the time of the disability in the calculation. If you entered on or after 8 September 1980, however, then you use an average of your "high-three" monthly basic pay. The 1986 reforms did not affect disability retirement, though, so to determine disability retirement pay, everyone uses 2.5 percent, no matter when they entered service.

There are some exemptions in the personal income tax code that pertain to disability retirement pay. If your disability resulted from combat duty, then your disability pay is not subject to income tax. If the disability is not combat related, and you use the percent-disability method to compute your pay, the pay is still not taxable. But if your disability is not combat related and you use the length-of-service method, then some portion of the retirement pay is taxable. For servicemembers who have been in the service for close to twenty years and who have low-rated disabilities, this taxation

TABLE 16-2
Calculating Disability Retirement Pay

	O-3 with 5 Years of Service and 40% Disability	E-8 with 26 Years of Service and 40% Disability
Length-of-service method		
Basic pay	$ 2,348.90[a]	$ 2,808.60[b]
× 2.5%	× .025	× .025
× Years of service	× 5	× 26
= Retirement pay	$ 293.61	$1,825.59
Percent-disability method		
Basic pay	$ 2,347.90[a]	$ 2,808.60[b]
× Percent disability	× .40	× .40
= Retirement pay	$ 939.56	$ 1,123.44
Monthly retirement pay received	$ 939.56	$ 1,825.59
Plus severance pay[c]	$23,489.00 (10 months)	$67,406.40 (24 months)

Notes
[a] Average of "high three" basic pays under Systems 2 and 3, because anyone with five years of service must have entered the service after 8 September 1980. Numbers are based on FY93 pay tables.
[b] Full basic pay at time of disability.
[c] Assuming a favorable LOD investigation.

consideration might affect the method you should use. For more information, consult your local finance and accounting office.

Finally, all disability retirement pay is fully indexed to the CPI.

Temporary Disability

It is also possible to be retired for a temporary disability. If this happens, you calculate your retirement pay as you would for a permanent disability, but there is one difference. If you have a temporary disability, your disability retirement pay will be either one-half your basic pay at the time of the disability or the amount that you calculate for permanent disability, whichever is higher.

You will also be given periodic medical examinations, at least once every eighteen months. If the disability disappears, you will be recalled from retirement at your former grade. If it does not disappear in five years, you will be permanently retired.

Severance Pay

Each disability retirement will be accompanied by a line-of-duty investigation. If the disability is not due to your intentional misconduct or willful neglect and if it was not incurred while AWOL, then you are entitled to disability severance pay in the amount of two months' basic pay per year of service up to a maximum of twelve years. For example, the O-3 in Table 16-2 would receive ten (2 x 5) months' basic pay, while the E-8 would receive the maximum allowable twenty-four months' basic pay (2 × 26 = 52, which is greater than the maximum allowable twenty-four months' basic pay).

DUAL COMPENSATION

Retired military personnel often take jobs with the federal government. These retirees can offer considerable experience and expertise gained during their military careers, and the government is always happy to benefit from that expertise. But due to the nature of the military retirement system, which permits early retirement compared with civilian employment, the government is perceived to be, in effect, paying twice to obtain it.

Congress has addressed this so-called double dipping from the federal treasury on several occasions. The bottom line on these dual compensation laws is that retired military members are entitled to hold jobs with the federal government, but if their combined civil service and retirement salary exceeds a certain level, the retirement salary will be reduced. You should consult your finance and accounting office and civilian personnel office to determine the precise impact in your situation. The two most important restrictions are discussed here.

The Dual Compensation Act

In 1964, Congress passed the Dual Compensation Act (PL 88-448), which affects retired regular officers and warrant officers. Retired reserve officers and enlisted retirees are exempt from the provisions of this law, as are regular officers and warrant officers who retire due to combat disability.

Under most conditions, then, retired regular officers and warrant officers will receive a reduced retirement pay if they take a job with the federal government. The amount of the retirement pay is equal to some base amount (approximately $700) plus one-half the difference between the base and the normal retirement amount. That means that the O-5 from Table 16-1 who retires after twenty years under System 1 will receive a monthly retirement check of about $1,470 ($700 + ½ [$2,240 – $700]) if he takes a job with the federal government. It is worth repeating that he will also draw the full civil service salary.

One other provision of this law should be mentioned here. Regardless of your rank, you must wait at least 180 days after you retire to take a job with the Department of Defense unless you have the written permission of the appropriate service secretary.

The Civil Service Reform Act of 1978

The Civil Service Reform Act of 1978 (PL 95-454) applies to all military retirees. Combined civil service and retirement salaries cannot exceed the amount paid to Executive Level V civil servants, which in 1993 was $108,200 annually. This means, for example, that if a retired servicemember exceeds $108,200 in combined pay, then the retired pay will be reduced until that Executive Level V pay cap is reached. A retired officer or warrant officer will automatically have his retired pay reduced under the provisions of the Dual Compensation Act. If, after that reduction, the combined pay still exceeds the Executive Level V cap, then the retired pay will be reduced further.

OTHER RETIREMENT BENEFITS

Commissary and Exchange

You, your family members, and unmarried surviving spouses are authorized to use the commissary and exchange on military installations when those facilities are considered adequate to support retirees without causing hardship to their active-duty customers. The local installation commander makes this determination, and the availability of this benefit varies by location.

Medical and Dental Care in an Active-duty Facility

You are eligible for the same medical and dental care you received while on active duty, but on a space-available basis. Your dependents and spouse may also be entitled to medical and dental care in an active-duty facility, again depending on the availability of resources. The decision on whether to provide the care in a military facility is made by the local commander of the medical or dental facility. Except in cases of emergency, you should visit a military medical facility before seeking hospitalization at a civilian institution. Please see chapter 7 for further information on retiree medical benefits.

Medical Care under CHAMPUS

Sometimes you will not be able to get to a military health care facility. You are still eligible to use CHAMPUS. You must remember that CHAMPUS is not free; the government will pay up to 75 percent of the costs, but it will not bear the entire cost. Also, CHAMPUS is not available for all medical procedures. Consult the CHAMPUS advisor at the nearest military health care facility for the most current information. See chapter 7 for more detailed information on the CHAMPUS program for retirees.

FORMER SPOUSES

In 1983, Congress passed 10 USC 1408, the "Uniformed Services Former Spouses Protection Act." The Act was amended by the "1991 DOD Authorization Act" (Public Law 101-510, 5 November 1990, Section 555). This law, as amended, allows a former spouse to be awarded up to 50 percent of the retiree's disposable retired pay. If you have a former spouse, check with your finance office on how this law could affect your retired pay.

CONCLUSION

The military retirement plan is generally quite generous and recognizes the sacrifices made by members of the armed forces. It is not, however, lavish. While the indexing provisions of the plan compare favorably with corresponding civilian pensions, Congress has not provided full inflation indexation; thus, retirement pay will be eroded by inflation over time. One can only expect that this trend will continue in the coming periods of fiscal austerity. These considerations make it clear that you will need to supplement your retirement income, so you should plan your finances now. One final note: Direct deposit/electronic transfer of your retirement pay is now mandatory.

SUGGESTED REFERENCES

DOD Manual 1340.12-M: *Military Retirement Pay and Allowances.*
Public Law 88-448, The Dual Compensation Act; and Public Law 95-454, The Civil Service Reform Act of 1978.
Sharff, Lee E., ed. *Uniformed Services Almanac,* 1991. Falls Church, VA: Uniformed Services Almanac, Inc., 1991.

17

Estate Planning

EVERYONE HAS AN estate. Although you may not have thought much about it, you have an estate, too. Your estate provides security for you and your family both now and after you die. Most people desire a larger estate, to provide this security better. While you may not be able to control the size of your estate, you can certainly restructure it to provide the best balance of security during your family's lifetime. While most of this book emphasizes accumulating an estate through financial planning and providing protection for your family through insurance, this chapter considers ways to preserve and dispose of an estate after it is accumulated. Estate planning requires organizing your financial affairs to facilitate transactions while you are alive and to ensure the desired transition of your estate upon your death. This chapter discusses six important topics:

1. Legal forms of ownership.
2. Power of attorney.
3. Wills and other estate-planning documents.
4. Trusts.
5. Income shifting.
6. The necessity of using expert assistance.

Much of estate planning seems arcane and even a bit scary to many people. This is understandable, considering the "legalese" involved and the stuffy images conjured up by "trusts" and "income shifting." Don't be put off by these concerns. Estate planning is driven by common sense and instinctive motivations that you already understand: a desire to provide security for your family, to avoid legal tangles and excessive taxation, and to ensure that your wishes are executed when you are gone. You may also wish to sleep soundly in the interim, avoiding the gnawing worries that accompany an unplanned or poorly planned estate. By properly attending to these matters, you can assure your family of the best possible use of your property throughout your life, and even after your death.

Fortunately, we in the armed services can turn to legal assistance officers when building our estate plans. Your commander and your legal assistance officer want you to arrange your legal affairs so that you will have the confidence that your wishes and your family's security will be provided for, even if you are gone. The time to address estate planning is now so that when an unexpected crisis or deployment occurs, you will be able to concentrate on your duty with your unit knowing that your loved ones have the wills, powers of attorney, and other provisions that they need. This is especially important if you are one of the 6.5 percent of the armed forces who is either a single parent or dual military couple. During the Persian Gulf War, for example, 37,000 children were separated from either their single parent or both of their parents who deployed to the Gulf. Many of those families and thousands of other spouses did not have adequate legal preparation for their servicemembers' extended absence. Your only cost of a well-planned estate is a little of your time today; the benefits to your family's security and your peace of mind in the future may be immeasurable.

THE OWNERSHIP OF PROPERTY

During your lifetime you will accumulate property as part of your "estate." It can be either personal property (such as personal effects, household furnishings, automobiles, money, or stocks), real property (land and associated buildings or fixtures), or mixed property. You may hold complete title to the property, in which case it belongs to you alone, or you may share ownership with another person or with a corporation. There are three common variations of joint ownership:

Tenancy in Common. Ownership is divided among the tenants and each has the right to sell, assign, or convey his or her share in the property.

Joint Tenancy with Right of Survivorship. Each tenant owns an undivided share in the property, and if one tenant dies, title automatically passes to the surviving tenants.

Tenancy by the Entirety. A special form of joint tenancy; the tenants must be husband and wife.

Quite often a servicemember will hold property jointly with a spouse or children to reduce administrative problems and costs if one owner should die. Property held jointly passes outside of the will, and thus avoids some of the expenses and problems associated with probate, which is the legal term for proving the authenticity of a will before proper judicial authority.

Before creating a joint tenancy with right of survivorship, you should get legal advice on the advantages and disadvantages because state laws vary. Real estate may be owned in joint tenancy with right of survivorship under proper deed. Joint title to personal property (such as a car), however, may make your spouse subject to personal property taxes on half or all of its value to the state where you are temporarily living because of your military duty.

Another common use of joint ownership is a joint bank account from which either party can draw funds. In a few states, funds in the account would not be available to the survivor until a tax release had been obtained. Be sure to check your specific situation when you see your legal assistance officer to draft your will.

Some states have laws recognizing all property of married couples as "community" property. Laws of those states pose special problems for the servicemember's estate, for there are strict definitions for community property and community income. In certain instances, purchases by either spouse are considered community property if earned "community" funds were used in the purchase. Separate purchases made by either spouse while residing in other states might also be declared community property upon moving into one of the community-property states. Special care must be taken in planning life insurance benefits and estate-tax deductions to avoid paying excessive taxes in these states. In most instances a service member can exempt life insurance benefits in any state from estate taxes by transferring policy ownership to his or her spouse as a gift. Good legal advice is critical. The community-property states are Arizona, California, Idaho, Louisiana, Nevada, New Mexico, Texas, and Washington.

POWER OF ATTORNEY

Because servicemembers are frequently absent or not immediately accessible when matters of personal business arise, it is advisable to designate an agent or "attorney" to act in the servicemember's name. Through a power of attorney, you give authority to act in your name and on your behalf to a family member or other person in whom you have complete trust and confidence.

The requirements of a legally effective power of attorney vary considerably among states, so it is impossible for one to draft a standardized form. The power of attorney should be made under the advice of your legal assistance officer, who is familiar with the laws of the state where it will be used. Do not use a standardized form unless the need is urgent and counsel is not available; even then, consider it a temporary expedient to be replaced as quickly as possible.

Most servicemembers would need a power of attorney in case of deployment or extended absence to allow someone to perform specific tasks in their place, such as the following:

- To ship and receive household goods or other property.
- To cash paychecks.
- To sell, buy, or receive a car.
- To request medical care for children (if they are not staying with your spouse).
- To accept or clear government quarters.

In most of these cases, your legal assistance officer will have a preprinted special power of attorney that complies with the laws of your state. It is a special power of attorney because it is limited to the time and purpose that it can be used. Whenever possible, use a special power of attorney, which gives you a greater degree of control over the agent's activities. It is generally desirable to provide for a certain date of termination, usually in two to three years. If you need to continue the power of attorney, you can complete a new power of attorney. Your agent (the person named in a power of attorney) need not be present for you to execute a new power of attorney. For example, if you are overseas, you could consult a legal assistance officer there to complete the power of attorney, and then mail it back to your agent.

As an alternative to the special power of attorney, you can sign a general power of attorney, which gives your agent unlimited power to act in your name. You should seek the advice of your legal assistance officer to determine which type of power of attorney is best for your particular situation. In any case, your agent should have three to six executed copies to meet prospective needs. You should retain one information copy.

Your power of attorney is valid only as long as you are alive and competent. A power of attorney can also be made durable, that is, written to remain valid even if you become incapacitated or incompetent. Remember, however, that death always nullifies any power of attorney, even one made durable. Therefore, a power of attorney should not be confused with or substituted for a will!

ESTATE-PLANNING DOCUMENTS

Wills

You and your spouse should have a will. If you die without a will ("intestate"), state law will determine the distribution of your property and the guardianship of your children. No matter how large or small your estate, not leaving a will results in some degree of hardship and inconvenience for your survivors. In some cases, it can result in an absurd disaster. Imagine a mother being required to sue to obtain custody of her own child because state law provides that the child becomes a ward of the state.

By making a will, you can specify who will receive your property, when, in what amounts, how it should be safeguarded, and by whom it should be handled. You can also settle the question of guardianship so that neither your spouse nor your children will have to endure the rigors of settling such a matter in the courts.

This section highlights some points you should be sure to ask about when you see your legal assistance officer about drafting your will. Don't use a standardized form for a will except in an emergency; if you do use such a will, replace it promptly with one developed by legal counsel. If you are married, you and your spouse should discuss these matters and go to see the lawyer together, but you must make separate wills. The following are topics and questions that you should consider before seeing your legal assistance officer:

Personal Representative. Your will specifies a person to act as your personal representative (sometimes called the executor of your will) to make decisions regarding your will. This is often your spouse or another trusted individual. You may also want to specify an alternate in case the person you designate is unable to act as your personal representative.

Domicile. Because of frequent changes in residence, it may be advisable to state your domicile in the will so that the will can be probated in the proper place.

Military Service. Your will should include the statement that you are now in (or have retired from, or served in) the active military or naval service of the United States, together with your grade and service (or Social Security) number.

Bequests. Your will specifies who is to receive your property and the manner in which it is to be divided upon your death. It covers property both that you own now and that you acquire after you execute your will. You can also make specific bequests that fully describe particular property and then specify the person who should receive it.

Common Disaster Clause. You should also include in your will a common disaster clause that names beneficiaries (usually children) should both spouses die in the same accident. This avoids any possible litigation by relatives as to which spouse died first and which spouse, therefore, was the owner of the entire estate at his or her death.

Guardianship. Your will should specify the legal guardian (and possibly alternate guardians) for your minor children. Your will should be consistent with that of your spouse to preclude legal conflicts in the unfortunate event that both of you die in the same calamity.

Testamentary Trust. A testamentary trust, discussed later in this chapter, helps protect the children's assets by putting them in a trust as specified in the will. This may substantially simplify matters for the children's guardian if both spouses die.

Events such as marriage, birth of children, divorce, or death of a named beneficiary or personal representative usually affect the provisions of a will. As circumstances change, you can always change your will and revoke, either partially or entirely, your previous will. The most recent properly executed will governs the disposition of your estate when you die. Hence the term "last will and testament" implies that that document replaces any previous wills. When a will is replaced by a new one, all copies of the previous will should be destroyed.

Only the original will should be signed. If you wish to keep a copy with you for reference or to give a copy to your personal representative or anyone else, it should be a "conformed" unsigned copy; that is, it should bear no signature, but your name as the maker and the names of witnesses should be printed or typed for information purposes.

Letters of Instruction

Along with a will, you should draw up a set of instructions for use by your personal representative and your survivors. This is an informational rather than a legal document that will help your personal representative and family to avoid confusion and major inconvenience in settling the estate. The best possible method for avoiding problems is to ensure that your spouse and children understand your plans and instructions now, before you die. This letter does not need to be notarized or prepared in any particular format, and it can be updated at any time. A letter of last instructions should contain the following:

- The location of all valuable documents (including birth certificates, Social Security cards, certificates of marriage and divorce, naturalization and citizenship papers, papers establishing your right to government benefits, service records, insurance policies, lists of savings accounts, bank accounts, stocks, bonds, deeds, and other evidence of ownership or debt).
- Instructions as to funeral and burial.
- Instructions concerning any business in which you may be involved.
- A statement of reasons for actions taken in your will, such as disinheritances.
- The location of your long-range planning charts, including instructions on how your assets can be used to satisfy the economic needs of the family.

Much of the information suggested here can be contained in some kind of personal affairs record form, such as that provided in appendix E. A conformed copy of your will and associated letter of last instructions should be left with your personal representative. A strongbox at home is probably a good place to keep these and other valuable documents.

You should not keep your will in a safe-deposit box. Often, when a person dies, the safe-deposit box may be sealed by the bank and opened only by court order.

TRUSTS

One of the most useful of all estate-planning tools is the trust, yet few people take advantage of it, probably because they don't understand it. Many people think of a trust as a complicated device involving a dour-looking trustee in a black frock coat (vaguely resembling a Dickens character), or a scheme used by the affluent to avoid taxes, or a financial straitjacket that deprives beneficiaries of the full enjoyment of property. It is none of these. Most couples should make use of at least one type of trust (a testamentary trust, described below) in their estate planning.

Trusts—and there are many variations to serve different objectives—are designed primarily to protect beneficiaries by providing more effective property management than an outright gift or bequest would provide. The advantage of a trust is that it provides increased protection for beneficiaries. The potential disadvantage is that it reduces the flexibility of the person who places assets into the trust. In some situations, tax savings can be realized even by persons with only moderate estates, although taxes usually are a collateral factor.

Essentially, a trust is simply a three-party relationship that separates ownership of the same property into two parts: the legal and the equitable. The person who establishes the trust might be called the trustor, grantor, settlor, maker, or donor (for consistency, we'll use trustor). The person (or corporation) to whom the property is transferred and who has legal title to it is the trustee. Those who have equitable ownership are referred to as the beneficiaries. Beneficiaries are divided into two categories: income beneficiaries, who have the benefit of the property for a certain period, such as the income for life; and remaindermen, who receive the property when the income beneficiaries' interests end. An example would be for you (trustor) to put a sum of money in a trust for your children (beneficiaries) under the control of a bank's trust department (trustee). If you instead had interest income from the trust going to your spouse (income beneficiary), and then had the remaining trust proceeds going to your children upon your spouse's death, they would be the remaindermen.

The two basic types of trusts used in estate planning are the living (or *inter vivos*) trust, which might be either revocable or irrevocable, and the testamentary trust (see Table 17-1). Another type we'll discuss later is the unfunded life insurance trust. Each has its own individual characteristics, and all offer a combination of advantages: separation of the burden from the benefit of property ownership; experienced management; strong legal safeguards; economy (a corporate trustee's fees usually are based on the value of the trust principal; from .25 to 1 percent a year is customary); protection for beneficiaries (especially important if the beneficiary is a minor or is financially inexperienced); assurance that the property will be used as the trustor desires; and continuity of assets and family income. Also, some trusts may offer significant savings in income and estate taxes.

Trust law is complex, so if you are wondering whether a trust is right for you, you should consult with a lawyer experienced in this specialized field and confer with a trust officer at your bank. There are also several good books on estate planning that cover trusts in detail. This section introduces you to trusts, highlighting some of the characteristics, possible uses, and principal consequences of the more common arrangements.

Revocable Living Trusts

As its name implies, a living trust is created and operates during the trustor's life. When the trustor has the right to cancel or modify its terms, the agreement is called a revocable trust.

The primary objective of an arrangement of this nature is, of course, property management during the trustor's life or during the lives of a husband and wife. Another important advantage is that the property could be transferred to the trustor's survivors without the normal delays (from several months to several years) and costs (such as attorney's fees and executor's commissions) involved in the probate process. For instance, the agreement might provide that after both spouses die, the trustee will divide the remaining trust estate and distribute it to their children, either all at once or at stated ages. If, however, the children already have adequate financial resources, it might direct that the trust continue, with the income to be paid to them during their lives, and with discretion in the trustee to use the principal for them if needed. When the children die, the principal could then go to grandchildren.

TABLE 17-1
Summary of Trusts

Type	Characteristics	Nontax Benefits	Income Tax	Estate Tax	Gift Tax
1. Irrevocable living	Settlor gives up property forever	Supervised control and investment; avoids probate	Taxed to beneficiary	Not taxable in settlor's estate	Taxable to settlor
2. Revocable living	Settlor can revoke	Same as 1	Taxable to settlor	Includable in settlor's estate	No liability
3. Testamentary	Created by will	Supervised control and investment	Same as 1	Includable in estate of creator	No liability

Because a revocable living trust does not involve a permanent surrender of control over property, trust income is taxable to the trustor (regardless of who the income beneficiary is) and is included in the estate for tax purposes. See Table 17-1 for a summary of trust characteristics.

Irrevocable Living Trusts

An irrevocable living trust is just what the name suggests: an arrangement under which the trustor gives up, either forever or for a stated period, any right to cancel or modify the agreement. It has most of the advantages of a revocable trust, including avoidance of probate, and it also permits some tax savings due to the income shifting. The income is not taxed to the trustor if he or she has relinquished all rights and control over it and transferred the future principal to a beneficiary. These savings could be substantial if you are in a high tax bracket and the beneficiaries are in a low bracket. Also, because the trustor has given up ownership of the property, its value would not be subject to death (estate) taxes.

Although a permanently irrevocable, nonreversionary agreement almost presupposes considerable wealth (and even then many people are reluctant to surrender permanent control over their property), there are a few situations in which such an arrangement might be useful. For example, a rich parent with a prodigal son might use an irrevocable trust to provide for his needs without indulging his excesses. An even more common use would be to provide a managed source of funds for a child's college education.

Testamentary Trusts

While a living trust can be quite useful in some situations, a testamentary trust, which is created by your will and does not operate until your death, deserves consideration by a broader range of people. Although no immediate income or estate tax savings are available, the other trust advantages should not be dismissed lightly. Any military family would probably benefit from establishing testamentary trusts in both spouses' wills. There are three reasons to consider establishing a testamentary trust:

Safety for spouse. If a significant amount of property is left outright to a surviving spouse, lack of investment experience or the influence of well-meaning but financially inexpert friends could lead to the loss of much of its value or purchasing power. (Weep for all the widows and widowers who, before the inflationary spurt of the late 1970s, used much of what their spouses left them to buy fixed-income annuities.) For a small annual fee, these risks can be avoided and the survivor can be relieved of the burden of managing the property.

Protection for children. A surviving spouse might remarry and later transfer title to the new spouse (and perhaps his or her children by a previous marriage), who might be enriched at the expense of the deceased's own children, who could end up with empty purses. The trust can easily be set up to pay income to the spouse and later provide the principal to surviving children.

Assistance for guardians. A testamentary trust can be established from your estate for any children who may survive you and your spouse. This helps protect the guardian and the children's assets from cumbersome and expensive reporting requirements that most states have to keep guardians from raiding their minors' inheritance.

The trust is simply a paragraph in your will, putting your estate in trust for your child, appointing a trustee (who could be the guardian or someone else), establishing any restrictions on use of the assets, and providing for eventual distribution of the assets to your children, in whatever way you choose. This way, you decide how your assets are managed when you are gone, and not the state. To prevent the trust approach from being thwarted if you die first, your spouse's will should have similar provisions. This type of trust is a contingent testamentary trust, contingent on the circumstances in which both spouses die.

Although a testamentary trust is not for everyone, anyone who has much more than a moderate estate should consider it. If, however, your estate consists mostly of nonprobate assets (such as jointly owned property or life insurance proceeds payable to a named beneficiary), so that relatively little would pass under the will, then you should consider some other way of achieving the same result (perhaps a life insurance trust, explained below).

Though legal assistance officers will not generally be able to set up complicated trusts for you, almost all legal assistance officers will add a contingent or testamentary trust to your will if you desire. This is an important benefit that you should definitely consider.

A final reason to consider trusts is that there may be tax advantages for your family. One common technique is to divide the estate into two parts: one for the surviving spouse, and the other in trust for the spouse's benefit while living, with whatever remains going to children or grandchildren after the spouse's death. Then, the trustee might be directed to distribute what is left to the children, either all at once or in whatever manner is specified. What such an arrangement does, essentially, is remove the principal of the trust from the spouse's estate for estate tax purposes, yet provide for the surviving spouse's needs as long as he or she lives.

Unfunded Life Insurance Trusts

A life insurance trust is merely a revocable trust that is funded with the proceeds of insurance on the trustor's life. Because the proceeds are not available until after death, the trust does not become effective until then, nor does it offer any immediate income or estate tax savings. Nevertheless, it meets the needs of some people because it provides professional management of life insurance proceeds.

If your estate consists of relatively little except a large amount of life insurance (a situation common in many young families), you could use the insurance to establish a trust for your spouse and children. After entering into a trust agreement, you direct the insurance companies to change the beneficiary to the trust. The trustee would hold the policies until your death, collect the proceeds, and then manage and distribute them according to the terms of the trust. The only expenses before your death are the attorney's fees for drafting the agreement (perhaps a few hundred dollars) and possibly a relatively small acceptance fee that some corporate trustees charge. You can change or revoke the trust at any time before your death.

Life insurance could be used to fund a testamentary trust, of course, but the unfunded life insurance trust has several advantages. For one thing, if the proceeds were used for a testamentary trust, the insured's estate would have to be the beneficiary, which would subject the proceeds to administration, claims against the estate, and inheritance taxation in some states. The avoidance of probate, with its costs and extended delays, is itself a sufficient reason not to make an estate the beneficiary of life insurance. Also, a life insurance trust can serve as a convenient receptacle for other estate assets, which can be "poured over" into it by the testator's will.

The dismal shortcomings of periodic payment settlement options offered by insurance companies become immediately apparent if compared with a life insurance trust. The most important advantage of a trust is its flexibility: If an unforeseen emergency arises, the principal could be drawn on to meet it. Under an insurance annuity, on the other hand, the beneficiary would receive no more or less than the monthly stipend, regardless of the circumstances.

Perhaps more important, a trust should provide greater protection against inflation. The "prudent man" standard of most states requires trust investments to be geared both to producing reasonable income and to preserving capital—and preservation means not just maintaining the same number of dollars, but also increasing capital to offset inflation. There is no assurance, of course, that the trust principal will appreciate, nor is there any certain small return like that which an insurer guarantees. There is, however, the potential for gain because, unless the trustor has directed otherwise, most corporate trustees usually invest the funds they manage in high-grade common stocks, bonds, and other securities.

Also, even if the trust principal does not appreciate, the income alone would probably exceed the payments guaranteed under a twenty-years-certain life insurance settlement option. What is more, when the trust beneficiary dies, the principal (less any amounts that might have been paid out of principal) would be available for the remaindermen. Conversely, with life insurance payments, on the death of the beneficiaries or at the end of the years-certain guarantee, nothing would remain for the children or others.

Contingent Unfunded Life Insurance Trusts

One variation of the typical unfunded life insurance trust is a contingent unfunded life insurance trust, in which the trustee is the contingent or secondary beneficiary. This arrangement might be used if you want your spouse to receive the insurance proceeds, but you want a trust for the children if your spouse dies.

Some of the advantages of a trust for minor children were mentioned earlier. First, a trust avoids the cost and inconvenience of appointing a guardian for their estates, the bonding expense, and the required periodic accounting by the guardian to the court. Second, the best guardian for your children may not have the financial expertise to manage the money that you have provided. Third, control of your children's assets is uncertain if the guardian dies during the guardianship period. Fourth, the guardian would have to pay each child his or her share when the child reaches majority (eighteen in most states), even though the child's experience and financial ability might be questionable. Finally, a guardian's control of the children's estate is subject to the continued jurisdiction of the probate court, which might be undesirable particularly if the children live in a state other than the one in which the will is probated.

Another limitation of naming young children as contingent beneficiaries of life insurance is that the proceeds would be divided equally among them. Better results are possible if the estate is used for the benefit of all the children, although their needs might be disparate. For example, assume that both parents die, survived by three minor children who, as contingent beneficiaries of life insurance, share $200,000 equally. If one child requires expensive medical care or special training, the costs would be borne by his or her share alone. After reaching majority, that child might have nothing left, but the other two might have sizable sums remaining. The parents can accomplish a more equitable division with a family trust that permits the trustee to "spray" or "sprinkle" the income and use the principal according to the individual needs of the beneficiaries, then distribute what remains when the children reach majority or when the trustor has directed.

Administrative and Distributive Arrangements

Deciding what administrative and distributive provisions would be best depends, of course, on several factors, such as the size and nature of the trust estate, the desires of the trustor, and the needs of the beneficiaries. A trust is a personal and complex instrument that requires custom drafting by a knowledgeable lawyer. It is not something you can do for yourself by filling in spaces on a printed form. To provide your lawyer with a clear understanding of your desires, however, there are a few general matters you should think about, starting with whom you want to appoint as trustee. Legal assistance officers will probably be willing to talk to you and advise you about trusts but will probably not draft trusts for you (other than testamentary trusts discussed above).

Selecting a Trustee

Similar to a personal representative, a trustee is a fiduciary and so is held to the highest standards of loyalty. Unlike a personal representative whose duties are short-term, a trustee is required to manage the trust productively over a long time.

Selecting a trustee has an important bearing on the effectiveness of a trust. In the past, individuals (often relatives or family lawyers) were the usual choices. One advantage of an individual trustee is that they are more likely to know the beneficiaries' needs and to have a personal interest in their welfare. Also, if a qualified relative or friend serves without compensation, the trust avoids the expense of a corporate trustee (.25 to 1 percent a year). Although these fees are reasonable, avoiding them means that more income is available for the beneficiaries. Often, however, the financial experience and abilities of individual trustees fall short of the competence needed. It also may not be fair to burden a friend or relative with such an onerous task without compensation.

Today, corporate trustees are more popular—over one-fifth of all banks have trust departments. They are not equally skilled, of course, but most are better equipped to perform investment duties than individuals. They provide continuity of management, and their long-term records are generally satisfactory. Although costs are too great to enable them to accept small individual trusts (perhaps less than $50,000 or $100,000, depending on the particular institution), most states permit corporate trustees to combine small trusts into a common trust fund. Some banks have different funds for different objectives (such as high income or appreciation potential) that permit you to select among them.

Sometimes, both a corporate trustee and the surviving spouse are appointed as co-trustee. This does not reduce costs, for most trust departments charge a full fee anyway, and as a practical matter, such an arrangement tends to be inefficient. As an alternative, the surviving spouse could be given power to direct the trustee in certain matters, or he or she could be appointed in an advisory capacity.

Occasionally, circumstances suggest that an individual serve as trustee. For most long-term, family-type trust arrangements, however, there are advantages of using an established institution with a proven record of satisfactory performance. Ask friends in your community for recommendations and visit several bank trust departments before you choose one.

Be sure to discuss "investment powers" with your trustee, so that you both understand desired limits and goals for investment of trust principal. Also discuss "invasion powers," to set the extent to which the trustee can dip into trust principal in case income alone is inadequate for the beneficiaries' needs. In this area, as in others, a little forethought and planning can often eliminate serious problems later.

Providing for the Guardian's Needs

Another provision that deserves consideration is whether part of the income can or should be used for the guardian's needs. If you have provided adequately for your family, your estate, supplemented by Social Security and other survivor benefits, is probably more than ample for your children alone. At the same time, their guardian might have limited income but large financial responsibilities, so that his or her own children are in a vastly different financial position than that of your children. Under these circumstances, the welfare of your children might be enhanced if the trustee is permitted to use some of the trust income to assist the guardian or the guardian's children, for they are the family that your children will then have.

Miscellaneous Other Provisions

There are many other matters that you should consider when planning a trust that are beyond the scope of this chapter. They include questions such as whether to include a "spendthrift" clause (to prevent a beneficiary from disposing of or encumbering his interest, and to protect the trust from creditors), how liberal the trustee's managerial powers should be, and at what ages distributions should be made to children (eighteen might not be best for a child, but is thirty-five too old?). You should discuss these and other concerns with your family, your lawyer, and the trustee.

INCOME SHIFTING

Many individuals would like to provide for children or elderly relatives and at the same time reduce the income tax liability associated with investing for this purpose. Most servicemembers in this category are primarily concerned with providing for their children's college education, and it is good that they are! According to the College Board, the total average annual expense in 1992–93 for a public college was $8,071. This was more than double the cost just ten years earlier. Using these numbers and assuming a 5 percent annual increase results in some alarming costs for our children's future education, as show in Table 17-2.

Providing for dependents while reducing income tax liability involves the transfer of income-producing assets to the low-income taxpayer so that assets are accumulated at their lower tax bracket. Most of us, however, want to maintain control over our investment until some time in the future. Unfortunately, retaining control may not allow you to shift your income tax.

TABLE 17-2
Higher Education Cost Projections

Average Annual College Expenses	Public College		Private College	
	2-Year	4-Year	2-Year	4-Year
1992–1993	$ 5,282	$ 8,071	$11,266	$17,027
2002–2003	$ 8,604	$13,146	$18,351	$27,735
2012–2013	$14,015	$21,415	$29,892	$45,177

Earlier in this chapter we noted that the primary purpose of most trusts is to protect the beneficiaries by providing responsible management for property. In some cases, you can realize income or estate tax savings, since most living trusts remove assets from the probate process. Many people, not just the rich, could benefit from a trust, but relatively few take advantage of the opportunities. Most people do, however, use various nontrust arrangements to avoid probate or to shift income from a higher to a lower tax bracket. This section discusses the characteristics, possible uses, and principal consequences of the more common arrangements. Probably the most familiar is joint tenancy or joint ownership (the "poor man's will") between a husband and wife. The following discussion summarizes some other methods of income shifting and/or avoiding probate; see also Table 17-3.

Outright Gifts

The most clear-cut way to reduce estate taxes and avoid probate is to dispose of property before death, and the simplest manner of doing so is to give it away. Consequently, if anyone has ample resources for present and future needs and could part with some assets while still alive, he or she should consider making outright gifts.

TABLE 17-3
Income Shifting Summary

	Postpone Minor's Control	Reduce Income Taxes	Avoid Probate	Reduce Death Taxes
Outright gifts	No	Yes	Yes	Yes
Custodian gifts to minors	Yes, to majority	Yes[1]	Yes	Yes[2]
Joint ownership with right of survivorship	No	No	Yes	No
Survivor bonds and pay-on-death accounts (Totten trust)	Yes, until donor's death	No	Yes	No
Family annuities	No	Yes	Yes	Yes
Revocable trust	Yes, to age desired	No	Yes	No
Irrevocable trust	Yes, to age desired	Yes	Yes	Yes

Notes
[1] Unless used to satisfy legal obligations of parent
[2] Unless donor or custodian dies before child's majority

ESTATE PLANNING

A gift not only shifts income and avoids probate, but in large estates it reduces estate taxes. To be effective, though, a present interest in the property must pass to the recipient. A "when I die it's yours" gift usually would not qualify.

Also, if a gift is sufficiently large, a tax on the transfer might be incurred. However, the federal law grants everyone an annual, noncumulative exclusion of $10,000 per recipient ($20,000 if a husband and wife make a gift to a third person). Purely from a cost perspective, a wealthy person should take advantage of the annual exclusion. If property left to someone other than the surviving spouse exceeds the exemption equivalent of the estate tax credit ($600,000), over one-third would be paid in taxes and never reach the beneficiaries.

Even parents who are not wealthy, for whom the savings might be more important, can stretch family dollars by making gifts of cash or preferably securities to their minor children. The difficulty, though, is that outright gifts of titled or registered property (other than government savings bonds or savings accounts) can be complicated. This is where the Uniform Gifts to Minors Act comes to the rescue.

Gifts to Minors

Every state has a Uniform Gifts to Minors Act (UGMA) or Uniform Transfers to Minors Act (UTMA). Both acts are similar and provide a simple procedure for giving money, securities, and other intangibles to minors, merely by placing them in the name of an adult. For example, a stock certificate could not be issued to a minor, but it could be registered as "Joan Adult, as custodian for Amy Child, under the Colorado UGMA." There may be only one custodian and only one beneficiary for each account or certificate. You can and should designate a successor custodian in writing. The custodian manages the property (including selling it and reinvesting the proceeds, if appropriate) until the minor reaches twenty-one, at which time it is transferred to the minor outright.

The UGMA technique merits consideration by even those persons who cannot afford more than a few hundred dollars a year to provide some degree of future financial security for their children. For example, assume that parents are able to save $100 a month for their child's later education or other use. If this is deposited in an interest-bearing account in the parents' names, the earnings would be taxable to them; if it is in the child's name, he or she could withdraw it without the parents' permission. If, instead, this sum is deposited in a custodial account or used to buy mutual funds or other securities under the UGMA or UTMA, not all the income would be taxable at the parents' rate, and the custodian would control the property until the child is twenty-one. The parent as custodian manages the child's money in the same way that they would for their own accounts. They simply sign documents and endorse checks "Joan Adult, for benefit of (FBO) Amy Child," and can buy or sell securities, mutual funds, or other assets as they desire.

For children under fourteen, the first $600 of unearned income (dividends and interest) is tax-free, the next $600 is taxed at the child's (presumably low) rate, and unearned income over $1,200 is taxed at the parents' marginal tax rate. For children fourteen or over, the first $600 is still tax-free, and the remainder is taxed at the child's tax rate. Thus, parents could place $6,000 in a mutual fund that earned 10 percent, or $600, annually, and under the UGMA or UTMA no one would pay taxes on that income. Here are some other points you should know about these transfers:

1. Once made, a gift is not revocable, so even if a once-cuddly bundle of joy grows into an ungrateful lout, what you gave them is now theirs.
2. This arrangement cannot be used to evade income taxes, of course, which would be the result if a parent-donor used the income in a way that was other than for the benefit of the child.
3. College financial aid formulas often require that all wealth available to the minor, which would include income in UGMA accounts, be exhausted before financial aid is considered. The parents' savings are also considered, but depending upon the college, the impact on financial aid may not be as great, especially if there are other children in the family.
4. If a parent-donor is custodian, the value of the property would be included in his or her estate if death occurs before the minor becomes twenty-one. This is advantageous if the parent's estate is below the estate tax threshold ($600,000), because property that has appreciated (such as shares of stock) receives a stepped-up tax basis at the time of the custodian's death. As such, the child would not have to pay taxes on the capital gains that occurred while the parent-donor is alive. If the estate is above $600,000, then the donor should consult a lawyer, because estate taxes may be avoided by designating the other parent or a third person as custodian.

Joint Bank Accounts

Large numbers of husbands and wives, as well as many parents and children, maintain what are known as joint bank accounts. These are not true joint tenancies, because either owner, acting independently, may withdraw any or all funds on deposit. The usual registration takes the form of "Robert or Jane Doe, as joint tenants with the right of survivorship." There is no gift tax liability if the joint owners are married.

When one joint owner dies, the survivor owns the account, although a release from the state inheritance tax authorities normally would be required before it (or all of it above a specified amount) could be released to the survivor. What is more, for nonspousal accounts, the entire value is included for estate tax purposes in the estate of the first to die, except insofar as the survivor can establish that his or her property contributed to the acquisition. Hence, although a joint bank account (with, for example, a parent and child as co-owners) can be convenient, it generally would not, contrary to popular belief, result in any savings in federal or state death taxes in large estates.

United States Savings Bonds

If you have college costs ahead, you may wish to buy Series EE savings bonds in your dependent child's name (with you as beneficiary rather than co-owner). This constitutes a completed gift but should be well within the annual exclusion. The first year, file a federal tax return in the child's name, listing accrued interest as income. This establishes your child's intent to report the increase in redemption value as interest each year (rather than reporting all the interest when the bond is cashed). Thereafter, no returns are necessary unless the child's unearned income exceeds $600. When he or she is ready for college, the bonds may be redeemed without incurring any additional tax liability.

Another possibility is to defer reporting income from the savings bonds until they are cashed in. This would only make sense for minors who already pay the "kiddie tax"—that is, they are already taxed at their parents' tax rate, since they report over $1,200 in annual interest income. This is not the case for the children of most military members.

Zero Coupon Bonds

A brokerage house will buy bonds or government securities and sell the bonds, less the coupons, to the investor at a discount (similar to a savings bond). For example, a ten-year, $1,000 bond will be sold at $400. When the $1,000 is paid at the end of ten years, a 9.6 percent annual return will be realized. The IRS has ruled that even though the interest is not paid until maturity, it is imputed each year. There is no advantage in this to the higher-tax-bracket taxpayer, but significant advantages may be available for the low-bracket taxpayer (your children). Zero coupon bonds could be purchased in a child's name with varying lengths of maturity times for college. See chapter 13 for additional information on zero coupon bonds.

Other Techniques

In the never-ending quest for ways to thwart the tax man and keep a larger portion of property or income within a family, taxpayers have resorted to various other arrangements. Apart from income-shifting techniques we have already considered, other methods of conserving assets within a family include loans and "private annuities," which offer unique advantages in some cases. For example, if reasonably wealthy elderly parents have responsible, adult children, they might transfer property to them in exchange for their promise to pay them a monthly income for life. Such an arrangement, in which the children serve essentially like the issuer of a commercial annuity, saves commissions and other costs, avoids the expense and delay of probate, and enables the parents to leave more to their offspring. Another technique involves a gift and borrow-back of property, or hiring a child or spouse in an income-producing activity. If you think that some such arrangement is for you, ask your lawyer or tax advisor for suggestions.

PROFESSIONAL ASSISTANCE

One of the philosophical tenets of this book is that all servicemembers should understand as much as possible concerning the management of their financial affairs. The better your understanding, the more chance you have of maximizing the satisfaction from your economic resources. If you do not take the few minutes required to make sound economic decisions (determining your insurance needs, properly preparing a will and letter of last instructions, and so on), you and your family will suffer the consequences.

Along with learning to do things yourself, however, you also need expert assistance at times. Whether it is your banker or your legal advisor, you should go to that professional with a basic understanding of your problem and the kinds of solutions that might be used to solve it. The more knowledge you have, the easier it is for your advisor to explain the reasons for the advice he gives, the easier it is for you to evaluate that advice, and the surer you are that the decisions you make are good ones. Do not neglect to get help from professionals. It is their business to know and to provide you with the latest information required for you to make rational decisions about your estate.

It has been said that one who is his or her own lawyer has a fool for a client. This sentiment can be extended to anyone going it alone when it comes to estate planning. Start with an appointment with your legal assistance officer, and then follow through by completing a will and any other tools that you discover you need. Your legal assistance office may have a list of lawyers in your area with particular specialties that you may be able to consult for complicated legal and financial matters. Sound financial and estate planning now will provide substantial benefits in the future.

18

Life Insurance

THE SUBJECT OF life insurance is one of the most important in personal financial planning. Unfortunately, life insurance is poorly understood, and tragic mistakes by breadwinners without insurance still cause great misfortune for their survivors. Today, many two-income families have adequate insurance on the husband but don't stop to think that without the wife's income, the family will suffer serious financial hardship. Less publicized but probably far more frequent problems are having too much or the wrong type of life insurance.

If you understand the life insurance principle and the nature of life insurance as commonly sold by U.S. companies, and if you have a clear evaluation of your financial obligations should death occur, you can find the life insurance protection you need at a cost your family can afford. The goal of this chapter is to help you buy the right amount and the right type of life insurance.

There is over $9 trillion of life insurance in force in the United States alone. It's big business. The life insurance industry is a business designed to produce a profit for the company and an income for the agent, as well as protecting your family's economic security. Because insurance agents operate primarily on a commission basis, they have a natural incentive to sell those policies that produce high commissions. Reputable agents will, of course, attempt to match an insurance program to your needs, but you should be aware of the substantial commissions involved and the possibility for high-pressure sales techniques.

Three factors complicate the buying process. The first is the emotional impact of confronting your own death. Second, some life insurance policies have both an insurance component and an investment component, which often makes it difficult to remember that the primary goal of life-insurance protection should be replacing family income in the event of a breadwinner's death. Finally, there is the somewhat mysterious nature of the life insurance business. The use of statistics and actuarial (life projection) techniques tends to discourage even the most careful shopper. Adding to the confusion are the special terms developed by the life insurance industry to make the subject more appealing and the product more marketable. The terms premium, permanent insurance, whole life insurance, and term insurance must be translated so that the typical buyer can understand the full range of options. Because of all this, many people are so confused that they decide to simply choose an agent rather than the best product.

Despite these obstacles, the basic concepts of life insurance are not difficult to grasp and the required computations are quite simple. After discussing the life insurance principle and the meaning of the terms commonly used in the industry, we suggest a procedure for determining your insurance needs and satisfying them as economically as possible. If you are already familiar with life insurance, you can skip to the section titled "Estimating Your Insurance Needs" (page 293).

THE PRINCIPLE OF INSURANCE

Insurance is based on a very simple commonsense concept: The cost of infrequent (but catastrophic) events can be spread among a large group with a small cost to each member. Individuals share the risk at a fraction of the cost of the catastrophic event. Life insurance is perhaps the best example of insurance that "pays off" for an event that happens most infrequently (once in a lifetime) but with truly catastrophic effects on the insured. It is not the insured that "life" insurance is designed to protect, however. Life insurance is for the future well-being of the survivors of the policyholder, who benefits only from the peace of mind that the insurance provides.

Of course, in a pure sense life cannot be insured because death is a certainty for all of us—only the date is unclear. What is actually being provided as "life insurance" is protection from the economic consequences of premature death. Insurance will not help with the emotional loss, although it should remove the fear of economic hardship. The amount of insurance does not demonstrate your love for your family, nor does it delay your departure from this world. Too much insurance results in high premiums that reduce your monthly budget and therefore your ability to enjoy other good things in life. A clear understanding of what one is buying, and why, is critical in developing a life insurance plan that is best for you, not your insurance company.

BASIC LIFE INSURANCE TERMS

The face amount, the policy period, the premium, and savings are part of any life insurance policy and can be varied to fit the individual needs of each policyholder.

Face Amount

The size of your insurance coverage is determined by the face amount of the policy. This amount would be paid to the beneficiary (a person designated by you) in the event of your death. The larger the face amount, the higher the benefit to the beneficiary but the higher the cost of the policy.

Policy Period

You can buy a life insurance policy for any length of time: a year or as long as your entire life. The premium you pay is often related to the length of the policy period. Although some policies are for a specific period, a policy can be renewed unless it is explicitly nonrenewable. Re-entry or guaranteed insurability policies can be renewed, but renewal requires a new physical examination, and the premiums may be recalculated based on the examination results. Renewable policies guarantee renewal without conditions, and the premium will change only with your age, not the condition of your health. Because with renewable policies the insurance company does not have the right to get out of its obligation to insure you or to raise your premiums should your health deteriorate, the premiums will be somewhat higher for these policies.

In general, nonrenewable policies and policies with shorter renewal periods or that base future premiums on new physical exams mean lower annual premiums today. Companies charge lower premiums for these policies because they have a chance to learn more at each renewal point about the factors (health, in particular) that affect the probability of death and to refuse insurance or raise premiums for very poor risks. If you are in excellent health, the cheapest possible coverage in the short run will be a one-year, nonrenewable term policy. If you want a renewable policy, you will have to pay more.

Premium

A premium is nothing more than a payment, like a car payment or a mortgage payment on a house. With certain types of policies, part of the payment goes to a form of "savings" after some point. Premiums can stay the same, increase, or decrease over the length of the policy depending on your policy type.

Savings

Permanent and variable insurance policies (discussed in the next section) accumulate a cash value and can be used as a method of savings. There are several advantages to this type of savings: You can borrow from your account (you will be charged interest for borrowing); after a period of years, your insurance policy can be paid up and you will no longer need to make premium payments; or you can end the policy and remove your "savings" portion to spend or invest elsewhere. There is also a disadvantage: You typically earn a lower rate of interest on these savings than on alternative financial investments.

TYPES OF LIFE INSURANCE POLICIES

There are three main types of life insurance: term (lasts for just a specific period, with no savings component), permanent (premiums are paid until your death but also build savings), and variable (has flexible structure designed to allow greater return on the savings portion of the policy). Within these major categories, there are many variations designed to meet the needs of the insured. As a policyholder gets older and the chances of a "premature" death increase, there may be a problem with steadily rising premiums. To avoid this problem, the insured may select level-term insurance or permanent insurance. Whatever the fine points, the underlying principle of distributing the risk over a large group to make it bearable remains the goal of any type of insurance. As we discuss each of the specialized types of life insurance, think about how the different options fit your personal needs.

Term Insurance

Term insurance protects the policyholder for a specified time period—one year, five years, twenty years, or more. It is pure insurance: protection of your survivors from the economic effects of your death. It has no savings feature and thus no "cash value," so you cannot borrow against the policy. Term insurance must be renewed when the "term" is completed. Normally, renewal requires a physical examination, although some companies may relax this requirement.

Since none of your premium is going toward "savings," term premiums are far lower than permanent policy premiums. Thus, a young person who has a need for a larger death benefit, perhaps in excess of $200,000, but whose income is low may be able to afford the needed coverage by using term insurance.

Term insurance (or "temporary" insurance as the agents like to call it) may sound somewhat undesirable. This is not necessarily true. Term insurance might be the most suitable alternative, depending on your situation. You should be aware, though, that many agents might try to steer you toward permanent insurance. Many agents sell both permanent (insurance plus savings) and term (insurance alone) insurance policies. Premiums for term insurance are based on the expected number of deaths per year for a given age group—and this number can be determined quite accurately using standard data, which makes for good competition among companies as they bid for your business with premiums only slightly above this base cost. By contrast, in permanent insurance policies, the savings component of the policies requires a larger premium, and since the premiums collected greatly exceed the expected payout for death benefits, the insurance company can make a good income investing the "excess premium" in bonds and stocks. As a result, few of the larger companies will "push" term insurance, and they adjust their commission incentives to make this very clear to their sales personnel. When they do sell term insurance (agents selling term insurance are called "termites" by some in the industry), it is often with the goal of converting the policy to "permanent" insurance as soon as the policyholder can be persuaded to do so. Fortunately, some good companies do specialize in term insurance, and a number cater especially to the military community.

There is an apparent disadvantage to term insurance. As you get older, the premiums increase. At age twenty, you might be able to get a $100,000 term policy for approximately $150 per year, but at age forty-five, that same policy could cost you over $300 per year. The increase in premiums would eventually make term more expensive than the premiums on permanent insurance (bought now) for the same face amount. As we will see later, however, the "insurance portion" of permanent insurance effectively has the same characteristics. Also, as you grow older, your insurance needs will likely peak and then lessen. Once children are through with school, your insurance needs should decrease. You may not even need any life insurance when you are older. If you do, however, several different types of term insurance are offered to partially alleviate this deficiency.

Level Term

The face value and the premium for level term insurance remain the same throughout the period of coverage. This type of insurance was designed to lower the high cost of term insurance in the later years of the policy. One method used to calculate the premiums averages the payments so that an equal payment is paid each month, in effect overpaying the first half of the policy period and underpaying the last half. Even if the term were forty-five years (perhaps until anticipated retirement), the premium would still be less than a permanent policy (discussed later) for the same amount of insurance, because there is no savings component to the policy.

Servicemen's Group Life Insurance (SGLI) is level term insurance. Currently, a servicemember may elect to take up to $200,000 of coverage for 80 cents per month per $10,000 of coverage, regardless of age. This is very inexpensive insurance for older officers and noncommissioned officers. In effect, the large numbers of young servicemembers make possible low premiums for the older servicemembers. For this reason, and also because it is convertible after you leave the service, SGLI should be the basic building block of your family's insurance program.

Decreasing Term

Decreasing term insurance has a constant premium over the term of the coverage, but the face value of the policy declines to reflect the higher risk of death as age increases. As an example, a $10 monthly premium might buy a twenty-five-year-old male insurance protection of $100,000; a man in his fifties would get only $15,000 of term insurance for this premium. A decreasing term policy may make a lot of sense if your insurance needs decrease as you get older. For instance, if you had an obligation that was decreasing, such as a home mortgage, then matching decreasing benefits would also make excellent sense. Mortgage insurance, a form of decreasing term, is a fairly common (but often expensive) way of dealing with this particular situation.

Deposit Term

Deposit term insurance rewards policyholders who keep the same term insurance coverage for long periods of time. In addition to your regular annual premium, you pay a deposit (usually about $10 per $1,000 of insurance coverage), which is placed in an interest-bearing account. If you maintain your insurance through the life of the policy, then you get back your deposit plus interest at the end of the period. If you cancel your insurance before the term outlined in the policy, you forfeit the deposit plus the earned interest. Deposit term insurance provides relatively low-cost insurance if you keep your policy for the full length and get your deposit back; it is one of the most expensive policies if you cancel your policy and forfeit your deposit. It is not as common as other forms of term insurance.

Renewable, Nonrenewable, and Re-entry Term

Renewable, nonrenewable, and re-entry term policies have special features that allow you to renew them at the end of the policy period if you meet certain standards. Renewable term eliminates the physical examination requirement: A person injured in combat or contracting cancer would still be able to renew the term policy. In this respect, term insurance is not really "temporary" at all. This renewal feature will not be available past age seventy, when term insurance is no longer available or becomes too expensive. We have already noted that you may not need insurance coverage in old age when your children are on their own and you have sufficient assets to provide a comfortable retirement. Most of the companies that cater to the military sell renewable term.

The second type, nonrenewable, means just that: The policy ends and the policyholder must purchase new insurance, qualifying for it with a new physical exam. Re-entry term is less expensive than renewable term insurance. You must, however, pass a physical after the end of the term in order to "re-enter" the low-cost policy. The danger is that if you fail the physical examination, you cannot "re-enter" and must pay a higher premium or find a different policy. Finding a new policy can be quite expensive (or even impossible) if you have failed a physical examination. As an example, let's see what happens with a thirty-five-year-old nonsmoking male who purchases a $250,000 five-year re-entry term policy. His annual premium starts out at $400 and gradually rises to $550 over the five-year term. At the re-entry point, the now forty-year-old male takes a new physical exam. If he passes, his premium goes down to $500 and gradually rises from there; but if he fails, his premium starts off at $750. At forty-five years of age, the numbers would be $600 (pass) and $1,100 (not pass), respectively.

In comparison, once you pass the initial physical examination for a renewable term policy, your premium is the same as for all others of the same age regardless of what subsequently happens to your health. Basically, re-entry term is best for only a very select group: people who need a substantial amount of insurance for a short period of time. For others, the cost of re-entry goes up when they can least afford it. For individuals seeking insurance, the risk of re-entry term probably outweighs the small savings.

Permanent Insurance

The words permanent, ordinary, and whole life insurance have the same meaning in the insurance industry. These policies combine pure insurance with an automatic savings feature (called "cash value") that provides the companies with funds that they invest to produce most of their profits. Insurance salespeople are offered the largest commissions for selling permanent policies and therefore emphasize them in their sales presentations to customers.

Perhaps "ordinary insurance" really refers to the fact that this is the type of insurance that a company would most prefer to sell. "Permanent" can be explained by the important cash value feature. As years go by, the interest earnings on the savings will accumulate, slowly at first, but then faster in later years, until there is enough in the account to cover the face value of the policy. This, in effect, gradually replaces the insurance with your own savings. The company eventually accumulates enough of a cash value for the policyholder to simply hand it back to the survivors when the policyholder dies. Permanent insurance is really term insurance of the decreasing type, with an enforced savings feature built onto it. The company, in paying off the "face value" totally out of "cash value," would no longer be providing any pure insurance. These accumulated savings represent a "cash value" that may be borrowed against—for interest—after some number of years.

An advantage of permanent insurance is that you are insured for your whole life, for a constant premium. No matter when you die, if your policy is still in force, the company will pay the face amount to your beneficiary. Although the payments are much higher than term insurance early in life, they are less later because of the accumulated savings portion of the premium.

The majority of permanent or whole life policies fall into two categories: straight life and limited-payment life.

Straight Life

Straight life (also called whole or ordinary life) is the most common form of life insurance sold. It provides both protection and savings for the policyholder, who pays premiums throughout his or her life and builds up a cash value in the policy. It has the same premium throughout the life of the policy (which is where the term *straight* comes from); the premium charged to you at age twenty is the same premium charged at fifty. The premium amount is determined primarily by your age when you buy the policy; the older you are when you start, the higher the premium. Your physical condition can also play a role.

Whole life policies build a cash value that steadily grows each year you have the policy. Be very careful concerning this savings feature. If you close out your account, especially in the first few years, you will not find much savings there. For example, one company's most popular permanent policy returns an average interest rate of .2 percent on the accumulating savings if you cancel it at the ten-year point. Policy cancellations are not unusual: A Senate subcommittee gathered data on sixty of the leading U.S. insurance companies and found that 25 percent of permanent policy buyers discontinue their policies within the first year, 46 percent within ten years, and nearly 60 percent before twenty years.

Although the industry's "average" policy has provided a return of 2.8 percent at the ten-year point, the return does depend on the length of time you keep the policy.

Most policies forfeit all cash value if the policy is in effect for less than two years, with the average "break-even point" at eight years, which is where your accumulated savings have earned a 0 percent return. At twenty years, the average interest earned on savings in whole life policies has been 4.4 percent. Interest does increase slightly after twenty years but stays near the 5 percent level up to fifty years. Generally, a savings account at your local bank will earn as much interest as, and in some cases even more than, the savings portion of a whole life policy. The whole life policy accumulates interest in a tax-deferred fashion, however; no taxes are paid on the gains in your account until the funds are actually withdrawn.

Another often-stated feature of whole life is the availability of loans against the cash value of the policy. In 1993, most companies charged 6 to 7.5 percent for policy loans. Although this is less expensive than most signature loans, you must realize that you are really borrowing from your own savings, which are left to accumulate at a lower rate. Policy loans may not have to be paid back; however, borrowing from your policy in this fashion will reduce the death benefits of the policy by the amount you withdraw. This feature can come in quite handy as a ready source for short-term loans.

Limited-payment Life

A limited-payment insurance policy provides life insurance protection throughout the policyholder's life similar to whole life. But instead of the same payment throughout, you pay the same premium for a limited number of years (perhaps for ten, twenty, or thirty years). At that point the policy is "paid up," meaning that no further premiums are required. In comparison, a whole life policy does not get paid up until you reach the age of 100. Insurance protection, in the sense that the beneficiaries get the face amount of the policy upon the policyholder's death, remains throughout the policyholder's life.

Of course, the sooner the policy is to be paid up, the greater the premium must be, so in the short run, these are usually the most expensive of all life insurance policy premiums. For example, a thirty-five-year-old man who purchases a $10,000, twenty-year limited-payment policy might pay $340 per year versus $220 for a whole life policy. Since the payments are so large, the amount of insurance that can be bought with a budgeted amount each month is smaller. Thus, a young couple using limited-payment life may be underinsured, even though they are paying a lot for insurance. They are also the most profitable for insurance companies, since more money comes to them "up front."

Variable Insurance

In the 1970s, high interest rates available on alternative savings vehicles made the low rates of return on the savings component in whole life and limited-payment life most unattractive. Sales of these products declined, and the insurance industry developed a whole new range of products with higher rates of return and increased flexibility. Some of these plans allow the policyholder to move between term and permanent insurance for a small fee, so that the savings and insurance components of the policies can be adjusted to meet the customer's needs over a period of years. Other new policies simply improve the return on the savings component of the policy. The most common types of these new policies are adjustable life, universal life, and variable life. Most of these policies also come in a "single-premium" flavor, with one massive up-front premium that would not appeal to most military people.

Adjustable Life

Adjustable life insurance lets policyholders move between term and permanent insurance as their needs change. Policies can start off as whole life and be converted to term insurance by lowering the premiums or increasing the face value of the policy. Or the policy can initially offer lower-cost term coverage with little or no cash value buildup. Then, when the policyholder is better able to pay, the policy can be changed to permanent insurance with higher premiums and the accumulation of cash value. Dividends can be used to pay premiums or to increase the face value of the policy. The major advantage of this type of policy is flexibility. The interest rate earned is not much better than with the standard whole life policies.

Universal Life

Universal life is a combination of term insurance with a tax-deferred savings account that earns a market interest rate. In many respects, universal life acts like an adjustable life policy in that the face value and premiums can be easily adjusted to meet changing needs. The major difference is that the interest rate paid on cash values in universal life is closer to market rates than in whole life policies, so the investment portion grows faster. Universal life usually invests the savings portion of the premium in short- or medium-term bond investments that in the past have offered superior rates of return compared with whole life returns. The return, however, is not guaranteed; what you earn depends on the actual performance of the insurance company's investment portfolios.

It is probably true that the rate of return on a universal life policy's savings component will be higher than the return on a similar whole life policy simply because the company attempts to tie the return to the performance of its investments. It is not clear, however, that the actual return you will earn on a universal policy will be much higher when all the additional fees and restrictions are considered. Beware of sales claims that advertise a rate of return paid on the cash value after all fees and costs have been deducted from your premium payment. The relevant rate of return should be calculated based on what you have paid in minus the amount necessary to pay for the pure insurance, an amount that may be approximated by the cost of a decreasing, renewable term policy.

It is important to shop for the best universal life policy, as different companies offer slightly different options. Some companies will pay only 3 percent interest on the first $1,000 in the savings portion of the account; other companies allow you to vary the amount of your insurance coverage without incurring additional fees; and still other companies charge high first-year fees. The return on universal life insurance policies is usually guaranteed for one year but then fluctuates up or down over the long term with market conditions. Many companies will guarantee a high rate for the first year, and then a nominal rate after that. Look for maximum flexibility, highest guaranteed minimum rates of return, and lowest fees.

Variable Life

Variable life policies are designed to allow the insured to earn higher rates of return by choosing to put the cash value component of the policy into higher-risk investments: common stocks, bonds, money market instruments, or government securities. There is no guaranteed cash surrender value, because the value depends on the return actually earned on the investments. Additionally, you will not know exactly what the face amount of your coverage is, although some minimum is normally guaranteed. If the investment portion of your policy is doing well, the cash surrender value and face amount of your policy will rise, and vice versa. It is important to recognize that the death benefit your survivors will receive from a variable life policy depends in part on the performance of the investment strategy you have the insurance company follow for you.

For example, if you choose to have the company invest the savings component of your variable life premium in common stocks, the death benefit paid to your survivors will be higher or lower, depending on how stock prices change. It is true that long-term bonds and common stocks have paid higher average returns in the past than more conservative investments, but it is also true that the variability of those returns has been much greater. Beware of counting on an assumed rate of return on your investment portfolio to deliver the insurance protection your family needs. The rates of return you may see in variable life sales literature are not guaranteed. Base the amount of insurance you buy on your family's needs and be sure what you need is guaranteed to be paid if you die. The potential gains from higher investment returns in variable life policies should be viewed as a means to earn higher expected returns on the cash value by accepting greater investment risk.

Permanent Life Insurance: A Tax Shelter?

In the aftermath of the tax reforms of 1986 (which restricted the benefits of Individual Retirement Accounts), insurance companies have been promoting permanent life insurance policies (whole, universal, variable life, and single-premium policies) as a way to accumulate assets for the future while avoiding current taxes on interest earned. Current tax laws do allow dividends and interest paid on permanent life insurance policies to accumulate tax deferred while the policy is in force, so that you pay no current tax on the increasing amount of your cash value in a permanent policy. The tax laws also allow loans to be taken against policy cash values without any tax on the amount borrowed. In the 1980s, rising interest rates enabled insurance companies to increase the interest rates paid on permanent policies, including whole life. The combination of increased interest returns on life insurance products, tax deferral on earnings, and tax-free loans has been touted as a way for you to earn tax-free income from a life-insurance investment. In fact, insurance companies now offer single-premium whole life policies that enable you to purchase a large policy with one large premium payment or, from your point of view, investment.

Let's see how such a life insurance investment might work. Suppose at age fifty-five you purchase, for $50,000 up front, a single-premium whole life insurance policy to accumulate assets for retirement. Your $50,000 investment will accumulate interest (let's assume 8 percent) and will offer a death benefit of about $140,000. If you let the cash value accumulate for ten years, when you are sixty-five you will be able to borrow about $8,000 per year against the policy and pay no taxes on the amount borrowed. Thus, your policy appears to be generating tax-free income—and in fact it does, as long as you keep the policy in force. When you die, your beneficiary receives the death benefit, which is also generally free of tax. This really does look like a good deal, but you should consider several possible pitfalls.

First of all, permanent insurance policies are very illiquid: It is expensive and difficult to get your money out of them if you change your mind about your investment. Commissions and fees consume a large part of your investment in the early years, so you may not earn a very high return (or may even lose money!) if you cancel the policy after only a few years.

Second, the earnings on permanent insurance are not tax-free, but tax deferred, which means that you will owe tax on all the earnings paid over the years if you decide to cash in the policy. This is a particular problem if you have been borrowing against the policy because you will owe tax on all those "tax-free" borrowings when you cash in the policy. It is even possible that you could owe almost as much in tax as the remaining surrender value of the policy. The same thing happens if you live long enough, say age ninety-five, to see the policy mature. At that point, the difference between your $50,000 investment and the accumulated cash value is taxable all at once. Finally, there is the risk that Congress will change the law that allows for tax-free borrowing against permanent life insurance policies. Remember, also, that these tax advantages mean very little to most servicemembers, who are typically in the lower tax brackets.

Changes in tax laws and more competitive interest returns in recent years have made permanent life insurance relatively more attractive as a savings vehicle. However, some major disadvantages, such as the potential tax traps mentioned above, remain. As we have noted already, a high proportion of permanent insurance policy owners cash in their policies earlier than they initially expected. Be sure you fully understand the implications of getting your money out of a policy before you buy it as a savings vehicle.

CHOOSING THE RIGHT POLICY

One of the major decisions in an insurance plan is how much of what type of insurance to buy. We have emphasized the advantages of low-cost term policies, because the rate of return on the savings portion of permanent life insurance is normally below the rates available on alternative savings vehicles. We think it is almost always better for young families with lower incomes and large insurance requirements to use term insurance, because it offers the only affordable means to get the protection needed. However, as you grow older and your income rises, there may be good reasons to consider permanent or cash value insurance for part of your insurance needs.

The first reason for purchasing permanent or variable insurance is the personal aspect of dealing with an agent who inspires trust. Ideally, your agent should be knowledgeable not only in insurance but also in general financial planning. Because the commission is substantial, the agent who sells you a permanent policy has the incentive to answer questions and tailor a program for your particular needs. The agent may be able to serve as an advisor for other types of insurance, offer limited financial advice, and perhaps assist your spouse and family should you die.

Be aware that in some cases the agents are trained in the basics of insurance and financial planning only as seen through the eyes of the parent company. It is up to you to realize that agents do not have the incentive to offer you the lowest-cost protection or the most impartial advice. If, however, you feel that you can trust an agent, and you do not have the time to do your own insurance planning, it may worthwhile to put yourself into the hands of a trustworthy professional insurance agent.

A second argument for permanent or variable insurance, which will seem trivial to many, is the "enforced saving" aspect of permanent life insurance. Many people who have difficulty saving regularly on their own find it easier to pay bills that they receive in the mail or that are paid out through a government allotment. Many agents argue that permanent life insurance is an effective means to get people to accumulate assets for retirement when they would otherwise not do so.

There is some truth to this argument. But, unfortunately, those who are forced to save through permanent insurance plans usually earn a lower rate of return than they could by saving on their own. Many financial advisors counsel clients to "buy term and invest the difference" between the lower term premium and the higher permanent policies premium. You can earn higher returns on your own savings than an insurance company will pay on accumulating cash value in a permanent policy. However, you will only be better off in the future if you really *do invest* the difference. If you spend it on current consumption, you will not have accumulated savings on which to live in retirement. Our advice to you is to know yourself: If you can save consistently and resist the temptation to dip into your savings, use term insurance and put what you save with lower premiums into your own investment program. If you feel that you will not discipline yourself to save regularly, however, then pay an insurance agent to make you save in a permanent insurance plan. But first make sure that you have accumulated an emergency reserve of savings. Otherwise, you may find yourself wiping out your "enforced savings" fund (your policy's cash value) or, even worse, discovering that you have *no* cash value yet, since first-year premiums go mainly to the salesman's commission.

By now it is probably apparent that choosing an appropriate insurance policy is an involved process. As we have emphasized, premiums and features can vary significantly among policies, and sales commissions can be high on permanent policies. USAA and several other reliable companies cater specifically to military personnel and offer "no load" (no sales commission) insurance policies that are often useful for comparison-shopping purposes. You can contact these companies by mail or phone for quotes on their policies; see their frequent advertisements in *Army, Air Force,* and *Navy Times.* Very good analyses of the current insurance market regularly appear in *Consumer Reports* (with costs and rankings) and occasionally can be found in other personal finance periodicals such as *Changing Times.*

ESTIMATING YOUR LIFE INSURANCE NEEDS

How much insurance should you have? The total insurance amount outstanding in the United States was almost $120,000 per household. That is far too much insurance for most single servicemembers, and far too little for those who are married. Rules of thumb by themselves are dangerous, so you should make your own estimate of how much insurance your family needs. Don't forget to do the analysis separately for your spouse as well as yourself! In many families, the wife is grossly underinsured, even if the husband's insurance plan is well thought out.

Step One: Establish Economic Consequences of Death

The first and most critical step in insurance planning is to estimate your family's actual financial needs when you die. Life insurance is *not* a measure of devotion to loved ones or a monument to your self-importance. It is insurance in case of premature death, and it should be used to protect dependents against undue financial hardship. If you are not alive to provide for your family, your insurance coverage should be sufficient to enable them to live as you would want them to live.

Method One: Net Present Value
You should plan for a basic monthly income for the family, plus additional needs such as education for the children, special medical care for known or predictable problems, and a reserve for unknown emergencies. Note that these needs usually arise during known periods. As you survive longer, some of the needs disappear; for example, if your children are grown and through college, there is no need to leave money for their education. In any case, there is never a requirement to make your family wealthy upon your death; buy only the coverage for identifiable needs. The following analyses should all be done in "today's" dollars and placed at the appropriate point on a time line that reflects the year in which you expect the income or expense to occur.

Estimate Expenses
We must first estimate family expenses. Some will be one-time expenses, such as for a funeral, while others will be ongoing, such as food and shelter. The following are some of the expenses that life insurance should cover:

Expenses Incidental to Death: These include illness expenses, hospital bills, burial costs, and possibly moving expenses for your family. Many of these expenses will not affect military families, because their benefits provide for them. You should refer to chapters 3, 16, 19, and 20 for the details. An insurance industry rule of thumb to cover these expenses is to buy insurance equal to one year's take-home pay; however, $6,000 (measured in 1993 dollars) should be sufficient for most military families.

Monthly Expenses: Simply estimate the monthly expenses you believe your survivors will be facing. If you do not know where to start in estimating these expenses, a good rule of thumb is two-thirds of your present monthly income for those years when children will be at home, and one-half after they have left.

One-time Expenses: Be sure to include one-time expenses such as a college education for the children, paying off a home mortgage, or purchasing a new car. You may also want to pay off any outstanding charge card bills and personal loans.

Estimate Income

Fortunately, military servicemembers' survivors continue to receive income from service-related sources, as explained in chapters 3 and 19. This income includes Social Security survivor benefits, Dependency and Indemnity Compensation, and, for the retirement-eligible or retired member, Survivor Benefit Plan benefits (see chapter 20). Other sources of income include a death gratuity, Social Security children's education benefits, war orphans educational assistance, lump-sum death payment, and even redeeming the accrued leave of the servicemember.

Your estate will provide at least a part of the established future needs. Your financial goal should be to accumulate enough assets to cover your family's financial requirements in the event of your death. To the extent you are successful in saving and investing, the protection provided by life insurance is less necessary. Remember that life insurance is needed only to provide an "instant estate" to meet the financial needs of survivors. You can easily estimate the amount of income your accumulated financial assets will provide by multiplying them by the interest rate (less the inflation rate) you think they will be earning. Your spouse's earning power should also be considered as a source of family income. Many spouses today are already working (or have valuable skills) and generating income that greatly reduces the requirement for insurance on your life. However, the earnings of a spouse probably ought to be covered with separate insurance on him or her. In some families, the required coverage may be dramatically reduced if no children are involved, and the spouse can go to school and learn a skill or profession.

Estimate Shortfalls or Windfalls

Once you have estimated your survivors' income and expenses for the years ahead, you need to find those time periods in which an "income gap" exists—where estimated expenses exceed estimated income. There may be years when estimated income is larger than estimated expenses. In those years, your survivors will be able to save to meet some of the future income gaps.

LIFE INSURANCE • 295

The Net Present Value of Your Insurance Needs

The net present value of all the income gaps, both positive (where expenses exceed income) and negative (where income exceeds expenses), is the amount of insurance protection you need to prevent financial hardship for your survivors. If you don't know how to calculate the net present value, refer to appendix D on present value and the time value of money. The real problem with finding the net present value is deciding what discount rate to use. And that requires some explanation. The net present value of the income gaps is the amount of money that, if you had it all today and invested it at a rate of interest equal to the discount rate, would grow to a sum large enough to cover all the income gaps you identify. Thus, if you assume the lump sum (that is, the proceeds from life insurance your family will receive if you die now) will accumulate interest at a high rate, you need less insurance. On the other hand, if you assume a low interest return on the insurance death benefit, you need to provide for a larger benefit.

Be realistic in assessing the rate of return your survivors will be able to earn. Perhaps more important, be sure your family understands that the insurance proceeds they receive if you die cannot be spent indiscriminately; they must be saved and invested to meet future needs. Since inflation is always a potential threat but was ignored in developing your income and expense numbers above, you should use a "real rate of interest"—the actual interest rate minus the projected rate of inflation (this concept was discussed in chapters 2 and 4). For example, if you expect the insurance proceeds to go into a money market account paying 7 percent interest and the annual inflation rate is 4 percent, then the purchasing power of the proceeds will earn a real interest rate of 3 percent. For your net present value calculations, you should then use 3 percent as the discount factor. Historically, in modern times, the real yields (interest rates) for very secure investments (such as bonds) are approximately 1 to 3 percent. More sophisticated investors can, by accepting greater risk, earn real rates of return of 4 percent or more. In our illustrations, we have used an assumed real rate of return of 3 percent per year.

When you have calculated the present value of all the income gaps, you have the amount of financial risk that should be covered by insurance on your life.

Estimating the amount of life insurance you need is a time-consuming but important exercise. Careful analysis is required if you are to get the amount of insurance you need but no more than that. To help you understand how the analysis is done, we present an example of an actual family situation.

An Example of the Net Present Value Method

In this example, we determine the life insurance needs for the family of a twenty-six-year-old O-3 with five years of military service, a twenty-four-year-old wife, and a two-year-old child. We assume the officer already has a $200,000 life insurance policy (e.g., SGLI). In the analysis, we establish the economic consequences of the officer's death by finding the gaps in the family's needs for future income and determining how much insurance is required to fill the gaps. This process is used by many insurance agents to show clients how much more insurance they need. Agents often present a computerized analysis based on information you provide, but as this example shows, you can do the same thing yourself. And you are less likely to overestimate the true amount by a large margin, as a few unscrupulous insurance salesmen might do.

The first step is to determine critical times when large expenses arrive and when major changes in benefits will occur. As discussed in chapter 19, for example, the amount survivors receive from Social Security depends on the number and ages of children. In our example, the important time phases are as follows:

- Phase 1 (Years from today 0–14): Child is less than sixteen; spouse and child collect Social Security.
- Phase 2 (Years 15–16): Child reaches sixteen; spouse loses Social Security payments.
- Phase 3 (Years 17–20): Child reaches eighteen and attends college.
- Phase 4 (Years 21–41): Spouse is alone and under sixty-five, no Social Security coverage.
- Phase 5 (Years 42–56): Time span covers period from age sixty-five to life expectancy of spouse (see Table 18-1 for life expectancies); spouse collects Social Security.

It is important to identify these phases, because they mark the points where significant changes in income or expenses will occur. In Phase 1, both the surviving

TABLE 18-1
Life Expectancies

Age	Expected Remaining Life	
	Male	Female
0	72.5	79.3
15	58.6	65.0
25	49.0	55.2
35	39.8	45.5
45	30.7	35.9
55	21.8	26.6
65	14.0	18.1
75	8.1	11.3
85	3.0	8.4

Example: A 25-year-old male has a life expectancy of 49.0 more years, for a projected total life of 74 years. A 25-year-old female has a life expectancy of 55.2 more years, for a total life of 80.2 years. The longer female lifetime is the reason life insurance is less expensive for women.

Source: *Statistical Abstract of the United States,* 1992

spouse and child will be eligible for Dependency and Indemnity Compensation (DIC) and Social Security benefits. When Phase 2 arrives, the spouse no longer is eligible for Social Security benefits because the child turns sixteen; however, the child's benefits continue until age eighteen. Phase 3 represents a point where both income and expenses will change significantly. Once the child reaches age eighteen, Social Security benefits end and major college expenses begin. In Phase 4, the spouse will be receiving DIC, as in Phases 1, 2, and 3, but will not be receiving Social Security. In Phase 5, the spouse reaches age sixty-five (reduced benefits could be taken at an earlier age) and will again receive both DIC and Social Security benefits. See chapters 3 and 19 for the details on eligibility for DIC and Social Security payments.

The second step is to estimate expenses the family will have in the phases above. Consider three categories: expenses incidental to death; large one-time expenses; and monthly living expenses for each phase. Because the officer is on active duty, most of the expenses for a funeral and burial will be borne by the government, but we will assume the need for $6,000 to pay any expenses not covered. Large one-time expenses include repayment of debts, college funds, and other such needs. We assume the family has debts of $18,000 that it would want to pay off in the event of the officer's death. To help with the child's college costs, the family wants to have $10,000 per year (in today's dollars) for the four years during Phase 3. Finally, for provision of monthly living expenses, while the child is still under eighteen, we allow for two-thirds of current income and, after the child leaves home in Phase 3, one-half of current income. Thus, for Phases 1 and 2, we want to provide $2,300 per month, and for Phases 3, 4, and 5, $1,700 per month. Don't forget about housing expenses—government quarters (or quarters allowance) will no longer be available to your family after you're gone.

The third step is to estimate income that will be available in each of the phases in the event the officer dies today and to inventory assets already accumulated that will be available to meet future needs. In our example, we assume that the family has available assets of $15,000 ($5,000 in a money market fund as an emergency reserve and another $10,000 in a stock mutual fund) set aside for the child's education. We decide not to count the $5,000 emergency reserve, as we want to leave it "untouched" for the family's use. We also need to know how much income DIC and Social Security will pay the officer's survivors in each phase.

Using the information in chapters 3 and 19, we identify the sources of income that will be available in the event of the officer's death:

1. Lump-sum payments at officer's death.
    - VA death gratuity: $6,000.
    - Social Security Death Benefit: $255.
    - 15 days accrued leave (assumed in this example): $1,700.
2. VA Survivor Benefits
    - Phases 1 and 2: $750 DIC plus $71 per child = $821 per month.
    - Phase 3: $750 DIC plus $404 per student = $1,154 per month.
    - Phases 4 and 5: $750 DIC per month.

298 • PERSONAL FINANCIAL PLANNING

3. Social Security Benefits: First we must calculate the primary insurance amount (PIA). For this officer, we estimate the PIA to be about $1,045. (See chapter 19 for PIA calculations, or contact your local Social Security office.) We can estimate the Social Security benefits as follows:
    - Phase 1: $1,045 times 0.75 for spouse plus $1,045 times 0.75 for child = $1,567 per month.
    - Phase 2: $1,045 times 0.75 for the child = $784 per month.
    - Phases 3 and 4: No Social Security benefits.
    - Phase 5: $1,045 for spouse.

The fourth step is to total up all the income and assets that will be available in each of the phases and do the same for the expenses. We will then look for gaps where the expenses exceed the income and assets available. It is these gaps that we need to fill with life insurance. Calculating the annual surplus or deficit in each phase, we find the following:

- At death
  Expenses:
      Incidental to death $ 6,000
      Pay off loans $18,000
  Minus
  Income:
      Liquid assets $10,000
      Lump-sum payments $ 7,955
  Equals
  Deficit or (Surplus) $6,045

- Phase 1: Years 0 to 14
  Expenses: $2,300 per month $27,600 per year
  Minus
  Income: $2,388 per month $28,656 per year
  Equals
  Phase 1 Deficit or (Surplus)   ($1,056) per year

- Phase 2: Years 15 to 16
  Expenses: $2,300 per month $27,600 per year
  Minus
  Income: $1,605 per month $19,260 per year
  Equals
  Phase 2 Deficit or (Surplus) $8,340 per year

- Phase 3: Years 17 to 20
  Expenses: $1,700 per month $20,400 per year
      For college $10,000 per year

    Minus
    Income: $1,154 per month   <u>$13,848 per year</u>
    Equals
    Phase 3 Deficit or (Surplus) $16,552 per year

- Phase 4: Years 21 to 41
    Expenses: $1,700 per month $20,400 per year
    Minus
    Income: $750 per month   <u>$ 9,000 per year</u>
    Equals
    Phase 4 Deficit or (Surplus) $11,400 per year

- Phase 5: Years 42 to 54
    Expenses: $1,700 per month $20,400 per year
    Minus
    Income: $1,795 per month   <u>$21,540 per year</u>
    Equals
    Phase 5 Deficit or (Surplus)   ($1,140) per year

Now all we need to do is to bring the annual figures back to their present value at an appropriate real rate of interest and add them up. The resulting sum is the amount of insurance required to cover future needs in the event of the officer's death. To find the present values, we use the techniques and present value tables illustrated in appendix D to convert annual amounts to equivalent lump sums and then convert those lump sums back to their present values. It may be helpful to organize the calculations on a worksheet like that shown in Table 18-2.

To complete the worksheet, we record data as follows:

Line 1: Write down the number of years until each phase begins.

Line 2: Write down the number of years in each phase.

Line 3: Write down the factor from Table D-1 that gives the present value of $1 received or paid N years in the future, using an appropriate interest rate; we used 3 percent. For line 3, N is the number of years until the phase begins, found on line 1.

Line 4: Write down the factor from Table D-2 that gives the present value of an equal annual flow of payments that lasts for N years, using an appropriate interest rate. For line 4, N is the length of the phase from line 2.

Line 5: Multiply the present value factors in lines 3 and 4 together. This number represents the *present value* of $1 received annually for the number of years in each phase.

Line 6: Write down the deficit or surplus for each phase you calculated above.

Line 7: Multiply the discount factor on line 5 by the number of dollars of annual surplus or deficit in each phase to find the present value of the surplus or deficit.

Line 8: Add the present value of all deficits (subtracting the present value of all surpluses) in each phase in line 7. One optional enhancement that we include is not to

TABLE 18-2
Life Insurance Worksheet

Line	Description	Phase 1	Phase 2	Phase 3	Phase 4	Phase 5
1	Start year	0	14	16	20	41
2	Length of phase	14	2	4	21	15
3	PV factor from start of phase (Appendix D-1, 3%)	1.0	.661	.623	.554	.298
4	Annuity factor for length of phase (Appendix D-2, 3%)	11.296	1.913	3.717	15.415	11.938
5	Discount factor (line 3 x line 4)	11.296	1.264	2.316	8.540	3.558
6	Annual deficit or (surplus)	($1,056)	$8,340	$16,552	$11,840	($1,140)
7	PV of phase deficit or (surplus) (5) x (6)	($11,929)	$10,542	$38,334	$97,356	(not counted)
8	Total of PVs for all phases' deficits (less surpluses)					$134,303
9	Add initial period deficit or (subtract surpluses)					$6,045
10	Subtract existing life insurance and assets					$200,000
11	Additional life insurance required					($59,652)

count any surplus occurring during the final phase. This makes sense because the Social Security laws change so frequently that it wouldn't be prudent to count on a surplus during your spouse's final years (taking the risk that later changes in the law would leave that spouse in poverty). Of course, you would always count a deficit in any period.

Line 9: Add the deficit (subtract the surplus) computed for the initial period.
Line 10: Subtract the amount of life insurance already provided; don't forget SGLI.
Line 11: The result is the amount of additional life insurance the family needs.

As stated previously, we assumed that the proceeds from the insurance policy would be invested to earn 3 percent after inflation and taxes. As we have shown in chapters 2 and 13, to earn even this much we will need to use a combination of bonds and stocks, because very safe investments like savings accounts historically have not provided a 3 percent rate of return after inflation and taxes. In Table 18-2, we have used data from the 3 percent column in Tables D-1 and D-2. You should check the tables against Table 18-2 to see how we found the present value factors used. In the case of the officer in our example, we find that his $200,000 SGLI policy provides adequate insurance coverage. However, in order to illustrate the steps that you would take to purchase additional life insurance, we will continue our discussion as if we found that additional insurance were required.

Present value analysis of life insurance needs is based on the assumption that survivors will not spend the proceeds immediately but will draw upon them only to cover the deficits identified in the plan. It is very important that survivors understand how the insurance plan is designed to work.

Method Two: A Simple Rule of Thumb

If finding the net present value of the future income gaps is more than you are willing to attempt, a very simple rule of thumb may give you an acceptable estimate of your insurance needs. Here is the rule: Have life insurance coverage equal to four years' gross pay, plus an extra year for each child you want to help through college. You may want more if you have no other assets or have a lot of debt. You may want less coverage if your spouse has marketable skills or you have extensive assets already.

If you have some special needs to consider, we strongly recommend you do a more careful analysis of your insurance requirements. One way to get the present value analysis done for you is to shop for life insurance with an agent who can do a computerized analysis of your needs. (You might even give the agent a copy of these pages on the net present value method and ask him do the analysis for you.) Since you have no obligation to buy, it cannot hurt to see what an agent will tell you about the amount of insurance you need. In any case, make sure your spouse is in on the process every step of the way, so he or she understands the insurance plan.

Step Two: Budget Resources to Pay Insurance Premiums

Having established the amount of insurance you need in Step One, you now need to identify resources available to pay the life insurance premium. This is part of developing a monthly budget from your goals, as outlined in chapter 4. Although planning and budgeting require a great deal of self-discipline, they must be done by anyone trying to reach any level of financial independence.

If you are unable to afford the premiums for the amount of insurance you need, you have a variety of options. First, reduce your monthly outlays in other areas of your budget. A second option would be to buy less insurance than you had calculated; this will help your monthly cash flow but it will not eliminate the need for insurance. Think of how important the financial well-being of your family is when compared to reducing spending in some other not-so-important area. A third and better option would be to choose an appropriate mix of lower-cost term with the more expensive permanent and variable life insurance policies. Refer back to the discussion on term, permanent, and variable life insurance to decide what type is best for your needs. We believe that most families can afford the life insurance protection they need if they use low-cost group term insurance policies that are offered to members of the military services.

Step Three: Shop for Insurance

Almost all active-duty members elect to take Servicemen's Group Life Insurance (SGLI). The maximum coverage currently is $200,000 in term insurance for $16 per month (80 cents for each $10,000 of coverage.) Check your Leave and Earnings Statement to see if you are paying for SGLI and are therefore covered. This low-cost term insurance should be turned down only after carefully reviewing your needs for insurance, and then only by those without any dependents. Be aware that SGLI can be converted to a five-year nonrenewable term insurance called Veterans Group Life Insurance (VGLI) upon separation or retirement from active duty. Within five years of separation, VGLI can be converted, without a physical, to an individual policy with one of several participating insurance companies.

For other term insurance, you must generally inquire about rates and collect data yourself. Since the profit margins are low with term insurance, many companies selling it do not have a sales force. You must decide on the amount of insurance you need and then go out and get the best deal you can find. Group term policies at very attractive rates are frequently advertised in the *Army, Air Force,* and *Navy Times.*

If you are shopping for permanent insurance, this step requires merely a telephone call or two—assuming you have not already received offers from agents. Remember, agents work on commission and usually are eager to show their products. Your job is to tone down that enthusiasm and purchase the right type and amount of insurance to fit your needs, not the agent's. This is not an easy thing to do. Remember, over half of the people who take out permanent policies cancel them within ten years. Your best offense is a good defense: Know something about your options and your insurance needs before the agent makes the sales pitch. Remember also that the insurance companies with the least expensive policies will probably not have a sales force, so don't expect the best deals to come knocking at your door!

Unfortunately, comparison shopping in the life insurance industry is tough at best. Even though the government has disclosure requirements, the names and types of policies vary, savings benefits vary each year in an uneven fashion, and interest rates vary with the performance of the U.S. economy. There is no conspiracy to confuse consumers, but as in any business, companies take great pains to market their policies as being the best possible product for you, the customer.

It is important that you select a financially secure company; insurance companies are subject to mismanagement, fraud, and poor economic conditions that can bankrupt weaker ones. You can find insurance company ratings in most libraries in *Best's Insurance Reports* and in magazines such as *Consumer Reports, Changing Times,* and *Money.* Each state also monitors the insurance companies licensed to sell policies within its jurisdiction. Information on problem companies and complaints about company performance can be directed to insurance commissioners in the various states.

Step Four: Periodic Review

You should periodically review your life insurance plan, particularly when your financial responsibilities undergo a significant change (divorce, remarriage, birth of a child, leaving the military). More subtle changes, such as a spouse's possible return to employment or development of a chronic medical problem, will also affect your need for life insurance. Proper insurance planning amounts to keeping a running count of all your obligations and ensuring that a sufficient estate is available to meet these responsibilities should you die.

Formulating an insurance plan is not a trivial undertaking, but after the initial analysis is completed, it should be relatively easy to maintain your plan. Knowing your family will be financially secure if you suddenly die should be ample reward for the effort.

SUGGESTED REFERENCES

Best's Insurance Reports. A. M. Best, Inc. Reports on the financial health of many insurance companies. It is available in many libraries.

Monthly periodicals including *Money, Consumer Reports,* and *Changing Times* cover developments in and rankings of life insurance products. They are available in most libraries.

19

Social Security and Department of Veterans Affairs Benefits

THIS CHAPTER HAS two sections: Social Security benefits and Department of Veterans Affairs benefits. A detailed and exhaustive treatment of these important topics is beyond the scope of this book, but we will attempt to provide you with a working knowledge of their essential components and their impact on your personal financial plan. For more detailed information, you should contact your nearest Social Security Administration or Department of Veterans Affairs office.

SOCIAL SECURITY BENEFITS

Social Security is actually a grouping of several programs designed to provide income insurance for American workers. The term Social Security is commonly used today to refer to only two of these programs: Old Age and Survivor's Insurance (OASI) and Disability Insurance (DI). There are several other major programs that come under the general heading of Social Security, including Medicare, Black Lung Benefits, and Supplemental Security Income. Also, the fifty states operate two other categories of "social security" programs: unemployment compensation and public assistance programs. This chapter is primarily concerned with Old Age and Survivor's Insurance and Disability Insurance.

According to the *Social Security Handbook,* Social Security is intended to provide for "the material needs of individuals and families, protecting aged and disabled persons against the expenses of illnesses that could otherwise exhaust their savings, keeping families together, and giving children the opportunity to grow up in health and security" (p. 2). Social Security benefits do not replace all the income lost when an insured worker retires, dies, or becomes disabled, but they help to maintain living standards. In 1992, the average retired worker drew Social Security benefits that replaced about 43 percent of preretirement income.

The first thing to understand about Social Security is how the system works. Social Security is not a savings plan. You do not pay your taxes into an account with your name on it, from which you draw payments after retirement. Instead, you pay taxes into general trust funds. The taxes you pay today are almost immediately paid out to today's retirees and disabled persons. In that sense, it is very much like other insurance programs: You pay your premiums now to insure against a future loss of income.

Social Security is a social contract. You agree to pay your taxes today for the benefit of today's aged folks on the understanding that the government will require that tomorrow's workers pay their taxes to take care of you in your retirement or disability. Thus, you should pay close attention to the decisions of political leaders concerning the future of Social Security. There is no guarantee that you will get back everything that you pay in. But, if productivity rises quickly, then wages will rise quickly and the tax base for Social Security will increase, ensuring that the system continues intact. If, however, productivity does not rise quickly or if life expectancy continues to increase, benefits may not rise as quickly as they have in the past.

The amount of benefits you can expect to receive has implications for the type and amount of savings plan you should undertake. This is not meant to be alarmist; the Social Security system is currently solvent by most estimations. The only moral to this discussion is that you should have some type of savings plan to supplement Social Security in your retirement. By itself, even the very generous system of today does not allow you to lead a truly comfortable lifestyle without other assets or income.

The Social Security Tax

Active-duty members of the uniformed services have been covered by Social Security on the same basis as civilian workers since 1957. Social Security is not optional—you must pay the Social Security tax, which is annotated "FICA" on your pay statements. For servicemembers, only basic pay is taxable for Social Security purposes, and taxes are mandatorily withheld in the full amount from each active-duty monthly paycheck. If you or your spouse have additional income from self-employment, you must pay self-employment tax to the IRS. You must also file Schedule SE, "Computation of Social Security Self-Employment Tax," with your tax return if your net annual earnings from self-employment are greater than $400.

In 1993, you paid a Social Security tax of 7.65 percent on your earnings. The 7.65 figure is apportioned so that 6.20 percent is applied to non-Medicare Social Security programs, with the remaining 1.45 percent collected to fund Medicare. This apportionment is important, for the non-Medicare rate applies only to income you earn up to a limit of $57,600, while the 1.45 percent Medicare tax applies to all income (as a result of the Budget Act of 1993). So the maximum (non-Medicare) Social Security tax you can pay is $3,571.20, while there is no maximum total Social

Security tax one may pay. The $57,600 limit will be automatically increased to account for inflation. Your employer matches every dollar that you pay in taxes, so the total tax is 15.30 percent. In 1992, the government disbursed over $280 billion in total Social Security benefits; retirement benefits accounted for slightly more than half of the total.

Eligibility for Social Security Benefits

Within the OASI and DI programs there are three major types of benefits: retirement, survivor, and disability. Eligibility for each type of benefit depends on your insurance status, which, in turn, depends on your employment history. Because servicemembers pay Social Security taxes, they become insured workers. Working spouses (who must also pay Social Security taxes) become insured workers in their own right. Nonworking spouses are eligible for Social Security benefits based on the benefits of their working spouses.

Becoming Insured

Within the Social Security Administration (SSA), individuals are identified by a Social Security account number. The first step to becoming insured is to get an account number by contacting your local Social Security office. You are now required to obtain a Social Security card for your children as well; you lose your income tax "exemption" for any children over the age of one who do not have a Social Security number.

The rules on how you get insured and how much money you are entitled to are a bit complex, but they are summarized below. In general, though, what matters is how long and how much you have "paid into" the Social Security system. Thus, the accuracy of your records at the SSA is crucial. You should request a statement of your earnings from the SSA every year or so. You can ask for a Personal Earnings and Benefit Statement from your local Social Security office, or call the SSA at (800) 772-1213. The SSA recommends calling after the middle of the month on a Wednesday or Thursday afternoon for the least waiting. Within six weeks after you have returned the completed form (SSA-7004), the SSA will send you a record of your earnings and an estimate of your projected benefits in today's dollars. Compare their numbers to your records (W-2 statements from your employer) and write back to correct any errors immediately. The government is not obligated to correct mistakes in your earnings record that are more than three years old.

There are three types of Social Security insured status: fully insured, currently insured, and specially insured. The requirements always depend on the number of calendar quarters in which a worker has been paid some minimum amount of pay (currently $590). Once a worker has received at least that minimum amount of pay (and paid taxes on it), he or she is covered for that calendar quarter. A calendar quarter is any one of the following three-month time periods: January through March, April through June, July through September, and October through December. Except under the most unusual circumstances, a servicemember can expect to earn four full quarters of coverage for each calendar year of military service.

For retirement benefits, you are fully insured once you have credit for forty quarters of coverage. In other words, anyone who has completed ten years of active-duty service will be fully insured. For the purpose of qualifying for survivor and/or disability benefits, you are fully insured if you have at least one quarter of coverage for each calendar year after your twenty-first birthday and before the year you die or become disabled. As a minimum, you must have at least six quarters of coverage to be fully insured. Therefore, all servicemembers are fully insured for Social Security survivor or disability benefits after they have been on active duty for a full year and a half.

Currently insured status is important as an alternative means of qualifying for survivors benefits. Individuals are currently insured if they have at least six quarters of coverage out of the thirteen quarters before death or disability.

Specially insured status is important for disability benefits. To be specially insured, an individual must have twenty quarters of coverage in the forty quarters preceding the disability. If you are disabled before age thirty-one, you must have coverage in one-half of the quarters since you turned twenty-one. A minimum of six quarters of coverage is required. Any active-duty servicemember who has not had a break in service is specially insured after eighteen months of service.

Explanation of Benefits

This section explains the three types of benefits. The amount of the benefit is based on a figure called the primary insurance amount, or PIA. We will show you how to calculate the PIA in the next section. We can provide only a sketch of the benefit calculations here. For further information, obtain the relevant pamphlets or get your own estimate of your projected benefits from the SSA.

Retirement Benefits
To qualify for retirement benefits, you must be fully insured. There are three options for retirement under Social Security. The normal option is retirement at age sixty-five. A fully insured worker who retires at age sixty-five receives the entire PIA. It is also possible to retire between the ages of sixty-two and sixty-five, but then you will receive a reduced monthly benefit. The earlier you retire, the larger the reduction. If you retire at sixty-two, for example, your monthly check will be 80 percent of the PIA. Similarly, you can choose to retire at age sixty-six or older and receive an increased monthly benefit. Monthly benefit increases are based on "increment months," defined as the months beyond normal retirement age (currently sixty-five) but prior to age seventy in which benefits are not drawn. For beneficiaries reaching age sixty-five after 1989, the monthly benefit amount is increased in accordance with the accompanying table (19-1).

TABLE 19-1
Chart of Delayed Retirement Credit Rates

Attain Age 65	Monthly Percentage	Yearly Percentage
Prior to 1982	1/2 of 1%	1%
1982–1989	1/4 of 1%	3%
1990–1991	7/24 of 1%	3.5%
1992–1993	1/3 of 1%	4%
1994–1995	3/8 of 1%	4.5%

This table is taken from the Social Security Handbook.

Note that the normal retirement age will gradually increase from sixty-five to sixty-seven as shown in Table 19-2. Workers who were born during or before 1937 (retire before 2002) can still retire normally at age sixty-five, while those born after 1937 cannot retire with normal benefits until a slightly later time. Those who were born during or after 1960 cannot retire with normal benefits until they are sixty-seven years old.

TABLE 19-2
Future Increases in Retirement Age

Year of Birth	Attainment of Age 62	Normal Retirement Age (years/months)	Age 62 Benefit as Percentage of Benefit at Normal Retirement Age
1937 or earlier	1999 or earlier	65/0	80.0%
1938	2000	65/2	79.2
1939	2001	65/4	78.3
1940	2002	65/6	77.5
1941	2003	65/8	76.7
1942	2004	65/10	75.8
1943–1954	2005–2016	66/0	75.0
1955	2017	66/2	74.2
1956	2018	66/4	73.3
1957	2019	66/6	72.5
1958	2020	66/8	71.7
1959	2021	66/10	70.8
1960 or later	2022 or later	67/0	70.0

This table is taken from the Social Security Administration pamphlet Retirement.

Early retirement at age sixty-two is still possible under the rules outlined in Table 19-2. Of course, because the normal retirement age is postponed, retiring exactly on your sixty-second birthday will mean that your monthly check will be an even smaller percentage of the PIA. For example, workers born after 1960 who retire at age sixty-two will receive only 70 percent of the PIA, as opposed to the 80 percent under the current system.

Survivor Benefits

An important goal of Social Security is the stability of families when an insured worker dies (if there are family members who are too young, old, or disabled to work). Benefits paid to the dependent family members of a deceased worker are called survivor benefits. There are many different categories of survivor benefits corresponding to the many circumstances that qualify someone to be a dependent family member of an insured worker. Table 19-3 presents information for four of the most frequently used categories of survivor benefits.

From the table you can see that each child under age eighteen receives a monthly check in the amount of 75 percent of the insured worker's PIA. There is, however, a maximum family payment that reduces the amount paid to each child if there are many children. (This family maximum benefit depends on the PIA. See Table 19-3 for the family maximum formula.) Notice also that nonworking spouses over age sixty who are not insured themselves are entitled to the benefits of their deceased spouses if the spouse was fully insured before dying. The benefit will range from 71.5 percent to 100 percent of the PIA of the deceased worker, depending on the age of the surviving spouse.

Divorced surviving spouses are entitled to the benefits of a deceased worker if the marriage lasted for ten years. One does not forfeit this entitlement by remarrying.

TABLE 19-3
Social Security Survivor Benefits

Benefit	Insurance Status	Amount of Payment
Payment to each child under 18	Full or current	75% of PIA
Payment to each child 18 or 19 and a full-time high school student	Full or current	75% of PIA
Payment to a widow(er) caring for any children under 16	Full or current	75% of PIA
Payment to a widow(er) over 60	Full	100% of PIA

There is a maximum benefit that can be paid to any one family. In 1993 the maximum family benefit was determined according to the following formulas:

If: $PIA \leq \$513.00$, then MAX = 150% of PIA.
If: $\$513.01 \leq PIA \leq \$740.00$, then MAX = $\$742.50 + (2.72) \times (PIA - 513)$.
If: $\$740.01 \leq PIA \leq \$966.00$, then MAX = $\$1338.18 + (1.34) \times (PIA - 740)$.
If: $\$966.01 \leq PIA$, then MAX = $\$1628.96 + (PIA - 966)$.

310 • PERSONAL FINANCIAL PLANNING

One final survivor benefit is the lump-sum death gratuity of $255. Surviving spouses living with an insured worker at the time of death are eligible; divorced spouses are not.

Disability Benefits

For the purposes of Social Security, disability means "the inability to engage in any substantial gainful activity by reason of any medically determinable physical or mental impairment which can be expected to result in death or which has lasted or can be expected to last for a continuous period of not less than 12 months" *(SSH,* p. 81). Clearly these benefits are meant for serious disabilities. To be eligible, a worker must be fully or specially insured. The benefit is the full PIA. Disability of a servicemember involves not only the SSA but perhaps also the VA and the military disability compensation system. In matters as complex as these, consult your legal assistance officer.

Calculating the Primary Insurance Amount (PIA)

The purpose of Social Security is to help maintain a reasonable portion of the standard of living that you achieved during your working lifetime. Therefore, the benefits you receive from Social Security will depend on the wages you earned (and the taxes you paid).

A secondary purpose of Social Security is to provide a minimum standard of living for all elderly persons. Therefore, workers who earned a lower level of wages will retain a larger percentage of those low wages in their benefits. For example, a lifetime minimum-wage worker will get a Social Security benefit of approximately 58 percent of his working wage, whereas a person who always earned the maximum covered earnings will receive a benefit of only about 24 percent of his working wage. The assumption is that the minimum-wage earner could not save enough to provide other income during retirement, while the well-paid worker could.

The primary insurance amount is based on your average indexed monthly earnings, or AIME. The idea behind the AIME is to adjust your actual earnings to reflect the effects of inflation. Once you know the AIME, you can calculate the PIA by using the formulas in Table 19-4.

Almost all servicemembers fall into the second and third wage brackets and would use one of the last two formulas shown in the table. The wage brackets ($400 and $2,420 of AIME in 1993; see Table 19-4) for calculating the PIA change each year. Call your local Social Security Administration office for the current figures.

You must now learn how to calculate the AIME (see Table 19-4). Essentially, there are three steps involved.

Step 1: Determine Your Actual Earnings Covered by Social Security

First, you must determine your actual earnings in every year in which you worked, including your base pay, any self-employment income that you reported and on which you paid Social Security taxes, and military service wage credits. Begin with the calendar year in which you turned twenty-one. You can determine your base pay for each year by looking at your income tax records, W-2 Forms, or Leave and Earnings Statements. You must determine any self-employment income from your personal records. Make sure that these numbers are also on record with the SSA by sending in Form SSA-7004, as mentioned above.

Wage credits reflect the fact that a considerable portion of military compensation comes in the form of allowances. In years prior to 1957, servicemembers earned a wage credit of $160 per month. From 1957 through 1977, they earned $300 for every quarter in which they earned military wages. Beginning in 1978, they earned a wage credit of $100 for each $300 of base pay they received, up to a maximum of $1,200 per year. Add the appropriate wage credit to your base pay in each year.

List your actual wages (including wage credits) for each year in column B of Table 19-4. Compare the actual wages to the maximum allowable amount in column A, and write the smaller of the two amounts in column C.

Step 2: Adjust Your Earnings Using the Index Factors
Multiply the number you wrote in column C by the index number in column D. This adjusts wages from the past for inflation. Write your answer in column E. (Note: The index factors are 1993 numbers. Call your Social Security Administration office for the current index numbers. Also, the index numbers in column D are rounded to only one decimal place. The actual numbers used by the SSA have several decimal places and are therefore more accurate. This exercise will still give you a good idea about the approximate size of your benefit.)

Step 3: Calculate Your Average Indexed Monthly Earnings (AIME)
Cross out the five lowest numbers in column E. You must, however, have at least two years to average together. For example, if you have worked for only six years, you may only cross off the four lowest years. Add the remaining numbers in column E and record this sum in the space marked "total indexed earnings" in Table 19-4. Now count the total number of years included in your total indexed earnings (do not count the years that you deleted), and record this number in the space provided. Multiply the total number of years by twelve and record the result in the "total number of months" space. Finally, divide the total indexed earnings by the total number of months to yield your average indexed monthly earnings, or AIME.

Other Factors Affecting Your Benefits

Earnings Test for Retirement Benefits
If you are receiving Social Security benefits and have a large amount of earnings, then your benefits may be reduced. Workers who retire from the full-time work force before the normal retirement age (currently sixty-five) will have their benefit reduced $1 for every $2 of income over $7,680 per year ($640 per month). For retired workers

TABLE 19-4
Calculating the Average Indexed Monthly Earnings (AIME) and the Primary Insurance Amount (PIA)

Year	Column A Maximum Earnings	Column B Actual Earnings	Column C Allowable Earnings	Column D Index Factor	Column E Indexed Annual Earnings
1951	3,600			7.8	
1952	3,600			7.3	
1953	3,600			6.9	
1954	3,600			6.9	
1955	4,200			6.6	
1956	4,200			6.2	
1957	4,200			6.0	
1958	4,200			5.9	
1959	4,800			5.7	
1960	4,800			5.4	
1961	4,800			5.3	
1962	4,800			5.1	
1963	4,800			5.0	
1964	4,800			4.8	
1965	4,800			4.7	
1966	6,600			4.4	
1967	6,600			4.2	
1968	7,800			3.9	
1969	7,800			3.7	
1970	7,800			3.5	
1971	7,800			3.4	
1972	9,000			3.1	
1973	10,800			2.9	
1974	13,200			2.7	
1975	14,100			2.5	
1976	15,300			2.4	
1977	16,500			2.2	
1978	17,700			2.1	
1979	22,900			1.9	
1980	25,900			1.7	
1981	29,700			1.6	
1982	32,400			1.5	
1983	35,700			1.4	
1984	37,800			1.4	
1985	39,600			1.3	
1986	42,000			1.3	
1987	43,800			1.2	

TABLE 19-4
(continued)

Year	Column A Maximum Earnings	Column B Actual Earnings	Column C Allowable Earnings	Column D Index Factor	Column E Indexed Annual Earnings
1988	45,000	_____	_____	1.1	_____
1989	48,000	_____	_____	1.1	_____
1990	51,300	_____	_____	1.0	_____
1991	53,400	_____	_____	1.0	_____
1992	55,500	_____	_____	1.0	_____
1993	57,600	_____	_____	1.0	_____

Total indexed earnings: [A]_____
Total number of years × 12 = Total number of months: [B]_____
Average indexed monthly earnings (AIME): [A] ÷ [B] = _____

If   AIME ≤ $401,   then PIA = .9 × AIME.
If $401 < AIME ≤ $2,420, then PIA = $360.00 + [.32 × (AIME − $401)].
If   AIME > $2,420, then PIA = $1006.98 + [.15 × (AIME − $2,420)].

Index factors are accurate for 1993. Factors change each year; call your SSA office for current factors.

between the normal retirement age and age seventy, benefits are reduced $1 for every $3 of income over $10,560 per year ($880 per month). If you are over seventy there is no earnings offset for retirement benefits, so you are eligible for the entire benefit no matter how much outside income you earn.

Taxation of Benefits

In addition to being offset in the manner described above, Social Security benefits may also be taxed as ordinary income when the retiree has substantial outside income. That is, benefits received after the earnings test offset will then be taxed as ordinary income when the retiree has outside income above specified levels. For taxation purposes, total income is the sum of adjusted gross income, nontaxable interest from municipal bonds, and one-half of the benefit actually received (after the offset).

Under the Revenue Reconciliation Act of 1993, the amount of benefits that is subject to taxation is up to 50 percent of the lesser of the benefit amount and the difference between total income and $25,000 ($32,000) for single (married filing jointly) recipients with total incomes between $25,000 ($32,000) and $34,000 ($44,000). For total income levels above these amounts, the portion of benefits subject to taxation rises by 85 cents for each $1 of earnings above the bracket limit until the total amount subject to taxation reaches 85 percent of the Social Security benefits.

Cost-of-Living Adjustments (COLA)

The COLA is probably the most valuable provision in Social Security. Once the benefit is determined, it is adjusted every year to protect its purchasing power from inflation. There is no standard formula for the COLA; the amount is determined by Congress each year.

Summary of Social Security Issues

This treatment of Social Security has necessarily made many simplifying assumptions. There are many exceptions to the rules for determining benefits as they are presented here. This chapter does not override the judgments made by those who administer the Social Security system. It should, however, give you a general idea of what to expect.

You should understand that Social Security is meant to replace only some portion of the income that you were earning before your retirement or disability. In the case of retirement, the average worker will replace about 43 percent of the preretirement income. This should demonstrate to you the importance of a savings plan for the quality of life you can expect to lead in your retirement. One final but very important reminder: You must apply for Social Security benefits before you will receive them. They are not paid automatically.

DEPARTMENT OF VETERANS AFFAIRS BENEFITS

The Department of Veterans Affairs (VA) oversees many programs designed to help military veterans. For ease of explanation, we have grouped the benefits into the following major categories: disability and survivor benefits, educational benefits, medical benefits, financial benefits, and employment benefits.

VA benefits affect your financial plan by subsidizing expenditures in these areas. When you are eligible for one (or more) of these benefits, using the VA program can free up funds for other activities.

For the purposes of this discussion, a veteran is someone who has at least twenty-four months of active-duty experience and who either is still on active duty or has received an honorable or a general discharge from the service. Bad-conduct discharges and dishonorable discharges disqualify one from VA benefits. Discharges under other-than-honorable conditions do not qualify for some benefits but do qualify for others.

As with Social Security benefits, VA benefits are subject to revision by the federal government. Legislation is being considered to create new programs and expand existing ones. Stay aware of the benefit changes that affect you; some of the information sources are your career-counselor NCO, the legal assistance officer, your local VA office and military personnel office, and periodicals such as the *Army, Navy,* or *Air Force Times.*

Disability and Survivor Benefits

Veterans who are disabled by injury or disease incurred in or aggravated by active service in the line of duty are entitled to monthly payments if the disability is rated at above 0 percent. That is, it is possible for a veteran to be determined to have a service-connected disability that is rated at 0 percent. In this case, no compensation is entitled. If the disabled veteran has dependents and if the disability is rated at 30 percent or higher, the benefit is increased. Except in cases of the most severe injuries, VA benefits really are supplemental income, and you usually will want to find other employment.

The dependents of servicemembers or veterans who die while on active duty or in certain cases stemming from disease or injury incurred in the line of duty are entitled to Dependency and Indemnity Compensation (DIC). The dollar amount of the DIC benefit is $750 (monthly) for spouses of either enlisted or officer personnel based upon a recent legislative change. DIC pays an additional $150 per month in FY94 (and $200 in FY95 and beyond) for each child under eighteen years of age.

When a servicemember dies on active duty, active duty training, or inactive duty training, the VA also pays a lump-sum death gratuity to the survivors. The amount of the benefit is equal to six months' base pay, plus incentive pay and hazardous duty pay, if applicable, but the gratuity will not exceed $3,000. The VA will also pay up to $1,500 for burial if the death results from a service-connected disability. If the death is not service-connected, the VA will pay $150 for burial costs, and may pay as much as $300 in some circumstances. Note that the VA will pay burial costs only if the veteran was receiving benefits from the VA at the time of his death or if the veteran dies in a VA hospital. If the death occurs while on active duty or after retirement from active duty, the deceased can be buried in a national cemetery. Finally, most veterans qualify for a burial flag to drape the coffin.

Education Benefits

Two different education assistance programs are offered by the VA. The original GI Bill expired on 31 December 1989. In its place, the VA administers the Veterans Educational Assistance Program (VEAP) and the Montgomery GI Bill, more popularly called the New GI Bill. Most active-duty servicemembers eligible for the original GI Bill will automatically convert to the New GI Bill if they have not had a break in service since 19 October 1984. Among the exceptions to this rule are servicemembers who graduated from the United States Military Academy after December 1976; they cannot convert from the original GI Bill. Under this conversion program, the monthly entitlement is $576 and total entitlements may not exceed thirty-six months.

To participate in VEAP, veterans must have entered the service between 1 January 1977 and 30 June 1985 and contributed to an education fund while on active duty. The government matches contributions on a two-for-one basis. These funds must be used for educational purposes within ten years of discharge, but unused contributions are returned.

The New GI Bill covers persons who enlisted in the service after 30 June 1985. Servicemembers must specifically elect not to participate in this program if they do not wish to do so. Participating servicemembers have $100 deducted from their pay for twelve months. As with the VEAP program, the government will match these contributions approximately on a two-for-one basis; unlike VEAP, however, unused contributions will not be returned. See your base or post education office for further details.

Medical Benefits

Veterans who qualify for VA disability payments, former POWs, veterans who receive Medicaid, and those exposed to Agent Orange or nuclear tests are eligible for hospital care through the VA. Other veterans are eligible for VA hospital care on a space-available basis. This care includes hospitalization, outpatient care (including prescriptions), alcohol and drug-abuse counseling, and readjustment counseling.

There is also a CHAMPVA program, which is similar to the CHAMPUS program covering active-duty servicemembers. CHAMPVA is essentially a health insurance program for dependents of disabled veterans and, in certain cases, for surviving dependents of deceased veterans.

Outpatient dental care is available for some veterans, but eligibility is restricted to those who have service-connected dental disabilities, whose disability is rated at 100 percent, or who were prisoners of war for more than six months.

In addition to these benefits, the VA also pays for nursing home care and in-home care in some cases.

Financial Benefits

The best-known VA benefit is probably the VA-backed home-mortgage loan. The VA guarantees that a loan will be repaid, and that guarantee permits the lender to offer a lower interest rate. Because the VA loan does not require a down payment, veterans can qualify for a larger loan than they otherwise might. See chapter 11 for more information.

Employment Benefits

Disabled veterans may qualify for vocational rehabilitation training that prepares them for employment in a vocation of their choosing. Also, veterans who served during a war period are given preference in job counseling, job information, and job placement services provided by the U.S. Employment Service.

Other Benefits

You may be entitled to other veterans' benefits, such as VGLI life insurance, one-time dental treatment on separation, employment assistance, and other benefits that are connected with separation from the military. Make sure that you are counseled thoroughly on these benefits before you leave the military. Also, don't forget to apply for unemployment compensation when you leave the service (if applicable).

SUGGESTED REFERENCES

Kingson, Eric R. *What You MUST Know about Social Security and Medicare.* New York: Pharos Books, 1987.

The U.S. Department of Health and Human Services publishes the *Social Security Handbook.* This reference provides very useful and detailed information, but it is written in a technical government style.

The most current edition of the *Uniformed Services Almanac* will give you much more detail about VA benefits than has been provided in this chapter.

One obvious source of information for Social Security Administration and Department of Veterans Affairs programs is the local office of each administration; check your local telephone directory under U.S. Government. They have pamphlets explaining each of their programs, which they will send you at no charge.

20

Retirement Survivor Benefits

THE SURVIVOR BENEFIT PLAN

The first voluntary system of survivor benefits for present and future military retirees was established on 21 September 1972 when Congress enacted PL 92-425. Called the Survivor Benefit Plan (SBP), the program allows retired uniformed service personnel to provide a monthly annuity (income) for their surviving dependents. Under the basic plan, a surviving spouse would receive 55 percent of the "base" amount of retired pay elected. If the participant retired after 31 December 1956 but before 1 October 1985, the SBP annuity would be subject to a Social Security offset when the surviving spouse reaches age sixty-two. The cost (monthly premium) and proceeds payable to survivors were established by Congress and based, in part, on actuarial reports furnished by the Department of Defense, the Life Insurance Association of America, the National Association of Life Underwriters, and the American Life Convention.

The Survivor Benefit Plan was improved for present and future retirees on 8 November 1985 when Congress passed the Defense Authorization Act of 1986 (PL 99-145). This provided for a two-tier SBP system and eliminated the Social Security offset. Those servicemembers retiring after 1 October 1985 would have their surviving spouses' annuities reduced to 35 percent of the base retirement pay upon reaching the age of sixty-two.

During 1989, Congress ordered an overhaul of the Survivor Benefit Plan that included a rollback in the premiums for buying basic benefits. That reduction took effect in March 1990. On 29 November 1989, Congress enacted Title XIV, Military Survivor Benefits Information Act of 1989 (PL 100-189), which made two significant changes to SBP. As of 1 April 1992, SBP participants have the option of purchasing supplemental coverage that would prevent the SBP annuity from being reduced when the surviving spouse turns sixty-two or when the retiree dies. In November 1990, the open season for enrollment in the program was extended until 1 April 1992 to give both the Department of Defense and military special-interest groups an opportunity to recommend alternatives to the current program. From April 1992 through March 1993, the Department of Defense launched an additional year-long open season to give military retirees another opportunity at signing up for the Survivor Benefit Plan with the new enacted benefits.

In this chapter, we explain the most current details of the SBP program as of this writing. The critical point is that SBP is voluntary, but final. Every retiring servicemember must decide whether or not to participate, based on a complete understanding of the program. The consequences of this decision are critically important and long lasting; this decision must not be taken lightly.

Purpose of the SBP Program

The purpose of SBP is to provide the military retiree's spouse (or children, in certain situations) with a monthly income after he or she dies. What few soldiers realize is that this program covers both the retired and retirement-eligible active-duty servicemember. As an active-duty member with sufficient time in service to retire, you are covered under the SBP plan at no cost until you actually retire. If you die before retirement, your spouse would receive 55 percent of the pay you would have been receiving had you been retired. If your retired pay would have been $2,100 per month, for example, the SBP annuity would be $1,155 per month until your spouse dies.

However, the annuity is reduced by any Dependency and Indemnity Compensation (DIC) payments, automatically paid by the Department of Veterans Affairs if death occurs on active duty. As of 1 January 1993, the amount of a surviving spouse's DIC payment was $750 per month regardless of the retiree's rank or time in service. For a widow receiving $750 per month from DIC, only the SBP excess (in this case $405) would be received, for a total payment of $1,155. If you die on active duty, your spouse will never receive less than the $750 per month DIC payment; however, the survivor benefits can be much greater than the DIC payment if the SBP benefit is sufficiently large.

For the retired servicemember, SBP is voluntary and the decision is an important one. Because of the consequences, the law states that spouses of servicemembers who do not elect SBP coverage, or who elect coverage below that of retired base pay, will be notified in writing of the implications of their choice. Sadly, some couples act impulsively and short-sightedly in this matter and later regret their decision.

It is important that you look at SBP as an integral part of your total estate planning. Decisions about participation should be based on family discussions and with the advice of qualified personnel officers, insurance agents, bank trust officers, or others qualified in estate planning.

Amount of Annuity and Costs

What does SBP do and how much does it cost? Basically, SBP continues to pay a portion of your retired pay to your surviving spouse after you die. The amount of the.

annuity is always 55 percent of what is referred to as the base amount, an amount that you choose. The maximum base is your gross monthly retired pay; the minimum is $300.

Some examples illustrate how the amount of the annuity is determined:

Gross Monthly Retired Pay	Base Amount That Retiree Elects	Monthly Spousal Annuity
$2,100	$2,100	$1,155 ($2,100 × 0.55)
$2,100	$1,000	$ 550 ($1,000 × 0.55)
$2,100	$ 300	$ 165 ($ 300 × 0.55)

Thus, you can ensure that your surviving spouse receives, for life, a monthly annuity check as low as $165 or as high as 55 percent of your retired gross pay in coverage for your spouse. The cost of the program will depend not only on the amount of coverage you elect, but also on whether you elect the coverage for spouse only, spouse and children, or children only. Let's now take a look at the costs.

Spouse-only Coverage

Computing the cost is just as easy as determining the base amount. Effective 1 March 1990, the cost is a flat 6.5 percent of the base amount. An example is provided below.

(Note: Prior to 1 March 1990, the first $300 of the base amount, or $165 in benefits, was always "costed" at the rate of 2.5 percent, or $7.50. The remainder was costed at the rate of 10 percent. If you became a servicemember before 1 March 1990, you have the option of having SBP costs calculated under the original formula. For small base amounts, that method will be cheaper.)

Gross Monthly Retired Pay	Base Amount That Retiree Elects	Monthly Spousal Annuity	Cost per Month
$2,100	$2,100 × 0.55 = $2,100 × 0.35 = (after spouse turns 62)	$1,155 or $ 735	$136.50 ($2,100 × 0.065) (or $187.50—see Note)
$2,100	$1,000 × 0.55 = $1,000 × 0.35 = (after spouse turns 62)	$ 550 or $ 350	$65.00 ($1,000 × 0.065) (or $77.50—see Note)
$2,100	$300 × 0.55 = $300 × 0.35 = (after spouse turns 62)	$ 165 or $ 105	$19.50 ($300 × 0.065) (or $7.50—see Note)

Note: Cost per month under the "old" pricing system (still available to retirees who had service time before March 1990) would be $187.50, $77.50, and $7.50, respectively, for the three options shown in this table.

The amount listed in the "Cost per Month" column will be deducted from your retirement check each month. As it is a deduction from income, it lowers your taxable income, which lowers your tax bill as well! Section 122 of the Internal Revenue Code exempts the cost of SBP from federal income tax. Only the cost is exempt, however; the annuity benefits to your spouse are considered taxable income. Furthermore, the SBP contribution, which is the amount deducted from retired pay to purchase SBP insurance, is exempt from state income tax in all states but Mississippi. The annuity, when received by the survivors, is treated as taxable income by the federal government. The tax treatment of the annuity varies by state; contact your state tax division for specifics.

In the event of death, the SBP annuity (plus cost-of-living increases) will be paid to surviving spouses as long as they live. Should your spouse remarry before age sixty, however, the annuity will end. But if that marriage terminates, the annuity is again payable. Should your spouse remarry after sixty, the annuity continues uninterrupted. If your spouse dies before you do, deductions from your retired pay for SBP stop.

Spouse and Children Coverage

The additional cost for children is based on the age of the youngest child and both spouses, and therefore varies tremendously. Your local personnel officer will be able to provide you with the factors for your specific situation. For example, let us consider a retiree who is forty-three, a spouse who is forty-one, and a youngest child who is ten. The cost factor for this particular situation is .0005. This factor must be added on to the cost of the annuity for the spouse in order to determine the total cost:

Gross Monthly Retired Pay	Base Amount That Retiree Elects	Monthly Spousal Annuity	Cost per Month
$2,100 plus children coverage	$2,100	$1,155	$136.50 ($2,100 × 0.065) $ 1.05 ($2,100 × 0.0005)
Total cost			$137.55

The total SBP proceeds will be paid to your spouse, then, if the spouse dies or remarries, to the unmarried children. When there is more than one child, the proceeds are shared by all of the children. Payments terminate when the youngest child reaches age eighteen, or twenty-two if the child is in college. Deductions for children coverage cease when the youngest child is no longer an eligible beneficiary. There is no age limit for eligible, incapacitated children. This includes unmarried children who are mentally or physically incapable of self-support because of a condition that existed before age eighteen (twenty-two if in school).

Children Only

Cost for the "children-only coverage" is based on your age and the age of the youngest child. However, the annuity payable is the same as for "spouse-only" or "spouse and children" coverage—always 55 percent of the base amount. For example, with your age of forty-three and your youngest child's age of ten, the cost factor is .0059.

Gross Monthly Retired Pay	Base Amount That Retiree Elects	Monthly Annuity	Cost per Month
$2,100	$2,100	$1,155	$12.39 ($2,100 × 0.0059)

Here, too, deductions from pay cease when the youngest child is no longer an eligible beneficiary. In the event of your death, the annuity would be shared equally by your eligible children. There are some additional combinations of coverage available in this program, including former-spouse coverage and retirees with no dependents.

Cost-of-Living Raises

Unlike ordinary insurance policies, SBP is fully protected by cost-of-living (COL) increases. Your retired pay is protected with COL Allowances (COLAs); hence the cost of the SBP program increases each time your retired pay rises. The cost will increase only by the amount of the COLA, however, and your real (inflation-adjusted) pay remains the same. And, of course, the benefit, or spousal annuity, increases as well. For example:

Gross Monthly Retired Pay	Base Amount That Retiree Elects	Monthly Annuity	Cost per Month
$2,100	$2,100	$1,155	$136.50 ($2,100 × 0.065)

After a 5 percent COLA increase (to $2,205) in your retired pay:

Gross Monthly Retired Pay	Base Amount That Retiree Elects	Monthly Annuity	Cost per Month
$2,205	$2,205	$1,212.75	$143.33 ($2,205 × 0.065)

So, although the COLA increases your monthly deduction, it also increases your spouse's benefit. Further, your spouse will continue to receive COLA increases after you die, even though you have stopped paying into the system. This is perhaps the greatest advantage of SBP—not only does the insurance benefit increase while you are buying it, but it keeps growing with inflation as long as your spouse receives benefits. This inflation protection is an extraordinarily valuable feature—you can't get inflation-indexed benefits like this with any commercial insurance product that we know of.

Social Security Entitlements

Many military people, secure in their own retirement and benefit programs, give scant attention to Social Security and what it can provide (see chapter 19). However, Social Security has a direct bearing on SBP benefits through what is known as the SBP offset. This essentially results in a two-tier SBP system. If you die before your spouse, the SBP annuity begins; however, once your spouse begins to receive your Social Security benefits, the SBP annuity will be reduced from 55 percent of the base amount elected to 35 percent.

The government, as your employer, contributes to the Social Security fund for active-duty personnel. In enacting the SBP law, Congress insisted that a spouse's annuity be reduced or offset by the value of the decedent's military-earned wage credits. Normally, the reduction begins when the surviving spouse reaches age sixty-two because that is when Social Security benefits can be paid. If you should die before your spouse is sixty-two, the SBP annuity will not be reduced before your spouse reaches that age unless there are dependent children in your household at the time of your death. Because a spouse with dependent children who are sixteen or younger also receives payments from Social Security, the SBP annuity may be reduced in such instances. Your spouse should contact the Social Security Administration, the Retired Officers Association, or the Army and Air Force Mutual Aid Association about current offset provisions if your survivors include dependent children.

The amount of SBP offset depends on a number of factors, but under an amendment to the SBP law on 1 March 1986, the offset will generally reduce the 55 percent annuity to 35 percent (applicable to those retiring after 1 October 1985). That is, in all but a few rare cases, the spousal annuity (benefit amount) will be 35 percent of the base amount when an SBP offset is in effect. Because Social Security benefits are generally greater than the reduction in SBP benefits, the surviving family's income from the two benefits will always be larger than SBP alone. Details about individual situations should be discussed with unit personnel officers.

SHOULD YOU TAKE SBP?

For any retiree, the question must certainly arise, "Is SBP a good deal?" We would reply, "Yes, but . . ." We carefully analyzed the program for the typical retiree with an average life expectancy, and came to two conclusions:

324 • PERSONAL FINANCIAL PLANNING

- A similar system could not be purchased at a lower cost "on the economy."
- It is an excellent program on its own merits.

But there are also important considerations that, for a few servicemembers, may make the selection of SBP unnecessary. Here we consider two ways of evaluating SBP: First is an *absolute* analysis, then we will analyze SBP in *relative* terms.

SBP versus No Insurance

First we address the question, "Am I better off with SBP or with nothing?" Clearly, for retirees who live longer than their spouses, SBP is a great expense with no benefit. On the other hand, if you die early and your spouse lives a long time after your death, the benefits received are very large in comparison to the costs.

In Table 20-1, we have illustrated the case of a male lieutenant colonel (O-5), age forty-two, with a forty-two-year-old spouse, retiring in 1993 after twenty years of service. To determine if SBP is beneficial, we go down the vertical axis to an assumed death age of sixty-five. We then go horizontally to an assumed spousal death age of seventy-five. Given these assumptions, we see that the retiree has paid in for twenty-three years and his wife receives an annuity for ten years. We hope that the value is at least zero, as this indicates that the present value (that is, allowing for the time value of money) of the amount paid is just equal to the payouts. In this case we see that the value is a positive $23,013, which means that the present value of the benefits paid to the surviving spouse is greater than the cost of the premiums paid by over $23,000 in today's dollars (a positive net present value).

Note that there are cases in which the net present value is negative. Clearly, if a retiree pays in for a number of years and the spouse dies first, there are no benefits, but the costs have still been paid and they are reflected in the negative number. This may also be true when the spouse dies soon after the military retiree. Using Table 20-1, you can get an idea of the circumstances under which SBP "pays off" by delivering more benefits than it costs. In general, this occurs when the retiree dies several years before the surviving spouse.

Obviously, we cannot know for certain how long we will live and how long our spouses will live. The purpose of insurance—and SBP is a form of insurance—is to reduce the financial risk arising from undesirable events. In this case, the undesirable event is the premature death of the military retiree, and the financial risk is a spouse being without sufficient income following the death.

Perhaps you have some reason to believe, based on family health history or the relative ages of you and your spouse, for example, that you or your spouse will live a long or short time after retirement or that one is highly likely to predecease the other. You can certainly use that information in making your decision about SBP, but you cannot eliminate completely the uncertainty. In any case, you may want to buy the insurance to protect your family. That raises the issue of the cost effectiveness of SBP as compared to privately available insurance. We analyze that issue in our relative analysis in the next section.

TABLE 20-1
Present Value of All SBP Costs and Benefits

Death Age of Retiree	Value of Payoff to Spouse Net of the Value of Your Payments Assuming Your Spouse Lives Until the Age of:											
	45	50	55	60	65	70	75	80	85	90	95	100
43	$18,895	$65,136	$106,237	$142,769	$168,323	$186,690	$203,016	$217,526	$230,424	$241,888	$252,078	$261,135
44	$7,584	$53,825	$94,926	$131,458	$157,013	$175,379	$191,705	$206,216	$219,113	$230,577	$240,767	$249,825
45	($3,463)	$42,778	$83,878	$120,411	$145,965	$164,332	$180,657	$195,168	$208,066	$219,530	$229,720	$238,777
50	($3,463)	($4,751)	$36,350	$72,882	$98,436	$116,803	$133,129	$147,639	$160,537	$172,001	$182,191	$191,248
55	($3,463)	($4,751)	($6,223)	$30,309	$55,864	$74,231	$90,556	$105,067	$117,965	$129,429	$139,619	$148,676
60	($3,463)	($4,751)	($6,223)	($7,905)	$17,650	$36,017	$52,342	$66,853	$79,751	$91,215	$101,405	$110,462
65	($3,463)	($4,751)	($6,223)	($7,905)	($9,826)	$8,541	$24,866	$39,377	$52,275	$63,739	$73,929	$82,986
70	($3,463)	($4,751)	($6,223)	($7,905)	($9,826)	($12,021)	$4,304	$18,815	$31,712	$43,176	$53,366	$62,424
75	($3,463)	($4,751)	($6,223)	($7,905)	($9,826)	($12,021)	($14,530)	($19)	$12,878	$24,343	$34,532	$43,590
80	($3,463)	($4,751)	($6,223)	($7,905)	($9,826)	($12,021)	($14,530)	($17,396)	($4,499)	$6,966	$17,155	$26,213
85	($3,463)	($4,751)	($6,223)	($7,905)	($9,826)	($12,021)	($14,530)	($17,396)	($20,671)	($9,207)	$983	$10,040
90	($3,463)	($4,751)	($6,223)	($7,905)	($9,826)	($12,021)	($14,530)	($17,396)	($20,671)	($24,414)	($14,224)	($5,167)
95	($3,463)	($4,751)	($6,223)	($7,905)	($9,826)	($12,021)	($14,530)	($17,396)	($20,671)	($24,414)	($28,689)	($19,632)
100	($3,463)	($4,751)	($6,223)	($7,905)	($9,826)	($12,021)	($14,530)	($17,396)	($20,671)	($24,414)	($28,689)	($33,575)

Notes: Based on a 42-year-old lieutenant colonel (0-5), retiring in 1993 with a 42-year old spouse.

Costs and benefits are after federal tax (28% bracket assumed); after-tax discount rates apply.

SBP Offset applied to all spousal benefits after age 62.

Present values calculated as of retirement date. Assumed 4% inflation, 9% before-tax interest rate.

SBP versus Commercial Life Insurance

Perhaps you do not feel comfortable without the basic insurance protection that SBP or some other form of life insurance provides. A second way to evaluate SBP is a *relative* analysis—compare it to privately offered insurance.

Some retirees say, "I can do it myself. All I have to do is purchase a commercial term life insurance policy, and I'll be able to replicate SBP at a fraction of the cost." Table 20-2 shows how we can compare the cost of SBP and the cost of commercial term life insurance to cover the income needs of surviving spouses should we die before them.

Basically, the decision is between participating in SBP (and accepting the lower retired pay that goes with it) and turning down SBP in favor of taking full retired pay and using part of it to buy term insurance. SBP is cheaper than the term insurance option if the present value of the retired pay you give up is lower than the present value of the premiums required to buy the same protection with term life insurance.

In Table 20-2, the key figures are in columns 4 and 8, where the annual cost of the SBP program and of the term insurance option are shown. The numbers in those two columns are compared in column 9 for each year's cost. For example, we see that the term option is cheaper (by $667) in the year after retirement. This cost difference is accumulated over time with interest in column 10. The table shows that the cumulative cost of a one-year term insurance policy may be cheaper in the short run. In the long run, though, the increasing year-to-year cost of attempting to maintain insurance protection for the cost-of-living increases and the rising cost of buying term insurance as your age increases will make the cost of the term insurance alternative greater than the cost of the SBP program. By comparing the figures in the table, you can see that if you die ten years after retirement (age fifty-two), the present value of the amount by which the cost of SBP exceeds the cost of insurance for the period from your retirement until your death is $2,849. Of course, this would be an unexpectedly early death. If you die around age eighty, the present value of your savings from electing SBP instead of purchasing term insurance would be $19,609.

If you are older than forty-two at retirement, term insurance will be more expensive than is shown here, and the analysis tilts more toward SBP. The opposite is true if you retire younger than forty-two. As we pointed out in our absolute analysis, if you have reason to believe you will have a relatively short life expectancy, you might want to consider using term insurance rather than SBP to protect your family after your death. But if you are uninsurable or expensive to insure (due to medical problems or smoking), SBP may be your best deal.

Some Additional Considerations

Our analysis shows that SBP is a reasonably cost-effective insurance plan for the typical retiree who lives a normal life expectancy. But there are some additional factors you should consider before you make your decision.

A Cost Comparison of SBP and Term Life Insurance

1	2	3	4	5	6	7	8	9	10
Death Year	Age of Retiree	Prior Year's Retirement Pay w/4% COLA	Net SBP Cost w/Tax Savings	After-tax SBP Benefit (28% tax rate)	Replacement Value of SBP Annuity	Monthly Cost of Term Per $1000	Annual Cost of Term	Annual Savings	PV of Cumulative Savings w/9% Interest
1994	43	$26,886	$1,258	$10,647	$189,507	$0.26	$591	($667)	($667)
1995	44	$27,961	$1,309	$11,073	$195,916	$0.29	$672	($636)	($1,147)
1996	45	$29,080	$1,361	$11,516	$202,476	$0.31	$764	($597)	($1,608)
1997	46	$30,243	$1,415	$11,976	$209,183	$0.35	$869	($547)	($1,995)
1998	47	$31,453	$1,472	$12,455	$216,033	$0.38	$987	($485)	($2,311)
1999	48	$32,711	$1,531	$12,954	$223,021	$0.42	$1,121	($410)	($2,555)
2000	49	$34,019	$1,592	$13,472	$230,139	$0.46	$1,272	($320)	($2,730)
2001	50	$35,380	$1,656	$14,011	$237,380	$0.51	$1,443	($213)	($2,837)
2002	51	$36,795	$1,722	$14,571	$244,733	$0.56	$1,637	($85)	($2,876)
2003	52	$38,267	$1,791	$15,154	$252,188	$0.61	$1,855	$64	($2,849)
2004	53	$39,798	$1,863	$15,760	$259,732	$0.67	$2,102	$239	($2,756)
2005	54	$41,390	$1,937	$16,390	$267,347	$0.74	$2,380	$443	($2,599)
2006	55	$43,045	$2,015	$17,046	$275,018	$0.82	$2,693	$678	($2,378)
2007	56	$44,767	$2,095	$17,728	$282,724	$0.90	$3,045	$950	($2,093)
2008	57	$46,558	$2,179	$18,437	$290,441	$0.99	$3,441	$1,262	($1,747)
2009	58	$48,420	$2,266	$19,174	$298,144	$1.09	$3,886	$1,620	($1,339)
2010	59	$50,357	$2,357	$19,941	$305,803	$1.19	$4,384	$2,027	($870)
2011	60	$52,371	$2,451	$20,739	$313,384	$1.31	$4,942	$2,491	($342)
2012	61	$54,466	$2,549	$21,569	$320,849	$1.45	$5,566	$3,017	$244
2013	62	$56,645	$2,651	$22,431	$328,157	$1.59	$6,262	$3,611	$889
2014	63	$58,911	$2,757	$23,329	$335,260	$1.75	$7,037	$4,280	$1,589
2015	64	$61,267	$2,867	$24,262	$342,105	$1.92	$7,899	$5,031	$2,345
2016	65	$63,718	$2,982	$25,232	$348,632	$2.12	$8,854	$5,872	$3,154
2017	66	$66,266	$3,101	$26,241	$354,777	$2.33	$9,912	$6,810	$4,015
2018	67	$68,917	$3,225	$27,291	$360,466	$2.56	$11,078	$7,852	$4,926
2019	68	$71,674	$3,354	$28,383	$365,616	$2.82	$12,359	$9,005	$5,884
2020	69	$74,541	$3,489	$29,518	$370,139	$3.10	$13,764	$10,275	$6,887
2021	70	$77,522	$3,628	$30,699	$373,934	$3.41	$15,295	$11,667	$7,931
2022	71	$80,623	$3,773	$31,927	$376,889	$3.75	$16,958	$13,184	$9,015
2023	72	$83,848	$3,924	$33,204	$378,882	$4.12	$18,752	$14,828	$10,132
2024	73	$87,202	$4,081	$34,532	$379,778	$4.54	$20,676	$16,595	$11,280
2025	74	$90,690	$4,244	$35,913	$379,426	$4.99	$22,722	$18,478	$12,452
2026	75	$94,318	$4,414	$37,350	$377,661	$5.49	$24,878	$20,464	$13,643
2027	76	$98,090	$4,591	$38,844	$374,300	$6.04	$27,123	$22,532	$14,846
2028	77	$102,014	$4,774	$40,398	$369,143	$6.64	$29,424	$24,650	$16,053
2029	78	$106,095	$4,965	$42,013	$361,969	$7.31	$31,737	$26,772	$17,257
2030	79	$110,338	$5,164	$43,694	$352,533	$8.04	$34,001	$28,837	$18,446
2031	80	$114,752	$5,370	$45,442	$340,567	$8.84	$36,131	$30,761	$19,609
2032	81	$119,342	$5,585	$47,259	$325,776	$9.73	$38,019	$32,433	$20,735
2033	82	$124,116	$5,809	$49,150	$307,836	$10.70	$39,517	$33,709	$21,808
2034	83	$129,080	$6,041	$51,116	$286,392	$11.77	$40,441	$34,400	$22,813

Note: This example is for a lieutenant colonel with 20 years of service, age 42, with a 42-year-old spouse. The spouse has a life expectancy of 89 years and will be in the 28% tax bracket. Inflation is assumed to be 4%. Nominal [illegible]

Do you need insurance at all? Remember that the only reason for participation in SBP is to provide for your survivors' needs if you should die before they do and your retired pay stops as a result. If you have substantial financial assets that meet your survivors' needs to provide them secure income or if they have valuable work skills, you may not need SBP or more term insurance to protect them. It makes little sense to buy insurance of any kind that you do not need.

SBP is inflation protected and term insurance is not. A unique feature of SBP benefits is that they are regularly adjusted upward as the cost of living rises. With term insurance, the amount of coverage is fixed and cannot be adjusted for inflation. You have to raise the face amount of the policy to keep up with inflation; you cannot do this without a medical exam, company approval, and a lot of extra cost and uncertainty.

Commercial insurance proceeds can be passed on to children. SBP cannot be paid to children who are older than twenty-two unless they are disabled. With term insurance, the face value of the policy is paid to your surviving spouse (or other beneficiary) at your death; the survivor then can decide what to do with that money: use it all for support or pass some of it along to your children. SBP benefits, by contrast, stop when your spouse dies or when your last child reaches twenty-two.

The SBP program is heavily subsidized by the government. This means that the average SBP participant is "buying" protection at a substantial discount from the "fair" price, and the government makes up the difference. This is certainly not the case for commercial insurance policies. Unless you have some special consideration that makes SBP unattractive to you and your family, it is unlikely that you will find better protection for the price.

If you are thinking about not taking any SBP at all, strongly consider taking at least the minimum base amount at the 2.5 percent reduced cost rate, if that is an option for you. At $7.50 a month, this might be too good a deal for you to pass up.

CHANGES IN COVERAGE

Except as permitted under the SBP open enrollment period, participation in SBP cannot be changed or modified once your application becomes effective. Deductions from your retired pay continue as long as you have an eligible beneficiary for the annuity. Deductions from your retirement pay will be discontinued if your spouse dies before you do, you are granted a divorce, or your marriage is annulled. If the retiree remarries (on or after 1 March 1986), he has the option not to provide coverage for the new spouse. The member's new spouse must be notified, and the option must be exercised within one year of remarrying.

SUPPLEMENTAL SURVIVOR BENEFIT PLAN (SSBP)

Effective 1 April 1992 (PL 101-189), eligible retirees of the uniformed services can enroll in Supplemental SBP, which is a program that replaces some or all of the SBP annuity reduction when a surviving spouse or former spouse reaches the age of sixty-two. This SSBP annuity is payable in increments of 5, 10, 15, or 20 percent. When increments are added to the "standard" SBP annuity (35 percent of base amount at age sixty-two or older), the total annuity to the surviving spouse or former spouse will equal 40, 45, 50, or 55 percent of monthly gross military retired pay. Retirees are eligible to elect SSBP only if the annuity will be computed under the two-tier method at age sixty-two, and not the Social Security offset method.

SSBP premiums are added to SBP premiums, which are 6.5 percent of the base amount elected, and depend on the retiree's age at the time he elects to add the supplemental annuity to his SBP. Once SSBP premiums are established, they will be treated in the same manner as SBP premiums. SSBP will be increased like SBP premiums and suspended whenever SBP premiums are suspended. SSBP rates can be obtained by consulting the references at the end of this chapter or talking with your local military pay division.

If the retiree marries or remarries after retiring, he may elect, within one year of marriage or remarriage, to provide an SSBP annuity for his spouse as long as he is providing maximum SBP coverage (55 percent of monthly gross retired pay). The SBP coverage may be increased to its maximum before electing SSBP coverage. The retiree may not, however, reduce a maximum SBP annuity that he already had elected upon remarriage.

THE BOTTOM LINE

The choice to participate in or pass up SBP and SSBP is very important, especially because the choice is irreversible. You cannot decide later to join SBP nor can you later drop out of the program unless your spouse dies before you. Our advice is to analyze SBP as an insurance policy and buy it only if you need the insurance protection that it provides.

Considering the benefits of SBP and SSBP and their costs in comparison with other means of providing for your family after you die, we think SBP is a good program for most retirees because it provides excellent coverage for most retirees and, together with Social Security survivor payments, can guarantee a secure income that your spouse cannot outlive and that cannot be eroded by inflation. The peace of mind that those benefits offer to many retirees may be well worth the cost of the reduced retirement check.

SUGGESTED REFERENCES

Gryczynski, Edward S., Lewis J. Tolleson, and Elizabeth H. Audie. *SBP Made Easy: The Survivor Benefit Plan.* Alexandria, VA: The Retired Officers Association, 1994. Updated annually; send $3 to TROA, 201 N. Washington St., Alexandria, VA 22314-2529.

SBP—It's Your Choice. Department of Defense brochure (updated periodically; title may change).

Part VI

APPENDIXES

Appendix A

Sources of Assistance

MILITARY ORGANIZATIONS AND ASSOCIATIONS

These nonprofit and commercial associations serve servicemembers and former servicemembers. Many advertise regularly in newspapers and magazines that serve active-duty and retired personnel. For detailed information about specific services, you should contact the appropriate organization directly. No endorsement of any company is meant or implied.

Air Force Association
1501 Lee Highway
Arlington, VA 22209
800-727-3337
   Services include group term life and health insurance, accident insurance, flight pay insurance, and employment transition service.

Air Force Sergeants Association
P.O. Box 50
Temple Hills, MD 20748
800-638-0594 or 0595
   Services available include life, auto, and health insurance; travel service; prescription program.

American Military Retirees
P.O. Box 973
Saranac Lake, NY 12983
518-563-9479
   Services include life and health insurance, travel service.

American Veterans of World War II, Korea, and Vietnam
4647 Forbes Boulevard
Lanham, MD 20706
301-459-9600
   Services include life and health insurance, counseling.

Armed Forces Insurance
P.O. Box G
Fort Leavenworth, KS 66027
800-255-6792
   Services include all-risk personal property and household insurance, comprehensive personal liability insurance, credit card insurance, homeowners' package policy.

Armed Forces Benefit Association
909 N. Washington St.
Alexandria, VA 22314
800-776-2322
   Services include group term life insurance with family plan rider available.

Armed Services Mutual Benefit Association (ASMBA)
P.O. Box 4646
Madison Building
Nashville, TN 37216
800-251-8434
   Services include group term, survivor income, and family plan insurance.

Army and Air Force Mutual Aid Association
Fort Myer
Arlington, VA 22211
800-336-4538
   Services include ordinary life insurance, twenty-payment life insurance, thirty-payment life insurance, retirement and survivor assistance, records storage.

Association of the United States Army
2425 Wilson Blvd.
Arlington, VA 22201
800-336-4570
   Services include group term life insurance with family rider available, health insurance, extra cash income hospital insurance.

Coast Guard Chief Petty Officer's Association
5520G Hempstead Way
Springfield, VA 22151
703-941-0395
   Services include life and health insurance.

SOURCES OF ASSISTANCE • 335

Disabled American Veterans
807 Maine Avenue, SW
Washington, DC 20024
202-554-3501
   Services include assistance in obtaining veterans benefits and claims, employment assistance.

Enlisted Association of the National Guard
One Massachusetts Avenue, NW
Washington, DC 20001
800-234-3264
   Services include life insurance.

Fleet Reserve Association
1303 New Hampshire Avenue, NW
Washington, DC 20036
202-785-2768
   Services include life and health insurance, representation with VA for claims and grievances.

Marine Corps League
c/o Membership Services
1304 Vincent Place
McClean, VA 22101
800-234-1304 or 703-821-0556
   Services include life and health insurance, representation with VA for claims and grievances.

Marine Corps Reserve Officers Association
201 North Washington Street, Suite 206
Alexandria, VA 22314
703-548-7607
   Services include life insurance, accidental disability and dismemberment insurance.

National Association for Uniformed Services
NAUS Insurance Program
5535 Hempstead Way
Springfield, VA 22151
703-750-1342
   Services include life, health, CHAMPUS supplement, hospital indemnity, and accident insurance; prescription medicine discounts; VISA credit cards.

Naval Enlisted Reserve Association
6703 Farragut Avenue
Falls Church, VA 22042
703-534-1329
   Services include life and health insurance, assistance with retirement processing.

Naval Reserve Association (NRA)
1619 King Street
Alexandria, VA 22314
703-548-5800
   Services include life, health, and accidental death and disability insurance.

Navy Mutual Aid Association (NMAA)
Arlington Annex, Room G070
Washington, DC 20370
800-628-6011
   Services include term and whole life insurance.

Navy League of the United States
2300 Wilson Boulevard
Arlington, VA 22201
800-356-5760
   Services include life and health insurance.

Non Commissioned Officers Association (NCOA)
P.O. Box 33610
San Antonio, TX 78235
512-653-6161
   Services include life and health insurance, car rental and new car discounts, auto club, telephone buying services.

Officers Benefit Association (OBA)
#2 Metroplex Drive, Suite 204
Birmingham, AL 35209
800-633-4632
   Services include group term life insurance with family plan rider available.

Reserve Officers Association
1 Constitution Avenue, NE
Washington, DC 20002
202-479-2200
   Services include life and health insurance, travel services, car rentals and leases.

The Retired Enlisted Association
P.O. Box 50584
Washington, DC 20004
800-843-2043
   Services include term and whole life and health insurance, CHAMPUS and Medicare supplemental insurance, auto and homeowners' insurance.

The Retired Officer's Association
201 North Washington Street
Alexandria, VA 22314
800-245-8762
   Services include life and health insurance, car rental, major appliance purchase discounts, auto leasing and purchase discounts, employment and counseling services.

Uniformed Services Benefit Association (USBA)
3822 Summit
Kansas City, MO 64111
800-821-7912
   Services include group ordinary life insurance, group decreasing and level term life insurance with accidental death and dismemberment coverage included, family plan riders, hospitalization insurance.

United Services Automobile Association (USAA)
USAA Building
San Antonio, TX 78288
800-531-8100
   Services include automobile insurance, boatowners' insurance, comprehensive personal liability insurance, fire and homeowners' insurance, household goods and personal effects floater, personal articles floater, term and whole life insurance, universal life insurance, credit cards (VISA/MasterCard), banking services, discount brokerage services, auto leasing and buying services, travel services.

U.S. Army Warrant Officers Association
462 Herndon Pkwy., Suite 207
Herndon, VA 22070
703-742-7727
   Services include life and health insurance, car rental discounts, CHAMPUS supplemental insurance.

Veterans of Foreign Wars of the United States
200 Maryland Avenue, NE
Washington, DC 20002
202-543-2239
   Services include life and health insurance, assistance with VA matters, counseling.

Appendix B

Glossary of Financial Terms

abstract of title A history of the ownership of real property from some moment in the past down to the present, generally required in a real estate transaction.

accidental death clause A guarantee in the life insurance policy providing additional proceeds if the insured dies as a result of an accident. It is also called a double-indemnity clause.

accumulation plan An arrangement that enables an investor to purchase mutual fund shares regularly, usually with provisions for the reinvestment of income dividends and the acceptance of capital gains distributions in additional shares. Plans are of two types, voluntary and contractual.

actuary Primarily a person who applies to life insurance the principles that underlie all its computations, such as those of premiums, reserves, surrender values, apportionment of dividends, and the like. The word has now acquired a broader meaning and might be defined as "one versed in the mathematics, bookkeeping, law, and finance of life insurance."

add-on method A computational method where (1) the finance charge for an installment credit contract as a whole equals the add-on rate times the principal amount of credit at the start of the contract times the number of years in the credit contract; (2) the finance charge is added to the principal; and (3) the credit user receives the principal and pays back the principal plus the finance charge in monthly (or other periodic) installments.

adjustable rate mortgage (ARM) A mortgage loan for which interest rates are not fixed but vary with market interest rates.

adjusted-balance method of computing interest Interest is charged on the balance outstanding after it has been adjusted for payments and credits.

amenities The features of a property that are not a part of the space occupied and that create special attraction, such as recreation rooms, saunas, and pools, or "natural amenities," such as a view or ocean frontage.

amortization The process of retiring debt or writing off an asset. As regards a direct reduction of self-amortizing mortgage, amortization represents the principal repayment portion of an installment payment. An amortization table is shown in Table 6-1.

annual percentage rate (APR) The effective interest rate applicable to a loan. See the formula for APR in Chapter 6, Table 6-1.

annual report The formal financial statement issued yearly by a corporation to its shareowners. The annual report shows assets, liabilities, earnings, how the company stood at the close of the business year, and how it fared in profit during the year.

annuity A stated sum of money, payable periodically at the end of fixed intervals.

annuity, certain An annuity payable throughout a fixed (certain) period of time, irrespective of the happening of any contingency, such as the death of annuitant.

annuity, contingent An annuity contingent upon the happening of an event that may or may not take place.

annuity, deferred An annuity modified by the condition that the first payment will not be due for a fixed number of years. Thus, an annuity deferred for twenty years is one on which the first payment is made at the end of twenty-one years, provided the annuitant is then alive.

annuity, life A fixed sum payable periodically so long as a given person's life continues.

annuity, survivorship An annuity payable throughout the lifetime of one person after the death of another person or persons.

annuity, variable A form of whole life insurance where the face value and cash value vary according to the investment success of the insurance company.

appraisal The estimation of market value of property.

assessed value The value assessed by the taxing authority for purpose of establishing real estate taxes. This value may not be directly related to market value.

assessment A charge against real estate made by a unit of government to cover a proportionate cost of an improvement such as a street or sewer.

assets The total monetary value of all property in a company's possession at a given time. Also, everything that a person owns, whether the items are paid for or not.

assumption clause A mortgage loan clause that allows the owner of a house to transfer the mortgage to a later buyer.

assumption of mortgage The taking of title to property by a grantee, wherein the grantee assumes liability for payment of an existing note or bond secured by a mortgage against a property and becomes personally liable for the payment of such mortgage debt.

ATM card Automatic Teller Machine card, issued by your bank, which allows you to withdraw cash and perform other simple banking transactions.

automatic paid-up insurance An amount of insurance, which, without further action by the insured and upon failure to pay a premium when due, is continued as paid-up insurance. (A lesser value than the original protection guaranteed by the policy.)

average-daily-balance method of computing interest Interest is charged on the average daily balance outstanding. The average balance is calculated by adding the balances outstanding each day and dividing by the number of days in the billing month. Payments made during the billing month reduce the average balance outstanding.

balanced mutual fund   A mutual fund that invests in both stocks and bonds.

balance sheet   A listing of what a person or business owns and owes at a certain point in a certain time period. It has three categories: assets, liabilities, and net worth.

bank credit cards   Credit cards issued by banks. The most widely used ones are MasterCard and VISA.

bankruptcy   A legal procedure that allows a person or an organization to give up certain assets in return for release from certain financial obligations.

bear   A person who believes stock prices will go down; a "bear market" is a market of declining prices.

beneficiary   The individual or organization that receives the proceeds of a life insurance policy when the insured dies. The primary beneficiary has the first right to proceeds, and contingent beneficiaries receive the proceeds if the primary beneficiary is no longer living.

bid and asked   The bid is the highest price anyone has declared willing to pay for a security at a given time; the asked is the lowest price anyone will take at the same time. In mutual fund shares, bid price means the net asset value per share, less a nominal redemption charge in a few instances. The asked price means the net asset value per share plus any sales charge. It is often called the "offering price."

blue chip stocks   Stock of highly stable and financially strong firms.

bond mutual fund   A mutual fund that emphasizes safety and invests in high-grade bonds.

bonds   A bond is essentially an IOU. The person who invests money in a bond is lending a company or government a sum of money for a specified time, with the understanding that the borrower will pay it back and pay interest for using it.

book value   The book value of a firm is equal to its total assets minus total liabilities.

budgeting   A system of record keeping involving detailed planning to account for all incomes and expenses.

bull   A person who believes stock prices will rise; a "bull market" is one with rising prices.

business risk   Risk associated with changes in the firm's sales.

buying on margin   The investor borrows a portion of funds from the brokerage house to buy securities.

call loan   A loan that may be terminated, or "called," at any time by the lender or borrower.

cancellation clause   A unilateral clause in a lease or purchase and sale that terminates an agreement.

capital gain   Income that results from the sale of an asset not in the usual course of business.

capital improvement   Any structure erected as a permanent improvement to real estate, usually extending the useful life and increasing value of property. (The replacement of a roof would be considered a capital improvement.)

capital loss A loss from the sale of an asset not in the usual course of business.

cash surrender value The amount available in cash upon voluntary termination of a policy before it becomes payable by death or maturity.

closed-end investment company A mutual fund that invests in the shares of other companies. There are a fixed number of shares, and shares are available in the market only if original investors are willing to sell them.

closing The culmination of a real estate purchase and sale when the title passes and certain financial transactions occur.

closing costs Costs paid at closing, such as operating cost adjustments, legal and financial expenses, brokerage commissions, and transfer taxes.

closing date The date upon which the buyer takes over the property.

collateral Property, or evidence of it, deposited with a creditor to guarantee the payment of a loan.

commission With respect to insurance policies, usually means a percentage of the premium paid to an agent as remuneration for services; for stocks or real estate, a sum due a broker for services in that capacity.

common stock Evidence of an ownership interest in a corporation.

common stock mutual fund A mutual fund that invests in the common shares of properties.

community property Property owned in common or held together by husband and wife within the statutes of certain states.

conditional sales contract A sales contract in which title to the goods remains with the lender, while the buyer has physical possession of them. The title goes to the buyer when the loan is repaid. This type of contract is often used with items such as appliances and furniture.

condominium ownership A form of ownership wherein a multi-unit building is divided so that each owner has individual ownership of his unit and joint ownership in the common areas of the buildings and grounds. Condominiums are frequently used for residential housing and sometimes for office space. In addition to the initial purchase price, each owner in a condominium is liable on an annual basis for a predetermined portion of the expenses of maintaining the common areas.

contingency fund A fund that provides cash to be used if an emergency arises.

conventional mortgage A mortgage that is not insured by the FHA or guaranteed by the VA.

conversion A right to change from a term insurance policy to a whole life policy without a medical examination. This feature is also called a convertability option.

conversion price The price of common stock at which a convertible security can be converted.

convertible A bond, debenture, or preferred share that may be exchanged for other stock in a company.

cooperative ownership A method of indirectly owning a unit in a multi-unit property through a cooperation. A specially created legal corporation owns the building completely. Each shareholder of that corporation owns a predetermined number of shares that entitle him to a long-term lease on a specific apartment. After paying for the purchase of his shares, each shareholder is liable for an annual maintenance charge to support the basic services and debt financing in the multi-unit building.

corporate bonds Debt securities issued by corporations.

cost index An index developed by the insurance industry allowing you to compare different policy costs. A surrender cost index is used to determine the value of your policy if you decide to terminate coverage. A net payment cost index determines the value of your policy assuming you do not surrender the policy and take the cash value.

coupon interest Refers to the rate of interest on bonds implied by the annual dollar amount of interest paid and the bond's face value.

credit card A bank card (e.g., VISA, MasterCard) that allows purchases or cash advances on "open-account" credit up to your credit limit.

credit life insurance Term insurance designed to pay off the remaining balance on a loan in case of the borrower's death.

creditor A person, group, or company that extends credit; one to whom a borrower owes money.

credit union An institution whose depositors are also its owners. It lends money only to its owners.

cumulative preferred stocks Preferred stock that requires that any dividends missed be paid before dividends can be paid on common stock.

current yield For a bond, its annual interest divided by its current market price.

custodianship account for minors An account set up for a child in the form of gifts (the gifts cannot exceed $30,000) and managed by an adult other than the grantor.

debenture A bond not secured by liens against specific assets of the firm.

debit card Like a credit card, except purchases are deducted from your checking account—there is no "line of credit."

debt consolidation loan A loan that is taken out to repay debts outstanding. One loan payment is substituted for many debt payments.

declarations section of an insurance policy The section that contains the basic identifying details of the policy. It consists of the name of the policy owner, what is insured, the amount of insurance, the cost of the policy, and the time period covered by the insurance.

declination The rejection of an application for life insurance, usually for reasons of the health or occupation of the applicant.

decreasing term life insurance Insurance in which the amount of benefits declines over the life of the policy.

deductible clause A clause in an insurance policy that allows the insured to retain the loss equal to the deductible amount.

deed A legal document transferring title from owner to buyer, typically recorded with the clerk of the county in which the property is located.

deed restrictions Limitations placed on the use of the real property through deed covenants such as land coverage, setback requirements, architectural approval, or construction timing.

demand deposit An account in a bank or other financial institution subject to withdrawal by check.

depreciation The decline in value of property due to normal wear and tear.

disability waver premium   A guarantee that premiums will be paid on your policy should you become disabled.

discount broker   A firm that processes securities transactions for relatively low commissions.

diversification   Spreading one's investments among the companies in different industries. A company producing various lines of products is also considered diversified.

dividend   In insurance, the part of the premium returned to you after the company pays its expenses. Dividends are paid only on participating term or whole life policies. For stocks, a dividend is usually paid quarterly, distributing some portion of earnings to shareholders.

dividend payout ratio   Dividends per share of stock divided by earnings per share.

dividend yield   Dividends per share of stock times 100 percent divided by the market value of a share.

dollar cost averaging (DCA)   Buying a fixed dollar amount of securities at regular intervals. Under this system the investor buys by the dollars' worth rather than by the number of shares. DCA can be an effective way to limit risk while building assets in stock and mutual funds.

double indemnity   An optional life insurance clause that provides payment of twice the face amount of the policy in death benefits if the insured is killed in an accident.

Dow Jones Industrial Average   Daily index of stock prices of thirty large industrial corporations; a popular measure of the stock market's performance.

down payment   The amount of money that the buyer puts up toward the purchase of a house, car, or other asset; does not include closing costs.

earnings per share   Net income divided by shares of the stock outstanding.

effective rate, annual or monthly   The finance charge as a percentage per unit of time of the average unpaid balance of the credit contract during its scheduled life. Also called actual rate or annual effective rate.

endorsement (insurance)   A statement attached to an insurance policy, changing the terms of the policy.

endowment life insurance   A life insurance policy that is fully paid up (endowed) after either a specified time period or when the insured attains a certain age.

Equal Credit Opportunity Act of 1975   Prohibits credit discrimination on the basis of sex or marital status.

equity   The interest in or value of a property or estate that belongs to an owner, over and above the liens against it; asset value minus liabilities.

escalator clause   A contract or lease clause providing for adjustment of payments in the event of certain specified contingencies such as an increase in real estate taxes or certain operating expenses.

escrow account   Most mortgage lenders require that borrowers make monthly payments equal to one-twelfth of anticipated real estate taxes and insurance into this account. This assures the lender that there are funds from which the taxes and insurance can be paid.

estate   All a person's assets, including the appropriate portion of any jointly owned property.

estate building   Accumulating or saving wealth.

estate planning The systematic accumulation, management, and transfer of a person's estate to achieve family goals.

estate taxes Taxes levied on the transfer of estates that are larger than a certain specified sum.

evidence of insurability Evidence of your health that helps the insurer decide if you are an acceptable risk.

exclusive agency An agreement of employment of a broker to the exclusion of all other brokers; if sale is made by any other broker during term of employment, the broker holding exclusive agency is entitled to commissions in addition to the commissions payable to the broker who effected the transaction.

executor A person or a corporate entity or any other type of organization named or designed in a will to carry out its provisions as to the disposition of the estate of a deceased person.

Federal Deposit Insurance Corporation (FDIC) A government agency that provides insurance for accounts held at banks; most banks carry FDIC insurance.

Federal Housing Authority (FHA) A government agency that provides mortgage loan insurance to financial institutions.

fiduciary A person who on behalf of or for the benefit of another individual transacts business or manages financial assets; such relationship implies great confidence and trust.

finance charge The dollar charge or charges for consumer credit.

finder's fee In real estate, a payment made for aid in obtaining a mortgage loan or for locating a property or tenant.

foreclosure The procedure through which property pledged as security for a debt is "repossessed" and sold to secure payment of the debt in event of default in payment or terms. The rights of debtors and creditors in foreclosure vary from state to state.

grace period Additional time allowed to perform an act or make a payment before a default occurs. In insurance, a period of time where if the premium is not paid, it is still in effect with or without penalty conditions. Generally in insurance the grace period is thirty-one days after the premium due date. Some credit cards have a twenty-five-day grace period to avoid finance charges.

growth stock Stock that is characterized by the prospect of its increase in earnings and in market value rather than by the cash dividends it earns for the stockholder.

guaranteed insurability clause A provision allowing policyholders to purchase additional insurance without having to pass a physical examination.

home loan A real estate loan for which the security is a residential property; in Federal Home Loan Bank Board statistics, a loan on a residential structure housing one to four families.

homeowners' form 2 (HO-2) Also known as the basic form of homeowner's insurance. It covers certain perils such as fire, lightning, explosion, riots, vandalism, and theft.

homeowners' form 3 (HO-3) Also known as the special form of homeowner's insurance. It covers a wide variety of perils.

homeowners' warranty (HOW) program Builders in this program guarantee that their workmanship, materials, and construction are up to established standards.

"house poor" Buying more house than one can afford to buy.
income bond A corporate bond that pays interest only if corporate earnings reach a specified level.
income shifting The process of transferring income from a high-income taxpayer to a lower-income taxpayer or from a high-tax year to a low-tax year.
incontestability In insurance, a provision that the payment of the claim may not be disputed by the company for any cause whatsoever except for nonpayment of premium. A life insurance policy in force for at least two years cannot be contested.
insurance, paid-up Insurance on which there remain no further premiums to be paid.
interest In practice, a payment for the use of money.
interest rate The percentage of a sum of money charged for its use.
intestacy The condition resulting from a person's dying without leaving a valid will.
investor An individual whose principal concerns in the purchase of a security are regular dividend income, safety of the original investment, and, if possible, capital appreciation. (See **speculator**.)
joint account A checking or savings account in the name of two or more persons. There are two types of joint accounts. One type allows any owner to withdraw funds. The other type requires the permission of all owners before funds can be withdrawn.
joint and survivorship annuity An annuity that continues payment to a secondary beneficiary if the primary one dies; this annuity guarantees income for life to the surviving beneficiary.
joint ownership Two or more persons jointly own the property in question. It is in three forms: (1) joint tenancy; (2) tenancy in common; (3) tenancy by the entirety.
joint tenancy A type of ownership wherein property is held by two or more persons together, with the distinct character of survivorship. In other words, during the life of both, they have equal rights to use the property and share in any benefits from it. Upon the death of either, the property automatically passes to the survivor(s).
junk bonds Bonds that investment advisors consider to be risky investments.
Keogh plan A retirement plan limited to self-employed individuals.
landlord One who rents property to another.
lapse The voidance of a policy, in whole or in part, by the nonpayment of a premium or installment on a premium date.
lease A contract, written or oral, between owner and tenant for the possession and use of land and/or improvements, and for rent or other income and other conditions of occupancy.
lease-option A lease written in conjunction with an option agreement, wherein the payments may be credited toward the purchase price if the option is exercised.
lessee The party contracting to use the property under a lease.
lessor The owner who contracts to allow property to be used under a lease.
lien A legal encumbrance upon a property interest created to ensure repayment of a debt or discharge of obligation.
limited payment whole life insurance Life insurance requiring premiums to be paid only for a specific time period but remaining in force after the payment period is over (e.g., twenty-pay life).
limited warranty A guarantee that is much more restrictive than a full warranty.

liquid assets Cash and other investments that can be converted into cash quickly, such as money in checking and savings accounts.

liquidity The cash position measured by the cash on hand and assets quickly convertible into cash.

listed stock The stock of a company traded on a securities exchange for which a listing application and a registration statement, giving detailed information about the company and its operations, have been filed with the Securities and Exchange Commission, unless otherwise exempted, and the exchange itself.

listing agreement A written employment contract between a property owner and a real estate broker whereby the agent is authorized to sell or lease certain property within specified terms and conditions.

load The portion of the offering price of shares of open-end investment (mutual fund) companies that covers sales commissions and all other costs of distribution. The load normally is incurred only on purchase. Some funds also charge a "back-end" load or "redemption charge" when the shares are sold, or an annual "12b-1" charge.

loading That addition to the net insurance premium that is necessary (1) to cover the policy's proportionate share in the expense of operating the company and (2) to provide a fund deemed sufficient to cover contingencies.

loan value The amount of money that can be borrowed from the insurance company, using the policy's cash value as collateral.

market value The highest price that a buyer, willing but not compelled to buy, would pay, and the lowest a seller, willing but not compelled to sell, would accept.

maturity The time at which a bond or insurance policy is due and payable. In insurance, the date at which the face value of an endowment policy is paid to the insured of still living.

mortality The statistical measure of the probability of death at each age group. The same age groups can have different rates depending on the amount of group risk. For example, a lower rate is charged a twenty-five-year-old nonsmoking male than a twenty-five-year-old male who uses tobacco.

mortality rate (death rate) The ratio of those who die at a stated age to the total number who are exposed to the risk of death at that age per year.

mortgage A legal document pledging a described property for the performance of promise to repay a loan under certain terms and conditions. The law provides procedures for foreclosure. The notations "first," "second," and so forth refer to the priority of the liens, with the lower number representing greater security for the mortgage holder. A direct-reduction mortgage involves a constant periodic payment that will eventually repay the entire loan, providing a specified return to the mortgagee.

mortgagee The party who lends money and takes a mortgage to secure the payment thereof.

mortgagor The person who borrows money and gives a mortgage on the person's property as security for the payment of the debt.

multiple listing An arrangement among Real Estate Board of Exchange members whereby each broker presents the broker's listings to the attention of the other members so that if a sale results, the commission is divided between the broker bringing the listing and the broker making the sale.

mutual wills Separate wills made by two or more persons (usually but not necessarily husband and wife) containing similar provisions in favor of each other or of the same beneficiary.

national charge cards Examples are American Express, Diners Club, and Carte Blance. They are very similar to bank credit cards in use except that (1) while bank cards are sometimes free, national cards charge an annual fee; (2) national cards do not offer revolving credit as bank cards do; and (3) banks cards are accepted by substantially more businesses than are national cards.

negative cash flow Situation when cash inflows are less than cash outflows.

net asset value of a mutual fund The value of one share of a mutual fund. It is equal to the fund's total market value, less its liabilities, divided by the number of its shares outstanding.

net cost In insurance, the total gross premiums paid, less total dividends credited for a given period.

net surrendered cost The total gross premiums paid, less the total dividends credited for the given period and the surrender or cash value of the policy, plus the surrender charge (if any) for an insurance policy.

net worth What a person or business would own after paying off all liabilities. Assets minus liabilities equals net worth. The same as "equity."

no-fault insurance A form of automobile insurance where the insured collects from his own company regardless of who was at fault.

no-loan mutual fund A mutual fund that does not charge a sales commission on the sale of its stock.

nominal interest rate The stated or advertised interest rate.

noncontributory pension plan A pension plan in which the employee does not make any contributions. Military retirement is an example.

nonforfeiture provisions Provisions whereby, after the payment of a given number of premiums, the contract may not be completely forfeited because of nonpayment of a subsequent premium but is held good for some value in cash, paid-up insurance, or extended term insurance. These values are usually stipulated in a table printed in the policy. One of the two latter options is usually effective automatically; any other option is generally available only upon surrender of the policy.

notary public A public officer who is authorized to take acknowledgments to certain classes of documents, such as deeds, contracts, or mortgages, and before whom affidavits may be sworn.

note A legal document in which the borrower promises to repay the loan under agreed-upon terms.

NOW account (negotiable order of withdrawal) Equivalent to checking accounts paying interest on the funds on deposit. Also, super-NOW account.

odd lot An amount of stock less than the established 100-share unit of trading: from one to ninety-nine shares for the great majority of issues.

offer An initial, brief written contract submitted by a potential buyer of real estate for approval by the seller, giving the price and limited other details.

open-end investment company A company, popularly known as a mutual fund, issuing redeemable shares, that is, shares that normally must be liquidated by the fund on demand of the shareholders. Such companies continuously offer new shares to investors.

open-end mortgage   A mortgage under which the mortgaged property stands as security not only for the original loan but for the future advances the lender may be willing to make. Similar to a home equity line of credit.

open listing   A listing given to any number of brokers without liability to compensate any except the one who first secures a buyer ready, willing, and able to meet the terms of the listing, or secures the acceptance by the seller of a satisfactory offer; the sale of the property automatically terminates the listing.

option   A legal agreement that permits the holder for a consideration to buy, sell, or otherwise obtain or dispose of a property interest within a specified time on specified terms described in the agreement.

over-the-counter   A market for securities made up of securities dealers who may not be members of a securities exchange. Thousands of companies have insufficient shares outstanding, stockholders, or earnings to warrant listing on a stock exchange. Securities of these companies are traded in the over-the-counter market between dealers and customers. The over-the-counter market is the chief market for U.S. government bonds, municipal bonds, and bank and insurance stock. NASDAQ is an organized, computerized OTC market handling a large number of stocks.

"paid-up" limited payment whole life insurance   Life insurance for which payments are made until the policy holder achieves a target age, after which the policy becomes "paid up."

participating preferred stock   A preferred stock that shares with common stock in exceptionally large corporate earnings, thus getting a rate higher than the stated maximum rate.

personal property   Property that is not attached to land, such as furniture, appliances, clothing, and other personal belongings.

points   A loan fee charged by lenders. Each point equals 1 percent of the amount of the loan. Points are payable up front and add to the effective cost of a loan.

policy   The life insurance contract between the life insurance company and the owner of the policy. The policy outlines the terms and conditions for both the company and the policyholder.

policy, installment   A contract under which the sum insured is payable in a given number of equal annual installments.

policy, joint life   A policy under which the company agrees to pay the amount of insurance at the death of the first of two or more designated persons.

policy, limited payment   A policy that stipulates that only a limited number of premiums are to be paid.

policy loan   A loan made to the policyholder by the insurance company based upon the cash value in a whole life or other permanent insurance policy.

policy, nonparticipating   A policy that is not entitled to receive dividends. Such a policy is usually written at a lower rate of premium than a corresponding participating policy.

policy, participating   A policy that participates (receives dividends) in the surplus as determined and apportioned by the company.

policy year The year beginning with the due date of an annual premium.

portfolio Holdings of securities by an individual or institution. A portfolio may contain bonds, preferred stocks, and common stocks of various types of enterprises. A more expanded definition would include holdings of all forms of investment wealth.

postdated check A check that has a date on it that is later than the date on which it was written.

power of attorney A written instrument duly signed and executed by an owner of property that authorizes an agent to act on behalf of the owner to the extent indicated in the instrument.

premium A stated sum charge by a company in return for insurance. It may be payable in a single sum or in a limited number of payments, or periodically throughout the duration of the policy.

premium, level A premium of a fixed and uniform amount, in lieu of a varying or increasing premium.

prepayment clause A clause in a consumer loan contract that provides for a refund to a debtor who chooses to repay an installment account early. Or a clause in a mortgage that gives a mortgagor the privilege of paying the mortgage indebtedness before it becomes due.

property Real property consists of land and, generally, whatever is erected or growing upon or affixed to it, including rights issuing out of, annexed to, and exercisable within or about the same. (See **personal property**.)

prospectus The official circular that describes the shares of a company and offers them for sale. It contains definitive details concerning the company issuing the shares, the determination of the price at which the shares are offered to the public, and so on, as required by the Securities and Exchange Commission's rules.

purchase and sales agreement A legal contract between buyer and seller of real estate that details the terms of the transaction.

rating The basis for an additional charge to the standard premium because the person to be insured is a greater than normal risk. A rating can result from anything from a dangerous occupation to poor health.

real estate investment trust (REIT) Similar to a closed-end investment company; specializes in buying real estate properties.

real estate syndicate A partnership formed for participation in a real estate venture. Partners may be limited or unlimited in their liability.

real property Land, buildings, and other kinds of property that legally are classified as real, as opposed to personal property.

Realtor A coined word that may be used only by an active member of a local real estate board affiliated with the National Association of Real Estate Boards.

redlining The refusal to lend money or issue insurance within a specific area for various reasons. This practice is illegal.

reduced paid-up insurance A form of insurance available as a nonforfeiture option. It provides for continuation of the original insurance plan, but for a reduced amount, and no further premiums.

reinstatement Restoring a lapsed policy by paying all unpaid premiums and charges by the policyholder.

renewable term insurance Term insurance that can be renewed at the end of the term, at the option of the policyholder and without evidence of insurability, for a limited number of successive terms. The rates increase at each renewal as the age of the insured increases.

rent The payment for use of someone else's property; the compensation paid for the use of real estate.

reserve (policy reserves) The amount that an insurance company allocates specifically for the fulfillment of its policy obligations. Reserves are so calculated that, together with future premiums and interest earnings, they will enable the company to pay all future claims.

retained earnings On an income statement, changes in retained earnings come from net income minus dividends paid for the year. On the balance sheet, this is cumulated from year to year.

retirement To give up one's work or business, especially because of age.

revenue bonds Municipal bonds backed by special sources of income.

reverse annuity mortgage Contract under which a homeowner can receive monthly income by borrowing against the equity in a home.

revocable trust A trust that is controlled by the grantor and can be revoked by him or her.

revolving credit A continuing credit arrangement between seller and buyer in which the buyer (1) agrees to make monthly payments equal to a stipulated percentage of the amount owed at the start of the month plus interest and (2) is permitted to make additional credit purchases as long as the total debt owed does not exceed an agreed-upon limit.

rider Any additional agreement to the insurance policy usually adding a benefit at an additional cost. A rider becomes part of the insurance policy.

rights or warrants When a company wants to raise more funds by issuing additional stock, it may give its stockholders the opportunity, ahead of others, to buy the new stock. The piece of paper evidencing this privilege is called a right or warrant. Because the additional stock is usually offered to stockholders below the market price, rights ordinarily have a market value of their own and are actively traded. Failure to exercise or sell rights may result in actual loss to the holder.

round lot A unit of trading or a multiple thereof. On the New York Stock Exchange the unit of trading is generally 100 shares in stock and $100,000 par value in the case of bonds.

sale-leaseback A transaction in which the vendor simultaneously executes a lease and retains occupancy of the property concurrently sold.

sales charge The amount charged in connection with the distribution to the public of mutual fund shares. It is added to the net asset value per share in the determination of the offering price and is paid to the dealer and underwriter. Also called a "load."

sales contract A contract by which the buyer and seller agree to terms of sale.

savings Amount of income not spent.

savings account An interest-bearing liability of a bank, redeemable in money on demand or after due notice, not transferable by check.

savings and loan associations   Financial institutions that have historically specialized in offering savings accounts and in providing mortgage funds.
savings banks   Located in New England and eastern states, these banks provides services very similar to services provided by commercial banks.
secondary financing   A loan secured by a mortgage or trust deed that is secured by a lien subordinate to that of another instrument.
secondary markets   Buying and selling of securities that takes place between investors.
second mortgage   A mortgage next in priority to a first mortgage.
secured installment loans   Loans that are backed up by collateral; examples are loans for cars, home improvements, boats, furniture, appliances, and other durable goods.
securities   Literally, things given, deposited, or pledged to assure the fulfillment of an obligation. In this narrow sense a mortgage is a security, but the term is now generally used in a broader sense to include stock as well as bonds, notes, and other evidences of indebtedness.
Securities Exchange Commission (SEC)   A federal agency that oversees securities trading.
Securities Investor Protection Corporation (SIPC)   A federal agency that insures investors' accounts at brokerage houses.
securities markets   Places or networks where stocks, bonds, and other financial instruments are traded.
selling short   Selling borrowed securities with the expectation of buying them back later at a lower price.
Series EE bond   A nonnegotiable U.S. savings bond. Interest on these bonds is received only upon redemption.
Series HH bond   A nonnegotiable U.S. savings bond that pays periodic interest, can be redeemed after six months, and has a maturity period of ten years.
service contract   An agreement purchased by an appliance owner to keep the appliance in working order.
simple-interest method   A computation method where the finance charge for a given month of an installment contract equals the monthly rate times the loan balance at the end of each month.
single-premium deferred annuity   An insurance product with a large up-front payment to provide for retirement income and tax savings for high-bracket taxpayers.
speculator   One willing to assume a relatively large risk in the hope of gain. His principal concern is to increase his capital rather than his dividend income. Safety of principal is a secondary factor. (See **investor**.)
Standard & Poors 500 (S&P500)   An index of 500 large stocks, a broad measure of the stock market's performance.
stock dividend   A dividend payable in stock rather than cash.
subletting   A leasing by a tenant to another, who holds under the tenant.
suicide clause   A provision in a life insurance contract that cancels the proceeds from a policy should the insured commit suicide within two years of taking out a life insurance policy. Illegal in some states.

surrender (cash) value The amount the insurer will pay the policyholder if the life insurance policy is canceled. Term insurance polices have no surrender value.

survey The process by which a parcel of land is measured and its area ascertained; also the blueprint showing the measurements, boundaries, and area.

tenancy in common The means of holding property by two or more persons, each of whom has an undivided interest. The undivided interest passes to the owner's estate and heirs rather than to the surviving tenants in common in event of the owner's death.

tenant One who is given possession of real estate for a fixed period or at will.

term policy An insurance policy that provides that the amount of the policy shall be payable only in event of death within a specified term.

testamentary trust A trust that is created by placing an appropriately worded clause in the testator's will. The clause places the trust principal under the trustee's control on the testator's death.

testator A person who has made and left a valid will at death.

time deposit account A savings account in which the account owner receives interest but cannot withdraw funds prior to maturity without a penalty.

time-share homes The buyer buys the use of the house for a short time period. The time varies from one week to six months.

title The right to ownership of a property.

title abstract A history of the ownership of the property.

title insurance A policy of insurance that indemnifies the holder for loss sustained by reason of defects in the title.

title search An examination of the public records to determine the ownership and encumbrances affecting real property.

traveler's checks Checks that are readily accepted as payment because the person must buy them in order to use them. They are safer to carry than cash as they can be replaced if stolen.

trust A fiduciary relationship in which one person (the trustee) is the holder of the legal title to property (the trust property) subject to an obligation to keep or use the property for the benefit of another person.

trustee A person who manages a trust.

trustor A person who establishes a trust.

underwrite The insurance company's decision on whether you qualify for life insurance based on reviews of your occupation, health, age, and so on. Also means the sale of original securities in the primary market.

usury Claiming a rate of interest in excess of that permitted by statute.

value averaging An accumulation method, like dollar-cost averaging, where you make periodic securities transactions to keep the value of your portfolio increasing at a preset target rate. See chapter 14.

variable annuity An annuity in which the dollar amount of benefits depends on the investment performance of the insurance company's fund managers.

variable rate mortgage A mortgage loan for which interest rates are not fixed. The rate applicable to the mortgage goes up or down as interest rates in general go up or down.

vesting The gaining of rights by a worker to the pension contributions made by an employer on the worker's behalf.

waiver-of-premium clause A provision committing the life insurance company to make premium payments for a policyholder who suffers an injury or illness causing a disability.

warranty The consumer's assurance that the product will work as it is supposed to. They are guarantees issued by manufacturers or suppliers of goods and services that explain their obligation and, generally, the user's or buyer's responsibilities also.

warranty deed The safest deed for the buyer, since it guarantees that title is free of any legal claims. There are two kinds of warranty deeds, general warranty deeds and special warranty deeds. A general warranty deed contains a promise by the grantor to "defend the property against every person or persons whomsoever"; in other words, it is a promise of protection against the whole world. A special warranty deed contains the more limited promise "to defend the property against every person or persons whomsoever lawfully claiming the same or any part thereof by, from, through, or under him." In other words, it is a promise to protect against the grantor, his heirs, or his assigns.

whole life insurance Life insurance that remains in force as long as the insured continues to pay the insurance premiums. The premiums remain level and fixed as long as the policy remains in force and the excess premiums collected in the early years of the policy's life accumulate interest as "cash value."

will A legally enforceable declaration of a person's wishes in writing regarding matters to be attended to after his death and inoperative until his death. A will usually relates to the testator's property, is revocable or amendable up to the time of his death, and is applicable to the situation that exists at the time of his death.

"window sticker" price Lists the manufacturer's suggested list price for a car and the itemized prices of the options.

yield The dividends or interest paid expressed as a percentage of the current price or, if you own the security, of the price you originally paid.

zero bracket amount An amount of income, based on filing status, below which a taxpayer does not have to pay taxes.

Appendix C

Military Pay, Benefit, and Entitlement Tables

C-1   Monthly Basic Pay, Officers
C-2   Monthly Basic Pay, Enlisted Members
C-3   Reserve Drill Pay, Officers
C-4   Reserve Drill Pay, Enlisted Members
C-5   Monthly Basic Allowance for Quarters
C-6   Other Special and Incentive Pay Categories
C-7   Aviation Career Incentive Pay
C-8   Aviation Crew Member Hazardous Duty Incentive Pay
C-9   Air Weapons Controller Pay
C-10 Career Sea Pay
C-11 Submarine Pay
C-12 Medical Officers' Special Pays
C-13 Dental Officers' Special Pays
C-14 Dependency and Indemnity Compensation (DIC) Monthly Payments to Surviving Spouses

TABLE C-1
Monthly Basic Pay, Officers
(Effective January 1, 1994)

YEARS OF COMMISSIONED SERVICE

Grade	Under 2	2	3	4	6	8	10	12	14	16	18	20	22	24	26
\multicolumn{16}{c}{COMMISSIONED OFFICERS}
O-10	6801.60	7040.70	7040.70	7040.70	7040.70	7311.00	7311.00	7716.00	7716.00	8267.70	8267.70	8821.50	8821.50	8821.50	9371.10
O-9	6027.90	6185.70	6317.40	6317.40	6317.40	6478.20	6478.20	6747.60	6747.60	7311.00	7311.00	7716.00	7716.00	7716.00	8267.70
O-8	5459.70	5623.50	5756.70	5756.70	5756.70	6185.70	6185.70	6478.20	6478.20	6747.60	7040.70	7311.00	7491.30	7491.30	7491.30
O-7	4536.60	4845.00	4845.00	4845.00	5062.20	5062.20	5355.60	5355.60	5623.50	6185.70	6611.10	6611.10	6611.10	6611.10	6611.10
O-6	3362.40	3694.20	3936.30	3936.30	3936.30	3936.30	3936.30	3936.30	4070.10	4713.60	4954.20	5062.20	5355.60	5536.80	5808.60
O-5	2689.20	3157.50	3375.90	3375.90	3375.90	3375.90	3478.20	3665.40	3911.10	4203.90	4444.50	4579.50	4739.40	4739.40	4739.40
O-4	2266.80	2760.30	2944.50	2944.50	2999.10	3131.40	3345.30	3533.10	3694.20	3856.50	3962.70	3962.70	3962.70	3962.70	3962.70
O-3	2106.30	2355.30	2517.90	2785.80	2919.00	3023.70	3187.50	3345.30	3427.20	3427.20	3427.20	3427.20	3427.20	3427.20	3427.20
O-2	1836.90	2005.80	2410.20	2491.20	2542.80	2542.80	2542.80	2542.80	2542.80	2542.80	2542.80	2542.80	2542.80	2542.80	2542.80
O-1	1594.80	1659.90	2005.80	2005.80	2005.80	2005.80	2005.80	2005.80	2005.80	2005.80	2005.80	2005.80	2005.80	2005.80	2005.80
\multicolumn{16}{c}{COMMISSIONED OFFICERS WITH MORE THAN FOUR YEARS ACTIVE DUTY AS ENLISTED OR WARRANT OFFICERS}
O-3E	0.00	0.00	0.00	0.00	2785.80	2919.00	3023.70	3187.50	3345.30	3478.20	3478.20	3478.20	3478.20	3478.20	3478.20
O-2E	0.00	0.00	0.00	0.00	2491.20	2542.80	2623.50	2760.30	2866.20	2944.50	2944.50	2944.50	2944.50	2944.50	2944.50
O-1E	0.00	0.00	0.00	0.00	2005.80	2143.20	2222.10	2302.50	2382.60	2491.20	2491.20	2491.20	2491.20	2491.20	2491.20
\multicolumn{16}{c}{WARRANT OFFICERS}
W-5	0.00	0.00	0.00	0.00	0.00	0.00	0.00	0.00	0.00	0.00	0.00	3662.70	3801.60	3911.40	4076.10
W-4	2146.20	2302.50	2302.50	2355.30	2462.40	2570.70	2678.70	2866.20	2999.10	3104.40	3187.50	3290.40	3400.50	3506.40	3665.40
W-3	1950.60	2115.90	2115.90	2143.20	2168.10	2326.80	2462.40	2542.80	2623.50	2701.80	2785.80	2894.40	2999.10	2999.10	3104.40
W-2	1708.50	1848.30	1848.30	1902.00	2005.80	2115.90	2196.30	2276.70	2355.30	2438.10	2517.90	2597.10	2701.80	2701.80	2701.80
W-1	1423.20	1632.00	1632.00	1768.20	1848.30	1927.50	2005.80	2088.90	2168.10	2248.80	2326.80	2410.20	2410.20	2410.20	2410.20

Monthly Basic Allowance for Subsistence: $142.46

Note: Basic pay is limited to $9,016.80 per month by level V of the executive pay schedule

TABLE C-2
Monthly Basic Pay, Enlisted Members
(Effective January 1, 1994)

YEARS OF SERVICE

Pay Grade	Under 2	2	3	4	6	8	10	12	14	16	18	20	22	24	26
E-9	0.00	0.00	0.00	0.00	0.00	0.00	2496.90	2552.70	2610.60	2670.60	2730.30	2783.40	2929.20	3043.20	3214.20
E-8	0.00	0.00	0.00	0.00	0.00	2093.70	2153.70	2210.40	2267.70	2327.70	2381.10	2439.60	2582.70	2697.90	2870.40
E-7	1461.60	1578.00	1636.20	1693.80	1751.40	1807.20	1865.10	1923.30	2010.30	2067.30	2124.60	2152.20	2296.80	2411.10	2582.70
E-6	1257.60	1370.70	1427.70	1488.60	1544.40	1599.90	1658.70	1744.20	1798.80	1857.00	1885.20	1885.20	1885.20	1885.20	1885.20
E-5	1103.40	1201.20	1259.70	1314.30	1401.00	1458.00	1515.60	1571.40	1599.90	1599.90	1599.90	1599.90	1599.90	1599.90	1599.90
E-4	1029.30	1087.20	1151.10	1239.90	1288.80	1288.80	1288.80	1288.80	1288.80	1288.80	1288.80	1288.80	1288.80	1288.80	1288.80
E-3	969.90	1023.00	1063.80	1105.80	1105.80	1105.80	1105.80	1105.80	1105.80	1105.80	1105.80	1105.80	1105.80	1105.80	1105.80
E-2	933.30	933.30	933.30	933.30	933.30	933.30	933.30	933.30	933.30	933.30	933.30	933.30	933.30	933.30	933.30
E-1	832.80	832.80	832.80	832.80	832.80	832.80	832.80	832.80	832.80	832.80	832.80	832.80	832.80	832.80	832.80
E-1 with less than 4 months	$770.10														

Basic Allowance for Subsistence:
On leave or granted permission to mess separately. $6.80 per day
When rations in kind are not available. $7.67 per day
When assigned to duty under emergency conditions where no government messing facilities are available. $10.16 per day

TABLE C-3
Reserve Drill Pay, Officers
(Effective January 1, 1994)

Below are the one-day drill rates. In general, a weekend drill is worth four one-day drills.

Pay Grade	Under 2	2	3	4	6	8	10	12	14	16	18	20	22	24	26
						COMMISSIONED OFFICERS									
O-10	226.72	234.69	234.69	234.69	234.69	243.70	243.70	257.20	257.20	275.59	275.59	294.05	294.05	294.05	312.37
O-9	200.93	206.19	210.58	210.58	210.58	215.94	215.94	224.92	224.92	243.70	243.70	257.20	257.20	257.20	275.59
O-8	181.99	187.45	191.89	191.89	191.89	206.19	206.19	215.94	215.94	224.92	234.69	243.70	249.71	249.71	249.71
O-7	151.22	161.50	161.50	161.50	168.74	168.74	178.52	178.52	187.45	206.19	220.37	220.37	220.37	220.37	220.37
O-6	112.08	123.14	131.21	131.21	131.21	131.21	131.21	131.21	135.67	157.12	165.14	168.74	178.52	184.56	193.62
O-5	89.64	105.25	112.53	112.53	112.53	112.53	115.94	122.18	130.37	140.13	148.15	152.65	157.98	157.98	157.98
O-4	75.56	92.01	98.15	98.15	99.97	104.38	111.50	117.77	123.14	128.55	132.09	132.09	132.09	132.09	132.09
O-3	70.21	78.51	83.93	92.86	97.30	100.79	106.25	111.50	114.24	114.24	114.24	114.24	114.24	114.24	114.24
O-2	61.23	66.86	80.34	83.04	84.76	84.76	84.76	84.76	84.76	84.76	84.76	84.76	84.76	84.76	84.76
O-1	53.16	55.33	66.86	66.86	66.86	66.86	66.86	66.86	66.86	66.86	66.86	66.86	66.86	66.86	66.86
			COMMISSIONED OFFICERS WITH MORE THAN FOUR YEARS ACTIVE DUTY AS ENLISTED OR WARRANT OFFICERS												
O-3E	0.00	0.00	0.00	0.00	97.30	100.79	106.25	111.50	115.94	115.94	115.94	115.94	115.94	115.94	115.94
O-2E	0.00	0.00	0.00	83.04	84.76	87.45	92.01	95.54	98.15	98.15	98.15	98.15	98.15	98.15	98.15
O-1E	0.00	0.00	0.00	66.86	71.44	74.07	76.75	79.42	83.04	83.04	83.04	83.04	83.04	83.04	83.04
						WARRANT OFFICERS									
W-5	0.00	0.00	0.00	0.00	0.00	0.00	0.00	0.00	0.00	0.00	0.00	122.09	126.72	130.38	135.87
W-4	71.54	76.75	76.75	78.51	82.08	85.69	89.29	95.54	99.97	103.48	106.25	109.68	113.35	116.88	122.18
W-3	65.02	70.53	70.53	71.44	72.27	77.56	82.08	84.76	87.45	90.06	92.86	96.48	99.97	99.97	103.48
W-2	56.95	61.61	61.61	63.40	66.86	70.53	73.21	75.89	78.51	81.27	83.93	86.57	90.06	90.06	90.06
W-1	47.44	54.40	54.40	58.94	61.61	64.25	66.86	69.63	72.27	74.96	77.56	80.34	80.34	80.34	80.34

TABLE C-4
Reserve Drill Pay, Enlisted Members
(Effective January 1, 1994)

Below are the one-day reserve drill rates. In general, a weekend drill is worth four one-day drills.

Pay Grade	Under 2	2	3	4	6	8	10	12	14	16	18	20	22	24	26
E-9	0.00	0.00	0.00	0.00	0.00	0.00	83.23	85.09	87.02	89.02	91.01	92.78	97.64	101.44	107.14
E-8	0.00	0.00	0.00	0.00	0.00	69.79	71.79	73.68	75.59	77.59	79.37	81.32	86.09	89.93	95.68
E-7	48.72	52.60	54.54	56.46	58.38	60.24	62.17	64.11	67.01	68.91	70.82	71.74	76.56	80.37	86.09
E-6	41.92	45.69	47.59	49.62	51.48	53.33	55.29	58.14	59.96	61.90	62.84	62.84	62.84	62.84	62.84
E-5	36.78	40.04	41.99	43.81	46.70	48.60	50.52	52.38	53.33	53.33	53.33	53.33	53.33	53.33	53.33
E-4	34.31	36.24	38.37	41.33	42.96	42.96	42.96	42.96	42.96	42.96	42.96	42.96	42.96	42.96	42.96
E-3	32.33	34.10	35.46	36.86	36.86	36.86	36.86	36.86	36.86	36.86	36.86	36.86	36.86	36.86	36.86
E-2	31.11	31.11	31.11	31.11	31.11	31.11	31.11	31.11	31.11	31.11	31.11	31.11	31.11	31.11	31.11
E-1	27.76	27.76	27.76	27.76	27.76	27.76	27.76	27.76	27.76	27.76	27.76	27.76	27.76	27.76	27.76
E-1 with less than 4 months	$25.67														

TABLE C-5
Monthly Basic Allowance for Quarters (1994)

	Rate with Dependents	Rate without Dependents
E-1	$320.10	$179.10
E-2	320.10	201.30
E-3	336.30	247.80
E-4	361.50	252.30
E-5	415.50	290.10
E-6	462.30	314.70
E-7	500.10	347.40
E-8	538.50	407.10
E-9	584.10	443.40
W-1	444.00	337.20
W-2	513.30	402.60
W-3	558.00	453.60
W-4	608.70	539.70
W-5	663.90	607.50
O1-E	510.00	378.30
O2-E	552.00	44.10
O3-E	611.70	517.50
O-1	434.40	320.10
O-2	486.30	380.10
O-3	569.40	479.40
O-4	687.90	598.20
O-5	780.30	645.30
O-6	809.70	670.20
O-7	899.10	730.50
O-8	899.10	730.50
O-9	899.10	730.50
O-10	899.10	730.50

TABLE C-6
Other Special and Incentive Pay Categories

All Servicemembers	
Hostile fire or imminent danger pay	$110/month
Incentive pay for hazardous duty (flying duty as non-crew member, parachute jumping, demolitions duty, handling toxic fuel, flight deck operations, experimental stress duty)	110/month
High altitude–low opening (HALO) pay	165/month
Foreign language proficiency pay (selected specialties)	25–100/month

Enlisted Members	
Special pay for diving duty-not to exceed $300 per month for master divers	
Foreign duty pay, E-7 through E-9	$22.50/month
E-6	20.00
E-5	16.00
E-4	13.00
E-3	9.00
E-1 through E-2	8.00

Officers

Special pay for Navy nuclear-qualified officers:
  Nuclear Career Accession Bonus: Not to exceed $8,000
  Continuation Pay for 3, 4, or 5-year period of obligated active service in an amount not to exceed $12,000 (not paid with nuclear career annual incentive bonus)
  Nuclear career incentive bonus: Not to exceed $10,000 for unrestricted line officers and $4,500 for limited duty officers and warrant officers (not paid with continuation pay)
Special pay for diving duty: Not to exceed $200/month

TABLE C-7
Aviation Career Incentive Pay

Monthly Rate	Years of Aviation Service as an officer*
Phase I	
$125	2 or less
156	over 2
188	over 3
206	over 4
650	over 6
Phase II	
$585	over 18
495	over 20
385	over 22
385	over 24
250	over 25
Warrant Officer	
$125	2 or less
156	over 2
188	over 3
206	over 4
650	over 6

*ACIP for officers in the grade of O-7 is limited $200 per month, and to $206 per month for officers in grade O-8 or above.

TABLE C-8
Aviation Crew Member
Hazardous Duty Incentive Pay

Pay Grade	Monthly
O-7–O-10	$110
O-6	250
O-5	250
O-4	225
O-3	175
O-2	150
O-1	125
W-4	250
W-3	175
W-2	150
W-1	125
E-9	200
E-8	200
E-7	200
E-6	175
E-5	150
E-4	125
E-3	110
E-2	110
E-1	110

TABLE C-9
Air Weapons Controller Pay

Years of Service as an Air Weapons Controller

Pay Grade	2 or Less	Over 2	Over 3	Over 4	Over 6	Over 8	Over 10	Over 12	Over 14	Over 16	Over 18	Over 20	Over 22	Over 24	Over 25
O-7	$200	$200	$200	$200	$200	$200	$200	$200	$200	$200	$200	$200	$200	$200	$110
O-6	225	250	300	325	350	350	350	350	350	350	350	300	250	250	225
O-5	200	250	300	325	350	350	350	350	350	350	350	300	250	250	225
O-4	175	225	275	300	350	350	350	350	350	350	350	300	250	250	225
O-3	125	156	188	206	350	350	350	350	350	350	300	275	250	225	200
O-2	125	156	188	206	250	300	300	300	300	300	275	245	210	200	180
O-1	125	156	188	206	250	250	250	250	250	250	245	210	200	180	150

TABLE C-10
Career Sea Pay

Pay Grade	Under 1	Over 1	Over 2	Over 3	Over 4	Over 5	Over 6	Over 7	Over 8	Over 9	Over 10	Over 11	Over 12	Over 13	Over 14	Over 15	Over 16	Over 17	Over 18	Over 19	Over 20
O-1				$150	$160	$185	$190	$195	$205	$215	$225	$225	$240	$240	$250	$250	$260	$260	$270	$270	$280
O-2				150	160	185	190	195	205	215	225	225	240	240	250	250	260	260	270	270	280
O-3				150	160	185	190	195	205	215	225	225	240	240	260	260	270	270	280	280	290
O-4				185	190	200	205	215	220	220	225	225	240	240	270	270	280	280	290	290	300
O-5				225	225	225	225	230	245	250	260	265	265	265	285	285	300	300	315	315	340
O-6				225	230	230	240	255	265	280	290	300	310	310	325	325	340	340	355	355	380
W-1	$130	$135	$140	150	170	175	200	250	270	300	325	325	340	340	360	360	375	375	375	375	375
W-2	150	150	150	150	170	260	265	265	270	310	340	340	375	375	400	400	400	400	400	400	400
W-3	150	150	150	150	170	270	280	285	290	310	350	375	400	400	425	425	425	425	450	450	450
W-4	150	150	150	150	170	290	310	310	310	310	350	375	400	400	450	450	450	450	500	500	500
E-4	50	60	120	150	160	160	160	160	160	160	160	160	160	160	160	160	160	160	160	160	160
E-5	50	60	120	150	170	315	325	350	350	350	350	350	350	350	350	350	350	350	350	350	350
E-6	100	100	120	150	170	315	325	350	350	365	365	365	380	395	410	410	425	425	450	450	450
E-7	100	100	120	175	190	350	350	375	390	400	400	410	420	450	475	475	500	500	500	500	500
E-8	100	100	120	175	190	350	350	375	390	400	400	410	420	450	475	475	500	500	520	520	520
E-9	100	100	120	175	190	350	350	375	390	400	400	410	420	450	475	475	520	520	520	520	520

Note: Grades E-1 through E-3 and O-7 through O-10 do not receive Career Sea Pay.

TABLE C-11
Submarine Pay

Pay Grade	Under 2	Over 2	Over 3	Over 4	Over 6	Over 8	Over 10	Over 12	Over 14	Over 16	Over 18	Over 20	Over 22	Over 26
\multicolumn{15}{l}{Officers: Years of Service as a Commissioned Officer}
O-1	$175	$175	$175	$175	$175	$175	$355	$355	$355	$355	$355	$355	$355	$355
O-2	235	235	235	235	235	235	355	355	355	355	355	355	355	355
O-3	355	355	355	390	595	595	595	595	595	595	595	595	595	595
O-4	365	365	365	405	595	595	595	595	595	595	595	595	595	595
O-5	595	595	595	595	595	595	595	595	595	595	595	595	595	595
O-6	595	595	595	595	595	595	595	595	595	595	595	595	595	595
O-7	355	355	355	355	355	355	355	355	355	540	535	535	410	355
O-8,9,10	355	355	355	355	355	355	355	355	355	355	355	355	355	355
\multicolumn{15}{l}{Warrant Officers: Years of Service as a Warrant Officer}
W-1-4	235	310	310	355	355	355	355	355	355	355	355	355	355	355
\multicolumn{15}{l}{Enlisted Members: Years of Accrued Submarine Service}
E-1	75	75	75	75	75	75	75	75	75	75	75	75	75	75
E-2	75	90	90	90	90	90	90	90	90	90	90	90	90	90
E-3	80	90	95	95	140	90	90	90	90	90	90	90	90	90
E-4	80	95	100	170	175	175	175	175	175	175	175	175	175	175
E-5	140	155	155	175	190	195	195	195	195	195	195	195	195	195
E-6	155	171	175	215	230	245	255	265	265	265	265	265	265	265
E-7	225	225	225	250	255	265	275	295	310	310	310	310	310	310
E-8	225	225	225	250	270	295	310	315	330	330	345	345	345	345
E-9	225	225	225	270	295	310	315	330	345	355	355	355	355	355

TABLE C-12
Medical Officers' Special Pays

Creditable Service	Variable Special Pay	Additional Special Pay	Board Certified Pay	Incentive Special Pay
		O-6 and Below		
Internship	$1,200	N/A	N/A	N/A
O-6 years	5,000	$15,000	$2,500	up to $36,000
6-8 years	12,000	15,000	2,500	up to $36,000
8-10 years	11,500	15,000	2,500	up to $36,000
10-12 years	11,000	15,000	3,500	up to $36,000
12-14 years	10,000	15,000	4,000	up to $36,000
14-18 years	9,000	15,000	5,000	up to $36,000
18-22 years	8,000	15,000	6,000	up to $36,000
Over 22 years	7,000	15,000	6,000	up to $36,000
		O-7 and Above		
Over 18 years	7,000	15,000	6,000	N/A

Notes: *Variable Special Pay*. Payable to all military physicians depending on years of creditable service. Payable monthly.
Additional Special Pay: Paid to all military physicians not in internship or residency. Officers must execute a written agreement to remain on active duty for one year.
Board Certified Pay: Payable to all military physicians who have achieved board certification in a medical specialty. Rates depend on years of creditable service.
Incentive Pay. Paid to physicians in selected critical specialties (primarily surgical specialties).
Special Pay for Active-duty Reserve Medical Officers. $450 additional paid monthly for less than 1 year active duty as a medical officer.

TABLE C-13

Dental Officers' Special Pays

Years of Service	Variable Special Pay	Additional Special Pay	Board Certified Pay
O-6 and Below			
Interns	$1,200	—	—
0–3 years	1,200	—	$2,000
3–6 years	2,000	$6,000	2,000
6–10 years	4,000	6,000	2,000
10–12 years	6,000	6,000	2,000
12–14 years	6,000	6,000	3,000
14–18 years	4,000	8,000	4,000
Over 18 years	3,000	10,000	4,000
O-7 and Above			
Over 18 years	1,000	10,000	4,000

Notes: Variable Special Pay. Payable to all military dentists depending on years of creditable service. Payable monthly.

Additional Special Pay. Payable to all military dentists not in internship or residency. Officers must execute a written agreement to remain on active duty for one year. Payable in a lump sum.

Board Certified Pay. Paid to all dental officers who have achieved board certification in a dental specialty. Rates depend on years of creditable service.

TABLE C-14
Dependency and Indemnity Compensation (DIC)
Monthly Payments to Surviving Spouses

E-1	$ 594
E-2	612
E-3	629
E-4	668
E-5	686
E-6	701
E-7	735
E-8	776
E-9	811
E-9 (top NCO in each service)	875
W-1	$ 752
W-2	785
W-3	805
W-4	852
O-1	$ 752
O-2	776
O-3	831
O-4	879
O-5	969
O-6	1,094
O-7	1,181
O-8	1,295
O-9	1,389
O-10	1,524
O-10 (Service Chief of Staff)	1,633

Notes: Additional benefits $178–265 are allotted for certain disabled surviving spouses. Add $68 to surviving spouse benefit for each child under 18.

For children over 18 years of age, DIC and the Dependents' Education Act contain certain educational benefits that may overlap. Contact the VA for additional information.

Where there is *no widow entitled* benefits for children under 18 are as follows:

1 child	$299
2 children	431
3 children	557
each additional	110

Appendix D

Time Value of Money and Present Value Tables

VIRTUALLY ALL SERVICEMEMBERS will at some time in their lives buy a home, take out a loan, invest in real estate, stocks, or bonds, decide on which type of life insurance to buy, or analyze a home improvement project. An understanding of the time value of money can greatly assist in making good decisions.

The most basic idea here is that we value less something for which we must wait. All of us would prefer to have a new sports car today rather than a year from now. We are impatient to consume and would probably pay more today for the sports car if we could have it right away than we would pay today for the right to receive the car a year from now.

An additional idea is that we have the opportunity to invest: Assets we have now can be deposited at interest so that later, say in a year, they will be worth more.

Consider the following example: A local bank decides to support local students by offering $1,000 to each student on graduation day, which is one year away. The prize is worth $1,000 one year from today. What is the prize worth today?

Suppose your teenage neighbor offers to sell you his prize today, one year from the time it will be worth $1,000. How much should you pay for the right to receive $1,000 one year from now?

If you could collect the $1,000 prize today you would be willing to pay $1,000 to your neighbor, but since you must wait to collect the money, you will be reluctant to pay that much. On the other hand, your neighbor's prize is worth a lot more than nothing. You might reason as follows:

1. "I can earn 5 percent per year on money I have in my savings account." (Economists call that the opportunity to invest.) "I should not earn less than that by investing in my neighbor's prize."

2. "My neighbor's prize will be worth $1,000 next year. How much money invested in my savings account at 5 percent interest per year will give me $1,000 in a year?" Let X represent the amount in the account now. Then:

$$\$X(1.05) = \$1.000$$

$$X = \frac{\$1.000}{1.05} = \$952.38$$

3. "I could take $952.38 out of savings today, buy my neighbor's prize, hold it for a year, and be no worse off."

You offer your neighbor $952.38 for the prize. Your neighbor, impatient to consume, agrees to accept $952.38 for his prize today because he does not want to wait a year.

Notice two important points about this transaction:

1. You valued the prize at less than its $1,000 face value because you would have to wait to receive the $1,000.
2. Your neighbor was willing to accept less today than the face value of the prize because he could have the money immediately.

APPLICATION TO LOANS

These principles determine the basis upon which consumer loans are made. The borrower takes a sum of money from a lender today and agrees to pay back a larger sum later, perhaps in monthly installments. The lender agrees to loan the money today in exchange for a larger sum later. In the above example, you were the lender, and your neighbor (the borrower) agreed to give up $1,000 next year in exchange for $952.38 this year.

Let's look at a typical installment loan. You want to borrow $1,000 today from the bank and agree to repay that sum plus interest in three annual installments. Since you receive the $1,000 today, we call it the present value (PV) of the loan. Your three annual payments (PMT) will be made at the end of each of the three years the loan is outstanding and will, of course, add up to more than the PV. The rate of interest charged on the loan is (1+r).

$$PV = \frac{PMT}{1+r} + \frac{PMT}{(1+r)^2} + \frac{PMT}{(1+r)^3}$$

For example, if the annual interest rate is 5 percent, then $1 + r = 1.05$, and

$$\$1,000 = \frac{PMT}{1.05} + \frac{PMT}{(1.05)^2} + \frac{PMT}{(1.05)^3}$$

$$PMT = 367.21$$

TIME VALUE OF MONEY AND PRESENT VALUE TABLES • 371

Notice that you will actually pay a total of $1,101.63 ($367.21 × 3) as you repay the $1,000 loan. This difference is the finance charge.

$$\$1,101.63 - \$1,000 = \$101.63 = \text{finance charge}$$

Most people are confused by the interest rate exponents in equations like those above. The exponents represent the number of periods (years in this example) between now and the time the payment (PMT) is made. Think back to the graduation prize example:

$$PV = \$952.38 = \frac{PMT}{(1+r)^1} = \frac{\$1,000}{(1.05)^1}$$

The exponent on the interest rate in that case was 1, because we had to wait one period to receive the payment of $1,000. If we had to wait two years to receive the $1,000 prize, we would pay less than $952.38 for it today. In fact, we would pay only

$$\frac{\$1,000}{(1.05)^2} = \$907.03$$

because $907.03 invested at 5 percent for two years gives us $1,000 in two years.

$$(907.03) \times (1.05)^2 = \$1,000$$

Use of a Time Line

For more complex problems you may find it helpful to use a time line to portray graphically when payments will be made. For example, the time line for the loan example above is:

```
PV = $1,000
    ↑         t = 1      t = 2      t = 3        time in years
    |_____|_____|_____|
  t = 0         ↓          ↓          ↓
              367.21     367.21     367.21
```

Amounts you receive are shown above the line; amounts you must pay are indicated below the line. The exponents correspond to the time period in which the payment is due.

VALUATION OF ASSETS

The concepts above can be extended to use in valuing productive assets such as factories, land, or investment opportunities in general. The time value of money is important because in many situations in our lives we invest funds today and receive returns in the future. For example, suppose you are buying a new car, an option on which is a five-speed overdrive transmission that will save you gas. You must pay for the option today and wait to receive the gas savings over a period of years. You calculate that the overdrive transmission will save you $33 per year in gas. You plan to keep the car for five years, then sell it. Resale value will be $50 higher then if you have the five-speed. What is the value of the option?

$$PV = \frac{33}{1+r} + \frac{33}{(1+r)^2} + \frac{33}{(1+r)^3} + \frac{33}{(1+r)^4} + \frac{33}{(1+r)^5} + \frac{50}{(1+r)^5}$$

If the extra money you pay for the option would otherwise earn 5 percent per year, $1 + r = 1.05$. If you are borrowing the money for the car, use the loan rate of interest, say $1 + r = 1.12$, or 12 percent per year.

$$PV = \$182.05 \quad \text{if } 1 + r = 1.05$$
$$PV = \$147.33 \quad \text{if } 1 + r = 1.12$$

PV indicates the value of the option today. You should not pay more than PV for the option because it is not worth it, at least not on the basis of gas savings and increased resale value.

APPLICATION TO ASSETS IN GENERAL

An asset is an "article of goods or property available for the payment of a person's obligations or debts." In general, an asset is anything that can be used as a store of value. You can use the methodology outlined above to determine the value of any asset. All you need to know is:

1. How much the asset will return to you in the future.
2. When those returns will be made.
3. The interest rate or "discount factor" that gives the opportunity cost to you of investing funds in a given asset rather than the next best alternative of equivalent risk.

Some additional considerations affect the practical use of the concepts above:

1. The interest rate you use must be the rate of interest per period. For example, if you are making or receiving monthly payments, $1 + r$ in your equations must be the monthly interest rate. If you know the annual effective interest rate, the gross monthly rate is the twelfth root of the gross annual rate:

$$(1 + r) = \text{annual rate} = (1 + i)^{12} \text{ where}$$
$$1 + i \text{ is the monthly interest rate}$$
Thus:
$$i = (1 + \text{annual rate})^{12}$$

But since many stated interest rates (e.g., mortgages, car loans, credit cards) are simply the monthly rate times 12, you will not require the procedure above. You simply divide the stated annual rate by 12 to get the actual rate for monthly use.

2. At times, you know the PV and the PMT values and you want to find the rate of return, called the internal rate of return, on the asset or investment project.

Let's return to the example of the five-speed transmission; say it costs $200 extra. You could draw a time line to illustrate the payments and receipts (in this case receipts are gas savings and higher resale value).

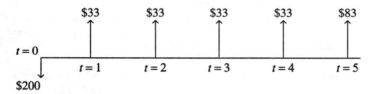

You must pay $200 now, so that is the PV. We equate PV with the stream of future earnings discounted by $1 + r$, the unknown rate of return on "investing" in this gas-saving transmission.

$$\$200 = \frac{33}{1+r} + \frac{33}{(1+r)^2} + \frac{33}{(1+r)^3} + \frac{33}{(1+r)^4} + \frac{83}{(1+r)^5}$$

The problem now is to find $1 + r$ that makes the equation balance. Using a hand calculator (a programmable one helps), you can solve this problem by trail and error by trying $1 + r$ values in computing the right-hand side of the equation. The value of $1 + r$ that makes the right-hand side equal $200 is the rate of return on your investment. In this case, $1 + r$ is 1.021, or 2.1 percent.

Obviously, the $200 five-speed is not a good buy if your money can earn a higher rate of return elsewhere. For example, if you can earn 5 percent on invested funds elsewhere, you would be foolish to invest them in the five-speed (if your objective was to save money). This is not surprising; remember we found previously that you should not pay more than $182.04 for the transmission if you can earn 5 percent on your assets elsewhere.

This analysis should help you avoid investing your scarce assets in projects that do not provide an adequate return. Inexpensive calculators can do the necessary calculations for you. For a small investment of your time and effort, you can easily make much better financial decisions using these techniques.

USING FINANCIAL TABLES

Financial tables are provided at the end of this appendix to help you make some of the more common calculations referred to in the text. All calculations can be easily made

374 • PERSONAL FINANCIAL PLANNING

using one of the modern financial calculators, and we recommend that servicemembers buy one and learn to use it. It is possible, however, to make close estimates of loan payments and other such amounts using the tables provided below.

Table D-1, "Present Value of $1," shows today's value of money that will be received in the future (the number of years shown down the left-hand column) at various interest rates (as shown along the top of the table). For example, the present value of $1 to be received in ten years when the interest rate you can earn on your savings is 6 percent is shown in the table to $.558, or about 56 cents. Table D-1 is useful for estimating the amount you need to set aside now in order to have a specified amount of money at some future time. Suppose you want to have $20,000 for a child's education in ten years and you can earn 6 percent on your savings for those ten years. According to Table D-1, $.558 will grow to $1 in ten years at 6 percent interest. So if you want to have $20,000 in ten years, you must set aside .558 times $20,000 now, or about $11,160.

Table D-2, "Present Value of $1 Received Annually for N Years," shows today's value of savings at various interest rates (shown across the top of the table) for various periods (the number of years is shown along the left column). This table is useful for calculating the amount of savings you will have to accumulate in order to pay yourself a specified amount per year in retirement or to provide for your family in the event of your death. For example, suppose you can earn 6 percent on your savings and want to have your savings provide $6,000 per year for twenty years after you retire. Table D-2 enables you to determine the amount of savings that will be required when you retire. Looking at D-2 for a 6 percent interest rate and twenty years, we find 11.470. This means that the amount of money required to provide $1 per year for twenty years when the money is earning 6 percent is $11.47. Since you want to have $6,000 per year for twenty years, the amount of money you will need at retirement is 6,000 times 11.47, or $68,820. If you are currently ten years from retirement, you need to deposit .558 times that amount, or about $38,400, now so that it will grow to the required amount in ten years. (See the example for Table D-1).

Present Value of $1 Received in N Years

Periods Until Payment	0.5%	1%	2%	3%	4%	5%	6%	7%	8%	9%	10%	11%	12%	13%	14%	15%	16%	17%	18%	19%	20%
1	0.995	0.990	0.980	0.971	0.962	0.952	0.943	0.935	0.926	0.917	0.909	0.901	0.893	0.885	0.877	0.870	0.862	0.855	0.847	0.840	0.833
2	0.990	0.980	0.961	0.943	0.925	0.907	0.890	0.873	0.857	0.842	0.826	0.812	0.797	0.783	0.769	0.756	0.743	0.731	0.718	0.706	0.694
3	0.985	0.971	0.942	0.915	0.889	0.864	0.840	0.816	0.794	0.772	0.751	0.731	0.712	0.693	0.675	0.658	0.641	0.624	0.609	0.593	0.579
4	0.980	0.961	0.924	0.888	0.855	0.823	0.792	0.763	0.735	0.708	0.683	0.659	0.636	0.613	0.592	0.572	0.552	0.534	0.516	0.499	0.482
5	0.975	0.951	0.906	0.863	0.822	0.784	0.747	0.713	0.681	0.650	0.621	0.593	0.567	0.543	0.519	0.497	0.476	0.456	0.437	0.419	0.402
6	0.971	0.942	0.888	0.837	0.790	0.746	0.705	0.666	0.630	0.596	0.564	0.535	0.507	0.480	0.456	0.432	0.410	0.390	0.370	0.352	0.335
7	0.966	0.933	0.871	0.813	0.760	0.711	0.665	0.623	0.583	0.547	0.513	0.482	0.452	0.425	0.400	0.376	0.354	0.333	0.314	0.296	0.279
8	0.961	0.923	0.853	0.789	0.731	0.677	0.627	0.582	0.540	0.502	0.467	0.434	0.404	0.376	0.351	0.327	0.305	0.285	0.266	0.249	0.233
9	0.956	0.914	0.837	0.766	0.703	0.645	0.592	0.544	0.500	0.460	0.424	0.391	0.361	0.333	0.308	0.284	0.263	0.243	0.225	0.209	0.194
10	0.951	0.905	0.820	0.744	0.676	0.614	0.558	0.508	0.463	0.422	0.386	0.352	0.322	0.295	0.270	0.247	0.227	0.208	0.191	0.176	0.162
11	0.947	0.896	0.804	0.722	0.650	0.585	0.527	0.475	0.429	0.388	0.350	0.317	0.287	0.261	0.237	0.215	0.195	0.178	0.162	0.148	0.135
12	0.942	0.887	0.788	0.701	0.625	0.557	0.497	0.444	0.397	0.356	0.319	0.286	0.257	0.231	0.208	0.187	0.168	0.152	0.137	0.124	0.112
13	0.937	0.879	0.773	0.681	0.601	0.530	0.469	0.415	0.368	0.326	0.290	0.258	0.229	0.204	0.182	0.163	0.145	0.130	0.116	0.104	0.093
14	0.933	0.870	0.758	0.661	0.577	0.505	0.442	0.388	0.340	0.299	0.263	0.232	0.205	0.181	0.160	0.141	0.125	0.111	0.099	0.088	0.078
15	0.928	0.861	0.743	0.642	0.555	0.481	0.417	0.362	0.315	0.275	0.239	0.209	0.183	0.160	0.140	0.123	0.108	0.095	0.084	0.074	0.065
16	0.923	0.853	0.728	0.623	0.534	0.458	0.394	0.339	0.292	0.252	0.218	0.188	0.163	0.141	0.123	0.107	0.093	0.081	0.071	0.062	0.054
17	0.919	0.844	0.714	0.605	0.513	0.436	0.371	0.317	0.270	0.231	0.198	0.170	0.146	0.125	0.108	0.093	0.080	0.069	0.060	0.052	0.045
18	0.914	0.836	0.700	0.587	0.494	0.416	0.350	0.296	0.250	0.212	0.180	0.153	0.130	0.111	0.095	0.081	0.069	0.059	0.051	0.044	0.038
19	0.910	0.828	0.686	0.570	0.475	0.396	0.331	0.277	0.232	0.194	0.164	0.138	0.116	0.098	0.083	0.070	0.060	0.051	0.043	0.037	0.031
20	0.905	0.820	0.673	0.554	0.456	0.377	0.312	0.258	0.215	0.178	0.149	0.124	0.104	0.087	0.073	0.061	0.051	0.043	0.037	0.031	0.026
21	0.901	0.811	0.660	0.538	0.439	0.359	0.294	0.242	0.199	0.164	0.135	0.112	0.093	0.077	0.064	0.053	0.044	0.037	0.031	0.026	0.022
22	0.896	0.803	0.647	0.522	0.422	0.342	0.278	0.226	0.184	0.150	0.123	0.101	0.083	0.068	0.056	0.046	0.038	0.032	0.026	0.022	0.018
23	0.892	0.795	0.634	0.507	0.406	0.326	0.262	0.211	0.170	0.138	0.112	0.091	0.074	0.060	0.049	0.040	0.033	0.027	0.022	0.018	0.015
24	0.887	0.788	0.622	0.492	0.390	0.310	0.247	0.197	0.158	0.126	0.102	0.082	0.066	0.053	0.043	0.035	0.028	0.023	0.019	0.015	0.013
25	0.883	0.780	0.610	0.478	0.375	0.295	0.233	0.184	0.146	0.116	0.092	0.074	0.059	0.047	0.038	0.030	0.024	0.020	0.016	0.013	0.010
26	0.878	0.772	0.598	0.464	0.361	0.281	0.220	0.172	0.135	0.106	0.084	0.066	0.053	0.042	0.033	0.026	0.021	0.017	0.014	0.011	0.009
27	0.874	0.764	0.586	0.450	0.347	0.268	0.207	0.161	0.125	0.098	0.076	0.060	0.047	0.037	0.029	0.023	0.018	0.014	0.011	0.009	0.007
28	0.870	0.757	0.574	0.437	0.333	0.255	0.196	0.150	0.116	0.090	0.069	0.054	0.042	0.033	0.026	0.020	0.016	0.012	0.010	0.008	0.006
29	0.865	0.749	0.563	0.424	0.321	0.243	0.185	0.141	0.107	0.082	0.063	0.048	0.037	0.029	0.022	0.017	0.014	0.011	0.008	0.006	0.005
30	0.861	0.742	0.552	0.412	0.308	0.231	0.174	0.131	0.099	0.075	0.057	0.044	0.033	0.026	0.020	0.015	0.012	0.009	0.007	0.005	0.004
40	0.819	0.672	0.453	0.307	0.208	0.142	0.097	0.067	0.046	0.032	0.022	0.015	0.011	0.008	0.005	0.004	0.003	0.002	0.001	0.001	0.001
50	0.779	0.608	0.372	0.228	0.141	0.087	0.054	0.034	0.021	0.013	0.009	0.005	0.003	0.002	0.001	0.001	0.001	0.000	0.000	0.000	0.000

Example: What amount invested today at 2% interest (after inflation) would cover a $10,000 education in 10 years?
Present value = (.820 × $10,000) = $8,200

Note: By interpolation you can estimate value for "periods of payment" between 30 and 40 and between 40 and 50.

TABLE D-2
Present Value of $1 received Annually for N Years

Years Payments Received	0.5%	1%	2%	3%	4%	5%	6%	7%	8%	9%	10%	11%	12%	13%	14%	15%	16%	17%	18%	19%	20%
1	0.995	0.990	0.980	0.971	0.962	0.952	0.943	0.935	0.926	0.917	0.909	0.901	0.893	0.885	0.877	0.870	0.862	0.855	0.847	0.840	0.833
2	1.985	1.970	1.942	1.913	1.886	1.859	1.833	1.808	1.783	1.759	1.736	1.713	1.690	1.668	1.647	1.626	1.605	1.585	1.566	1.547	1.528
3	2.970	2.941	2.884	2.829	2.775	2.723	2.673	2.624	2.577	2.531	2.487	2.444	2.402	2.361	2.322	2.283	2.246	2.210	2.174	2.140	2.106
4	3.950	3.902	3.808	3.717	3.630	3.546	3.465	3.387	3.312	3.240	3.170	3.102	3.037	2.974	2.914	2.855	2.798	2.743	2.690	2.639	2.589
5	4.926	4.853	4.713	4.580	4.452	4.329	4.212	4.100	3.993	3.890	3.791	3.696	3.605	3.517	3.433	3.352	3.274	3.199	3.127	3.058	2.991
6	5.896	5.795	5.601	5.417	5.242	5.076	4.917	4.767	4.623	4.486	4.355	4.231	4.111	3.998	3.889	3.784	3.685	3.589	3.498	3.410	3.326
7	6.862	6.728	6.472	6.230	6.002	5.786	5.582	5.389	5.206	5.033	4.868	4.712	4.564	4.423	4.288	4.160	4.039	3.922	3.812	3.706	3.605
8	7.823	7.652	7.325	7.020	6.733	6.463	6.210	5.971	5.747	5.535	5.335	5.146	4.968	4.799	4.639	4.487	4.344	4.207	4.078	3.954	3.837
9	8.779	8.566	8.162	7.786	7.435	7.108	6.802	6.515	6.247	5.995	5.759	5.537	5.328	5.132	4.946	4.772	4.607	4.451	4.303	4.163	4.031
10	9.730	9.471	8.983	8.530	8.111	7.722	7.360	7.024	6.710	6.418	6.145	5.889	5.650	5.426	5.216	5.019	4.833	4.659	4.494	4.339	4.192
11	10.677	10.368	9.787	9.253	8.760	8.306	7.887	7.499	7.139	6.805	6.495	6.207	5.938	5.687	5.453	5.234	5.029	4.836	4.656	4.486	4.327
12	11.619	1.255	10.575	9.954	9.385	8.863	8.384	7.943	7.536	7.161	6.814	6.492	6.194	5.918	5.660	5.421	5.197	4.988	4.793	4.611	4.439
13	12.556	12.134	11.348	10.635	9.986	9.394	8.853	8.358	7.904	7.487	7.103	6.750	6.424	6.122	5.842	5.583	5.342	5.118	4.910	4.715	4.533
14	13.489	13.004	12.106	11.296	10.563	9.899	9.295	8.745	8.244	7.786	7.367	6.982	6.628	6.302	6.002	5.724	5.468	5.229	5.008	4.802	4.611
15	14.417	13.865	12.849	11.936	11.118	10.380	9.712	9.108	8.559	8.061	7.606	7.191	6.811	6.462	6.142	5.847	5.575	5.324	5.092	4.876	4.675
16	15.340	14.718	13.578	12.561	11.652	10.838	10.106	9.447	8.851	8.313	7.824	7.379	6.974	6.604	6.265	5.954	5.668	5.405	5.162	4.938	4.730
17	16.259	15.562	14.292	13.166	12.166	11.274	10.477	9.763	9.122	8.544	8.022	7.549	7.120	6.729	6.373	6.047	5.749	5.475	5.222	4.990	4.775
18	17.173	16.398	14.992	13.754	12.659	11.690	10.828	10.059	9.372	8.756	8.201	7.702	7.250	6.840	6.467	6.128	5.818	5.534	5.273	5.033	4.812
19	18.082	17.226	15.678	14.324	13.134	12.085	11.158	10.336	9.604	8.950	8.365	7.839	7.366	6.938	6.550	6.198	5.877	5.584	5.316	5.070	4.843
20	18.987	18.046	16.351	14.877	13.590	12.462	11.470	10.594	9.818	9.129	8.514	7.963	7.469	7.025	6.623	6.259	5.929	5.628	5.353	5.101	4.870
21	19.888	18.857	17.011	15.415	14.029	12.821	11.764	10.836	10.017	9.292	8.649	8.075	7.562	7.102	6.687	6.312	5.973	5.665	5.384	5.127	4.891
22	20.784	19.660	17.658	15.937	14.451	13.163	12.042	11.061	10.201	9.442	8.772	8.176	7.645	7.170	6.743	6.359	6.011	5.696	5.410	5.149	4.909
23	21.676	20.456	18.292	16.444	14.857	13.489	12.303	11.272	10.371	9.580	8.883	8.266	7.718	7.230	6.792	6.399	6.044	5.723	5.432	5.167	4.925
24	22.563	21.243	18.914	16.936	15.247	13.799	12.550	11.469	10.529	9.707	8.985	8.348	7.784	7.283	6.835	6.434	6.073	5.746	5.451	5.182	4.937
25	23.446	22.023	19.523	17.413	15.622	14.094	12.783	11.654	10.675	9.823	9.077	8.422	7.843	7.330	6.873	6.464	6.097	5.766	5.467	5.195	4.948
26	24.324	22.795	20.121	17.877	15.983	14.375	13.003	11.826	10.810	9.929	9.161	8.488	7.896	7.372	6.906	6.491	6.118	5.783	5.480	5.206	4.956
27	25.198	23.560	20.707	18.327	16.330	14.643	13.211	11.987	10.935	10.027	9.237	8.548	7.943	7.409	6.935	6.514	6.136	5.798	5.492	5.215	4.964
28	26.068	24.316	21.281	18.764	16.663	14.898	13.406	12.137	11.051	10.116	9.307	8.602	7.984	7.441	6.961	6.534	6.152	5.810	5.502	5.223	4.970
29	26.933	25.066	21.844	19.188	16.984	15.141	13.591	12.278	11.158	10.198	9.370	8.650	8.022	7.470	6.983	6.551	6.166	5.820	5.510	5.229	4.975
30	27.794	25.808	22.396	19.600	17.292	15.372	13.765	12.409	11.258	10.274	9.427	8.694	8.055	7.496	7.003	6.566	6.177	5.829	5.517	5.235	4.979
40	36.172	32.835	27.355	23.115	19.793	17.159	15.046	13.332	11.925	10.757	9.779	8.951	8.244	7.634	7.105	6.642	6.233	5.871	5.548	5.258	4.997
50	44.143	39.196	31.424	25.730	21.482	18.256	15.762	13.801	12.233	10.962	9.915	9.042	8.304	7.675	7.133	6.661	6.246	5.880	5.554	5.262	4.999

Example: How much would you have to invest today at 8% to draw out $6,000 at the end of each year for 20 years?

Appendix E

Sample Personal Affairs Record

PERSONAL AFFAIRS RECORD OF

(Name)   (Grade) (Service No.)   (Component)

1. **Personal Data**
   Religious preference _____
   Birthdate _____ Place of birth _____
   Permanent legal address _____
   Local (or emergency) address _____
       Telephone No. _____
   Father's name and address _____
       Father's date and place of birth _____
   Mother's name and address _____
       Mother's date and place of birth _____
   Names, addresses, and ages of brothers and sisters:
   _____
   _____
   _____

   Date and place of marriage _____
   Location of marriage certificate _____
   Name of spouse _____ Social Security No. _____
   Spouse's permanent legal address _____
   Spouse's birthdate _____
   Spouse's place of birth _____

Children's names, date and place of birth _____
_____
_____
_____

Birth certificates located as follows:
Myself _____ Spouse _____
Children _____

Social Security cards located at _____
Pay Status
    Base pay _____
    Quarters allowance _____
    Subsistence _____
    Hazardous duty pay _____
    Other pay _____
        Total _____
Former service numbers _____
Entered military service on _____ at _____
Military service (list here or separately all military service including units, grades, and periods of service) _____
_____
_____

II. Will

Date and location of will _____
Where made _____
Executor's name and address _____
Spouse or joint will? _____
Date and location of spouse's will _____
Where made _____
Executor's name and address _____

III Power of Attorney

Does a power of attorney exist? _____
Type (general, limited). If limited, for what purpose? _____
Date of execution _____ Date of expiration _____
Name and address of grantee _____

IV. Taxes

Federal income taxes paid through calendar year _____
State income taxes paid through calendar year _____
Real estate taxes paid until _____
Personal property taxes paid until _____
Location of tax return records _____

V. Property Ownership

1. Real estate _____
   Description of real estate owned _____
   _____
   Names in which held _____
   Dates acquired _____
   Purchase price _____ Estimated present value _____
   Mortgage amount _____ Held by _____
   Name and address of insurance company _____
   Policy No. _____ Expiration date _____
   in the amount of $ _____
   against _____
   (fire, damage, liability, etc.)
   Lease on rented property expiration date _____
   Pertinent documents located at _____

2. Automobile Record
   Make _____ Model _____ Year _____
   Serial no. _____ Motor no. _____ Color _____
   License plate no. _____ Year _____ State _____
   Title no. _____ Title state _____ Date _____
   Insurance company _____
   Address _____
   Insurance policy no. _____ Expiration date _____

Insured Against:	Yes	No	Limits
Bodily injury	_____	_____	_____
Property damage	_____	_____	_____
Public liability	_____	_____	_____
Collision	_____	_____	_____
Comprehensive	_____	_____	_____
Other (explain)	_____	_____	_____

   Name and address of finance company _____
   Balance due _____ Monthly payments _____
   Automobile papers located at _____

3. Other personal property (jewelry, boats, trailers, etc.)

List property of great value	Amt. of lien and monthly payment	Lien held by	Insurance (company, limits, policy no., exp. date)
_____	_____	_____	_____
_____	_____	_____	_____
_____	_____	_____	_____
_____	_____	_____	_____
_____	_____	_____	_____

VI. Credit Cards

Company	Card No.	No. of Cards	Expiration Date

Credit card insurance? _____ Amount _____
Name of insurance company _____ Policy no. _____

VII. Bank Accounts and Savings Deposits

Name and Address of Bank	Type Account	Account Number

Bonds are located at _____

VII. U.S. Bonds

Denomination	Number	In Name Of

Bonds are located at _____

IX. Stocks, Mutual Funds, and Other Securities

Company	Date Purchased	Purchase Price	Certificate Number

Carried in account number _____ maintained with _____
_____
(Name and address of broker)

X. Insurance

1. I (do) (do not) have government life insurance.
    This insurance is (U.S. government life insurance)
        (National Service Life Insurance)
        (Servicemen's Group Life Insurance)
    The policy number is _____ Type of insurance _____
    Amount of government insurance _____
    The policy is located at _____

2. I have in effect the following commercial life insurance:
   Company   Address   Policy Number   Amount
   _____
   _____

   These policies are locate at _____
   The following loans are outstanding against these policies:
   _____

3. I have accomplished an insurance program that outlines the manner in which the proceeds of each are to be paid. It is located at _____

4. Primary beneficiary _____
   Contingent beneficiaries _____

5. Life insurance in effect upon the lives of my wife and children:
   Name and relationship   Company Policy no.   Amount   Premium due
   _____
   _____

6. The property and casualty insurance policies presently in effect are:
                        Company   Address   Policy No.
   Personal property   _____   _____   _____
   Personal liability   _____   _____   _____
   Hospitalization
      and health   _____   _____   _____

XI. Moneys Owed to Me
Amount   Debtor
_____
_____

XII. Liabilities (Loans, notes not previously listed)
Amount   Lender   Date Made   Date Due
_____
_____

XIII. Safe Deposit Box
Location of box _____
Safe deposit box key located at _____

XIV. Burial
I desire to be interred at _____
I desire (that the government grave marker be utilized) (that a monument be erected at the place of my interment at a cost not to exceed $ _____).

XV. Other Pertinent Information and Instructions:

_____
_____
_____

XVI. This record was last checked on _____

Notes

Birth and marriage certificates should be obtained as part of estate planning. At least fifteen copies of each should be on hand, as they are generally required for pensions, Social Security, and sometimes by commercial insurance companies.

Burial may be at a post or national cemetery. A government grave marker is furnished gratuitously.

Some rights of surviving spouses:
1. Entitled to purchase at commissary and post exchanges.
2. Entitled to medical care and hospitalization when facilities are available.
3. May be entitled to state bonus.
4. Eligible, if unremarried, for GI home or business loans to same extent as veteran.
5. Entitled to preference in federal civil service examination.
6. Entitled to transportation of self, children, and household goods to new home.
7. Entitled to GI educational benefits.

Index

Air Force Times, 293, 302, 314
Air weapons controller pay (table), 363
All States Income Tax Guide, 97, 98
Allowances
    clothing, 17
    difference from pay, 16
    family separation, 18
    housing, 16
    housing (table), 359
    subsistence, 17
    temporary duty, 21–22
    travel, 19–21
    see also Benefits; Pay
Appraisals, 148
Arlington National Cemetery, 24
Armed Forces Insurance, 179
Army Times, 293, 302, 314
Assets, formulas for calculating present values of, 372–73
Associations, military, list of, 333–37
Automobile insurance, 106
    checklist, 133–35
    collision coverage, 129–30
    comprehensive coverage, 130
    leased car coverage, 132
    liability coverage, 127–29
    medical payments coverage, 129
    optional coverage, 132
    overview of, 125–27
    rental car coverage, 131–32
    rental reimbursement, 132
    towing and labor coverage, 132–33
    uninsured motorist coverage, 130–31
Automobiles
    affordability of, determining, 103–4
    buying from dealer, 114–19
    comparative analysis (worksheet), 113
    dealer cost vs. retail cost, 115–16
    dealing with a dealer, 116–19
    depreciation, 107–8
    how long to keep, 123–24
    insurance, 106, 125–35
    leasing, 121–22
    loans, 104–6, 109–12
    maintenance expenses, 106
    new, 114–19
    operating expenses, 106
    operating expenses (table), 119
    optional equipment, 113–14
    payments, 104–6
    requirements, 112–13

selling your old, 122–23
total expenses, 108–9
trading in your old, 122–23
used, 119–21
using a pricing/buying service, 116

Balance sheet, 4–5
Balloon loans, 57
Bankcard Holders of America, 69
Banks
automobile loans from, 111–12
certificates of deposit, 53–54
checking accounts, 47–50
emergency fund account, 43
joint accounts, 278
loans, 44
savings, long-term, 43–44
savings accounts, 50–53
selecting, 44–47
services, 41–44, 47–54
transactions account, 42–43
Basic Allowance for Quarters (BAQ), 16
Basic pay, 16
tables, 354–58
Benefits
dental, 22, 80–81
disability, 257–59, 315
education, 315–16
employment, 316
financial, 316
funeral and burial, 23–24
life insurance, 22, 317
medical, 22, 71–90, 316
retirement, 253–61
Social Security, 304–14
supplemental survivor (SSBP), 328–29
survivor, 22–24, 315, 318–28
veterans, 22, 314–17
Best's Insurance Reports, 302
Bond mutual funds, 215
stock combination, 216

Bonds, 190–92
convertible, 200
corporate, 192–93
exchangeable, 200
government agency, 192
municipal, 192
savings, 189–90, 279
treasury, 190–92
zero coupon, 279
Brokers, stock, 197
Budgets, 33–38
mechanics of, 34–38
principles of, 33–34
worksheet, 36–37
Business Week, 219, 221
Buyer's Guide to Insurance: What Companies Won't Tell You, 179

Capital gains, 8
The Car Guide, 106, 126
Cars. *See* Automobiles
Certificates of deposit (CDs), 44, 50, 53–54, 188–89
CHAMPUS, 72, 74–78
auxillary services for handicapped, 78
benefits, 75–76
eligibility for, 75
organizations providing supplemental insurance for, 85–88
payment for, 76–78
reforms, 83–84
retirement benefits, 261
supplemental, 82–83
Changing Times, 209, 221, 293, 302
Checking accounts, 47–50, 187–88
interest-bearing, 47–48, 49–50
joint, 278
minimum balances, 48–49
negotiable order of withdrawal (NOW), 47
Chiropractors, special pay for, 19
Civil Service Reform Act of 1978, 260

Civilian Health and Medical Program of the Uniformed Services. *See* CHAMPUS
Clothing allowances, 17
COLA (cost-of-living allowances), 21, 314, 322–23
Collateral, 61
Collectibles, investing in, 247, 249
College fund investments, 8
Commodities, 200–1
Consumer Reports, 302
Consumer Reports Annual Buying Guide, 106, 120, 126
Cost-of-living allowances. *See* COLA
Credit, 44
  borrowers' rights, 69–70
  cards, 63–66
  debit cards, 66–67
  history, 69
  sources for, 63
  see also Loans
Credit cards, 63–66
  abusers, 68–69
  cost of, 64–66
  premium, 67–68
  travel and entertainment, 67
Credit unions, automobile loans from, 111–12

Debit cards, 66–67
Defense Enrollment Eligibility Reporting System (DEERS), 72
Dental care
  for dependents, 80–81
  retirement benefits, 260
Dentists, special pay for, 19
  table, 367
Department of Defense Military Pay and Allowances Entitlements Manual, 15
Department of Veterans Affairs benefits. *See* Veterans benefits

Dependency and Indemnity Compensation (DIC), table, 368
DIC. *See* Dependency and Indemnity Compensation
Disability benefits
  permanent, 257–58
  severance pay, 259
  social security, 310
  temporary, 258–59
  veterans, 315
Dislocation allowance (DLA), 21
Diving duty pay, 18
DLA. *See* Dislocation allowance
Doctors, special pay for, 19
  table, 366
Donoghue's, 219
Duel Compensation Act, 259–60

Earthquake insurance, 179
Edmund's New Car Prices, 115
Education benefits, 315–16
Estate planning
  income shifting, 275–80
  letters of instruction, 266–67
  overview of, 262–63
  power of attorney, 264–65
  professional assistance for, 280
  property ownership, 263–64
  trusts, 267–75
  wills, 265–66

Family separation allowances, 18
Federal Benefits for Veterans and Dependents, 160
FHA loans, 160–61
FICA. *See* Social Security taxes
Financial institutions. *See* Banks
Financial planning
  basics, 3, 6–14
  personal affairs record, 377–82
  setting goals, 25–33
Financial terms, definitions of, 338–53
Flood insurance, 178

Flying duty pay, 19
Forbes magazine, 219, 221
Foreign duty pay, 18
Foreign language proficiency pay, 19
Foreign mutual funds, 216

Gates, William, 194
Gems, investing in, 247
Goals, setting, 25–33
   brainstorming, 27
   calculating the "lump sum," 29–32
   calculating the monthly allotment, 32–33
   determining the appropriate investment, 33
   determining today's cost of, 27
   priorities, 33
   target date, 29
   worksheet, 28
Gold stocks, 13
Government insurance, 180

Hazardous duty pay, 17
Health care, 71–72
   active-duty, 72
   CHAMPUS, 74–78
   dental, for dependents, 80–81
   dependents, 73–74
   retirement benefits, 78–79, 260, 261
   summary of, 79–80
   supplemental insurance, 81–83
   Uniformed Services Health Benefits Program, 72–79
   veterans benefits for, 316
Home-equity loans, 62
Homeowners' insurance, 149, 173–79
   and additional insurance requirements, 178–79
   Armed Forces Insurance, 179
   checklist, 182–83
   coverage, 176–78
   types of, 174
   types of (table), 175
   USAA, 179
Hostile fire pay, 18
Housing
   affordability of, determining, 141–43
   allowances, 16
   allowances (table), 359
   appraisals, 148
   buying, 140–64
   checklist for home buyers, 169–71
   down payment sources, 151–53
   down payments, 153
   homeowners' insurance, 149
   inspections, 149
   mortgages, 144, 148–64
   renting, 137–40
   renting vs. buying, 167–69
   searching for the right home, 143–46
   selling, 165–67
   tax considerations, 164–65
   your needs concerning, 136–37
How to Buy a Car, 112

Imminent danger pay, 18
Income shifting
   gift and borrow-back of property, 279
   gifts, 276–78
   joint bank accounts, 278
   overview of, 275–76
   private annuities, 279
   savings bonds, 279
   zero coupon bonds, 279
Individual Investor's Guide to No-Load Mutual Funds, 219, 220, 221
Individual Retirement Accounts (IRAs), 7–8
   as down payment source, 151–52
Inflation, 9–10
Installment loans, 57–63
   collateral, 61
   home–equity, 62
   prepayment penalties, 60–61

sources for, 63
true interest rates, 57–60
Insurance. See specific types
Interest rates, 11
 true, 57–60
Investments, 7–8
 certificates of deposit, 188–89
 checking accounts, 187–88
 commodities, 200–201
 corporate bonds, 192–93
 government agency securities, 192
 municipal bonds, 192
 mutual funds, 207–30
 real assets, 231–50
 real estate, direct, 232–45
 real estate, indirect, 245–46
 risk factors, 12–14, 204–5
 savings accounts, 188
 savings bonds, 189–90
 scams, 201–2
 stocks, 193–200
 tax deferrals, 202–4
 that protect against inflation, 10
 tips, 205
 treasury bills, notes, and bonds, 190–92
IRAs. See Individual Retirement Accounts

Joint Travel Regulations for the Uniformed Services, 19, 21

Kelley Blue Book, 108, 120
Klein, David, 12

Leave and Earnings Statement (LES), 15
Life insurance, 22
 budgeting resources for premiums, 301
 choosing the right, 291–93
 estimating your needs, 293–301
 face amount, 282–83
 overview of, 281–82
 permanent, 286–88
 policy period, 283
 premiums, 283
 principle of, 282
 reviewing your, 302–3
 savings, 283
 SGLI, 301–2
 shopping for, 301–2
 vs. survivor benefit plan, 326
 tax deferred, 290–91
 term, 11, 284–86
 trusts, 271–73
 types of, 284–91
 variable, 288–90
 VGLI, 302, 317
 whole, 10
 worksheet, 300
Loans
 balloon, 57
 formulas for calculating present values of, 370–71
 installment, 57–63
 single-payment, 57
 see also Credit; Loans, automobile; Mortgages
Loans, automobile, 104–6, 109–12
 bank, 111–12
 collateralized, 112
 credit union, 111–12
 duration of, 111–12
 payments, 104–6
 self-financing, 111
Lynch, Peter, 199

Medical expenses. See Health care
Medical insurance. See Health care
Metals, investing in, 247, 248–49
Military Net Pay Advice, 15
Money magazine, 219, 221, 302
Money market mutual funds, 213–15
Mortgage insurance, 150
 life, 179

Mortgages, 153–54
  adjustable- or variable-rate, 154–56
  ARM vs. fixed rate (table), 156
  closing costs, 148–51
  conventional, 157–58
  costs, 156–57
  down payments, 153
  FHA, 160–61
  fixed-rate, 154
  length of, 161–62
  monthly principal and interest payments (table), 144
  paying off early, 162
  refinancing, 162–64
  seller financing, 157
  sources of money for closing costs, 151–53
  sources of money for down payment, 151–53
  VA, 158–60
Motor Trend magazine, 120, 126
Mutual funds, 14
  advantages of, 228–29
  bond, 215
  categories and risk (table), 214
  closed-end, 212
  combination stock and bond, 216
  contractual, 208–9
  disadvantages of, 229
  foreign, 216
  investment strategies, 222–23
  load, 208–9
  management fees, 209–11
  money market, 213–15
  no-load, 209
  open-end, 212–17
  overview of, 207–8
  prices, 211–12
  real asset, 216–17
  returns, 226–27
  selecting, 217–22
  selling, 226
  stock, 215
  tax considerations concerning, 228
  tracking performance of, 223–26
  12b-1 fees, 210–11
  types of, 212–17
  worksheet, 218

NADA Official Used Car Guide, 120
National Insurance Consumers Organization, 179
Navy Times, 293, 302, 314
New York Times, 211
Notes, 190–92
Nuclear duty pay, 18
Nurse anesthesists, special pay for, 19

OHA. *See* Overseas Housing Allowance
One Up on Wall Street, 199
Opportunity cost, 10–11
Optometrists, special pay for, 19
Organizations, military, list of, 333–37
Overseas Housing Allowance (OHA), 21
Overseas Station Allowances, 21

Pay:
  air weapons controller (table), 363
  basic, 16
  basic (tables), 354–58
  before and after tax, 7–9
  difference from allowances, 16
  diving duty, 18
  flying duty, 19
  foreign duty, 18
  foreign language proficiency, 19
  hazardous duty incentive, 17
  health-care professionals, 19
  health-care professionals (tables), 366, 367
  hostile fire/imminent danger, 18
  incentive (tables), 360–62
  nuclear duty, 18
  overview of, 15–16

sea duty, 18
sea duty (table), 364
severance, 259
submarine duty, 18
submarine duty (table), 365
see also Allowances; Benefits
Personal Earnings and Benefit Statement, 306
Power of attorney, 264–65
Precious metals, investing in, 247, 248–49
Present value of money, tables, 373–76

RAM Research's Cardtrak, 69
Rates of return, 26–27, 30
  historical averages for real (table), 29
Real asset mutual funds, 216–17
Real assets
  collectibles, 249
  formulas for calculating present values of, 371–72
  overview of, 231
  precious metals, 248–49
Real assets investments
  analysis of, 247–48
  collectibles, 247
  common metals, 246
  precious gems, 247
  precious metals, 246
  real estate, direct, 232–45
  real estate, indirect, 245–46
Real estate agents, 146–48
Real estate investments:
  and being a landlord, 244–45
  direct, 232–45
  indirect, 245–46
  partnerships, 245
  residential properties, 240–41
  risk factors, 246
  taxes, 235–37
  time-sharing properties, 241–44
  trusts (REITs), 246
  vacation properties, 241

REITs (real estate investment trusts), 246
Rent Plus program, 16
Renters' insurance, 180
Residences, legal, 95–98
Retirement benefits
  commissary and exchange, 260
  disability, permanent, 257–58
  disability, temporary, 258–59
  dual compensation, 259–60
  former spouses, 261
  length-of-service, 254–57
  medical and dental care, 260
  overview of, 253
  social security, 307–9

Savings accounts, 50–53, 188
  joint, 278
Savings bonds, 188–90, 279
  Series EE, 8
SBP. *See* Survivor benefit plan
Sea pay, 18
  table, 364
Servicemen's Group Life Insurance (SGLI), 22, 301–2
Severance pay, 259
SGLI. *See* Servicemen's Group Life Insurance
Social Security benefits:
  becoming insured, 306–7
  cost-of-living adjustments (COLA), 314
  disability, 310
  earnings test for, 311–13
  overview of, 304–5
  primary insurance amount (PIA), 310–11
  retirement, 307–9
  survivor, 309–10
  survivor benefit plan and, 323
  taxation of, 313
  types of, 307–10
Social Security Handbook, 304

Social Security taxes (FICA), 305–6
The Soldiers' and Sailors' Relief Act, 98
SSBP. *See* Supplemental Survivor Benefit Plan
Stock mutual funds, 215
   bond combination, 216
Stocks, 193–200
   analyzing, 197–200
   assessing value of, 195–96
   brokers, 197
   investment advice, 196–97
   overview of, 194–95
Submarine pay, 18
   table, 365
Subsistence allowances, 17
Supplemental Survivor Benefit Plan (SSBP), 328–29
Sure Pay account, 5
Survivor Benefit Plan (SBP)
   amount of annuity and costs, 319–20
   changes in coverage, 328
   children-only coverage, 321–22
   cost-of-living increases, 322–23
   overview of, 318–19
   purpose of, 319
   Social Security entitlements and, 323
   spouse-and-children coverage, 321
   spouse-only coverage, 320–21
   supplemental (SSBP), 328–29
   vs. life insurance, 328
   vs. no insurance, 324

Tax forgiveness, 91–92
Taxes, 89–90
   deductions for homeowners, 164–65
   deferrals on life insurance, 290–91
   federal income, 90–94
   filing returns, 92–100
   income tax brackets (table), 30
   investment deferrals, 202–4
   local, 9, 94–98
   on mutual funds, 228
   nontaxable income, 93
   on real estate investments, 235–37
   revisions, 98–100
   sales, 9
   Social Security (FICA), 305–6
   on Social Security benefits, 313
   state, 9, 94–98
   taxable income, 92–94
Temporary duty allowances, 21–22
Temporary Lodging Expense (TLE), 21
Time value of money
   formulas for calculating, 370–73
   overview of, 369–70
Title insurance, 178–79
TLE. *See* Temporary Lodging Expense
Travel allowances, 19–21
Treasury bills, 190–92
Trusts, 267–68
   life insurance, 271–73
   living, 268–70
   providing for guardian's needs, 274–75
   real estate investment, 246
   and selecting a trustee, 273–74
   testamentary, 270–71

U.S. savings bonds. *See* Savings bonds
Umbrella insurance policies, 181–82
Uniformed Services Active Duty Dependents Dental Plan, 80
Uniformed Services Former Spouses Protection Act, 261
Uniformed Services Health Benefits Program, 72–79
USAA, 179
   Automobile Pricing/Auto Purchase Service, 112, 116

VA benefits. *See* Veterans benefits
Variable Housing Allowance (VHA), 16
Veterans benefits, 22
   disability and survivor, 315
   education, 315–16

employment, 316
financial, 316
life insurance, 317
medical, 316
mortgages, 158–60
overview of, 314
Veterans Group Life Insurance (VGLI), 302, 317
Veterinarians, special pay for, 19

VGLI. *See* Veterans Group Life Insurance
VHA. *See* Variable Housing Allowance

Wall Street Journal, 211, 224
Wills, 265–66
   and letters of instruction, 266–67

Zero coupon bonds, 279

NOTES

NOTES

NOTES

100
 30   OPP
 40   ATT
 30   MC